# you are mistaken

Sean Wai Keung has been published in various magazines, journals and anthologies, including *Lunar Poetry*, *The Suburban Review* and *Blue of Noon*. He studied at Roehampton University and the University of East Anglia. He began attending and organising poetry open mics and events in 2013 and was awarded the Farrago Zoo Award for Best Debut Performance in 2014, as well as the Funniest Poem Award as part of the Cafe Writers Open Poetry Competition 2015. *you are mistaken* is his debut pamphlet and won The Rialto's first Open Pamphlet Competition.

# you are mistaken

SEAN WAI KEUNG

THE RIALTO

## ACKNOWLEDGEMENTS

Sincere thanks to the editors at the *Glasgow Review of Books, The Suburban Review* and the *UEA Poetry Anthology 2016*, in which some of these poems first appeared. Thank you also to everyone at the Café Writers 2015 Open Poetry Competition, for which '+ so i said to the guy what...' won the Funniest Poem Award. The author would lastly like to gratefully acknowledge Tiffany Atkinson for her editorial encouragement and feedback during the development of many of these poems, as well as all the support received from friends, workshop groups and open mic-ers over the years.

First published in 2017.

*The Rialto* PO Box 309 Aylsham Norwich
England NR11 6LN



ISBN 9781909632073

The Publisher acknowledges financial assistance from Grants For Arts.

LOTTERY FUNDED

The Rialto is a Registered Charity No. 297553
Typeset in Berling 10 on 12.5pt
Design by Starfish, Norwich
Printed in England by Page Bros, Norwich, Norfolk
Cover illustration from a reproduction of a woodcut. A prodigious monster, 1655. Original image: Wellcome Library, London. V0007455

# CONTENTS

## funeral

the most important principle is the principle
of never looking back even if you are
in a yorkshire church misted with
incense smoke + even if instead of you
its your cousin standing at the altar
looking more chinese than you ever will
+ even if the poor kind christian minister
sitting in the back has no idea
whats going on + you have no idea
whats going on but you know
that part of never looking back is never
asking why + in the pub afterwards
when someone asks you how to properly
show respect without offending
your culture you must be honest + say
that you dont know the rules
+ then thank them for worrying
+ then thank them for asking

## 'i think i want to write about race'

really
thats really cool
can you do that arent you white
o so you decided to go full american then
will you send me your poems
i think thats a good move for you
are they going to be performance poems
i thought you hated that sort of thing
what do you think of sarah howe
sweet
is that because you feel under pressure to write about that
thats so needed in this country especially after brexit
i thought you were going to write about honesty
no offence but why bother
have you told your mum
have you read sarah howe
you should ask for funding so you can go back to hongkong
o thats actually pretty interesting
great move thats what the arts council likes
i thought you were going to write about performance poems
o that makes sense i guess
didnt someone do that last year or was it the year before
good on you
yes yes yes yes excellent
have you really experienced that sort of thing then
yes
o good i hoped that you would
thats kind of brave of you
i thought you were going to write about food
will you get to go back to hongkong
isnt that the sort of thing you normally hate doing
is this because you did that thing at soas last year
that is so super exciting
im so glad
can i read it after

樸

pu describes pure simplicity or rawness
as in the rawness of an untouched tree
+ its from that rawness of simple nature
that everything that exists was born
+ its in that rawness that tao can act
+ tao is the universal truth
its what creates all the things that are real
including us but excluding the things
we create to distract us from rawness
like nuclear warheads or ice cream cones
the things that make the world more empty
the things that change the rawness around us
things like untruthful art are poisonous
your laptop is filled with dead ancestors

## 道

tao can also be spelled dao but most
people prefer the letter t over the letter
d because t looks more alive like a person
jumping with arms stretched out saying
*lets all group hug* whereas d looks more
like a potato sprouting an ugly root + tao
is not a potato but then it could be a potato
because a potato is beyond language + tao
is beyond language as well much like x which
is not only a letter but also a mathematical
symbol indicating two separate things should be
combined into one which is very like tao yet
we cant use x + call it xao because xao sounds
nothing like tao so the t will simply have to do

## a gift

a couple with a baby come into work + my
coworker says to me quietly dont you
think its strange that in this city you only
ever see white men with asian women +
never the other way around + i dont
immediately think of my white father or
my asian mother instead i think about my
white self + also my asian self + all of my
past relationships + by the time i realise
that i really am not thinking of my white
father or my asian mother my coworker
is gone + the couple are at my checkout +
when its time for them to pay they raise a
red packet filled with money + without
meaning to i say out loud that i havent
had a red packet since i was a kid + i dont
think they hear me but maybe they do +
they are simply choosing to ignore me
which i dont blame them for [i mean they
do have a baby to watch over they dont
need me] but then as they leave the baby
looks at me + i guess i look back or
something because it makes some sort of
noise + then the father bends down + says
something reassuring + the mother bends
down + smiles with real joy + then they
leave + i feel really angry at the couple +
the baby + my coworker too but i cant
think about that right now i have more
customers to serve +
i need all the money i can get

## 三寶 [慈 - 儉 - 不敢為天下先]

sanpao are the three treasured virtues
classically translated as compassion
frugality + humility but those
translations arent completely right
since the first treasure which is ci
really means a specific type of motherly love
which is not at all like the virtue of compassion
in confucianism which is not it at all
+ then the second is jian which is simplicity
of desire as in dont take more when you
already have enough + then the third is
dont dare to be before others in the world
or something similar to that its a little hard because its six characters long
but it really is important in case you become poor

**cny 2016**

over the phone
they say they had a big meal
twice-cooked belly pork
sea bass
whole duck

they say they all drank brandy
together – raised a toast

they say they missed me

they say they visited the cemetery
that everyone got proper
emotional round the grave

they say that it was too windy to light
the incense that they needed me there
to do it

they say a spirit rose
from the ground
screamed + cried
asked where i was
what i was doing

they say none of them knew
what to say to the spirit + that it chased them out

they say that the spirit followed them
back to the house
calling out my name
asking if i was a success
if i was rich
if i was married

they say they said i was none of those things

but dont worry
its not a big deal

i say i love you all
+ i hang up

—

over skype you tell me you are much happier now you arent in norwich
+ i feel this shooting pain somewhere because im in norwich without
you i feel less grounded its like theres less structure somehow as if
the time we spent together when you were here was a perfectly
dimensioned cube + now its more like fragments of varying shapes
+ sizes + i cant help but wish you were here now even though i am happy
that you are happy now + you ask me how im finding norwich now
+ i launch into this story about some guy with an air pistol who i saw walking
down my street he was shooting at street lights + from my position by
the third floor window of my bedsit he looked kind of sad + it reminded me
of the time i got attacked by a crow i felt its claws on my head + i turned
to look at it + it was wearing this frantic bashful expression as if to say
*i dont know why im doing this + i dont know why im here*
*but at least we are both defining ourselves in somesortaway*

**stealing table sauces from wetherspoons**

at lunch       you tell me you miss going to church
the rituals       the something
to fill up the lack

i am eyeing up
the sauce basket
beside you

its not enough
you say
this
isnt
enough

after lunch my pockets are bulging
with colmans mustard/hp/cholula
hot in the rain you tell me       im a bad human being
you ask       me why

i try to explain the comfort of it
the complete relief of having a fridge
filled up a shelf perfectly lined
the safe knowledge that with enough
condiments any meal is edible

you say       but what about
their business models

i tell you not to worry
this happens all the time

anything they lose
they can always simply replace

# 太極

taiji is the great movement which occurs
during most interactions + that is why
it can also mean an exercise which is commonly
translated as tai chi instead + during
tai chi people move in all sorts of ways
mostly slowly because most great movement
works slowly just look at tectonic plates + the fact
that asia + europe used to be the same
massive place but now they arent
or the fact that childhood friends so often
drift away to become adult strangers
who only barely recognise each other + even when
they do finally realise who the other person is
all it leads to are surreal feelings of smallness

## departure

everywhere is an airport
if you try hard enough
all you have to do is wait
until you turn into your
parents or your grandparents
or your great grandparents +
then its just a case of choosing
where in the world you will go
what in the world you will be
how you will walk how your
children will walk how your
grandchildren will walk how
your great grandchildren will walk
+ how long will they have to wait
before they build airports
of their own

**earnings**

at the checkout
i daydream

you are there

beep

i think about boats the size of cities
machines which could take us
any where

beep

i think about winning awards
for my poems or for being
a good human being
beep
i think about what it would be like
to not have to worry about rent
beep
i think about us

i mean

imagine all the great things we could do

if only we had the money if only we had the money if only we had the money
if only we had the money if only we had the money if only we had the money
if only we had the money if only we had the money if only we had the money
beep if only we had the money if only we had the money if only we had the money
if only we had the money beep if only we had the money beep if only we had the money beep
if only we had the money if only we had the money if only we had the money
if only we had the money if only we had the money if only we had the money
if only we had the money if only we had the money if only we had the money

if only we had the money if only we had the money if only we had the money
if only we had the money if only we had the money if only we had the money
if only we had the money if only we had the money if only we had the money
beep if only we had the money if only we had the money if only we had the money
if only we had the money beep if only we had the money beep if only we had the money beep
if only we had the money if only we had the money if only we had the money
if only we had the money if only we had the money if only we had the money
if only we had the money if only we had the money if only we had the money

## 無爲

wuwei is the practice of doing
without acting in other words
allowing yourself to be driven
by forces beyond your control
like when you have to decide
between staying in one place
or moving to another so you
flip a coin + if its heads you will
stay + if its tails you will go +
when it lands on tails + you end
up moving it turns out to not
be too bad + to not be too good
either but at least where you live
now the rent is slightly cheaper

**16 slices**

| | |
|---|---|
| sliced ham contains ////// more water than pork + in this way s liced ham is more like a human than any other form of process ed sliced meat //////////////// | ///////////// if you rip open a pack of sliced ham + // throw //// each slice in the air //////// its possible to divine th e future fortunes of your love life ///// or indeed your age //// of death ///// |
| during the process of making slice d ham scraps gather at the bottom of the machines + these can be us ed to make reformed ham ///// as c an /// mechanically / deboned meat | after going through //// the deboning process //// potassium nitrate /// is us ed as a natural preservative ///// potas sium nitrate can also be used to make fireworks / but is mostly used for ham |
| the most popular sliced ham reci pe is the ham sandwich which o ften also uses // other ingredients such as cheese tomato or lettuce to create an efficient lunch meal | water is used to bulk out each s lice of ham so as to create the i llusion of eating real carved por k sliced from a cured joint /////// ////////////////////////////////// |
| the blood /// from each pig //// used in the deboning process ///// can be used to make a completely fresh pig ripe for slicing //// + therefore slice d ham is a ////// sustainable business | frozen sliced ham ////// can be us ed as an effective //////// form of eyemask in certain circumstances due to the healing properties foun d in pork ///////////////////////// |
| ////////////////////////////////// the inclusion of sliced ham is the main difference between special fried rice + house fried rice in ma ny british-chinese takeaways //// | sodium //// ascorbate ///// protects each slice of ham //// from bad bacte ria as well as /// providing consume rs with a good source of vitamin c // which they wouldnt /// normally get |
| one review /// of a certain brand of sl iced ham described each slice as A M ASS OF PALE PINK WITH ROGUE DARK ER CIRCLES ////// another simply said ////////// UNOFFENSIVE /////////// | sliced ham ///// pigs ////// are now known to be /////// the happiest /// pigs in the world ////// with their o nly real complaint being their lack of sliced ham to eat /////////////// |
| professional sliced ham eaters do exi st albeit only in the remotest parts of clacton /// their life expectancy rates are surprisingly average // but their e yes are filled ///////////// with magic | sliced ham is often seen as inferior to other processed meats such as b acon //// however more sliced ham is consumed annually worldwide th an any other processed ////// meat |
| ///// sliced ham has been used as a symbol of societal progression sin ce the very first sliced ham factor y opened in the early 1900s to pro vide cheap sliced ham for all /////// | according to the united states depar tment of agriculture the shelf life o f an unopened /////// pack of sliced h am is generally thought to be 1-200 0 years past / the printed sell-by date |

陰

yin is the feminine founding element
which isnt to say that yin promotes
the buying of daughters or the
hollywood dragon lady archetype
in which an asian woman is defined
by her aggressive + domineering
behaviour [see: lucy lius character
in kill bill] + in fact a truer example of yin
is to be found in the deepest parts
of pornhub.com where under a video
titled busty bigdick asian gives self
pleasure the top comment reads
i wish i had that all the way inside me
right the way into my stomach

陽

yang is the masculine founding element
which isnt to say that yang promotes
patriarchs selling daughters or the
hollywood yellowface archetype
in which a white male actor plays
a stereotypical asian man [see: mickey
rooneys character in breakfast at tiffanys]
+ in fact a truer example of yang
is to be found in the deepest parts
of pornhub.com where under a video
titled busty bigdick asian gives self
pleasure the top comment reads
i wish i had that all the way inside me
right the way into my stomach

**cleansing ritual**

the tao that is the true tao
is the tao you make up when
steaming in your shower
+ all you can think about
is how at the party
you didnt feel like you
just kept drinking more
+ more until finally the world
turned into elements + you
turned into elements too
+ you couldnt wait to be
in your shower again
scrubbing water on skin
that fakest of tao + now
you are in that shower
+ maybe you are crying
or maybe you are not
but at least you are doing
so honestly

**i am on the floor cutting roast duck into bits**

the portrait on the kitchen wall is slanted

there are three plug sockets –kettle –microwave –electric incense
only one is being used

sometimes i wish i was catholic
–gold+white is a better aesthetic
than red+brown

from the other room
麻將 is being played
everyone is yelling

i get shouted at
to focus on cutting each duckbit equally

except the offerings–
they have to be smaller

but i dont know how small

just three little pieces

from the body

i have yet to figure out how best to structure
each of my prayers into language

—

+ so i said to the guy what do you
mean you dont sell poems this
is a bookshop you should sell poems
+ he said sorry but poems
just dont really sell but we do sell
shakespeare we actually have a
discount on the collected works of
shakespeare right now + i said
that is not right at all + he said
do you mean right as in correct
or right as in morally acceptable
+ i said i just want some poems
why are there no poems in this city + he said
why are you crying sir why are you crying
do you want me to get in trouble with my manager

**you are mistaken**

no my life isnt more interesting than yours no i dont watch anime no im not especially good at maths no i dont want to go back to hongkong no my mum speaks english to me albeit in a slightly northern accent no i dont eat roasts every sunday no i think english food is ok too no i dont think im exotic no i dont have any siblings isnt it strange how theres a whole spectrum of familial emotion i will never have access to no i havent seen every hongkong film ever no i dont have anything in common with the other half-chinese person you know no im not rich at all no i dont think racism is getting bad i think racism has always been bad no i cant grow facial hair no i dont blame white people no i dont think china should own hongkong no i dont write translation poetry no i dont dye my hair black no i dont know any triads no i wont tell you anything about my dick just read my poems no i can definitely say the letter L correctly no im not ok no i dont cosplay no i havent lived in china no i dont want to write angry poems about my life no i dont want to be labelled as a political or racial poet no i do think the world is a pretty good place no i cant set you up with any hot asian girls no i dont drive an audi no i dont want to go to japan at least not until they apologise for their warcrimes no i dont think jackie chan is the greatest living martial artist no i havent read much classical chinese literature no i havent read much classical english literature no i dont know why chinese guys wont date you no ive never eaten dog no ive never seen the queen no i dont want to take your job if anything i would quite like to not have to work no i dont think that asian racism is more acceptable than black racism or white racism or female racism or male racism or trans racism no i dont think i know everything no i wont stop using + no i do want a hug no i dont want to watch sailor moon no i havent always been this way no i dont like pandas no im not malaysian no im not a very happy boy no i dont remember the handover no im not asleep my eyes are just like this no i cant grow body hair no i dont want to ignore my own privileges no im not hardworking because im chinese im hardworking because working hard is the only way to make the day go faster no im not quiet because im chinese im quiet because i dont have much to say to you no i dont know kungfu no i do still worry about the future no i dont wish i was fully one way or another no i dont want to talk about politics with you this is a fucking garden party not the houses of parliament no i dont have an english nose no im not interested in hearing your funny story about your time backpacking in china no my childhood was mostly ok no i dont think ai wei wei is the greatest living artist no i really am chinese trust me no my views on things change all the time is that really a bad thing no i dont think im a better human being than you no ive never brought a rice cooker in with me to my university library so that i can cook rice at the same time as studying although i do admit its a pretty good idea no im fine really no i think fortune cookies are disgusting in all possible ways no im not a buddhist i actually find buddhism to be really depressing i mean its all about suffering + suffering + suffering + suffering + escaping from suffering instead of accepting it no i wont join your asian writers group unless you pay me because fuck knows i need the money no i cant get you a discount at your local chinese takeaway no i dont want to be the next sarah howe no i really am british trust me no im not academically gifted no i dont want to have sex with robots no i wont speak chinese for you no i dont write poems in chinese no i hate long flights no i have no idea how to fix your iphone no i dont think charlie chan as a character was a turning point for white attitudes towards the portrayal of asian men in western media no im not a communist no im not singaporean no i dont have many chinese friends no i was never part of a chess club no i dont think race is talked about enough in british poetry no i actually know embarrassingly little about the history of britain no i do think china does some things better for instance customer service no i do think britain does some things better for instance pub culture no ive never been to beijing no i dont love shakespeare no i dont read manga no i still dont believe that i fully understand myself no i wont look over that poem you wrote about a chinese girl you used to know no i dont like prawn crackers no i dont like hentai no i dont think china is going to take over the world no i dont enjoy the british museum no i wont stop being who i am dont you know its impossible for me to artificially change like that + of course if i was given the choice i would change a few things about myself no i dont think anyone ever doesnt want to change some things about themselves no i dont always follow my own principles that would completely defeat the point of having them

## 無極

wuji is without limit
it can be used to explain what came
before our universe of tao
as in before there was tao there was something
much like before the big bang
there was something + those somethings
didnt have beginnings or if they did they are
unknowable at least within our current
limitations + so whats the point
in thinking about them too much
especially when the universe which exists
in the now of today is much more interesting
for instance just look out of the window now look
how did that get there

# TRACTION MAINTENANCE AND SERVICING DEPOT CODES

The following list covers all BR depots at which traction receives scheduled maintenance. This is only a general guide as to the main Sectors for which each depot is responsible and the type of traction normally maintained at that location. Some depots only carry out smaller exams and brake block changes and may not have an allocation and facilities for full maintenance.

| Code. | Depot | Sector(s) | Stock maintained. |
|---|---|---|---|
| AB | Aberdeen SD | I | SL |
| AF | Chart Leacon T&RSMD (Ashford) | N | SL, EMU |
| AL† | Aylesbury TMD | N | DMU |
| AN | Allerton SD | F | SL |
| AY | Ayr SD | F | SL |
| BD | Birkenhead North EMUD | P | BL, EMU |
| BI | Brighton EMUD | N | EMU |
| BJ | Bristol Barton Hill CSMD | R | NPCCS |
| BL | Blyth (Cambois) SD | F | DL, SL |
| BM | Bournemouth West EMUD | N | EMU |
| BN | Bounds Green T&RSMD (London) | I | DL★, EL, HCS |
| BQ | Bury EMUD | P | EMU |
| BR | Bristol Bath Road TMD | I,P,R | DL★, DMU. |
| BS | Bescot TMD | F,D | DL |
| BX | Buxton SD | F | DL |
| BY | Bletchley TMD | N,P | SL, DMU, EMU. |
| BZ | St Blazey SD | F | DL |
| CA | Cambridge TMD | N,R | DMU, NPCCS. |
| CC | Clacton EMUD | N | EMU |
| CD | Crewe DMD | I,F,P,R | DL |
| CE | Crewe ETD | F,R | EL |
| CF | Cardiff Canton T&RSMD | F,P | DL, DMU |
| CH | Chester TMD | P | DMU |
| CK | Corkerhill TMD | P | DMU |
| CL | Carlisle Upperby TMD | P,F | SL, HCS |
| CP | Crewe CS | P | |
| CR | Colchester SD | F | DL |
| DR | Doncaster SD | F | DL, SL |
| DY | Derby Etches Park T&RSMD | I,P,R | SL, DMU, HCS, NPCCS |
| EC*f* | Edinburgh Craigentinny T&RSMD | I,P,R | DL★, HCS, NPCCS |
| ED | Eastfield TMD (Glasgow) | I,P,F | DL, DMU. |
| EH | Eastleigh T&RSMD | N,D | DL, SL, DEMU, EMU, HCS |
| EM | East Ham EMUD | N | EMU |
| EN | Euston Downside CSD | I,R | HCS, NPCCS. |
| FH | Frodingham SD | F | DL |
| FR $ | Fratton EMUD | N | EMU |
| FW | Fort William SD | P | DL, DMU, HCS |
| GD | Gateshead SD | R | SL |
| GI | Gillingham EMUD | N | EMU |
| GL | Gloucester SD | F | SL |
| GM | Grangemouth SD | F | DL, SL |
| GW | Glasgow Shields ETMD | P | EMU |
| HA | Haymarket TMD | P | SL, DMU |
| HE | Hornsey EMUD | N | BL, EMU |
| HM | Healey Mills SD | F | DL |
| HO | Holbeck SD (Leeds) | R, D | |
| HR | Hall Road EMUD (Liverpool) | P | EMU |
| HT | Heaton T&RSMD | I,P,R | DL, DMU, HCS, NPCCS |
| IL‡ | Ilford ETMD | I,N,R | DL, EL, EMU |
| IS | Inverness T&RSMD | I,P,F | DL, SL, DMU, HCS |
| KY | Knottingley SD | F | DL, SL |
| LA | Laira T&RSMD | I,N,P,F,D | DL★, SL, DMU, HCS |
| LE | Landore TMD (Swansea) | I,P | SL, DMU, HCS★ |
| LG | Longsight EMD (Manchester) | I,P | EL, EMU |
| LL | Liverpool Downhill | P | HCS |
| LO | Longsight DMD | F,P | SL, DMU |
| LR | Leicester SD | F | DL |
| MA | Longsight CSMD | I,R | HCS, NPCCS |
| ME | Marylebone TMD | N | DMU |
| MG | Margam SD | F | SL |
| ML | Motherwell TMD | F | DL, SL |
| MR | March SD | F,D | DL |
| NC‡ | Norwich Crown Point T&RSMD | I,P,R | EL, SL, DMU, HCS, NPCCS |
| NH | Newton Heath TMD | P | DMU |
| NL | Neville Hill T & RSMD | I,P | DL, SL, DMU, HCS |

| | | | |
|---|---|---|---|
| OC | Old Oak Common TMD | N,D | DL, SL. |
| OM | Old Oak Common RSMD | I,N | HCS |
| ON | Orpington EMUD | N | EMU |
| OO | Old Oak Common HST & DMU Shed | I,N | DL★, DMU, HCS★ |
| OY | Oxley CSMD | I,F | HCS, NPCCS |
| PB | Peterborough SD | F | DL, SL |
| PC | Polmadie (Glasgow) CSMD | I,F | HCS, NPCCS |
| PH | Perth SD | I,D | SL, HCS |
| PM | St Philips Marsh HSTD (Bristol) | I | DL★, HCS★ |
| PY | Pylle Hill CSD (Bristol) | R | NPCCS |
| PZ | Penzanze SD | I | DL★, HCS★ |
| RE | Ramsgate EMUD | N | EMU, NPCCS |
| RG | Reading TMD | N, F | SL, DMU |
| RL | Ripple Lane SD | F | SL, DL |
| RY | Ryde IOW | N,D | SL, EMU |
| SA | Salisbury CSMD Exhibition | I | NPCCS |
| SF | Stratford TMD | F,D | DL |
| SG | Slade Green EMUD | N | EMU |
| SH | Strawberry Hill CMEED | N,D | EMU |
| SL | Stewarts Lane T&RSMD | I,F | DL, EDL, EMU |
| SP | Springs Branch SD | F,D | DL |
| SR | Stratford Major Depot.(DMEE) | I,N,F,R,D | DL, EL, SL |
| SU | Selhurst T&RSMD | N | SL, DEMU, EMU |
| SY | Saltley SD | F | DL |
| TO | Toton TMD | F | DL, SL |
| TS | Tyseley TMD | P | DMU |
| WB | Wembley CSMD | I | HCS, NPCCS |
| WC | Waterloo EMUD (W&C) | N | EMU |
| WD | Wimbledon (East) EMUD | N | EMU |
| WN | Willesden TMD | I | EL, SL |
| WY | Westbury SD | F | DL |
| YK | York CED | D | SL |
| HQ | BRB Headquarters. (New stock awaiting acceptance, Research stock, Private Owner stock, Stored stock awaiting decision). | | |
| ZF | BRML Doncaster Major Depot. | | |
| ZG | BRML Eastleigh Works. | | |
| ZH | BRML Springburn (Glasgow) Major Depot. | | |
| ZL | BR Cathays Maintenance Depot. | | |
| ZN | BRML Wolverton Major Depot. | | |

**Private companies maintaining BR stock.**

| | |
|---|---|
| - | Hunslet-Barclay, Kilmarnock. |
| KN | RFS Industries, Kilnhurst |
| ZB | RFS Industries (Doncaster & Kilnhurst). |
| ZC | BREL Crewe Works. |
| ZE | BREL Derby Locomotive Works |
| ZR | BREL York Carriage Works. |

† Aylesbury depot is being constructed for Chiltern Lines Class 165 DMUs, delivery due to commence February 1991. The location is currently used only as a stabling point.

*ƒ* Provincial Sector ceases to maintain stock at Craigentinny from May 1990.

$ Fratton is due to close May 1990. EMU maintenance facilities will be opened at Eastleigh from this date.

‡ InterCity electric locomotive maintenance to be transferred from Ilford to Norwich October 1990.

**STOCK:**

| | |
|---|---|
| BL | Battery locomotives. |
| DL | Diesel locomotives. |
| DMU | Diesel multiple units. |
| EL | Electric locomotives. |
| EMU | Electric multiple units. |
| HCS | Hauled passenger coaching stock. |
| NPCCS | Non passenger carrying coaching stock. |
| SL | Shunting locomotives. |

★ Maintains/Services InterCity 125 (HST) locomotives and/or coaches.

**SECTORS:**

| | |
|---|---|
| D | Departmental. |
| F | Railfreight. |
| I | InterCity. |
| N | Network SouthEast. |
| P | Provincial. |
| R | Parcels. |

Above: BREL built Mk3 DVT No 82143 leads the 09.54 Blackpool North–Euston through Bushey on 18 March, Class 90 No 90003 at the rear provides power.
Below: Class 08 No 08740 seen at Stratford Major Depot (SR). Note the absence of any sub-Sector decals from the two-tone Railfreight livery (F–).

# SUB-SECTOR (POOL) CODES:

**Locomotives:** See allocation summary on page 8.

**Multiple Units and Hauled Coaching Stock:** All official codes are of FOUR characters. The fourth character 'X' on passenger carrying stock indicates a normal stock status and for convenience is thus omitted herein; where a different character applies details are given below.

*DME:* Director of Mechanical & Electrical Engineering (Service stock).
*IAN:* InterCity, Anglia Region.
*ICC:* InterCity, Cross-Country services.
*ICH:* InterCity, Special Services Group (Charter).
*ICHB:* InterCity Charter, Vacuum brake, refurbished.
*ICHC:* InterCity Charter, Vacuum brake, non-refurbished.
*ICHD:* InterCity Charter, Air braked.
*ICHE:* InterCity Charter, Exhibition van fleet.
*ICHM:* InterCity Charter, Manchester fleet.
*ICHS:* InterCity Charter, steam-haulage fleet.
*ICHV:* InterCity Charter, VIP fleet.
*IEC:* InterCity, East Coast route.
*IML:* InterCity, Midland main line.
*IVG:* InterCity, Gatwick Express service.
*IWC:* InterCity, West Coast main line.
*IWR:* InterCity, Western Region.
*NBT:* Network SouthEast Boat Trains (Victoria-Folkestone).
*NGB:* Network SouthEast Gospel Oak-Barking & Kensington Olympia-Clapham Junction.
*NGE:* Network SouthEast Great Eastern lines (Liverpool St.– Southend Victoria/Parkeston Quay/Clacton and branches).
*GN:* Network SouthEast Great Northern lines (King's Cross/Moorgate - Cambridge/Huntingdon)
*NKC:* Network SouthEast Kent Coast services.
*NKS:* Network SouthEast Kent Suburban services.
*NML:* Network SouthEast Midland Lines.
*NMY:* Network SouthEast Chiltern Lines (Marylebone – Aylesbury/Banbury).
*NNE:* Network SouthEast West Anglia lines (Liverpool St – Kings Lynn and branches).
*NNL:* Network SouthEast North London lines (Richmond-Woolwich, Corby-Kettering-Bedford-Bletchley)
*NNW:* Network SouthEast North-West lines (Euston-Northampton).
*NSB:* Network SouthEast Surrey & Berkshire (South-Western lines outer suburban)
*NSL:* Network SouthEast South London (Victoria & Waterloo inner suburban services)
*NSS:* Network SouthEast Solent and Sarum (Waterloo-south Hampshire/Weymouth/Exeter)
*NSX:* Network SouthEast Sussex (Victoria-Sussex coast and branches)
*NTS:* Network SouthEast London, Tilbury & Southend line (Fenchurch St.–Shoeburyness)
*NWR:* Network SouthEast Thames lines (Paddington-Oxford/Newbury and branches)
(Note: Routes given are the official NSE boundaries. In some instances through semi-fast services are provided by NSE by arrangement with Provincial Sector beyond these points (eg to Birmingham, Ipswich and Peterborough).

*P—:* Provincial Sector. All stock in normal service for this Sector has the 2nd & 3rd digits of its code corresponding to the owning maintenence depot.
DXX, IXX, NXX, PXX General, not allocated to operating traffic.
General Suffixes to passenger carrying fleet:
*D:* Driver training train.
*L:* On loan to sub-Sector shown.
*H:* Hold – to await instructions.
*R:* Vehicle internally refurbished (not all such vehicles are so coded).
*Z:* To be scrapped or transferred to Departmental Service fleet.

*RPAC:* Parcels, NRX, airline container traffic
*RPIC:* InterCity use, BGs with security cage.
*RPIP:* InterCity use, BGs for general use.
*RPIT:* InterCity use, temporary.
*RPMA:* Parcels, AC electric multiple-units, Class 302.
*RPMB:* Parcels, AC electric multiple-units, Class 307.
*RPMD:* Parcels, DC electric multiple-units.
*RPOA:* Parcels, Post Office vans, Anglia Region.
*RPOC:* Parcels, Post Office, General van pool.
*RPOE:* Parcels, Post Office vans, Eastern Region.
*RPOM:* Parcels, Post Office vans, London Midland Region.
*RPOW:* Parcels, Post Office vans, Western Region.
*RPOZ:* Parcels, Post Office vans, Scottish Region.
*RPPA:* Parcels, Newspaper vans, Anglia Region.
*RPPE:* Parcels, Newspaper vans, Eastern Region.
*RPPM:* Parcels, Newspaper vans, London Midland Region.
*RPPW:* Parcels, Newspaper vans, Western Region.
*RPXA:* Gangwayed Brake, NEA (100mph) Anglia Region.
*RPXB:* Parcels, General, NDX (dual brake) series.
*RPXC:* Parcels, General, NDV (vacuum brake only) series.
*RPXD:* Parcels, General, NJV & NKV (vacuum brake only) series.
*RPXE:* Parcels, General, NJA (air brake only) & NJX (dual brake) series.
*RPXG:* Parcels, General, Courier vans.
*RPXH:* Gangwayed Brake, NEA (100mph) & NHA (110mph), Eastern Region.
*RPXM:* Gangwayed Brake, NEA (100mph) & NHA (110mph), London Midland Region.
*RPXN:* Parcels, diesel multiple-units.
*RPXT:* Parcels, General, surplus to requirements.
*RPXW:* Gangwayed Brake, NEA (100mph) Western Region.
*RPXX:* Parcels, General, condemned.
*RPXZ:* Gangwayed Brake, NEA (100mph) & NHA (110mph), Scottish Region.

## LIVERIES

The British Rail policy on liveries has changed frequently in recent years and although supposedly now standardised minor variations continue depending on where the painting is carried out. Network SouthEast is the main Sector to have it's stock specially stopped for painting in the official livery. With official shopping periodicity on traction and rolling stock varying between 18 months and 10 years plus many varieties can be seen. Much stock remains in 'old' colours of Rail Blue for locomotives and BG type Parcels Sector vans, blue and grey for multiple units, hauled passenger stock and GUV type (Mk.1 design) parcels vans. These are the liveries being replaced and therefore in this book no reference appears where this scheme currently applies. Other liveries are shown by a code as follows:

*B:* Rail blue (DMUs only).
*BA:* British Airports Authority, green and white.
*Bg:* Rail blue and grey (Parcels stock only).
*F:* Railfreight, old style, single light grey (some have red solebar).
*F–:* Railfreight without sub-Sector decals.
*F+:* Railfreight without sub-Sector decals, spray painted.
*Fa:* Railfreight, Construction (brush painted) Two-tone grey. Decals blue and yellow blocks.
*Fb:* Railfreight, Construction (spray painted) Two-tone grey. Decals blue and yellow blocks.
*Fe:* Railfreight, Coal (brush painted) Two-tone grey. Decals black diamonds on yellow background.
*Ff:* Railfreight, Coal (spray painted) Two-tone grey. Decals black diamonds on yellow background.
*Fg:* Railfreight Distribution (brush painted) Two-tone grey. Decals red diamonds on yellow background.
*Fh:* Railfreight Distribution (spray painted) Two-tone grey. Decals red diamonds on yellow background.
*Fm:* Railfreight Steel (brush painted) Two-tone grey. Decals blue chevrons on yellow background.
*Fn:* Railfreight Steel (spray painted) Two-tone grey. Decals blue chevrons on yellow background.
*Fp:* Railfreight Petroleum (brush painted) Two-tone grey. Decals blue wavy lines on yellow background.
*Fq:* Railfreight Petroleum (spray painted) Two-tone grey. Decals blue wavy lines on yellow background.
*Fx:* Railfreight General (brush painted). Two-tone grey. Decals red and yellow blocks.
*I:* InterCity (locomotives with name branding sic *'INTERCITY'* or 'InterCity', coaching stock with or without branding)
*IB:* InterCity, traditional Pullman.
*IG:* InterCity Gatwick Express.
*IM:* InterCity, maroon.
*Im:* InterCity, Motorail.
*IP:* InterCity Pullman.
*IT:* InterCity Tourist (West Highland), green and cream.
*Iw:* INTERCITY with swallow insignia.
*ML:* BR Main Line (locomotives only).
*Ms:* BR Main Line with 'ScotRail' name branding.
*N:* Network SouthEast.
*NL:* (NSE) London and South East Sector (Brown, orange & grey).
*Pb:* Provincial two-tone blue.
*PC:* Provincial Highland Rail, green and cream.
*PE:* Provincial Express. (Black and fawn with blue stripes).
*PM:* Provincial, Greater Manchester PTE, orange.
*PN:* Provincial Network North West, two-tone blue with red band.
*PP:* Provincial, Trans-Pennine.
*PS:* Provincial, Strathclyde PTE, orange.
*Ps:* Provincial Main Line with ScotRail branding.
*PT:* Provincial Tyne and Wear, yellow.
*PW:* Provincial, chocolate and cream.
*PY:* Provincial, West Yorkshire PTE, crimson red and cream.
*R:* Parcels, red with yellow lining (including Royal Mail branded vehicles).
*R:* Parcels, red and grey (Locomotives).
*ZG:* BR General. (Dark grey, unlined).
★: Special – see below.

## LOCOMOTIVES:

Black: 08601 08642 08730 08867 08907
Blue (Great Eastern): 08833
Blue (NSE): 73004 73005
Green (BR): 08011 08168 08556 08604 08647 08691 08772 08793 08846 08869 08944 20030 20064 37350 47484 47500 50007
Green (LNER): 08793
Green (SR): 08892
Red (Railfreight): 08500
Red and blue (BRB Research): 97403
Red and cream (BRB Research): 31970
(Hunslet-Barclay and RFS Industries apply their own liveries, subject to DoT safety requirements if operating on BR lines).

## DIESEL MULTIPLE UNITS:

Chocolate and cream (GWR): 51368 51410 59520
Green (BR): 53964 54247

# LOCOMOTIVES COSTING CENTRES/POOLS

This summary shows the normal duties for which locomotives are currently maintained.

**CYPD: Private owner, Hunslet-Barclay, Class 20/9**
20901 20902 20903 20904 20905 20906

**CYPO: Private owner, Foster Yeoman, Class 59**
59001 59002 59003 59004 59005

**DBMS: Departmental, Shunters, BRML**
08484(ZN) 08629(ZN) 08647(ZF) 08881(ZH) 08883(ZH)

**DCAA: Departmental, RCE Anglia SF**
31135 31165 31181 31186 31187 31190 31191
31196 31219 31224 31250 31263 31268
37140 37216
47346 47366

**DCBS: Departmental, RCE Midland, Shunters, BY**
08011 08628 08656 08789 08807 08909 08914
08922 08927

**DCEA: Departmental, RCE Eastern IM:**
31106 31230 31252 31282 31285
31541 31444 31547 31552 31453 31456 31458
37003 37066 37071 37095 37104 37184 37232
37251 37408
47331 47332 47344 47348 47352

**DCEB: Departmental, RCE Eastern, Shunters YK**
08499 08500 08525 08605 08657 08662 08719
08777

**DCEW: Departmental, RCE Eastern weekend duties IM**
31212 31221 31223 31249

**DCHA: Departmental, RCE Scottish ED**
26011 26014 26015 26021 26023 26024 26026
26027 26028 26035 26036 26039
37072 37087 37153 37156 37170 37175 37196
37240 37407
47467 47550 47604

**DCHB: Departmental, RCE Scottish, Shunters PH**
08712 08762

**DCLS: Departmental, RCE Midland, Shunters LO**
08611 08619 08624 08666 08673 08676 08721
08744 08790 08891 08915

**DCMA: Departmental, RCE Midland Region**
TO: 20030 20064
BS: 31107 31110 31119 31235
31422 31430 31433 31445 31448 31455
CD: 47005 47053 47108 47116 47117
47329 47333 47353 47372

**DCMB: Departmental, ACE Birmingham TO**
20025 20035 20048 20070 20072 20096 20110
20127 20145 20228

**DCMC: Departmental, ACE Crewe**
TO: 20034 20042 20043 20069 20092 20102
20139 20160
BS 31237
31407 31435 31446 31451 31454 31465

**DCML: Departmental, ACE Liverpool BS**
31113 31145 31147 31158 31166 31174

**DCMM: Departmental, ACE Manchester CD**
47340 47356 47357 47436

**DCMN: Departmental, ACE Nottingham**
TO: 20029 20031 20056 20063 20095 20176
20189 20227
CD: 31162 31409 31419 31437

**DCMP: Departmental, ACE Preston CD**
47339 47343 47358 47426 47431 47450 47453

**DCMW: Departmental, ACE Watford BS**
31112 31178 31317
31405 31411 31420 31424 31434 31568

**DCQA: Departmental DCE Track Test CD**
31412 31414 31416 31426
47531 47546

**DCSA: Departmental, RCE Southern**
EH: 33002 33035 33057 33065
33108 33109 33111 33113
SL: 73101 73103 73105 73108 73110 73111
73114 73117 73118 73119 73126 73128 73129
73131 73132 73133 73138 73139

**DCSB: Departmental, RCE Southern, Shunters SU**
08854
09003 09004 09005 09006 09007 09009 09010
09012 09014 09016 09020

**DCSC: Departmental, RCE Southern, Shunters, AF**
08600 08637 08796 08950
09002 09011 09018 09019 09021 09022 09023
09024

**DCSM: Departmental RCE Southern, Meldon EH**
33008 33026 33101 33102 33103 33106 33110
33114 33117 33118 33201

**DCSW: Departmental RCE Southern, stored SL**
73003 73004

**DCWA: Departmental, RCE Western Region**
EH: 33116
SL: 33208
CF: 37133 37141 37142 37146 37158 37162
37174 37207 37221 37230 37263 37264 37372
OC: 47315 47334 47341 47364
47472 47484 47540
LA: 50004 50008 50009 50015 50023 50031
50034 50036 50042

**DCWC: Departmental RCE Western, Class 97**
CF: 97651 97653
RG: 97654

**DMEA: Departmental DMEE Nationwide, HQ**
TO: 20206 20213
ED: 26010 26042 26043 26046
TE: 31171 31248 31264 31305 31320
BS: 31101 31105 31272 31290 31402 31403
31415 31417 31423 31457 31459 31461 31462
31464 31466 31467
EH: 33025 33030
SL: 73001 73002 73106 73107 73136

**DMEC: Departmental DMEE, battery-electrics**
BD: 97701 97702
HE: 97703 97704 97705 97706 97707 97708

**DOPA: Departmental Director of Operations CF**
97806

**DRTC: Departmental Railway Technical Centre**
TO: 20058 20087
CD: 31970 47971 47972 47973
HQ: 97403 97404u

**DXXD: Departmental, stored.**
20224 50019 50020

**FABT: R'freight Construction (Stone), Buxton TI**
37411 37422 37425
37676 37677 37678 37679 37680 37681 37682
37683 37684 37685 37686 37687 37688

**FACM: Railfreight Construction (Cement) ML**
37370 37373 37379

**FAGS: Railfreight Construction SF**
31116 31128 31134 31149 31155 31164 31180
31209 31234 31247 31271 31289 31293 31294
31296 31301 31306 31308 31327
37144 37211 37218 37219 37354
47007 47325 47328 47367 47430

**FALY: Railfreight Construction (Cement) TE**
31123 31124 31184 31215 31229

**FAME: Railfreight Construction (Cement) ED**
47004 47006 47114 47210

**FASB: Railfreight Construction (Stone) SL**
33004 33006 33009 33012 33019 33020 33021
33023 33027 33029 33033 33040 33042 33046
33047 33048 33050 33051 33052 33053 33056
33058 33060 33063 33064
33202 33204 33207
73140 73141

**FAWK: R'freight Construction (Stone), Westbury CF**
47033 47063
56001 56031 56032 56034 56035 56036 56037
56038 56039 56040 56041 56043 56044 56046
56048 56049 56050 56051 56052 56053 56055
56056

**FAXN: R'freight Construction (Stone), Leicester TO**
56033 56045 56054 56057 56058 56059 56060
56061 56062 56063 56064 56065 56070 56078
56103 56105 56110

**FAXX: Railfreight Construction, Stored**
56042

**FCLL: Railfreight Distribution, China-clay, St. Blazey LA**
37412 37414
37669 37670 37671 37672 37673 37674 37675

**FCTY: Railfreight Distribution (Chemicals) TE**
37378 37415 37417 37420
47301 47302 47303 47304 47305 47361 47362
47363

**FDAT: Railfreight Distribution, TI Class 47**
47016 47018 47019 47049 47051 47052 47060
47079 47095 47099 47105 47107 47112 47142
47144 47145 47147 47150 47152 47156 47157
47186 47187 47188 47201 47204 47205 47206
47207 47209 47211 47213 47214 47217 47218
47219 47220 47225 47226 47227 47228 47229
47231 47234 47236 47237 47238 47241 47245
47249 47256 47258 47270 47279 47280 47281
47283 47284 47285 47286 47287 47288 47289
47290 47291 47292 47293 47296 47297 47298
47306 47307 47308 47309 47310 47311 47312
47313 47317 47321 47323 47335 47337 47345
47351 47359 47360 47370 47371 47375 47376
47377 47378

**FDBT: Railfreight Distribution, 1989/90 Hit List TI**
47002 47003 47096 47098 47100 47102 47118
47120 47121 47123 47146 47200 47314 47316
47338

**FDCC: R'freight Distribution (Chems Coal & Cons) CD**
47320 47322 47323 47330 47347 47349 47350
47354 47355 47365
47423 47425 47438 47439 47440 47441 47442
47445 47446 47447 47449 47451 47452 47454
47457 47473 47479 47485 47491 47532 47588
47594 47599 47600 47605 47615

**FDET: Railfreight Distribution, TI Class 37**
37008 37009 37013 37015 37019 37029 37031
37032 37045 37047 37053 37054 37055 37057
37059 37063 37065 37068 37073 37074 37077
37079 37101 37107 37116 37178 37185 37194
37198 37209 37238 37242 37251 37252 37271
37272 37285 37298 37358

**FDHC: Railfreight Distribution, CE Class 85**
85015 85018 85026 85031 85034 85040

**FDIB: Railfreight Distribution, Dover Linkspan SL**
33203 33205 33206

**FDOT: Railfreight Distribution, TI Class 31**
31102 31125 31132 31142 31144 31146 31159
31160 31206 31232 31242

**FDPC: Railfreight Distribution, CE Classes 86 & 87**
86403 86404 86405 86406 86410 86411 86412
86414 86415 86418 86423 86428 86431 86437
86438 86439
86602 86607 86608 86609 86613 86620 86621
86622 86627 86632 86633 86634 86635 86636
87101

**FDQC: Railfreight Distribution, CE Class 90**
90021 90022 90023 90024 90025 90026 90027
90028 90029 90030 90031 90032 90033 90034
90035 90036 90037 90038 90039 90040 90041
90042 90043

**FDRC: Railfreight Distribution, Class 85/1 CE**
85101 85102 85103 85104u 85105 85106 85108
85109 85110 85112

**FDSE: Railfreight Distribution, ED Class 20**
20118 20119 20122 20124 20137 20138 20156
20165 20198 20211 20212

**FDTE: Railfreight Distribution, ED Class 37**
37401 37402 37403 37404 37405 37406 37409
37410 37413 37423 37424

**FDUV: Railfreight Distribution, IS**
37113 37114 37128 37154 37261 37262

**FDYX: Railfreight Distribution, stored or *to be delivered.***
20051 20065 20099 20173 20208
37096
47009 47017
85013 85020
*90044 90045 90046 90047 90048 90049 90050*

**FDZX: Railfreight Distribution, Stored**
81010

**FEAN: Railfreight Coal, West Midlands TO**
58001 58003 58004 58005 58006 58007 58009
58010 58011 58012 58013 58014 58015 58017

**FEBN: Railfreight Coal, East Midlands Cl.58 TO**
58002 58008 58016 58018 58019 58020 58021
58022 58023 58024 58025 58026 58027 58028
58029 58030 58031 58032 58033 58034 58035
58036 58037 58038 58039 58040 58041 58042
58043 58044 58045 58046 58047 58048 58049
58050

**FECN: Railfreight Coal, Midlands TO**
56002 56003 56004 56005 56006 56007 56008
56009 56010 56011 56012 56013 56014 56015
56016 56017 56018 56019 56020 56021 56022
56023 56024 56025 56026 56027 56028

**FEDN: Railfreight Coal, Yorkshire TO**
56029 56030 56047 56066 56067 56068 56069
56071 56072 56073 56074 56075 56076 56077
56079 56080 56081 56082 56083 56084 56085
56086 56087 56088 56089 56090 56091 56092
56093 56094 56095 56096 56097 56098 56099
56100 56101 56102 56104 56106 56107 56108
56109 56111 56123

**FEEN: Railfreight, Coal, Trainload, Blyth TO**
56112 56113 56114 56115 56116 56117 56118
56119 56120 56121 56122 56124 56125 56126
56127 56128 56129 56130 56131 56132 56133
56134 56135

**FEFN: Railfreight Coal, East Midlands Cl.20 TO**
20004 20007 20026 20040 20047 20052 20053
20059 20078 20081 20084 20085 20088 20094
20103 20104 20105 20108 20129 20136 20142
20151 20157 20163 20166 20170 20177 20186
20187 20190 20196 20197 20210 20214 20215

**FEGN: Railfreight Coal, Non-E.Midlands TO**
20006 20010 20013 20016 20019 20020 20021
20023 20028 20045 20055 20057 20071 20073
20075 20080 20082 20090 20106 20113 20117
20120 20121 20128 20130 20131 20132 20133
20135 20140 20141 20143 20154 20159 20168
20169 20172 20175 20182 20194 20195

**FEKK: Railfreight Coal, Trainload, Aberthaw CF**
37701 37702 37703 37704 37796 37797 37798
37799 37800 37801 37802 37803 37887 37889
37894 37895 37896 37897 37898 37899

**FEPE: Railfreight Coal Lothians, ED**
26001 26002 26003 26004 26005 26006 26007
26008
37165 37229 37375 37376 37380
37693 37694

**FHAC: Railfreight Coal (Flask), CD**
31120 31130 31200 31217 31270 31275 31276
31312 31324

**FHBK: Railfreight Coal (Train-load), CF**
37689 37690 37691 37692 37695 37696 37697
37698 37699

**FHSH: Railfreight Coal, Shunters KY**
08309 08449 08516 08659 08706 08707 08773
08776 08782 08783 08806

**FHTA: Railfreight Coal, Shunters LE**
08390 08646 08756 08780 08798 08895 08896
08897 08993 08994 08995

**FHUB: Railfreight Coal, Shunters BL**
08421 08441 08442 08512

**FHWN: Railfreight Coal, Shunters TO**
08416 08511 08597 08623 08829

**FHZR: Railfreight Coal, Shunters AY**
08561 08586 08591 08675 08693 08727 08735

**FMAK: Railfreight Steel, CF Class 37/0**
37038 37197 37254 37278 37293

**FMGM: Railfreight Steel, Hunterston ML**
37010 37026 37037 37040 37049 37051 37088
37092 37097 37099 37108 37111 37137 37145
37152 37190 37201

**FMHK: Railfreight Steel, CF Classes 37/7 & 37/9**
37710 37711 37712 37713 37714 37715 37716
37717 37718 37719 37883 37884 37885 37886
37901 37902 37903 37904 37905 37906

**FMMT: Railfreight Steel, Shunters TI Class 09**
09008 09013

**FMMY: Railfreight Steel, TE Class 60**
60008

**FMSK: Railfreight Steel, Shunters CF**
08375 08479 08481 08493 08589 08649 08652
08654 08660 08664 08668 08787 08804 08818
08822 08835 08836 08848 08932 08940 08942
09001 09015

**FMST: Railfreight Steel, Shunters TI**
08308 08434 08436 08492 08508 08509 08543
08691 08749 08857 08870 08878 08879 08880
08919

**FMTY: Railfreight Steel, TE**
37004 37023 37042 37046 37048 37054 37058
37069 37070 37075 37083 37098 37100 37109
37110 37202 37203 37227 37241 37250 37255
37258
37501 37502 37503 37504 37505 37506 37507
37508 37509 37510 37511 37512 37513 37514
37515 37516 37517 37518 37519 37520 37521
37667 37668

**FMYI: Railfreight Steel, IM**
20046 20061 20093 20098 20107 20112
37106 37225 37275 37351 37377 37381

**FPAE: Railfreight Petroleum & Chemicals ED**
20066 20148 20185
26025 26032 26037 26038 26040 26041
37035 37080 37188 37191 37245
37359
37707 37708

**FPBC: Railfreight Petroleum, Stanlow CD**
IM: 37426 37430
CD: 47125 47190 47193 47194 47195 47196
47233 47278 47324 47368

**FPCI: R'freight Petroleum (Oil, Chemical, Construction), IM (excluding Class 60)**
31108 31126 31154 31156 31163 31168 31185
31188
31201 31203 31205 31207 31210 31233
31238
31243 31255 31257 31273 31286 31288
31309 31319
47010 47054 47085 47115 47119 47212 47221
47223 47224 47276 47294 47299
47319 47336 47369 47373 47374 47379 47380

**FPDI: Railfreight Petroleum, IM Class 60**
60007

**FPEK: Railfreight Petroleum, South Wales CF**
37012 37078 37138 37215 37220 37248 37273
37280 37294 37350 37371
47094 47197 47277 47318 47326 47327 47381

**FPFR: Railfreight Petroleum, North Thames IM**
37705 37706 37709 37888 37890 37891 37892
37893

**FPXA: Railfreight Petroleum, 1989/90 hit list IM**
31199 31302 31304
47222 47295 47401 47402

**FPZA: Railfreight Petroleum, Shunters IM**
08388 08397 08401 08405 08445 08537 08583
08632 08665 08734 08743 08745 08751 08871
08877

**FQCK: Railfreight Distribution (Network Coal) CF**
37131 37139 37167 37212 37213 37214 37217
37222 37223 37235 37239 37244 37274

**FSAE: Railfreight Distribution, Shunters EH**
RY: 03079 03179
ZG: 08642 08892
EH: 08760 08830 08831 08845 08847 08933
09025 09026

**FSBM: Railfreight Distribution, Shunters ML**
08565 08568 08581 08622 08732 08733 08738
08853 08938 08952

**FSCG: Railfreight Distribution, Shunters GM**
08630 08725 08731

**FSDH: Railfreight Distribution, Shunters HA**
08570 08571 08620 08710 08718 08720 08730
08755 08761 08791 08793

**FSEP: Railfreight Distribution, Shunters NC**
08658 08685 08810 08859 08868 08869 08936

**FSFL: Railfreight Distribution Shunters LA**
08576 08584 08641 08644 08645 08792 08799
08801 08839 08840 08849 08937 08941 08945
08953 08954 08955

**FSGB: Railfreight Distribution, Shunters BS**
08466 08517 08535 08601 08603 08604 08610
08616 08672 08692 08700 08746 08759 08765
08805 08832 08841 08893 08901 08920 08928

**FSHY: Railfreight Distribution, Shunters TE**
08411 08506 08519 08575 08582 08588 08770
08786 08817 08867 08906

**FSID: Railfreight Distribution, Shunters DR**
08418 08510 08514 08562 08595 08607 08682
08723 08729 08813 08824 08866 08876 08885
08903

**FSJS: Railfreight Distribution, Shunters SF**
08393 08407 08413 08414 08417 08460 08498
08527 08530 08531 08533 08541 08542 08593
08627 08655 08689 08698 08708 08709 08715
08724 08740 08748 08750 08752 08758 08767
08772 08775 08828 08833 08834 08873 08923
08956 08957 08958

**FSKC: Railfreight Distribution, Shunters CA**
08495 08496 08526 08528 08529 08538 08539
08540 08580 08594 08631 08638 08705 08711
08713 08714 08757 08865 08889

**FSLC: Railfreight Distribution, Shunters CL**
08419 08447 08534 08690 08768 08808 08826
08844 08910 08911 08912

**FSMA: Railfreight Distribution, Shunters AN**
08402 08415 08482 08485 08532 08569 08615
08686 08688 08694 08703 08809 08815 08827
08856 08858 08884 08894 08902 08913 08916
08917 08918 08924 08925 08939

**FSNC: Railfreight Distribution, Shunters CD**
08472 08585 08599 08613 08633 08635 08695
08699 08702 08737 08739 08742 08784 08823
08907 08921

**FSPG: Railfreight Distribution, Shunters GL**
08778 08781 08795

**FSQA: Railfreight Distribution, Shunters BR**
08410 08483 08643 08800 08819 08900 08935
08949 08951

**FSRO: Railfreight Distribution, Shunters RG**
08523 08803 08821 08850 08946

**FSSO: Railfreight Distribution, Shunters OC**
08454 08480 08573 08612 08634 08651 08653
08670 08811 08825 08837 08887 08904 08905
08929 08944 08947 08948

**FXXA: Railfreight, General**
60001(A) 60005(A) 60002(P) 60003(P) 60004(E)
60006(A) 60012(A) 60009(A) 60010(A) 60011(A)
60013(P) *(60014–60100)*
Latest advised provisional operating allocations :
Construction: Hither Green (FAHH): 60001/06/15–19;
Leicester: 60005/9–12; Westbury: 60039–43
Petroleum: Immingham (FPDI) : 60002/03/13/14/24–28;
Immingham or Cardiff: 60033/34/35/63/64/65
Coal: Toton: 60004/66–75; Springs Branch: 60044–48;
Toton/Crewe: 60055–61
Steel: Thornaby (FMMY): 60020-23/36/37/38/49/50/52/53/54
Thornaby or Motherwell: 60029/30/31/32(a)/62(b)
(a= Sponsored by Coal sub-Sector
b= Sponsored by Petroleum sub-Sector)

**FXXX: Railfreight, General stored**
08704 85107

**IABB: InterCity, Shunters AB**
08680 08855 08882

**IANA: InterCity Anglia IL**
86214 86215 86216 86217 86218 86220 86221
86223 86227 86230 86232 86235 86238 86244
86246 86259

**ICCA: InterCity, Cross-Country LG**
CE: 85008 85030 85037
WN: 86206 86207 86222 86228 86231 86233
86234 86240 86245 86248 86250 86255 86258
86260
87009 87031 87032 87035

**ICCP: InterCity Cross-Country 125 Power Cars LA/PM†**
43012 43016 43019 43035† 43036† 43037† 43126†
43163 43164 43165 43166 43171† 43172† 43173†
43174† 43175† 43177 43178 43179 43181 43182
43183 43184 43185 43186

**ICDA: InterCity, CD Class 47**
47432 47456 47459 47462 47471 47478 47483
47500 47508 47512 47517 47519 47520 47525
47527 47555 47586
47803 47831 47836 47837 47838 47839 47840
47841 47842 47843 47844 47845 47846 47847
47848 47849 47850 47851 47852 47853

**ICHA: InterCity Charter**
WN: 86212 86256
OC: 97251
CL: 97252

**IEBA: InterCity, Euston-W.Mids with DVT WN**
86204 86208 86209 86210 86213 86219 86224
86225 86236 86242 86247 86249 86253 86257

**IECA: InterCity East Coast main line BN**
IM: 47406 47407 47413 47417 47418
BN: 89001
91001 91002 91003 91004 91005 91006 91007
91008 91009 91010 91011 91012 91013
(to be delivered 91014 - 91031)

**IECP: InterCity Eastern 125 Power Cars BN/EC†/HT$/NL‡**
43013 43014 43040† 43041† 43042 43052‡ 43053‡
43054‡ 43056‡ 43057‡ 43058‡ 43062 43063 43065
43068 43069† 43070† 43071† 43074 43075 43078†
43079† 43080 43081 43082 43083 43084 43085
43086† 43087† 43088† 43089† 43090† 43091† 43092†
43093† 43094† 43095$ 43096$ 43097$ 43098$ 43099$
43100† 43101† 43102$ 43103$ 43104$ 43105$ 43106
43107 43108‡ 43109‡ 43110‡ 43111‡ 43113$ 43114‡
43115† 43116‡ 43117‡ 43118‡ 43119‡ 43120‡ 43121‡
43122‡ 43123 43154‡ 43155‡ 43194‡ 43195‡ 43196‡
43197‡ 43198‡

**IEDA: InterCity ED**
47470 47509 47518 47562 47578 47593 47595
47617 47633 47636 47641 47643 47644

**IISB: InterCity, Shunters IS**
08717 08753 08754

**ILRA: InterCity, Long range fuel Class 47/4 BR**
47801 47802 47804 47805 47806 47807 47808
47809 47810 47811 47812 47813 47814 47815
47816 47817 47818 47819 47820 47821 47822
47823 47824 47825 47826 47827 47828 47829
47830 47832 47833 47834 47835

**IMLP: InterCity Midland Lines 125 Power Cars NL**
43038 43039 43043 43044 43045 43046 43047
43048 43049 43050 43051 43055 43059 43060
43061 43064 43066 43072 43073 43076 43077
43112 43152 43153 43193

**IPSA: InterCity, West Coast Pullman TDM WN**
87005 87007 87010 87011 87012 87019 87021
87024 87025
90001 90003 90004 90005 90008 90009 90011
90012 90013 90015

**IVGA: InterCity, Victoria-Gatwick SL**
73135
73201 73202 73203 73204 73205 73206 73207
73208 73209 73210 73211 73212

**IWCA: InterCity West Coast main line WN**
81012 81017
86101 86102 86103
86205 86226 86229 86237 86251 86252
87001 87002 87003 87004 87006 87008 87013
87014 87015 87016 87017 87018 87020 87022
87023 87026 87027 87028 87029 87030 87033
87034
90002 90006 90007 90010 90014

**IWNB: InterCity, Shunters WN**
08451 08556 08609 08614 08617 08625 08648
08677 08683 08696 08890 08926 08934

**IWRP: InterCity Western 125 Power Cars LA‡/PM/OO†**
43002‡ 43003‡ 43004‡ 43005‡ 43006‡ 43007‡ 43008‡
43009‡ 43010‡ 43011‡ 43015‡ 43017 43018 43020‡
43021‡ 43022‡ 43023‡ 43024‡ 43025‡ 43026‡ 43027‡
43028‡ 43029‡ 43030 43031 43032 43033 43034
43124 43125 43127 43128 43129 43130 43131
43132 43133 43134 43135 43136 43137 43138
43139 43140† 43141† 43142† 43143‡ 43144† 43145†
43146† 43147† 43148† 43149 43150 43156‡ 43157‡
43158‡ 43159‡ 43160‡ 43161‡ 43162‡ 43167 43168
43169 43170 43176 43180 43187‡ 43188‡ 43189‡
43190‡ 43191‡ 43192‡

**NSSA: Network SouthEast, Solent and Sarum LA**
50001 50002 50003 50005 50007 50016 50017
50018 50024 50026 50027 50028 50029 50030
50033 50035 50037 50043 50044 50045 50046
50048 50049 50050

**NSSB: Network SouthEast, Solent and Sarum SL**
73005
73104 73109 73112 73130 73134

**NWRA: Network SouthEast, Thames line OC**
47521 47530 47547 47573 47576 47579 47581
47582 47583 47587 47596 47598
47705 47707 47714 47715 47716 47717

**NXXA: Network SouthEast, General**
50032u
73006

**PCDA: Provincial, CD Class 47/4**
47422 47424 47434 47443 47444 47448 47475
47477 47488 47503 47597

**PCDB: Provincial, CD Class 31/4**
31400 31404 31406 31408 31431 31449 31460
31463 31469

**PCFA: Provincial CF**
37427 37428 37429 37431

**PEDA: Provincial ED**
47701 47702 47703 47704 47706 47708 47709
47710 47711 47712

**PISA: Provincial IS Class 47**
47460 47461 47492 47541 47630 47635 47640
47642

**PISB: Provincial, IS Class 37**
37416 37418 37419 37421

**PNLA: Provincial, Shunters NL**
08389 08590 08661 08667 08766 08794 08874
08875 08908

**PXXA: Provincial, General**
08567(YK)

**RXLA: Parcels, Shunters GD**
08489 08507 08515 08521 08544 08577 08578
08587 08701 08771 08802 08886 08888 08931

**RXLB: Parcels. CD Class 31/4**
31410 31413 31418 31421 31425 31427 31428
31429 31432 31438 31439 31442 31450

**RXLC: Parcels, CD Class 47/4**
47421 47433 47458 47463 47465 47474 47479
47481 47489 47522 47523 47526 47559 47567

**RXLD: Parcels, BR & OC† Class 47/4**

| | | | | | | |
|---|---|---|---|---|---|---|
| 47466 | 47468 | 47476 | 47482 | 47490 | 47501 | 47513 |
| 47515 | 47524 | 47528 | 47533† | 47534† | 47535† | 47536 |
| 47537 | 47538 | 47539 | 47543† | 47549 | 47557 | 47558 |
| 47564 | 47565 | 47566 | 47568 | 47569 | 47572 | 47574 |
| 47575 | 47580 | 47584 | 47585 | 47592 | 47603 | 47616 |
| 47624 | 47625 | 47626 | 47627 | 47628 | 47631 | 47634 |

**RXLE: Parcels, AC Electric CE**

| | | | | | | |
|---|---|---|---|---|---|---|
| 85003 | 85011 | | | | | |
| 86239 | 86241 | 86243 | 86254 | 86261 | | |
| 86401 | 86416 | 86417 | 86419 | 86424 | 86425 | 86426 |
| 86430 | | | | | | |
| 90016 | 90017 | 90018 | 90019 | 90020 | | |

**RXLS: Parcels, Shunters DY**

| | | | | | | |
|---|---|---|---|---|---|---|
| 08399 | 08428 | 08448 | 08536 | 08697 | 08788 | 08814 |
| 08838 | 08842 | 08899 | | | | |

**RXXA: Parcels, stored**

08618 08741 08747 08797 08872

**PRIVATE OWNER LOCOMOTIVES:**

**BREL, Shunters:**

08168(ZR) 08470(ZC) 08846(ZD)

**RFS Engineering:**

08164 08331 08602 08764

Above: Class 60 No 60006 *Great Gable* in Railfreight Construction livery (Fb) stands at Hither Green depot on 28 January, where it has been loaned for crew training prior to introduction on Channel Tunnel construction materials trains.

Below: The first two Class 90s in Railfreight Distribution livery (Fg) are seen at the builders, BREL Crewe Works (ZC), on 7 November 1989. They were not handed over to BR until April.

## CLASS 03 — 204hp BR Shunter (Mechanical) — 0-6-0

| | | | |
|---|---|---|---|
| 03079 | | FSAE | RY |
| 03179 | N | FSAE | RY |

## CLASS 08/0 — 400hp BR Shunter (Electric) — 0-6-0

| | | | |
|---|---|---|---|
| 08011 | ★ | DCBS | BY |
| 08308 | | FMST | TI |
| 08309 | Fe | FHSH | KY |
| 08375 | | FMSK | CF |
| 08388 | Fp | FPZA | IM |
| 08389 | | PNLA | NL |
| 08390 | | FHTA | LE |
| 08393 | ZG | FSJS | SF |
| 08397 | | FPZA | IM |
| 08399 | | RXLS | DY |
| 08401 | | FPZA | IM |
| 08402 | ZG | FSMA | AN |
| 08405 | | FPZA | IM |
| 08407 | F- | FSJS | SF |
| 08410 | | FSQA | BR |
| 08411 | | FMZA | TE |
| 08413 | ZG | FSJS | SF |
| 08414 | | FSJS | SF |
| 08415 | | FSMA | AN |
| 08416 | | FHWN | TO |
| 08417 | ZG | FSJS | SF |
| 08418 | Fg | FSID | DR |
| 08419 | | FSLC | CL |
| 08421 | | FHUB | BL |
| 08428 | | RXLS | DY |
| 08434 | | FMST | TI |
| 08436 | | FMST | TI |
| 08441 | | FHUB | BL |
| 08442 | | FHUB | BL |
| 08445 | | FPZA | IM |
| 08447 | | FSLC | CL |
| 08448 | | RXLS | DY |
| 08449 | | FHSH | KY |
| 08451 | | IWNB | WN |
| 08454 | | FSSO | OC |
| 08460 | F- | FSJS | SF |
| 08466 | F | FSGB | BS |
| 08472 | | FSNC | CD |
| 08479 | | FMSK | CF |
| 08480 | | FSSO | OC |
| 08481 | | FMSK | CF |
| 08482 | | FSMA | AN |
| 08483 | | FSQA | BR |
| 08484 | F- | DBMS | ZN |
| 08485 | | FSMA | AN |
| 08489 | F- | RXLA | GD |
| 08492 | | FMST | TI |
| 08493 | | FMSK | CF |
| 08495 | | FSKC | CA |
| 08496 | | FSKC | CA |
| 08498 | | FSJS | SF |
| 08499 | F- | DCEB | YK |
| 08500 | ★ | DCEB | YK |
| 08506 | F- | FSHY | TE |
| 08507 | | RXLA | GD |
| 08508 | | FMST | TI |
| 08509 | F- | FMST | TI |
| 08510 | | FSID | DR |
| 08511 | | FHWN | TO |
| 08512 | F- | FHUB | BL |
| 08514 | | FSID | DR |
| 08515 | | RXLA | GD |
| 08516 | F- | FHSH | KY |
| 08517 | | FSGB | BS |
| 08519 | | FSHY | TE |
| 08521 | | RXLA | GD |
| 08523 | | FSRO | RG |
| 08525 | F- | DCEB | YK |
| 08526 | | FSKC | CA |
| 08527 | F- | FSJS | SF |
| 08528 | F- | FSKC | CA |
| 08529 | | FSKC | CA |
| 08530 | | FSJS | SF |
| 08531 | F- | FSJS | SF |
| 08532 | | FSMA | AN |
| 08533 | | FSJS | SF |
| 08534 | F- | FSLC | CL |
| 08535 | F | FSGB | BS |
| 08536 | | RXLS | DY |
| 08537 | F | FPZA | IM |
| 08538 | | FSKC | CA |
| 08539 | | FSKC | CA |
| 08540 | | FSKC | CA |
| 08541 | | FSJS | SF |
| 08542 | F- | FSJS | SF |
| 08543 | | FMST | TI |
| 08544 | | RXLA | GD |
| 08556 | ★ | IWNB | WN |
| 08561 | | FHZR | AY |
| 08562 | | FSID | DR |
| 08565 | | FSBM | ML |
| 08567 | | PXXA | YK |
| 08568 | | FSBM | ML |
| 08569 | | FSMA | AN |
| 08570 | I | FSDH | HA |
| 08571 | | FSDH | HA |
| 08573 | | FSSO | OC |
| 08575 | | FSHY | TE |
| 08576 | | FSFL | LA |
| 08577 | | RXLA | GD |
| 08578 | | RXLA | GD |
| 08580 | | FSKC | CA |
| 08581 | | FSBM | ML |
| 08582 | | FSHY | TE |
| 08583 | | FPZA | IM |
| 08584 | | FSFL | LA |
| 08585 | | FSNC | CD |
| 08586 | | FHZR | AY |
| 08587 | | RXLA | GD |
| 08588 | | FSHY | TE |
| 08589 | | FMSK | CF |
| 08590 | | PNLA | NL |
| 08591 | | FHZR | AY |
| 08593 | | FSJS | SF |
| 08594 | | FSKC | CA |
| 08595 | | FSID | DR |
| 08597 | | FHWN | TO |
| 08599 | | FSNC | CD |
| 08600 | N | DCSC | AF |
| 08601 | ★ | FSGB | BS |
| 08603 | | FSGB | BS |
| 08604 | ★ | FSGB | BS |
| 08605 | | DCEB | YK |
| 08607 | | FSID | DR |
| 08609 | | IWNB | WN |
| 08610 | | FSGB | BS |
| 08611 | | DCLS | LO |
| 08612 | | FSSO | OC |
| 08613 | | FSNC | CD |
| 08614 | | IWNB | WN |
| 08615 | | FSMA | AN |
| 08616 | | FSGB | BS |
| 08617 | | IWNB | WN |
| 08618 | | RXXA | HQ |
| 08619 | | DCLS | LO |
| 08620 | | FSDH | HA |
| 08622 | | FSBM | ML |
| 08623 | | FHWN | TO |
| 08624 | | DCLS | LO |
| 08625 | | IWNB | WN |
| 08627 | | FSJS | SF |
| 08628 | | DCBS | BY |
| 08629 | | DBMS | ZN |
| 08630 | | FSCG | GM |
| 08631 | N | FSKC | CA |
| 08632 | | FPZA | IM |
| 08633 | | FSNC | CD |
| 08634 | | FSSO | OC |
| 08635 | | FSNC | CD |
| 08637 | | DCSC | AF |
| 08638 | | FSKC | CA |
| 08641 | | FSFL | LA |
| 08642 | ★ | FSAE | ZG |
| 08643 | | FSQA | BR |
| 08644 | F- | FSFL | LA |
| 08645 | F- | FSFL | LA |
| 08646 | F- | FHTA | LE |
| 08647 | ★ | DBMS | ZF |
| 08648 | ZG | IWNB | WN |
| 08649 | | FMSK | CF |
| 08651 | | FSSO | OC |
| 08652 | | FMSK | CF |
| 08653 | | FSSO | OC |
| 08654 | | FMSK | CF |
| 08655 | | FSJS | SF |
| 08656 | | DCBS | BY |
| 08657 | | DCEB | YK |
| 08658 | | FSEP | NC |
| 08659 | | FHSH | KY |
| 08660 | | FMSK | CF |
| 08661 | | PNLA | NL |
| 08662 | | DCEB | YK |
| 08664 | | FMSK | CF |
| 08665 | F- | FPZA | IM |
| 08666 | | DCLS | LO |
| 08667 | | PNLA | NL |
| 08668 | | FMSK | CF |
| 08670 | | FSSO | OC |
| 08672 | | FSGB | BS |
| 08673 | I | DCLS | LO |
| 08675 | | FHZR | AY |
| 08676 | | DCLS | LO |
| 08677 | | IWNB | WN |
| 08680 | | IABB | AB |
| 08682 | | FSID | DR |
| 08683 | | IWNB | WN |
| 08685 | | FSEP | NC |
| 08686 | | FSMA | AN |
| 08688 | | FSMA | AN |
| 08689 | | FSJS | SF |
| 08690 | | FSLC | CL |
| 08691 | ★ | FMST | TI |
| 08692 | | FSGB | BS |
| 08693 | | FHZR | AY |
| 08694 | | FSMA | AN |
| 08695 | | FSNC | CD |
| 08696 | | IWNB | WN |
| 08697 | | RXLS | DY |
| 08698 | | FSJS | SF |
| 08699 | | FSNC | CD |
| 08700 | | FSGB | BS |
| 08701 | | RXLA | GD |
| 08702 | | FSNC | CD |
| 08703 | | FSMA | AN |
| 08704 | | FXXX | HQ |
| 08705 | | FSKC | CA |
| 08706 | | FHSH | KY |
| 08707 | | FHSH | KY |
| 08708 | | FSJS | SF |
| 08709 | | FSJS | SF |
| 08710 | | FSDH | HA |
| 08711 | | FSKC | CA |
| 08712 | | DCHB | PH |
| 08713 | | FSKC | CA |
| 08714 | | FSKC | CA |
| 08715 | | FSJS | SF |
| 08717 | | IISB | IS |
| 08718 | | FSDH | HA |
| 08719 | | DCEB | YK |
| 08720 | Pb | FSDH | HA |
| 08721 | ★ | DCLS | LO |
| 08723 | | FSID | DR |
| 08724 | | FSJS | SF |
| 08725 | | FSCG | GM |
| 08727 | | FHZR | AY |
| 08730 | ★ | FSDH | HA |
| 08731 | | FSCG | GM |
| 08732 | | FSBM | ML |
| 08733 | | FSBM | ML |
| 08734 | | FPZA | IM |
| 08735 | | FHZR | AY |
| 08737 | F- | FSNC | CD |
| 08738 | ZG | FSBM | ML |
| 08739 | | FSNC | CD |
| 08740 | F- | FSJS | SF |
| 08741 | | RXXA | HQ |
| 08742 | | FSNC | CD |
| 08743 | | FPZA | IM |
| 08744 | | DCLS | LO |
| 08745 | | FPZA | IM |
| 08746 | | FSGB | BS |
| 08747 | | RXXA | HQ |
| 08748 | | FSJS | SF |
| 08749 | | FMST | TI |
| 08750 | | FSJS | SF |
| 08751 | | FPZA | IM |
| 08752 | | FSJS | SF |
| 08753 | | IISB | IS |
| 08754 | | IISB | IS |
| 08755 | | FSDH | HA |
| 08756 | | FHTA | LE |
| 08757 | F- | FSKC | CA |
| 08758 | | FSJS | SF |
| 08759 | | FSGB | BS |
| 08760 | | FSAE | EH |
| 08761 | | FSDH | HA |
| 08762 | | DCHB | PH |
| 08765 | ★ | FSGB | BS |
| 08766 | | PNLA | NL |
| 08767 | | FSJS | SF |
| 08768 | | FSLC | CL |
| 08770 | F- | FSHY | TE |
| 08771 | | RXLA | GD |
| 08772 | ★ | FSJS | SF |
| 08773 | | FHSH | KY |
| 08775 | | FSJS | SF |
| 08776 | | FHSH | KY |
| 08777 | | DCEB | YK |
| 08778 | ZG | FSPG | GL |
| 08780 | | FHTA | LE |
| 08781 | | FSPG | GL |
| 08782 | | FHSH | KY |
| 08783 | | FHSH | KY |
| 08784 | | FSNC | CD |

| | | | |
|---|---|---|---|
| 08786 | | FSHY | TE |
| 08787 | | FMSK | CF |
| 08788 | | RXLS | DY |
| 08789 | | DCBS | BY |
| 08790 | | DCLS | LO |
| 08791 | F- | FSDH | HA |
| 08792 | | FSFL | LA |
| 08793 | ★ | FSDH | HA |
| 08794 | | PNLA | NL |
| 08795 | | FSPG | GL |
| 08796 | | DCSC | AF |
| 08797 | | RXXA | GD |
| 08798 | | FHTA | LE |
| 08799 | | FSFL | LA |
| 08800 | | FSQA | BR |
| 08801 | | FSFL | LA |
| 08802 | | RXLA | GD |
| 08803 | | FSRO | RG |
| 08804 | | FMSK | CF |
| 08805 | F | FSGB | BS |
| 08806 | F | FHSH | KY |
| 08807 | | DCBS | BY |
| 08808 | | FSLC | CL |
| 08809 | | FSMA | AN |
| 08810 | | FSEP | NC |
| 08811 | | FSSO | OC |
| 08813 | | FSID | DR |
| 08814 | | RXLS | DY |
| 08815 | | FSMA | AN |
| 08817 | | FSHY | TE |
| 08818 | | FMSK | CF |
| 08819 | | FSQA | BR |
| 08821 | | FSRO | RG |
| 08822 | | FMSK | CF |
| 08823 | | FSNC | CD |
| 08824 | F- | FSID | DR |
| 08825 | | FSSO | OC |
| 08826 | | FSLC | CL |
| 08827 | | FSMA | AN |
| 08828 | | FSJS | SF |
| 08829 | | FHWN | TO |
| 08830 | | FSAE | EH |
| 08831 | | FSAE | EH |
| 08832 | F | FSGB | BS |
| 08833 | ★ | FSJS | SF |
| 08834 | Fg | FSJS | SF |
| 08835 | | FMSK | CF |
| 08836 | | FMSK | CF |
| 08837 | F- | FSSO | OC |
| 08838 | | RXLS | DY |
| 08839 | | FSFL | LA |
| 08840 | | FSFL | LA |
| 08841 | | FSGB | BS |
| 08842 | | RXLS | DY |
| 08844 | | FSLC | CL |
| 08845 | F- | FSAE | EH |
| 08847 | | FSAE | EH |
| 08848 | | FMSK | CF |
| 08849 | | FSFL | LA |
| 08850 | | FSRO | RG |
| 08853 | | FSBM | ML |
| 08854 | | DCSB | SU |
| 08855 | | IABB | AB |
| 08856 | | FSMA | AN |
| 08857 | | FMST | TI |
| 08858 | | FSMA | AN |
| 08859 | | FSEP | NC |
| 08865 | | FSKC | CA |
| 08866 | | FSID | DR |
| 08867 | ★ | FSHY | TE |
| 08868 | | FSEP | NC |
| 08869 | ★ | FSEP | NC |
| 08870 | | FMST | TI |
| 08871 | | FPZA | IM |
| 08872 | | RXXA | HQ |
| 08873 | Iw | FSJS | SF |
| 08874 | | PNLA | NL |
| 08875 | | PNLA | NL |
| 08876 | | FSID | DR |
| 08877 | | FPZA | IM |
| 08878 | | FMST | TI |
| 08879 | | FMST | TI |
| 08880 | | FMST | TI |
| 08881 | ZG | DBMS | ZH |
| 08882 | | IABB | AB |
| 08883 | | DBMS | ZH |
| 08884 | | FSMA | AN |
| 08885 | | FSID | DR |
| 08886 | | RXLA | GD |
| 08887 | | FSSO | OC |
| 08888 | | RXLA | GD |
| 08889 | | FSKC | CA |
| 08890 | F- | IWNB | WN |
| 08891 | | DCLS | LO |
| 08892 | ★ | FSAE | ZG |
| 08893 | F | FSGB | BS |
| 08894 | | FSMA | AN |
| 08895 | | FHTA | LE |
| 08896 | | FHTA | LE |
| 08897 | ZG | FHTA | LE |
| 08899 | | RXLS | DY |
| 08900 | | FSQA | BR |
| 08901 | | FSGB | BS |
| 08902 | | FSMA | AN |
| 08903 | | FSID | DR |
| 08904 | | FSSO | OC |
| 08905 | | FSSO | OC |
| 08906 | | FSHY | TE |
| 08907 | ★ | FSNC | CD |
| 08908 | | PNLA | NL |
| 08909 | | DCBS | BY |
| 08910 | | FSLC | CL |
| 08911 | | FSLC | CL |
| 08912 | | FSLC | CL |
| 08913 | | FSMA | AN |
| 08914 | | DCBS | BY |
| 08915 | F- | DCLS | LO |
| 08916 | | FSMA | AN |
| 08917 | | FSMA | AN |
| 08918 | ZG | FSMA | AN |
| 08919 | | FMST | TI |
| 08920 | F- | FSGB | BS |
| 08921 | | FSNC | CD |
| 08922 | | DCBS | BY |
| 08923 | F- | FSJS | SF |
| 08924 | F- | FSMA | AN |
| 08925 | | FSMA | AN |
| 08926 | | IWNB | WN |
| 08927 | | DCBS | BY |
| 08928 | F | FSGB | BS |
| 08929 | | FSSO | OC |
| 08931 | | RXLA | GD |
| 08932 | | FMSK | CF |
| 08933 | | FSAE | EH |
| 08934 | | IWNB | WN |
| 08935 | | FSQA | BR |
| 08936 | | FSEP | NC |
| 08937 | | FSFL | LA |
| 08938 | | FSBM | ML |
| 08939 | | FSMA | AN |
| 08940 | | FMSK | CF |
| 08941 | | FSFL | LA |
| 08942 | | FMSK | CF |
| 08944 | ★ | FSSO | OC |
| 08945 | | FSFL | LA |
| 08946 | | FSRO | RG |
| 08947 | | FSSO | OC |
| 08948 | | FSSO | OC |
| 08949 | | FSQA | BR |
| 08950 | F- | DCSC | AF |
| 08951 | F- | FSQA | BR |
| 08952 | | FSBM | ML |
| 08953 | F- | FSFL | LA |
| 08954 | F- | FSFL | LA |
| 08955 | | FSFL | LA |
| 08956 | | FSJS | SF |
| 08957 | | FSJS | SF |
| 08958 | | FSJS | SF |

## CLASS 08/9 — 400hp BR Shunter (Electric) — 0-6-0

(Reduced height cab)

| | | | |
|---|---|---|---|
| 08993 | | FHTA | LE |
| 08994 | F | FHTA | LE |
| 08995 | Fe | FHTA | LE |

## CLASS 09 — 400hp BR Shunter (Electric) — 0-6-0

| | | | |
|---|---|---|---|
| 09001 | | FMSK | CF |
| 09002 | | DCSC | AF |
| 09003 | | DCSB | SU |
| 09004 | | DCSB | SU |
| 09005 | | DCSB | SU |
| 09006 | | DCSB | SU |
| 09007 | | DCSB | SL |
| 09008 | | FMMT | TI |
| 09009 | | DCSB | SU |
| 09010 | | DCSB | SU |
| 09011 | | DCSC | AF |
| 09012 | | DCSB | SU |
| 09013 | | FMMT | TI |
| 09014 | | DCSB | SU |
| 09015 | | FMSK | CF |
| 09016 | | DCSB | SU |
| 09018 | | DCSC | AF |
| 09019 | | DCSC | AF |
| 09020 | | DCSB | SU |
| 09021 | | DCSC | AF |
| 09022 | | DCSC | AF |
| 09023 | | DCSC | AF |
| 09024 | | DCSC | AF |
| 09025 | | FSAE | EH |
| 09026 | ZG | FSAE | EH |

## PRIVATE OWNER ex-CLASS 08 LOCOMOTIVES

**Used at works repairing BR rolling stock.**

| | | | |
|---|---|---|---|
| 08164 | | RFS | ZB |
| 08168 | ★ | BREL | ZR |
| 08331 | ★ | RFS | KN |
| 08470 | | BREL | ZC |
| 08602 | | RFS | ZB |
| 08764 | | RFS | ZB |
| 08846 | ★ | BREL | ZD |

(NB: Numbers shown may not be carried. See 'Locomotive Names' Section of this book.)

## CLASS 20 — TYPE 1 English Electric 1000hp. — Bo-Bo

| | | | |
|---|---|---|---|
| 20004 | | FEFN | TO |
| 20006 | | FEGN | TO |
| 20007 | | FEFN | TO |
| 20010 | F | FEGN | TO |
| 20013 | | FEGN | TO |
| 20016 | | FEGN | TO |
| 20019 | | FEGN | TO |
| 20020 | | FEGN | TO |
| 20021 | | FEGN | TO |
| 20023 | F | FEGN | TO |
| 20025 | | DCMB | TO |
| 20026 | | FEFN | TO |
| 20028 | | FEGN | TO |
| 20029 | | DCMN | TO |
| 20030 | ★ | DCMA | TO |
| 20031 | | DCMN | TO |
| 20032 | | DCMN | TO |
| 20034 | | DCMC | TO |
| 20035 | | DCMB | TO |
| 20040 | | FEFN | TO |
| 20042 | | DCMC | TO |
| 20043 | | DCMC | TO |
| 20045 | | FEGN | TO |
| 20046 | | FMYI | IM |
| 20047 | | FEFN | TO |
| 20048 | | DCMB | TO |
| 20051 | F | FDYX | HQ |
| 20052 | | FEFN | TO |

| | | | |
|---|---|---|---|
| 20053 | | FEFN | TO |
| 20055 | | FEGN | TO |
| 20056 | | DCMN | TO |
| 20057 | | FEGN | TO |
| 20058 | | DRTC | HQ |
| 20059 | F | FEFN | TO |
| 20061 | | FMYI | IM |
| 20063 | | DCMN | TO |
| 20064 | ★ | DCMA | TO |
| 20065 | | FDYX | HQ |
| 20066 | | FPAE | ED |
| 20069 | | DCMC | TO |
| 20070 | | DCMB | TO |
| 20071 | | FEGN | TO |
| 20072 | | DCMB | TO |
| 20073 | | FEGN | TO |
| 20075 | | FEGN | TO |
| 20078 | | FEFN | TO |
| 20080 | | FEGN | TO |
| 20081 | | FEFN | TO |
| 20082 | | FEGN | TO |
| 20084 | | FEFN | TO |
| 20085 | | FEFN | TO |
| 20087 | | DRTC | HQ |
| 20088 | F- | FEFN | TO |
| 20090 | F | FEGN | TO |
| 20092 | | DCMC | TO |
| 20093 | | FMYI | IM |
| 20094 | | FEFN | TO |
| 20095 | | DCMN | TO |
| 20096 | | DCMB | TO |
| 20098 | | FMYI | IM |
| 20099 | | FDYX | HQ |
| 20102 | | DCMC | TO |
| 20103 | | FEFN | TO |
| 20104 | F | FEFN | TO |
| 20105 | | FEFN | TO |
| 20106 | | FEGN | TO |
| 20107 | | FMYI | IM |
| 20108 | F | FEFN | TO |
| 20110 | | DCMB | TO |
| 20112 | | FMYI | IM |
| 20113 | | FEGN | TO |
| 20117 | | FEGN | TO |
| 20118 | | FDSE | ED |
| 20119 | | FDSE | ED |
| 20120 | | FEGN | TO |
| 20121 | | FEGN | TO |
| 20122 | F | FDSE | ED |
| 20124 | | FDSE | ED |
| 20127 | | DCMB | TO |
| 20128 | | FEGN | TO |
| 20129 | | FEFN | TO |
| 20130 | | FEGN | TO |
| 20131 | | FEGN | TO |
| 20132 | F | FEGN | TO |
| 20133 | | FEGN | TO |
| 20135 | | FEGN | TO |
| 20136 | | FEFN | TO |
| 20137 | F | FDSE | ED |
| 20138 | F | FDSE | ED |
| 20139 | | DCMC | TO |
| 20140 | | FEGN | TO |
| 20141 | F | FEGN | TO |
| 20142 | | FEFN | TO |
| 20143 | | FEGN | TO |
| 20145 | | DCMB | TO |
| 20148 | | FPAE | ED |
| 20151 | | FEFN | TO |
| 20154 | | FEGN | TO |
| 20156 | F | FDSE | ED |
| 20157 | | FEFN | TO |
| 20159 | | FEGN | TO |
| 20160 | | DCMC | TO |
| 20163 | F | FEFN | TO |
| 20165 | F | FDSE | ED |
| 20166 | | FEFN | TO |
| 20168 | | FEGN | TO |
| 20169 | | FEGN | TO |
| 20170 | F | FEFN | TO |
| 20172 | | FEGN | TO |
| 20173 | | FDYX | HQ |
| 20175 | F | FEGN | TO |
| 20176 | | DCMN | TO |
| 20177 | F | FEFN | TO |
| 20182 | F | FEGN | TO |
| 20185 | | FPAE | ED |
| 20186 | | FEFN | TO |
| 20187 | | FEFN | TO |
| 20189 | | DCMN | TO |
| 20190 | | FEFN | TO |
| 20194 | | FEGN | TO |
| 20195 | F | FEGN | TO |
| 20196 | F | FEFN | TO |
| 20197 | | FEFN | TO |
| 20198 | | FDSE | ED |
| 20206 | | DMEA | ED |
| 20208 | | FDYX | HQ |
| 20210 | | FEFN | TO |
| 20211 | | FDSE | ED |
| 20212 | | FDSE | ED |
| 20213 | | DMEA | ED |
| 20214 | | FEFN | TO |
| 20215 | F | FEFN | TO |
| 20227 | F | DCMN | TO |
| 20228 | | DCMB | TO |

## CLASS 20/9 TYPE 2 ENGLISH ELECTRIC 1000hp Bo-Bo

Owned by Hunslet-Barclay, Kilmarnock for hire operation on BR lines.

| | | | |
|---|---|---|---|
| 20901 | ★ | CYPD | HQ |
| 20902 | ★ | CYPD | HQ |
| 20903 | ★ | CYPD | HQ |
| 20904 | ★ | CYPD | HQ |
| 20905 | ★ | CYPD | HQ |
| 20906 | ★ | CYPD | HQ |

## CLASS 26/0 TYPE 2 BRCW 1160hp. Bo-Bo

| | | | |
|---|---|---|---|
| 26001 | Fe | FEPE | ED |
| 26002 | Fe | FEPE | ED |
| 26003 | Fe | FEPE | ED |
| 26004 | Fe | FEPE | ED |
| 26005 | Fe | FEPE | ED |
| 26006 | Fe | FEPE | ED |
| 26007 | Fe | FEPE | ED |
| 26008 | Fe | FEPE | ED |
| 26010 | F | DMEA | ED |
| 26011 | | DCHA | ED |
| 26014 | | DCHA | ED |
| 26015 | | DCHA | ED |

## CLASS 26/1. TYPE 2 BRCW 1160hp. Bo-Bo

| | | | |
|---|---|---|---|
| 26021 | | DCHA | ED |
| 26023 | F | DCHA | ED |
| 26024 | | DCHA | ED |
| 26025 | F | FPAE | ED |
| 26026 | F | DCHA | ED |
| 26027 | | DCHA | ED |
| 26028 | | DCHA | ED |
| 26032 | F | FPAE | ED |
| 26035 | F | DCHA | ED |
| 26036 | | DCHA | ED |
| 26037 | F | FPAE | ED |
| 26038 | F | FPAE | ED |
| 26039 | | DCHA | ED |
| 26040 | F | FPAE | ED |
| 26041 | F | FPAE | ED |
| 26042 | | DMEA | ED |
| 26043 | | DMEA | ED |
| 26046 | | DMEA | ED |

## CLASS 31/1 TYPE 2 Brush 1470hp. A1A-A1A.

| | | | |
|---|---|---|---|
| 31101 | | DMEA | BS |
| 31102 | F | FDOT | TI |
| 31105 | F | DMEA | BS |
| 31106 | | DCEA | IM |
| 31107 | F | DCMA | BS |
| 31108 | F | FPCI | IM |
| 31110 | F | DCMA | BS |
| 31112 | F | DCMW | BS |
| 31113 | ZG | DCML | BS |
| 31116 | F | FAGS | SF |
| 31119 | F | DCMA | BS |
| 31120 | Ff | FHAC | CD |
| 31123 | | FALY | TE |
| 31124 | | FALY | TE |
| 31125 | F | FDOT | TI |
| 31126 | F | FPCI | IM |
| 31128 | F | FAGS | SF |
| 31130 | Ff | FHAC | CD |
| 31132 | F | FDOT | TI |
| 31134 | F | FAGS | SF |
| 31135 | F | DCAA | SF |
| 31142 | F | FDOT | TI |
| 31144 | F | FDOT | TI |
| 31145 | F | DCML | BS |
| 31146 | F | FDOT | TI |
| 31147 | F | DCML | BS |
| 31149 | F | FAGS | SF |
| 31154 | F | FPCI | IM |
| 31155 | F | FAGS | SF |
| 31156 | | FPCI | IM |
| 31158 | F | DCML | BS |
| 31159 | F | FDOT | TI |
| 31160 | Fg | FDOT | TI |
| 31162 | | DCMN | BS |
| 31163 | F | FPCI | IM |
| 31164 | F | FAGS | SF |
| 31165 | F | DCAA | SF |
| 31166 | ZG | DCML | BS |
| 31168 | | FPCI | IM |
| 31171 | F | DMEA | TE |
| 31174 | F | DCML | BS |
| 31178 | F | DCMW | BS |
| 31180 | F | FAGS | SF |
| 31181 | F | DCAA | SF |
| 31184 | F | FALY | TE |
| 31185 | Fq | FPCI | IM |
| 31186 | F | DCAA | SF |
| 31187 | F | DCAA | SF |
| 31188 | F | FPCI | IM |
| 31190 | F | DCAA | SF |
| 31191 | F | DCAA | SF |
| 31196 | F | DCAA | SF |
| 31199 | F | FPXA | IM |
| 31200 | Ff | FHAC | CD |
| 31201 | Fq | FPCI | IM |
| 31203 | F | FPCI | IM |
| 31205 | F | FPCI | IM |
| 31206 | F | FDOT | TI |
| 31207 | Fq | FPCI | IM |
| 31209 | F- | FAGS | SF |
| 31210 | F | FPCI | IM |
| 31212 | | DCEW | IM |
| 31215 | F | FALY | TE |
| 31217 | Ff | FHAC | CD |
| 31219 | F | DCAA | SF |
| 31221 | | DCEW | IM |
| 31223 | | DCEW | IM |
| 31224 | F | DCAA | SF |
| 31229 | F | FALY | TE |
| 31230 | F | DCEA | IM |
| 31232 | F | FDOT | TI |
| 31233 | Fq | FPCI | IM |
| 31234 | F | FAGS | SF |
| 31235 | F | DCMA | BS |
| 31237 | F | DCMC | BS |
| 31238 | Fq | FPCI | IM |
| 31242 | F | FDOT | TI |
| 31243 | F | FPCI | IM |
| 31247 | F | FAGS | SF |
| 31248 | F | DMEA | TE |

Above: Railfreight Steel (formerly Metal) Sector Class 37/5 locomotives Nos 37504 *British Steel Corby* and 37521 seen at Skelton Bridge Junction, York in February with a Lackenby to Corby BSC Company coil freight train.

Below: Contrast in front end liveries on Class 43 IC125 power cars Nos 43038 and 43097 at King's Cross. The former was experimentally painted in this style at its home depot of Neville Hill (NL).

| | | | |
|---|---|---|---|
| 31249 | | DCEW | IM |
| 31250 | F | DCAA | SF |
| 31252 | F | DCEA | IM |
| 31255 | F | FPCI | IM |
| 31257 | | FPCI | IM |
| 31263 | F | DCAA | SF |
| 31264 | | DMEA | TE |
| 31268 | F | DCAA | SF |
| 31270 | Ff | FHAC | CD |
| 31271 | Fb | FAGS | SF |
| 31272 | F | DMEA | BS |
| 31273 | Fq | FPCI | IM |
| 31275 | Ff | FHAC | CD |
| 31276 | Ff | FHAC | CD |
| 31282 | F | DCEA | IM |
| 31285 | F | DCEA | IM |
| 31286 | | FPCI | IM |
| 31288 | | FPCI | IM |
| 31289 | | FAGS | SF |
| 31290 | F | DMEA | BS |
| 31293 | | FAGS | SF |
| 31294 | Fb | FAGS | SF |
| 31296 | Fa | FAGS | SF |
| 31299 | F | FPCI | IM |
| 31301 | F | FAGS | SF |
| 31302 | F | FPXA | IM |
| 31304 | F | FPXA | IM |
| 31305 | | DMEA | TE |
| 31306 | F | FAGS | SF |
| 31308 | F | FAGS | SF |
| 31309 | | FPCI | IM |
| 31312 | Ff | FHAC | CD |
| 31317 | F | DCMW | BS |
| 31319 | Fp | FPCI | IM |
| 31324 | Ff | FHAC | CD |
| 31327 | F | FAGS | SF |
| 31970 | ★ | DRTC | CD |

## CLASS 31/4 TYPE 2 Brush 1470hp. A1A-A1A

(Equipped for Electric Train Heating, Index 66).

| | | | |
|---|---|---|---|
| 31400 | | PCDB | CD |
| 31402 | | DMEA | BS |
| 31403 | | DMEA | BS |
| 31404 | | PCDB | CD |
| 31405 | | DCMW | BS |
| 31406 | | PCDB | CD |
| 31407 | | DCMC | BS |
| 31408 | | PCDB | CD |
| 31409 | | DCMN | BS |
| 31410 | | RXLB | CD |
| 31411 | | DCMW | BS |
| 31412 | ZG | DCQA | CD |
| 31413 | ★ | RXLB | CD |
| 31414 | | DCQA | CD |
| 31415 | | DMEA | BS |
| 31416 | | DCQA | CD |
| 31417 | ZG | DMEA | BS |
| 31418 | | RXLB | CD |
| 31419 | ZG | DCMN | BS |
| 31420 | | DCMW | BS |
| 31421 | | RXLB | CD |
| 31422 | | DCMA | BS |
| 31423 | ML | DMEA | BS |
| 31424 | ZG | DCMW | BS |
| 31425 | | RXLB | CD |
| 31426 | | DCQA | CD |
| 31427 | | RXLB | CD |
| 31428 | | RXLB | CD |
| 31429 | | RXLB | CD |
| 31430 | ★ | DCMA | BS |
| 31431 | | PCDB | CD |
| 31432 | | RXLB | CD |
| 31433 | | DCMA | BS |
| 31434 | | DCMW | BS |
| 31435 | | DCMC | BS |
| 31437 | | DCMN | BS |
| 31438 | | RXLB | CD |
| 31439 | | RXLB | CD |
| 31442 | | RXLB | CD |
| 31444 | | DCEA | IM |
| 31445 | | DCMA | BS |
| 31446 | | DCMC | BS |
| 31448 | | DCMA | BS |
| 31449 | | PCDB | CD |
| 31450 | | RXLB | CD |
| 31451 | ZG | DCMC | BS |
| 31453 | ZG | DCEA | IM |
| 31454 | ZG | DCMC | BS |
| 31455 | ZG | DCMA | BS |
| 31456 | | DCEA | IM |
| 31457 | ZG | DMEA | BS |
| 31458 | | DCEA | IM |
| 31459 | | DMEA | BS |
| 31460 | | PCDB | CD |
| 31461 | ZG | DMEA | BS |
| 31462 | ZG | DMEA | BS |
| 31463 | | PCDB | CD |
| 31464 | | DMEA | BS |
| 31465 | ZG | DCMC | BS |
| 31466 | ZG | DMEA | BS |
| 31467 | | DMEA | BS |
| 31469 | | PCDB | CD |

## CLASS 31/5 TYPE 2 Brush 1470hp. A1A-A1A

**(Electric Train Heating isolated. Maximum speed 60mph. DCxx Class 31/4 fleet to be renumbered {† by mid-May 1990 or ‡ by mid-October 1990}, altering third digit only to figure 5).**

| | | | |
|---|---|---|---|
| 31507† | | DCMC | BS |
| 31511† | | DCMW | BS |
| 31512‡ | | | |
| 31514‡ | | | |
| 31516‡ | | | |
| 31519† | ZG | DCMN | BS |
| 31522† | | DCMA | BS |
| 31524† | ZG | DCMW | BS |
| 31526‡ | | | |
| 31530† | ★ | DCMA | BS |
| 31533† | | DCMA | BS |
| 31537† | | DCMN | BS |
| 31541 | | DCEA | IM |
| 31544† | | DCEA | IM |
| 31545† | | DCMA | BS |
| 31546† | | DCMC | BS |
| 31547 | | DCEA | IM |
| 31548† | | DCMA | BS |
| 31551† | ZG | DCMC | BS |
| 31552 | ZG | DCEA | IM |
| 31553† | ZG | DCEA | IM |
| 31554† | ZG | DCMC | BS |
| 31555† | ZG | DCMA | BS |
| 31556† | | DCEA | IM |
| 31558† | | DCEA | IM |
| 31565† | ZG | DCMC | BS |
| 31568 | ZG | DCMW | BS |

31970 see end of Class 31/1 above.

## CLASS 33/0 TYPE 3 BRCW 1550hp. Bo-Bo.

| | | | |
|---|---|---|---|
| 33002 | ZG | DCSA | EH |
| 33004 | | FASB | SL |
| 33006 | | FASB | SL |
| 33008 | ZG | DCSM | EH |
| 33009 | | FASB | EH |
| 33012 | | FASB | SL |
| 33019 | | FASB | SL |
| 33020 | | FASB | SL |
| 33021 | Fa | FASB | SL |
| 33023 | | FASB | SL |
| 33025 | ZG | DMEA | EH |
| 33026 | ZG | DCSM | EH |
| 33027 | | FASB | SL |
| 33029 | | FASB | SL |
| 33030 | | DMEA | SL |
| 33033 | Fa | FASB | SL |
| 33035 | | DCSA | EH |
| 33040 | | FASB | SL |
| 33042 | Fa | FASB | SL |
| 33046 | | FASB | SL |
| 33047 | | FASB | SL |
| 33048 | | FASB | SL |
| 33050 | Fa | FASB | SL |
| 33051 | Fa | FASB | SL |
| 33052 | | FASB | SL |
| 33053 | Fa | FASB | SL |
| 33056 | Fa | FASB | SL |
| 33057 | ZG | DCSA | EH |
| 33058 | | FASB | SL |
| 33060 | | FASB | SL |
| 33063 | Fa | FASB | SL |
| 33064 | Fa | FASB | SL |
| 33065 | ZG | DCSA | EH |

## CLASS 33/1 TYPE 3 BRCW 1550hp. Bo-Bo.

**(Push-Pull fitted).**

| | | | |
|---|---|---|---|
| 33101 | | DCSM | EH |
| 33102 | | DCSM | EH |
| 33103 | ZG | DCSM | EH |
| 33106 | | DCSM | EH |
| 33108 | ZG | DCSA | EH |
| 33109 | | DCSA | EH |
| 33110 | | DCSM | EH |
| 33111 | | DCSA | EH |
| 33113 | | DCSA | EH |
| 33114 | | DCSM | EH |
| 33116 | | DCWA | EH |
| 33117 | | DCSM | EH |
| 33118 | | DCSM | EH |

## CLASS 33/2 TYPE 3 BRCW 1550hp. Bo-Bo.

| | | | |
|---|---|---|---|
| 33201 | ZG | DCSM | SL |
| 33202 | Fa | FASB | SL |
| 33203 | Fg | FDIB | SL |
| 33204 | Fa | FASB | SL |
| 33205 | Fg | FDIB | SL |
| 33206 | Fg | FDIB | SL |
| 33207 | Fa | FASB | SL |
| 33208 | | DCWA | SL |
| 33211 | | FDIB | SL |

## CLASS 37/0 TYPE 3 English Electric 1750hp. Co-Co

| | | | |
|---|---|---|---|
| 37003 | | DCEA | IM |
| 37004 | Fm | FMTY | TE |
| 37008 | F | FDET | TI |
| 37009 | | FDET | TI |
| 37010 | | FMGM | ML |
| 37012 | | FPEK | CF |
| 37013 | | FDET | TI |
| 37015 | Fg | FDET | TI |
| 37019 | Fg | FDET | TI |
| 37023 | | FMTY | TE |
| 37025 | ZG | DCEA | IM |
| 37026 | | FMGM | ML |
| 37029 | Fg | FDET | TI |
| 37031 | Fg | FDET | TI |
| 37032 | F | FDET | TI |
| 37035 | Fp | FPAE | ED |
| 37037 | Fm | FMGM | ML |
| 37038 | Fm | FMAK | CF |
| 37040 | Fm | FMGM | ML |
| 37042 | Fm | FMTY | TE |
| 37045 | Fh | FDET | TI |
| 37046 | | FMTY | TE |
| 37047 | Fg | FDET | TI |
| 37048 | Fm | FMTY | TE |
| 37049 | Fe | FMGM | ML |
| 37051 | Fm | FMGM | ML |
| 37053 | Fg | FDET | TI |
| 37054 | | FMTY | TE |
| 37055 | Fg | FDET | TI |
| 37057 | | FDET | TI |
| 37058 | F-h | FMTY | TE |
| 37059 | Fg | FDET | TI |
| 37063 | Fg | FDET | TI |
| 37065 | Fg | FDET | TI |
| 37066 | | DCEA | IM |
| 37068 | F | FDET | TI |
| 37069 | F- | FMTY | TE |
| 37070 | Fg | FMTY | TE |
| 37071 | ZG | DCEA | IM |
| 37072 | | DCHA | ED |
| 37073 | | FDET | TI |
| 37074 | Fg | FDET | TI |
| 37075 | F+ | FMTY | TE |
| 37077 | | FDET | TI |
| 37078 | Fp | FPEK | CF |
| 37079 | Fh | FDET | TI |
| 37080 | Fp | FPAE | ED |
| 37083 | | FMTY | TE |
| 37087 | ZG | DCHA | ED |
| 37088 | | FMGM | ML |
| 37092 | | FMGM | ML |
| 37095 | ZG | DCEA | IM |
| 37096 | | FDYX | HQ |
| 37097 | Fm | FMGM | ML |
| 37098 | | FMTY | TE |
| 37099 | Fm | FMGM | ML |
| 37100 | | FMTY | TE |
| 37101 | Fg | FDET | TI |
| 37104 | ZG | DCEA | IM |
| 37106 | Fm | FMYI | IM |
| 37107 | | FDET | TI |
| 37108 | | FMGM | ML |
| 37109 | Fm | FMTY | TE |
| 37110 | Fm | FMTY | TE |
| 37111 | Fm | FMGM | ML |
| 37113 | Fg | FGUV | IS |
| 37114 | Fg | FGUV | IS |
| 37116 | | FDET | TI |
| 37128 | | FGUV | IS |
| 37131 | | FQCK | CF |
| 37133 | ZG | DCWA | CF |
| 37137 | Fm | FMGM | ML |
| 37138 | Fa | FPEK | CF |
| 37139 | | FQCK | CF |
| 37140 | | DCAA | SF |
| 37141 | | DCWA | CF |
| 37142 | ZG | DCWA | CF |
| 37144 | Fa | FAGS | SF |
| 37145 | Fm | FMGM | ML |
| 37146 | | DCWA | CF |
| 37152 | | FMGM | ML |
| 37153 | | DCHA | ED |
| 37154 | | FGUV | IS |
| 37156 | ZG | DCHA | ED |
| 37158 | | DCWA | CF |
| 37162 | ZG | DCWA | CF |
| 37165 | Fe | FEPE | ED |
| 37167 | Fe | FQCK | CF |
| 37170 | | DCHA | ED |
| 37174 | | DCWA | CF |
| 37175 | | DCHA | ED |
| 37178 | | FDET | TI |
| 37184 | Fp | DCEA | IM |
| 37185 | | FDET | TI |
| 37188 | Fp | FPAE | ED |
| 37190 | Fm | FMGM | ML |
| 37191 | | FPAE | ED |
| 37194 | Fg | FDET | TI |
| 37196 | F | DCHA | ED |
| 37197 | Fm | FMAK | CF |
| 37198 | Fg | FDET | TI |
| 37201 | Fm | FMGM | ML |
| 37202 | Fm | FMTY | TE |
| 37203 | Fm | FMTY | TE |
| 37207 | ZG | DCWA | CF |
| 37209 | | FDET | TI |
| 37211 | Fa | FAGS | SF |
| 37212 | Fe | FQCK | CF |
| 37213 | F- | FQCK | CF |
| 37214 | | FQCK | CF |
| 37215 | Fp | FPEK | CF |
| 37216 | | DCAA | SF |
| 37217 | | FQCK | CF |
| 37218 | | FAGS | SF |
| 37219 | | FAGS | SF |
| 37220 | | FPEK | CF |
| 37221 | | DCWA | CF |
| 37222 | | FQCK | CF |
| 37223 | Fe | FQCK | CF |
| 37225 | | FMYI | IM |
| 37227 | Fm | FMTY | TE |
| 37229 | F- | FEPE | ED |
| 37230 | | DCWA | CF |
| 37232 | Fp | DCEA | IM |
| 37235 | Fe | FQCK | CF |
| 37238 | | FDET | TI |
| 37239 | Fe | FQCK | CF |
| 37240 | ZG | DCHA | ED |
| 37241 | Fm | FMTY | TE |
| 37242 | Fg | FDET | TI |
| 37244 | F- | FQCK | CF |
| 37245 | F- | FPAE | ED |
| 37248 | Fp | FPEK | CF |
| 37250 | | FMTY | TE |
| 37251 | ZG | DCEA | IM |
| 37252 | Fg | FDET | TI |
| 37254 | | FMAK | CF |
| 37255 | | FMTY | TE |
| 37258 | Fm | FMTY | TE |
| 37261 | | FGUV | IS |
| 37262 | ZG | FGUV | IS |
| 37263 | ZG | DCWA | CF |
| 37264 | | DCWA | CF |
| 37271 | Fg | FDET | TI |
| 37272 | Fg | FDET | TI |
| 37273 | Fp | FPEK | CF |
| 37274 | Fe | FQCK | CF |
| 37275 | Fm | FMYI | IM |
| 37278 | Fe | FMAK | CF |
| 37280 | Fp | FPEK | CF |
| 37285 | F- | FDET | TI |
| 37293 | Fm | FMAK | CF |
| 37294 | Fp | FPEK | CF |
| 37298 | | FDET | TI |

## CLASS 37/3 TYPE 3 English Electric 1750hp. Co-Co

**(Refurbished bogies).**

| | | | |
|---|---|---|---|
| 37350 | ★ | FPEK | CF |
| 37351 | F | FMYI | IM |
| 37354 | Fa | FAGS | SF |
| 37358 | | FDET | TI |
| 37359 | Fq | FPAE | ED |
| 37370 | F | FACM | ML |
| 37371 | F | FPEK | CF |
| 37372 | F | DCWA | CF |
| 37373 | F | FACM | ML |
| 37375 | F | FEPE | ED |
| 37376 | Fe | FEPE | ED |
| 37377 | F | FMYI | IM |
| 37378 | F | FCTY | TE |
| 37379 | F | FACM | ML |
| 37380 | F- | FEPE | ED |
| 37381 | Fm | FMYI | IM |

## CLASS 37/4 TYPE 3 English Electric 1750hp. Co-Co

**(Electric Train Heating, Index 30. Refurbished with alternator.).**

| | | | |
|---|---|---|---|
| 37401 | ML | FDTE | ED |
| 37402 | Fg | FDTE | ED |
| 37403 | Fg | FDTE | ED |
| 37404 | Fg | FDTE | ED |
| 37405 | | FDTE | ED |
| 37406 | ML | FDTE | ED |
| 37407 | | DCHA | ED |
| 37408 | | DCEA | IM |
| 37409 | ML | FDTE | ED |
| 37410 | Fg | FDTE | ED |
| 37411 | Fa | FABT | TI |
| 37412 | Fg | FCLL | LA |
| 37413 | | FDTE | ED |
| 37414 | Fg | FCLL | LA |
| 37415 | | FCTY | TE |
| 37416 | | PISB | IS |
| 37417 | | FCTY | TE |
| 37418 | | PISB | IS |
| 37419 | | PISB | IS |
| 37420 | | FCTY | TE |
| 37421 | | PISB | IS |
| 37422 | Fa | FABT | TI |
| 37423 | ML | FDTE | ED |
| 37424 | | FDTE | ED |
| 37425 | Fa | FABT | TI |
| 37426 | | FPBC | IM |
| 37427 | | PCFA | CF |
| 37428 | | PCFA | CF |
| 37429 | | PCFA | CF |
| 37430 | | FPBC | IM |
| 37431 | | PCFA | CF |

## CLASS 37/5 TYPE 3 English Electric 1750hp. Co-Co

**(Refurbished with alternator).**

| | | | |
|---|---|---|---|
| 37501 | Fm | FMTY | TE |
| 37502 | Fm | FMTY | TE |
| 37503 | Fm | FMTY | TE |
| 37504 | Fm | FMTY | TE |
| 37505 | Fm | FMTY | TE |
| 37506 | Fm | FMTY | TE |
| 37507 | Fm | FMTY | TE |
| 37508 | F | FMTY | TE |
| 37509 | Fm | FMTY | TE |
| 37510 | Fm | FMTY | TE |
| 37511 | Fm | FMTY | TE |
| 37512 | F | FMTY | TE |
| 37513 | F | FMTY | TE |
| 37514 | F | FMTY | TE |
| 37515 | F | FMTY | TE |
| 37516 | F | FMTY | TE |
| 37517 | F | FMTY | TE |
| 37518 | F | FMTY | TE |
| 37519 | Fm | FMTY | TE |
| 37520 | F | FMTY | TE |
| 37521 | Fm | FMTY | TE |
| 37667 | Fm | FMTY | TE |
| 37668 | Fm | FMTY | TE |
| 37669 | F | FCLL | LA |
| 37670 | Fg | FCLL | LA |
| 37671 | Fg | FCLL | LA |
| 37672 | F | FCLL | LA |
| 37673 | Fg | FCLL | LA |

| | | | |
|---|---|---|---|
| 37674 | F | FCLL | LA |
| 37675 | F | FCLL | LA |
| 37676 | F | FABT | TI |
| 37677 | F | FABT | TI |
| 37678 | F | FABT | TI |
| 37679 | F | FABT | TI |
| 37680 | F | FABT | TI |
| 37681 | Fb | FABT | TI |
| 37682 | F | FABT | TI |
| 37683 | F+ | FABT | TI |
| 37684 | Fb | FABT | TI |
| 37685 | Fb | FABT | TI |
| 37686 | F | FABT | TI |
| 37687 | Fb | FABT | TI |
| 37688 | Fa | FABT | TI |
| 37689 | Fe | FHBK | CF |
| 37690 | F | FHBK | CF |
| 37691 | F | FHBK | CF |
| 37692 | F | FHBK | CF |
| 37693 | Fe | FEPE | ED |
| 37694 | Fe | FEPE | ED |
| 37695 | F | FHBK | CF |
| 37696 | F | FHBK | CF |
| 37697 | F | FHBK | CF |
| 37698 | Fe | FHBK | CF |
| 37699 | F | FHBK | CF |

## CLASS 37/7 TYPE 3 English Electric 1750hp. Co-Co

**(Refurbished with alternator and ballast weighted bogies).**

| | | | |
|---|---|---|---|
| 37701 | F | FEKK | CF |
| 37702 | Fe | FEKK | CF |
| 37703 | F | FEKK | CF |
| 37704 | F | FEKK | CF |
| 37705 | Fp | FPFR | IM |
| 37706 | Fp | FPFR | IM |
| 37707 | Fp | FPAE | ED |
| 37708 | Fp | FPAE | ED |
| 37709 | Fp | FPFR | IM |
| 37710 | Fm | FMHK | CF |
| 37711 | Fm | FMHK | CF |
| 37712 | Fm | FMHK | CF |
| 37713 | Fm | FMHK | CF |
| 37714 | Fm | FMHK | CF |
| 37715 | Fm | FMHK | CF |
| 37716 | Fm | FMHK | CF |
| 37717 | Fm | FMHK | CF |
| 37718 | Fm | FMHK | CF |
| 37719 | Fm | FMHK | CF |
| 37796 | F | FEKK | CF |
| 37797 | F | FEKK | CF |
| 37798 | F | FEKK | CF |
| 37799 | F | FEKK | CF |
| 37800 | Fe | FEKK | CF |
| 37801 | F | FEKK | CF |
| 37802 | F | FEKK | CF |
| 37803 | F | FEKK | CF |
| 37883 | Fm | FMHK | CF |
| 37884 | Fm | FMHK | CF |
| 37885 | Fm | FMHK | CF |
| 37886 | Fm | FMHK | CF |
| 37887 | Fp | FEKK | CF |
| 37888 | Fp | FPFR | IM |
| 37889 | Fp | FEKK | CF |
| 37890 | Fp | FPFR | IM |
| 37891 | Fp | FPFR | IM |
| 37892 | Fp | FPFR | IM |
| 37893 | Fp | FPFR | IM |
| 37894 | F | FEKK | CF |
| 37895 | F | FEKK | CF |
| 37896 | F | FEKK | CF |
| 37897 | F | FEKK | CF |
| 37898 | F | FEKK | CF |
| 37899 | F | FEKK | CF |

## CLASS 37/9 TYPE 3 English Electric 1800hp. Co-Co

**(Experimental engines: 37901–04 Mirrlees, 37905/06 GEC Ruston).**

| | | | |
|---|---|---|---|
| 37901 | F | FMHK | CF |
| 37902 | Fm | FMHK | CF |
| 37903 | Fm | FMHK | CF |
| 37904 | Fm | FMHK | CF |
| 37905 | Fm | FMHK | CF |
| 37906 | Fm | FMHK | CF |

## CLASS 43 TYPE 4 BREL 2250hp. Bo-Bo

**(INTERCITY 125 POWER CARS. ¶TDM fitted to operate with Class 91 locomotives.)**
**(All Paxman engines except 43167-70 with experimental Mirrlees engines).**
**Livery: InterCity; latest 'Swallow' style where indicated.**

| | | | |
|---|---|---|---|
| 43002 | Iw | IWRP | LA |
| 43003 | Iw | IWRP | LA |
| 43004 | Iw | IWRP | LA |
| 43005 | Iw | IWRP | LA |
| 43006 | Iw | IWRP | LA |
| 43007 | Iw | IWRP | LA |
| 43008 | Iw | IWRP | LA |
| 43009 | Iw | IWRP | LA |
| 43010 | Iw | IWRP | LA |
| 43011 | Iw | IWRP | LA |
| 43012 | Iw | ICCP | LA |
| 43013¶ | Iw | IECP | BN |
| 43014¶ | Iw | IECP | BN |
| 43015 | Iw | IWRP | LA |
| 43016 | Iw | ICCP | LA |
| 43017 | Iw | IWRP | LA |
| 43018 | Iw | IWRP | PM |
| 43019 | Iw | ICCP | LA |
| 43020 | Iw | IWRP | LA |
| 43021 | Iw | IWRP | LA |
| 43022 | Iw | IWRP | LA |
| 43023 | Iw | IWRP | LA |
| 43024 | | IWRP | LA |
| 43025 | | IWRP | LA |
| 43026 | | IWRP | LA |
| 43027 | | IWRP | LA |
| 43028 | | IWRP | LA |
| 43029 | Iw | IWRP | LA |
| 43030 | | IWRP | PM |
| 43031 | | IWRP | PM |
| 43032 | Iw | IWRP | PM |
| 43033 | Iw | IWRP | PM |
| 43034 | | IWRP | PM |
| 43035 | Iw | ICCP | PM |
| 43036 | Iw | ICCP | PM |
| 43037 | Iw | ICCP | PM |
| 43038 | Iw | IMLP | NL |
| 43039 | Iw | IMLP | NL |
| 43040 | | IECP | EC |
| 43041 | | IECP | EC |
| 43042 | Iw | IECP | BN |
| 43043 | Iw | IMLP | NL |
| 43044 | | IMLP | NL |
| 43045 | Iw | IMLP | NL |
| 43046 | Iw | IMLP | NL |
| 43047 | Iw | IMLP | NL |
| 43048 | Iw | IMLP | NL |
| 43049 | | IMLP | NL |
| 43050 | Iw | IMLP | NL |
| 43051 | Iw | IMLP | NL |
| 43052 | | IECP | NL |
| 43053 | Iw | IECP | NL |
| 43054 | Iw | IECP | NL |
| 43055 | Iw | IMLP | NL |
| 43056 | Iw | IECP | BN |
| 43057 | Iw | IECP | BN |
| 43058 | Iw | IECP | NL |
| 43059 | Iw | IMLP | NL |
| 43060 | | IMLP | NL |
| 43061 | Iw | IMLP | NL |
| 43062 | | IECP | BN |
| 43063 | | IECP | BN |
| 43064 | Iw | IMLP | NL |
| 43065¶ | Iw | IECP | NL |
| 43066 | Iw | IMLP | NL |
| 43067¶ | Iw | IECP | BN |
| 43068¶ | Iw | IECP | BN |
| 43069 | | IECP | EC |
| 43070 | Iw | IECP | EC |
| 43071 | Iw | IECP | EC |
| 43072 | Iw | IMLP | NL |
| 43073 | Iw | IMLP | NL |
| 43074 | Iw | IECP | BN |
| 43075 | Iw | IECP | BN |
| 43076 | Iw | IMLP | NL |
| 43077 | Iw | IMLP | NL |
| 43078 | Iw | IECP | EC |
| 43079 | Iw | IECP | EC |
| 43080¶ | Iw | IECP | BN |
| 43081 | Iw | IECP | BN |
| 43082 | Iw | IECP | BN |
| 43083 | Iw | IECP | BN |
| 43084¶ | Iw | IECP | BN |
| 43085 | Iw | IECP | BN |
| 43086 | Iw | IECP | EC |
| 43087 | Iw | IECP | EC |
| 43088 | Iw | IECP | EC |
| 43089 | Iw | IECP | EC |
| 43090 | Iw | IECP | EC |
| 43091 | Iw | IECP | EC |
| 43092 | Iw | IECP | EC |
| 43093 | Iw | IECP | EC |
| 43094 | Iw | IECP | EC |
| 43095 | | IECP | HT |
| 43096 | Iw | IECP | HT |
| 43097 | Iw | IECP | HT |
| 43098 | Iw | IECP | HT |
| 43099 | | IECP | HT |
| 43100 | Iw | IECP | EC |
| 43101 | Iw | IECP | EC |
| 43102 | Iw | IECP | HT |
| 43103 | Iw | IECP | HT |
| 43104 | Iw | IECP | HT |
| 43105 | Iw | IECP | HT |
| 43106 | Iw | IECP | BN |
| 43107 | Iw | IECP | BN |
| 43108 | Iw | IECP | NL |
| 43109 | Iw | IECP | NL |
| 43110 | Iw | IECP | NL |
| 43111 | Iw | IECP | NL |
| 43112 | Iw | IMLP | NL |
| 43113 | Iw | IECP | HT |
| 43114 | Iw | IECP | NL |
| 43115 | Iw | IECP | EC |
| 43116 | Iw | IECP | NL |
| 43117 | Iw | IECP | NL |
| 43118 | Iw | IECP | NL |
| 43119 | Iw | IECP | NL |
| 43120 | | IECP | NL |
| 43121 | Iw | IECP | NL |
| 43122 | Iw | IECP | NL |
| 43123¶ | Iw | IECP | BN |
| 43124 | Iw | IWRP | PM |
| 43125 | Iw | IWRP | PM |
| 43126 | Iw | ICCP | PM |
| 43127 | Iw | IWRP | PM |
| 43128 | Iw | IWRP | PM |
| 43129 | Iw | IWRP | PM |
| 43130 | Iw | IWRP | PM |
| 43131 | Iw | IWRP | PM |
| 43132 | Iw | IWRP | PM |
| 43133 | Iw | IWRP | PM |
| 43134 | Iw | IWRP | PM |
| 43135 | Iw | IWRP | PM |
| 43136 | Iw | IWRP | PM |
| 43137 | Iw | IWRP | PM |
| 43138 | | IWRP | PM |
| 43139 | Iw | IWRP | PM |
| 43140 | Iw | IWRP | OO |
| 43141 | Iw | IWRP | OO |
| 43142 | Iw | IWRP | OO |
| 43143 | | IWRP | LA |
| 43144 | | IWRP | OO |
| 43145 | Iw | IWRP | OO |
| 43146 | Iw | IWRP | OO |
| 43147 | Iw | IWRP | OO |
| 43148 | Iw | IWRP | OO |
| 43149 | Iw | IWRP | PM |
| 43150 | Iw | IWRP | PM |
| 43151 | Iw | IWRP | PM |
| 43152 | Iw | IMLP | NL |
| 43153 | Iw | IMLP | NL |

| | | | |
|---|---|---|---|
| 43154 | Iw | IECP | NL |
| 43155 | | IECP | NL |
| 43156 | | IWRP | LA |
| 43157 | | IWRP | LA |
| 43158 | Iw | IWRP | LA |
| 43159 | | IWRP | PA |
| 43160 | | IWRP | LA |
| 43161 | Iw | IWRP | LA |
| 43162 | | IWRP | LA |
| 43163 | Iw | ICCP | LA |
| 43164 | Iw | ICCP | LA |
| 43165 | Iw | ICCP | LA |
| 43166 | Iw | ICCP | LA |
| 43167 | Iw | IWRP | PM |
| 43168 | Iw | IWRP | PM |
| 43169 | Iw | IWRP | PM |
| 43170 | Iw | IWRP | PM |
| 43171 | Iw | ICCP | PM |
| 43172 | | ICCP | PM |
| 43173 | | ICCP | PM |
| 43174 | | ICCP | PM |
| 43175 | | ICCP | PM |
| 43176 | | IWRP | LA |
| 43177 | | ICCP | LA |
| 43178 | Iw | ICCP | LA |
| 43179 | Iw | ICCP | LA |
| 43180 | Iw | IWRP | PM |
| 43181 | | ICCP | LA |
| 43182 | | ICCP | LA |
| 43183 | | ICCP | LA |
| 43184 | Iw | ICCP | LA |
| 43185 | Iw | ICCP | LA |
| 43186 | Iw | ICCP | LA |
| 43187 | Iw | IWRP | LA |
| 43188 | Iw | IWRP | LA |
| 43189 | Iw | IWRP | LA |
| 43190 | Iw | IWRP | LA |
| 43191 | Iw | IWRP | LA |
| 43192 | Iw | IWRP | LA |
| 43193 | | IMLP | NL |
| 43194 | Iw | IECP | NL |
| 43195 | Iw | IECP | NL |
| 43196 | Iw | IECP | NL |
| 43197 | Iw | IECP | NL |
| 43198 | Iw | IECP | NL |

## CLASS 43/2.

**Class 43/0 Power cars to be regeared for 100 mph push-pull single operation on InterCity Cross-Country services with TGS vehicle modified to DGS (see coaches 44201 et seq). Planned operation in 1991**

43201 to 43229.

## CLASS 47/0 TYPE 4 BR & Brush 2580hp. Co-Co

**(No train heating, speed restricted 75mph).**

| | | | |
|---|---|---|---|
| 47002 | | FDBT | TI |
| 47003 | | FDBT | TI |
| 47004 | Fa | FAME | ED |
| 47005 | | DCMA | CD |
| 47006 | Fa | FAME | ED |
| 47007 | Fa | FAGS | SF |
| 47009 | | FDYX | HQ |
| 47010 | Fq | FPCI | SF |
| 47014 | F | FDAT | TI |
| 47016 | F | FDAT | TI |
| 47017 | | FDYX | HQ |
| 47018 | F | FDAT | TI |
| 47019 | F | FDAT | TI |
| 47033 | | FAWK | CF |
| 47049 | Fg | FDAT | TI |
| 47050 | F | FDBT | TI |
| 47051 | | FDAT | TI |
| 47052 | Fg | FDAT | TI |
| 47053 | | DCMA | CD |
| 47054 | Fp | FPCI | IM |
| 47060 | Fg | FDAT | TI |
| 47063 | Fa | FAWK | CF |
| 47079 | Fa | FDAT | TI |
| 47085 | Fq | FPCI | IM |
| 47094 | Fp | FPEK | CF |
| 47095 | F | FDAT | TI |
| 47096 | | FDBT | TI |
| 47098 | | FDBT | TI |
| 47099 | F | FDAT | TI |
| 47100 | | FDBT | TI |
| 47102 | | FDBT | TI |
| 47105 | | FDAT | TI |
| 47107 | F | FDAT | TI |
| 47108 | | DCMA | CD |
| 47112 | F | FDAT | TI |
| 47114 | Fa | FAME | ED |
| 47115 | Fp | FPCI | IM |
| 47116 | | DCMA | CD |
| 47117 | Fg | DCMA | CD |
| 47118 | | FDBT | TI |
| 47119 | Fq | FPCI | IM |
| 47120 | | FDBT | TI |
| 47121 | | FDBT | TI |
| 47123 | | FDBT | TI |
| 47125 | Fq | FPBC | CD |
| 47142 | F | FDAT | TI |
| 47144 | Fg | FDAT | TI |
| 47145 | | FDAT | TI |
| 47146 | | FDBT | TI |
| 47147 | Fg | FDAT | TI |
| 47150 | Fg | FDAT | TI |
| 47152 | Fg | FDAT | TI |
| 47156 | Fg | FDAT | TI |
| 47157 | F- | FDAT | TI |
| 47186 | F | FDAT | TI |
| 47187 | Fg | FDAT | TI |
| 47188 | Fg | FDAT | TI |
| 47190 | Fq | FPBC | CD |
| 47193 | Fq | FPBC | CD |
| 47194 | Fq | FPBC | CD |
| 47195 | Fq | FPBC | CD |
| 47196 | Fq | FPBC | CD |
| 47197 | Fp | FPEK | CF |
| 47200 | | FDBT | TI |
| 47201 | Fg | FDAT | TI |
| 47204 | Fg | FDAT | TI |
| 47205 | Fg | FDAT | TI |
| 47206 | Fh | FDAT | TI |
| 47207 | Fg | FDAT | TI |
| 47209 | | FDAT | TI |
| 47210 | Fa | FAME | ED |
| 47211 | F+ | FDAT | TI |
| 47212 | Fp | FPCI | IM |
| 47213 | Fh | FDAT | TI |
| 47214 | F | FDAT | TI |
| 47217 | | FDAT | TI |
| 47218 | | FDAT | TI |
| 47219 | | FDAT | TI |
| 47220 | | FDAT | TI |
| 47221 | Fp | FPCI | IM |
| 47222 | | FPCI | IM |
| 47223 | Fq | FPCI | IM |
| 47224 | Fp | FPCI | IM |
| 47225 | Fg | FDAT | TI |
| 47226 | | FDAT | TI |
| 47227 | F | FDAT | TI |
| 47228 | F | FDAT | TI |
| 47229 | F | FDAT | TI |
| 47231 | Fg | FDAT | TI |
| 47233 | Fq | FPBC | CD |
| 47234 | F+ | FDAT | TI |
| 47236 | F+ | FDAT | TI |
| 47237 | F | FDAT | TI |
| 47238 | Fg | FDAT | TI |
| 47241 | Fg | FDAT | TI |
| 47245 | | FDAT | TI |
| 47249 | F | FDAT | TI |
| 47256 | Fh | FDAT | TI |
| 47258 | Fg | FDAT | TI |
| 47270 | | FDAT | TI |
| 47276 | Fp | FPCI | IM |
| 47277 | Fp | FPEK | CF |
| 47278 | Fq | FPBC | CD |
| 47279 | Fg | FDAT | TI |
| 47280 | F | FDAT | TI |
| 47281 | | FDAT | TI |
| 47283 | Fg | FDAT | TI |
| 47284 | | FDAT | TI |
| 47285 | F | FDAT | TI |
| 47286 | Fh | FDAT | TI |
| 47287 | | FDAT | TI |
| 47288 | F- | FDAT | TI |
| 47289 | Fg | FDAT | TI |
| 47290 | Fh | FDAT | TI |
| 47291 | F | FDAT | TI |
| 47292 | Fg | FDAT | TI |
| 47293 | Fg | FDAT | TI |
| 47294 | Fp | FPCI | IM |
| 47295 | | FPCI | IM |
| 47296 | Fg | FDAT | TI |
| 47297 | F | FDAT | TI |
| 47298 | | FDAT | TI |
| 47299 | | FPCI | IM |

## CLASS 47/3 TYPE 4 BR & Brush 2580hp. Co-Co

**(No train heating, speed restricted 75mph).**

| | | | |
|---|---|---|---|
| 47301 | F | FCTY | TE |
| 47302 | F | FCTY | TE |
| 47303 | F- | FCTY | TE |
| 47304 | | FCTY | TE |
| 47305 | Fp | FCTY | TE |
| 47306 | | FDAT | TI |
| 47307 | | FDAT | TI |
| 47308 | F- | FDAT | TI |
| 47309 | Fg | FDAT | TI |
| 47310 | | FDAT | TI |
| 47311 | Fg | FDAT | TI |
| 47312 | Fg | FDAT | TI |
| 47313 | | FDAT | TI |
| 47314 | | FDBT | TI |
| 47315 | ZG | DCWA | OC |
| 47316 | | FDBT | TI |
| 47317 | Fg | FDAT | TI |
| 47318 | F | FPEK | CF |
| 47319 | Fp | FPCI | IM |
| 47320 | F | FDCC | CD |
| 47321 | Fh | FDAT | TI |
| 47322 | F | FDCC | CD |
| 47323 | | FDAT | TI |
| 47324 | Fq | FPBC | CD |
| 47325 | F | FAGS | SF |
| 47326 | | FPEK | CF |
| 47327 | F | FPEK | CF |
| 47328 | Fa | FAGS | SF |
| 47329 | ZG | DCMA | CD |
| 47330 | | FDCC | CD |
| 47331 | F | DCEA | IM |
| 47332 | ZG | DCEA | IM |
| 47333 | ZG | DCMA | CD |
| 47334 | ZG | DCWA | OC |
| 47335 | Fg | FDAT | TI |
| 47336 | Fp | FPCI | IM |
| 47337 | F | FDAT | TI |
| 47338 | | FDBT | TI |
| 47339 | F | DCMP | CD |
| 47340 | F | DCMM | CD |
| 47341 | F- | DCWA | OC |
| 47343 | ZG | DCMP | CD |
| 47344 | | DCEA | IM |
| 47345 | F | FDAT | TI |
| 47346 | F | DCAA | SF |
| 47347 | Fm | FDCC | CD |
| 47348 | F | DCEA | IM |
| 47349 | Fg | FDCC | CD |
| 47350 | F | FDCC | CD |
| 47351 | | FDAT | TI |
| 47352 | ZG | DCEA | IM |
| 47353 | ZG | DCMA | CD |
| 47354 | Fg | FDCC | CD |
| 47355 | Fg | FDCC | CD |
| 47356 | F | DCMM | CD |
| 47357 | Fg | DCMM | CD |
| 47358 | F | DCMP | CD |
| 47359 | Fm | FDAT | TI |
| 47360 | | FDAT | TI |
| 47361 | Fg | FCTY | TE |
| 47362 | F | FCTY | TE |
| 47363 | F | FCTY | TE |
| 47364 | | DCWA | OC |
| 47365 | F- | FDCC | CD |
| 47366 | F | DCAA | SF |
| 47367 | F | FAGS | SF |
| 47368 | Fq | FPBC | CD |
| 47369 | Fp | FPCI | IM |

Two Class 47/4 locomotives with officially very different duties seen in pristine condition. *INTERCITY* Swallow livery (Iw) is carried by No 47835 *Windsor Castle* (above) unusually employed at Edinburgh Waverley on 4 March with the ScotRail General Manager's saloon No DM45020 for a media special to the Forth Bridge Centenary celebrations. Numbering in the 478xx series indicates its additional 575 gallon fuel capacity.

No 47568 *Royal Engineers Postal & Courier Services* (below) is seen at Long Marston on 20 March after a special naming ceremony. This locomotive carries Mainline livery (ML) and is the last of the Parcels Sector to be so painted.

| | | | | | | | | | | | | | | | |
|---|---|---|---|---|---|---|---|---|---|---|---|---|---|---|---|
| 47370 | F | FDAT | TI | 47373 | Fp | FPCI | IM | 47376 | | FDAT | TI | 47379 | Fp | FPCI | IM |
| 47371 | F | FDAT | TI | 47374 | F | FPCI | IM | 47377 | Fg | FDAT | TI | 47380 | Fp | FPCI | IM |
| 47372 | | DCMA | CD | 47375 | Fg | FDAT | TI | 47378 | F+ | FDAT | TI | 47381 | Fp | FPEK | CF |

## CLASS 47/4 TYPE 4 BR & Brush 2580hp. Co-Co

(Electric train heating, Index 66).

| | | | | | | | | | | | | | | | |
|---|---|---|---|---|---|---|---|---|---|---|---|---|---|---|---|
| 47401 | | FPXA | IM | 47461 | Ps | PISA | IS | 47523 | ML | RXLC | CD | 47580 | ML | RXLD | BR |
| 47402 | | FPXA | IM | 47462 | | ICDA | CD | 47524 | ML | RXLD | BR | 47581 | N | NWRA | OC |
| 47406 | ML | IECA | IM | 47463 | | RXLC | CD | 47525 | ML | ICDA | CD | 47582 | N | NWRA | OC |
| 47407 | | IECA | IM | 47465 | | RXLC | CD | 47526 | | RXLC | CD | 47583 | N | NWRA | OC |
| 47413 | | IECA | IM | 47466 | | RXLD | BR | 47527 | ML | ICDA | CD | 47584 | | RXLD | BR |
| 47417 | | IECA | IM | 47467 | | DCHA | ED | 47528 | ML | RXLD | BR | 47585 | | RXLD | BR |
| 47418 | | IECA | IM | 47468 | | RXLD | BR | 47530 | N | NWRA | OC | 47586 | Iw | ICDA | CD |
| 47421 | | RXLC | CD | 47470 | Ms | IEDA | ED | 47531 | | DCHA | ED | 47587 | N | NWRA | OC |
| 47422 | | PCDA | CD | 47471 | ML | ICDA | CD | 47532 | | FDCC | CD | 47588 | Fg | FDCC | CD |
| 47423 | | FDCC | CD | 47472 | | DCWA | OC | 47533 | ML | RXLD | OC | 47592 | ML | RXLD | BR |
| 47424 | | PCDA | CD | 47473 | | FDCC | CD | 47534 | | RXLD | OC | 47593 | ML | IEDA | ED |
| 47425 | | FDCC | CD | 47474 | R | RXLC | CD | 47535 | | RXLD | OC | 47594 | Fm | FDCC | CD |
| 47426 | | DCMP | CD | 47475 | Pb | PCDA | CD | 47536 | | RXLD | BR | 47595 | Iw | IEDA | ED |
| 47430 | Fa | FAGS | SF | 47476 | | RXLD | BR | 47537 | | RXLD | BR | 47596 | N | NWRA | OC |
| 47431 | | DCMP | CD | 47477 | | PCDA | CD | 47538 | ML | RXLD | BR | 47597 | | PCDA | CD |
| 47432 | | ICDA | CD | 47478 | | ICDA | CD | 47539 | | RXLD | BR | 47598 | N | NWRA | OC |
| 47433 | | RXLC | CD | 47479 | R | RXLC | CD | 47540 | | DCWA | OC | 47599 | Fm | FDCC | CD |
| 47434 | | PCDA | CD | 47481 | | RXLC | CD | 47541 | Ms | PISA | IS | 47600 | Fg | FDCC | CD |
| 47436 | | DCMM | CD | 47482 | | RXLD | BR | 47543 | | RXLD | OC | 47603 | | RXLD | BR |
| 47438 | | FDCC | CD | 47483 | ML | ICDA | CD | 47546 | | DCHA | ED | 47604 | | DCHA | ED |
| 47439 | ML | FDCC | CD | 47484 | ★ | DCWA | OC | 47547 | N | NWRA | OC | 47605 | F- | FDCC | CD |
| 47440 | | FDCC | CD | 47485 | | FDCC | CD | 47549 | ML | RXLD | BR | 47615 | F- | FDCC | CD |
| 47441 | | FDCC | CD | 47488 | | PCDA | CD | 47550 | ML | DCHA | ED | 47616 | ML | RXLD | BR |
| 47442 | | FDCC | CD | 47489 | R | RXLC | CD | 47555 | ML | ICDA | CD | 47617 | | IEDA | ED |
| 47443 | | PCDA | CD | 47490 | ML | RXLD | BR | 47557 | ML | RXLD | BR | 47624 | ML | RXLD | BR |
| 47444 | | PCDA | CD | 47491 | | FDCC | CD | 47558 | ML | RXLD | BR | 47625 | ML | RXLD | BR |
| 47445 | Fh | FDCC | CD | 47492 | Ms | PISA | IS | 47559 | | RXLC | CD | 47626 | | RXLD | BR |
| 47446 | | FDCC | CD | 47500 | ★ | ICDA | CD | 47562 | I | IEDA | ED | 47627 | ML | RXLD | BR |
| 47447 | | FDCC | CD | 47501 | Iw | RXLD | BR | 47564 | | RXLD | BR | 47628 | ML | RXLD | BR |
| 47448 | | PCDA | CD | 47503 | | PCDA | CD | 47565 | ML | RXLD | BR | 47630 | | PISA | IS |
| 47449 | | FDCC | CD | 47508 | ML | ICDA | CD | 47566 | ML | RXLD | BR | 47631 | | RXLD | BR |
| 47450 | | DCMP | CD | 47509 | I | IEDA | ED | 47567 | ML | RXLC | CD | 47633 | | IEDA | ED |
| 47451 | | FDCC | CD | 47512 | | ICDA | CD | 47568 | ML | RXLD | BR | 47634 | | RXLD | BR |
| 47452 | | FDCC | CD | 47513 | | RXLD | BR | 47569 | ML | RXLD | BR | 47635 | | PISA | IS |
| 47453 | | DCMP | CD | 47515 | ML | RXLD | BR | 47572 | | RXLD | BR | 47636 | | IEDA | ED |
| 47454 | | FDCC | CD | 47517 | | ICDA | CD | 47573 | N | NWRA | OC | 47640 | | PISA | IS |
| 47456 | | ICDA | CD | 47518 | | IEDA | ED | 47574 | | RXLD | BR | 47641 | | IEDA | ED |
| 47457 | | FDCC | CD | 47519 | | ICDA | CD | 47575 | | RXLD | BR | 47642 | Ms | PISA | IS |
| 47458 | | RXLC | CD | 47520 | I | ICDA | CD | 47576 | N | NWRA | OC | 47643 | Ms | IEDA | ED |
| 47459 | | ICDA | CD | 47521 | N | NWRA | OC | 47578 | | IEDA | ED | 47644 | | IEDA | ED |
| 47460 | | PISA | IS | 47522 | R | RXLC | CD | 47579 | N | NWRA | OC | | | | |

47/7 series below.

Long range fuel tank fleet:

| | | | | | | | | | | | | | | | |
|---|---|---|---|---|---|---|---|---|---|---|---|---|---|---|---|
| 47801 | ML | ILRA | BR | 47815 | | ILRA | BR | 47829 | ML | ILRA | BR | 47843 | Iw | ICDA | CD |
| 47802 | | ILRA | BR | 47816 | | ILRA | BR | 47830 | ML | ILRA | BR | 47844 | Iw | ICDA | CD |
| 47803 | ML | ICDA | CD | 47817 | | ILRA | BR | 47831 | ML | ICDA | CD | 47845 | | ICDA | CD |
| 47804 | Iw | ILRA | BR | 47818 | Iw | ILRA | BR | 47832 | ML | ILRA | BR | 47846 | | ICDA | CD |
| 47805 | | ILRA | BR | 47819 | | ILRA | BR | 47833 | ML | ILRA | BR | 47847 | | ICDA | CD |
| 47806 | | ILRA | BR | 47820 | | ILRA | BR | 47834 | Iw | ILRA | BR | 47848 | | ICDA | CD |
| 47807 | Iw | ILRA | BR | 47821 | Iw | ILRA | BR | 47835 | Iw | ILRA | BR | 47849 | ML | ICDA | CD |
| 47808 | | ILRA | BR | 47822 | | ILRA | BR | 47836 | Iw | ICDA | CD | 47850 | ML | ICDA | CD |
| 47809 | | ILRA | BR | 47823 | ML | ILRA | BR | 47837 | Iw | ICDA | CD | 47851 | Iw | ICDA | CD |
| 47810 | Iw | ILRA | BR | 47824 | Iw | ILRA | BR | 47838 | Iw | ICDA | CD | 47852 | ML | ICDA | CD |
| 47811 | | ILRA | BR | 47825 | Iw | ILRA | BR | 47839 | Iw | ICDA | CD | 47853 | ML | ICDA | CD |
| 47812 | | ILRA | BR | 47826 | Iw | ILRA | BR | 47840 | Iw | ICDA | CD | | | | |
| 47813 | | ILRA | BR | 47827 | Iw | ILRA | BR | 47841 | Iw | ICDA | CD | | | | |
| 47814 | | ILRA | BR | 47828 | ML | ILRA | BR | 47842 | Iw | ICDA | CD | | | | |

Class 47/4 Research Department Fleet

| | | | | | | | | | | | |
|---|---|---|---|---|---|---|---|---|---|---|---|
| 47971 | | DRTC | CD | 47972 | | DRTC | CD | 47973 | ML | DRTC | CD |

## CLASS 47/7 TYPE 4 BR & Brush 2580hp. Co-Co

(Electric train heating, Index 66. Push-pull equipped).

| | | | |
|---|---|---|---|
| 47701 | Ps | PEDA | ED |
| 47702 | Ps | PEDA | ED |
| 47703 | Ps | PEDA | ED |
| 47704 | Ps | PEDA | ED |
| 47705 | N | NWRA | OC |
| 47706 | Ps | PEDA | ED |
| 47707 | Ps | NWRA | OC |
| 47708 | Ps | PEDA | ED |
| 47709 | Ps | PEDA | ED |
| 47710 | Ps | PEDA | ED |
| 47711 | Ps | PEDA | ED |
| 47712 | Ps | PEDA | ED |
| 47714 | N | NWRA | OC |
| 47715 | Ps | NWRA | OC |
| 47716 | Ps | NWRA | OC |
| 47717 | Ps | NWRA | OC |

478xx series see above.

47971 et seq see above.

## CLASS 50 TYPE 4 English Electric 2700hp. Co-Co

(Electric Train Heating. Index 61. 'DCWA' fleet speed restricted 60mph).

| | | | |
|---|---|---|---|
| 50001 | N | NSSA | LA |
| 50002 | N | NSSA | LA |
| 50003 | N | NSSA | LA |
| 50004 | | DCWA | LA |
| 50005 | N | NSSA | LA |
| 50007 | ★ | NSSA | LA |
| 50008 | | DCWA | LA |
| 50009 | N | DCWA | LA |
| 50015 | | DCWA | LA |
| 50016 | N | NSSA | LA |
| 50017 | N | NSSA | LA |
| 50018 | N | NSSA | LA |
| 50019 | | DXXD | LA |
| 50020 | | DXXD | LA |
| 50023 | N | DCWA | LA |
| 50024 | N | NSSA | LA |
| 50026 | N | NSSA | LA |
| 50027 | N | NSSA | LA |
| 50028 | N | NSSA | LA |
| 50029 | N | NSSA | LA |
| 50030 | N | NSSA | LA |
| 50031 | | DCWA | LA |
| 50032 | N | NXXA | OC |
| 50033 | N | NSSA | LA |
| 50034 | N | DCWA | LA |
| 50035 | N | NSSA | LA |
| 50036 | | DCWA | LA |
| 50037 | | NSSA | LA |
| 50042 | | DCWA | LA |
| 50043 | N | NSSA | LA |
| 50044 | N | NSSA | LA |
| 50045 | N | NSSA | LA |
| 50046 | | NSSA | LA |
| 50048 | N | NSSA | LA |
| 50049 | N | NSSA | LA |
| 50050 | N | NSSA | LA |

## CLASS 56 TYPE 5 BREL & Electroputere 3250hp. Co-Co

($ Experimentally derated to 2400hp).

| | | | |
|---|---|---|---|
| 56001 | Fa | FAWK | CF |
| 56002 | F | FECN | TO |
| 56003 | F- | FECN | TO |
| 56004 | | FECN | TO |
| 56005 | F | FECN | TO |
| 56006 | Fe | FECN | TO |
| 56007 | Fe | FECN | TO |
| 56008 | | FECN | TO |
| 56009 | Fe | FECN | TO |
| 56010 | | FECN | TO |
| 56011 | F | FECN | TO |
| 56012 | Ff | FECN | TO |
| 56013 | Fe | FECN | TO |
| 56014 | Fe | FECN | TO |
| 56015 | Fe | FECN | TO |
| 56016 | Ff | FECN | TO |
| 56017 | Fe | FECN | TO |
| 56018 | F | FECN | TO |
| 56019 | Fe | FECN | TO |
| 56020 | | FECN | TO |
| 56021 | | FECN | TO |
| 56022 | | FECN | TO |
| 56023 | Fe | FECN | TO |
| 56024 | F | FECN | TO |
| 56025$ | Ff | FECN | TO |
| 56026 | Fe | FECN | TO |
| 56027 | Fe | FECN | TO |
| 56028 | Fe | FECN | TO |
| 56029 | Fe | FEDN | TO |
| 56030 | Fe | FEDN | TO |
| 56031 | Fb | FAWK | CF |
| 56032 | Fa | FAWK | CF |
| 56033 | Fa | FAXN | TO |
| 56034 | Fa | FAWK | CF |
| 56035 | F | FAWK | CF |
| 56036 | Fp | FAWK | CF |
| 56037 | Fa | FAWK | CF |
| 56038 | F | FAWK | CF |
| 56039 | Fa | FAWK | CF |
| 56040 | F | FAWK | CF |
| 56041 | F | FAWK | CF |
| 56042 | F+ | FAXX | HQ |
| 56043 | Fa | FAWK | CF |
| 56044 | F | FAWK | CF |
| 56045 | Fa | FAXN | TO |
| 56046 | Fa | FAWK | CF |
| 56047 | Fe | FEDN | TO |
| 56048 | | FAWK | CF |
| 56049 | F | FAWK | CF |
| 56050 | Fa | FAWK | CF |
| 56051 | Fa | FAWK | CF |
| 56052 | Fa | FAWK | CF |
| 56053 | Fa | FAWK | CF |
| 56054 | Fe | FAXN | TO |
| 56055 | Fa | FAWK | CF |
| 56056 | Fa | FAWK | CF |
| 56057 | F | FAXN | TO |
| 56058 | Fa | FAXN | TO |
| 56059 | F+ | FAXN | TO |
| 56060 | Fa | FAXN | TO |
| 56061 | Fa | FAXN | TO |
| 56062 | Fa | FAXN | TO |
| 56063 | Fa | FAXN | TO |
| 56064 | F | FAXN | TO |
| 56065 | Fb | FAXN | TO |
| 56066 | Fe | FEDN | TO |
| 56067 | F | FEDN | TO |
| 56068 | F | FEDN | TO |
| 56069 | Fe | FEDN | TO |
| 56070 | Fa | FAXN | TO |
| 56071 | Fe | FEDN | TO |
| 56072 | Fe | FEDN | TO |
| 56073 | Fe | FEDN | TO |
| 56074 | Fe | FEDN | TO |
| 56075 | Fe | FEDN | TO |
| 56076 | F | FEDN | TO |
| 56077$ | Fe | FEDN | TO |
| 56078 | Fa | FAXN | TO |
| 56079 | Fe | FEDN | TO |
| 56080$ | Fe | FEDN | TO |
| 56081 | Fe | FEDN | TO |
| 56082 | Fe | FEDN | TO |
| 56083 | F | FEDN | TO |
| 56084 | Ff | FEDN | TO |
| 56085 | Ff | FEDN | TO |
| 56086$ | Fe | FEDN | TO |
| 56087 | Fe | FEDN | TO |
| 56088 | Ff | FEDN | TO |
| 56089 | F | FEDN | TO |
| 56090$ | F+ | FEDN | TO |
| 56091 | Fe | FEDN | TO |
| 56092 | Fe | FEDN | TO |
| 56093 | | FEDN | TO |
| 56094 | Fe | FEDN | TO |
| 56095 | Fe | FEDN | TO |
| 56096 | Ff | FEDN | TO |
| 56097 | Fe | FEDN | TO |
| 56098 | Fe | FEDN | TO |
| 56099 | Fe | FEDN | TO |
| 56100 | F | FEDN | TO |
| 56101 | | FEDN | TO |
| 56102 | Fe | FEDN | TO |
| 56103 | Fa | FAXN | TO |
| 56104 | Fe | FEDN | TO |
| 56105$ | | FAXN | TO |
| 56106 | | FEDN | TO |
| 56107$ | F | FEDN | TO |
| 56108 | F | FEDN | TO |
| 56109 | | FEDN | TO |
| 56110$ | | FAXN | TO |
| 56111 | | FEDN | TO |
| 56112 | | FEEN | TO |
| 56113 | F+ | FEEN | TO |
| 56114 | | FEEN | TO |
| 56115 | F+ | FEEN | TO |
| 56116 | | FEEN | TO |
| 56117 | | FEEN | TO |
| 56118 | | FEEN | TO |
| 56119 | | FEEN | TO |
| 56120 | | FEEN | TO |
| 56121 | F- | FEEN | TO |
| 56122 | Fe | FEEN | TO |
| 56123 | Fe | FEDN | TO |
| 56124 | | FEEN | TO |
| 56125 | Fe | FEEN | TO |
| 56126 | | FEEN | TO |
| 56127 | Fe | FEEN | TO |
| 56128 | Fe | FEEN | TO |
| 56129 | Fe | FEEN | TO |
| 56130 | F- | FEEN | TO |
| 56131$ | Fe | FEEN | TO |
| 56132 | Fe | FEEN | TO |
| 56133 | Fe | FEEN | TO |
| 56134 | Fe | FEEN | TO |
| 56135 | Fe | FEEN | TO |

## CLASS 58 TYPE 5 BREL 3300hp. Co-Co

| | | | |
|---|---|---|---|
| 58001 | Fe | FEAN | TO |
| 58002 | Fe | FEBN | TO |
| 58003 | Fe | FEAN | TO |
| 58004 | Fe | FEAN | TO |
| 58005 | F | FEAN | TO |
| 58006 | Fe | FEAN | TO |
| 58007 | F | FEAN | TO |
| 58008 | F | FEBN | TO |
| 58009 | Fe | FEAN | TO |
| 58010 | Fe | FEAN | TO |
| 58011 | Fe | FEAN | TO |
| 58012 | Fe | FEAN | TO |
| 58013 | F | FEAN | TO |
| 58014 | Fe | FEAN | TO |
| 58015 | Fe | FEAN | TO |
| 58016 | Fe | FEBN | TO |
| 58017 | Fe | FEAN | TO |
| 58018 | Fe | FEBN | TO |
| 58019 | Fe | FEBN | TO |
| 58020 | Fe | FEBN | TO |

Above: Railfreight Coal liveried (Fe) Class 56 No 56130 crosses the River Ouse at York on 9 February with a merry-go-round service from Ryhope Grange (Sunderland) to York Yard North for onward movement to Fiddlers Ferry Power Station.

Below: Class 86/4 Nos 86404 and 86424 in multiple head past Shenfield on 18 August 1989 with a freightliner service from Stratford FLT to Felixstowe South. The former locomotive is due to be converted to Class 86/6 whilst the latter is officially owned by Parcels Sector and will not be so modified.

| | | | |
|---|---|---|---|
| 58021 | F | FEBN | TO |
| 58022 | Fe | FEBN | TO |
| 58023 | Fe | FEBN | TO |
| 58024 | Fe | FEBN | TO |
| 58025 | Fe | FEBN | TO |
| 58026 | Fe | FEBN | TO |
| 58027 | Fe | FEBN | TO |
| 58028 | Fe | FEBN | TO |
| 58029 | Fe | FEBN | TO |
| 58030 | Fe | FEBN | TO |
| 58031 | Fe | FEBN | TO |
| 58032 | F | FEBN | TO |
| 58033 | Fe | FEBN | TO |
| 58034 | F | FEBN | TO |
| 58035 | Fe | FEBN | TO |
| 58036 | Fe | FEBN | TO |
| 58037 | F | FEBN | TO |
| 58038 | Fe | FEBN | TO |
| 58039 | Fe | FEBN | TO |
| 58040 | F | FEBN | TO |
| 58041 | Fe | FEBN | TO |
| 58042 | F | FEBN | TO |
| 58043 | Ff | FEBN | TO |
| 58044 | Ff | FEBN | TO |
| 58045 | Ff | FEBN | TO |
| 58046 | F | FEBN | TO |
| 58047 | F | FEBN | TO |
| 58048 | F | FEBN | TO |
| 58049 | F | FEBN | TO |
| 58050 | F | FEBN | TO |

## CLASS 59/0 TYPE 5 General Motors 3300hp. Co-Co

(Owned and operated by Foster Yeoman Ltd, Merehead)

| | | | |
|---|---|---|---|
| 59001 | ★ | CYPO | HQ |
| 59002 | ★ | CYPO | HQ |
| 59003 | ★ | CYPO | HQ |
| 59004 | ★ | CYPO | HQ |
| 59005 | ★ | CYPO | HQ |

## CLASS 59/1 TYPE 5 General Motors 3300hp. Co-Co

(On order for ARC Ltd, Whatley Quarry)

59101
59102
59103
59104

## CLASS 60 TYPE 5 Brush Traction 3100hp. Co-Co

(Locomotives in process of delivery. Livery and Pool are those planned at time of publication)

| | | | |
|---|---|---|---|
| 60001 | Fb | FAHH | TO |
| 60002 | Fq | FPDI | IM |
| 60003 | Fq | FPDI | IM |
| 60004 | Ff | FE.. | TO |
| 60005 | Fb | FA.. | TO |
| 60006 | Fb | FAHH | TO |
| 60007 | Fq | FPDI | IM |
| 60008 | Fn | FMMY | TE |
| 60009 | Fb | FA.. | TO |
| 60010 | Fb | FA.. | TO |
| 60011 | Fb | FA.. | TO |
| 60012 | Fb | FA.. | TO |
| 60013 | Fq | FPDI | IM |
| 60014 | Fq | FPDI | IM |
| 60015 | Fb | FAHH | |
| 60016 | Fb | FAHH | |
| 60017 | Fb | FAHH | |
| 60018 | Fb | FAHH | |
| 60019 | Fb | FAHH | |
| 60020 | Fn | FM.. | |
| 60021 | Fn | FM.. | |
| 60022 | Fn | FM.. | |
| 60023 | Fn | FM.. | |
| 60024 | Fq | FPDI | |
| 60025 | Fq | FPDI | |
| 60026 | Fq | FPDI | |
| 60027 | Fq | FPDI | |
| 60028 | Fq | FPDI | |
| 60029 | Fn | FM.. | |
| 60030 | Fn | FM.. | |
| 60031 | Fn | FM.. | |
| 60032 | Fn | FM.. | |
| 60033 | Fq | FP.. | |
| 60034 | Fq | FP.. | |
| 60035 | Fq | FP.. | |
| 60036 | Fn | FM.. | |
| 60037 | Fn | FM.. | |
| 60038 | Fn | FM.. | |
| 60039 | Fb | FA.. | |
| 60040 | Fb | FA.. | |
| 60041 | Fb | FA.. | |
| 60042 | Fb | FA.. | |
| 60043 | Fb | FA.. | |
| 60044 | Ff | FE.. | |
| 60045 | Ff | FE.. | |
| 60046 | Ff | FE.. | |
| 60047 | Ff | FE.. | |
| 60048 | Ff | FE.. | |
| 60049 | Fn | FM.. | |
| 60050 | Fn | FM.. | |
| 60051 | | | |
| 60052 | Fn | FM.. | |
| 60053 | Fn | FM.. | |
| 60054 | Fn | FM.. | |
| 60055 | Ff | FE.. | |
| 60056 | Ff | FE.. | |
| 60057 | Ff | FE.. | |
| 60058 | Ff | FE.. | |
| 60059 | Ff | FE.. | |
| 60060 | Ff | FE.. | |
| 60061 | Ff | FE.. | |
| 60062 | Fn | FM.. | |
| 60063 | Fq | FP.. | |
| 60064 | Fq | FP.. | |
| 60065 | Fq | FP.. | |
| 60066 | Ff | FE.. | |
| 60067 | Ff | FE.. | |
| 60068 | Ff | FE.. | |
| 60069 | Ff | FE.. | |
| 60070 | Ff | FE.. | |
| 60071 | Ff | FE.. | |
| 60072 | Ff | FE.. | |
| 60073 | Ff | FE.. | |
| 60074 | Ff | FE.. | |
| 60075 | Ff | FE.. | |
| 60076 | | | |
| 60077 | | | |
| 60078 | | | |
| 60079 | | | |
| 60080 | | | |
| 60081 | | | |
| 60082 | | | |
| 60083 | | | |
| 60084 | | | |
| 60085 | | | |
| 60086 | | | |
| 60087 | | | |
| 60088 | | | |
| 60089 | | | |
| 60090 | | | |
| 60091 | | | |
| 60092 | | | |
| 60093 | | | |
| 60094 | | | |
| 60095 | | | |
| 60096 | | | |
| 60097 | | | |
| 60098 | | | |
| 60099 | | | |
| 60100 | | | |

## CLASS 73/0 ELECTRO-DIESEL BR 1420hp(E)/600hp(D) Bo-Bo

(Maximum speed 80mph)

| | | | |
|---|---|---|---|
| 73001 | | DMEA | SL |
| 73002 | | DMEA | SL |
| 73003 | | DCSW | HQ |
| 73004 | ★ | DCSW | HQ |
| 73005 | ★ | NSSB | SL |
| 73006 | | NXXA | SL |

## CLASS 73/1 ELECTRO-DIESEL BR 1420hp(E)/600hp(D). Bo-Bo

(Maximum speed 60mph)

| | | | |
|---|---|---|---|
| 73101 | ML | DCSA | SL |
| 73103 | ML | DCSA | SL |
| 73105 | ML | DCSA | SL |
| 73106 | ZG | DMEA | SL |
| 73107 | ML | DMEA | SL |
| 73108 | ZG | DCSA | SL |
| 73110 | ML | DCSA | SL |
| 73111 | ML | DCSA | SL |
| 73114 | ML | DCSA | SL |
| 73117 | ML | DCSA | SL |
| 73118 | ML | DCSA | SL |
| 73119 | ML | DCSA | SL |
| 73126 | ML | DCSA | SL |
| 73128 | ML | DCSA | SL |
| 73129 | ML | DCSA | SL |
| 73131 | ML | DCSA | SL |
| 73132 | ML | DCSA | SL |
| 73133 | ML | DCSA | SL |
| 73135 | ZG | DMEA | SL |
| 73136 | ZG | DMEA | SL |
| 73138 | ML | DCSA | SL |
| 73139 | ML | DCSA | SL |
| 73140 | ML | FASB | SL |
| 73141 | ML | FASB | SL |

## CLASS 73/2 ELECTRO-DIESEL BR 1420hp(E)/600hp(D) Bo-Bo
(Maximum speed 90mph)

| | | | | | | | | | | | | | | | |
|---|---|---|---|---|---|---|---|---|---|---|---|---|---|---|---|
| 73104 | ML | NSSB | SL | 73135 | ML | IVGA | SL | 73205 | ML | IVGA | SL | 73209 | ML | IVGA | SL |
| 73109 | ML | NSSB | SL | 73201 | Iw | IVGA | SL | 73206 | ML | IVGA | SL | 73210 | ML | IVGA | SL |
| 73112 | ML | NSSB | SL | 73202 | Iw | IVGA | SL | 73207 | ML | IVGA | SL | 73211 | ML | IVGA | SL |
| 73130 | ML | NSSB | SL | 73203 | ML | IVGA | SL | 73208 | ML | IVGA | SL | 73212 | ML | IVGA | SL |
| 73134 | ML | NSSB | SL | 73204 | ML | IVGA | SL | | | | | | | | |

## CLASS 81 AC ELECTRIC BRCW 3200hp. Bo-Bo
(Electric Train Heating. Index: 66. Restricted to 40mph).

| | | | | | | | | | | | |
|---|---|---|---|---|---|---|---|---|---|---|---|
| 81002 | IXXA | HQ | 81010 | FGZX | HQ | 81012 | IWCA | WN | 81017 | IWCA | WN |

## CLASS 85/0 AC ELECTRIC BR 3200hp. Bo-Bo
(Electric Train Heating. Index:66. '‡' locomotives restricted to 80mph).

| | | | | | | | | | | | |
|---|---|---|---|---|---|---|---|---|---|---|---|
| 85003 | RXLE | CE | 85013 | FDYX | HQ | 85026‡ | FDHC | CE | 85037‡ | ICCA | CE |
| 85005‡ | IXXA | HQ | 85015‡ | FDHC | CE | 85030‡ | ICCA | CE | 85040‡ | FDHC | CE |
| 85008‡ | ICCA | CE | 85018‡ | FDHC | CE | 85031‡ | FDHC | CE | | | |
| 85011 | RXLE | CE | 85020‡ | FDYX | HQ | 85034‡ | FDHC | CE | | | |

## CLASS 85/1 AC ELECTRIC BR 3200hp. Bo-Bo
(Maximum speed 75mph).

| | | | | | | | | | | | |
|---|---|---|---|---|---|---|---|---|---|---|---|
| 85101 | FGRC | CE | 85104 | FGRC | CEu | 85107 | FXXX | HQ | 85110 | FGRC | CE |
| 85102 | FGRC | CE | 85105 | FGRC | CE | 85108 | FGRC | CE | 85112 | FGRC | CE |
| 85103 | FGRC | CE | 85106 | FGRC | CE | 85109 | FGRC | CE | | | |

## CLASS 86/1 AC ELECTRIC English Electric 5000hp. Bo-Bo
(Electric Train Heating. Index 66 or 95 on stock with 600 amp wiring. Maximum speed 110mph).

| | | | | | | | | | | | |
|---|---|---|---|---|---|---|---|---|---|---|---|
| 86101 | ML | IWCA | WN | 86102 | ML | IWCA | WN | 86103 | ML | IWCA | WN |

## CLASS 86/2 AC ELECTRIC BR† & English Electric 4040hp. Bo-Bo
(Electric Train Heating. Index 66 or 95 on stock with 600 amp wiring.
Maximum speed 110‡/100mph. ¶ TDM equipped).

| | | | | | | | | | | | | | | | |
|---|---|---|---|---|---|---|---|---|---|---|---|---|---|---|---|
| 86204¶ | Iw | IEBA | WN | 86220¶ | ML | IANA | IL | 86235 | ML | IANA | IL | 86250¶ | I | ICCA | WN |
| 86205†¶ | I | IWCA | WN | 86221 | ML | IANA | IL | 86236¶ | I | IEBA | WN | 86251¶ | ML | IWCA | WN |
| 86206¶ | I | ICCA | WN | 86222† | I | ICCA | WN | 86237¶ | I | IWCA | WN | 86252¶ | ML | IWCA | WN |
| 86207¶ | I | ICCA | WN | 86223¶ | I | IANA | IL | 86238¶ | Iw | IANA | IL | 86253¶ | I | IEBA | WN |
| 86208¶ | ML | IEBA | WN | 86224¶‡ | ML | IEBA | WN | 86239†¶ | ML | RXLE | CE | 86254¶ | I | RXLE | CE |
| 86209¶ | ML | IEBA | WN | 86225¶‡ | I | IEBA | WN | 86240¶ | ML | ICCA | WN | 86255¶ | I | ICCA | WN |
| 86210¶ | Iw | IEBA | WN | 86226¶ | I | IWCA | WN | 86241†¶ | ML | RXLE | CE | 86256¶ | I | ICHA | WN |
| 86212¶ | ML | ICHA | WN | 86227 | ML | IANA | IL | 86242¶ | ML | IEBA | WN | 86257¶ | ML | IEBA | WN |
| 86213¶ | ML | IEBA | WN | 86228¶ | I | ICCA | WN | 86243¶ | ML | RXLE | CE | 86258†¶ | ML | ICCA | WN |
| 86214 | ML | IANA | IL | 86229¶ | ML | IWCA | WN | 86244 | ML | IANA | IL | 86259 | ML | IANA | IL |
| 86215¶ | ML | IANA | IL | 86230¶ | ML | IANA | IL | 86245¶ | ML | ICCA | WN | 86260¶ | ML | ICCA | WN |
| 86216 | I | IANA | IL | 86231¶‡ | ML | ICCA | WN | 86246†¶ | Iw | IANA | IL | 86261¶ | ML | RXLE | CE |
| 86217†¶ | Iw | IANA | IL | 86232 | ML | IANA | IL | 86247¶ | ML | IEBA | WN | | | | |
| 86218 | ML | IANA | IL | 86233†¶ | ML | ICCA | WN | 86248¶ | I | ICCA | WN | | | | |
| 86219¶ | ML | IEBA | WN | 86234¶ | ML | ICCA | WN | 86249¶ | ML | IEBA | WN | | | | |

## CLASS 86/4 AC ELECTRIC BR† & English Electric 4040hp. Bo-Bo
(Electric Train Heating. Index 66 or 95 on stock with 600 amp wiring. Maximum speed 100mph.
Multiple working with electric locomotives fitted with 36–way jumper cables. ¶ Also TDM fitted.

| | | | | | | | | | | | | | | | |
|---|---|---|---|---|---|---|---|---|---|---|---|---|---|---|---|
| 86401 | N | RXLE | CE | 86412 | I | FDPC | CE | 86419† | ML | RXLE | CE | 86430† | ML | RXLE | CE |
| 86403† | ML | FDPC | CE | 86414 | ML | FDPC | CE | 86423 | ML | FDPC | CE | 86431 | ML | FDPC | CE |
| 86404† | ML | FDPC | CE | 86415† | ML | FDPC | CE | 86424† | ML | RXLE | CE | 86437†¶ | ML | FDPC | CE |
| 86405 | ML | FDPC | CE | 86416¶† | I | RXLE | CE | 86425¶ | I | RXLE | CE | 86438† | ML | FDPC | CE |
| 86406† | ML | FDPC | CE | 86417 | ML | RXLE | CE | 86426 | ML | RXLE | CE | 86439 | ML | FDPC | CE |
| 86410† | ML | FDPC | CE | 86418 | ML | FDPC | CE | 86428 | I | FDPC | CE | | | | |
| 86411 | ML | FDPC | CE | | | | | | | | | | | | |

## CLASS 86/6 AC ELECTRIC BR† & English Electric 4040hp. Bo-Bo

(Maximum speed 75mph. Multiple working with electric locomotives fitted with 36-way jumper cables. ¶ Also TDM fitted).

| | | | | | | | | | | | | | | | |
|---|---|---|---|---|---|---|---|---|---|---|---|---|---|---|---|
| 86602¶ | Fx | FDPC | CE | 86610† | | | | 86620†¶ | ML | FDPC | CE | 86632¶ | ML | FDPC | CE |
| 86603† | | | | 86611 | | | | 86621¶ | ML | FDPC | CE | 86633¶ | ML | FDPC | CE |
| 86604† | | | | 86612† | | | | 86622¶ | Fg | FDPC | CE | 86634¶ | Fg | FDPC | CE |
| 86605 | | | | 86613†¶ | Fg | FDPC | CE | 86623 | | | | 86635†¶ | ML | FDPC | CE |
| 86606 | | | | 86614 | | | | 86627†¶ | Fx | FDPC | CE | 86636¶ | Fg | FDPC | CE |
| 86607¶ | ML | FDPC | CE | 86615† | | | | 86628 | | | | 86637 | | | |
| 86608 | Fg | FDPC | CE | 86618 | | | | 86631 | | | | 86639 | | | |
| 86609¶ | ML | FDPC | CE | | | | | | | | | | | | |

## CLASS 87/0 AC ELECTRIC BR 5000hp. Bo-Bo

(Electric Train Heating. Index 66 or 95 on stock with 600 amp wiring. Maximum speed 110mph.
(Multiple working with electric locomotives fitted with 36-way jumper cables. ¶ Also TDM fitted.

| | | | | | | | | | | | | | | | |
|---|---|---|---|---|---|---|---|---|---|---|---|---|---|---|---|
| 87001¶ | ML | IPSA | WN | 87010¶ | I | IPSA | WN | 87019¶ | ML | IPSA | WN | 87028 | Iw | IWCA | WN |
| 87002 | ML | IWCA | WN | 87011¶ | ML | IPSA | WN | 87020 | ML | IWCA | WN | 87029¶ | ML | IWCA | WN |
| 87003¶ | I | IPSA | WN | 87012¶ | I | IPSA | WN | 87021¶ | ML | IPSA | WN | 87030 | ML | IWCA | WN |
| 87004¶ | I | IWCA | WN | 87013¶ | I | IWCA | WN | 87022 | I | IWCA | WN | 87031¶ | I | ICCA | WN |
| 87005¶ | ML | IPSA | WN | 87014¶ | ML | IPSA | WN | 87023¶ | ML | IWCA | WN | 87032¶ | ML | ICCA | WN |
| 87006 | ML | IWCA | WN | 87015¶ | ML | IPSA | WN | 87024¶ | ML | IPSA | WN | 87033¶ | I | IWCA | WN |
| 87007¶ | ML | IPSA | WN | 87016¶ | ML | IPSA | WN | 87025¶ | ML | IPSA | WN | 87034 | I | IWCA | WN |
| 87008 | ML | IWCA | WN | 87017¶ | ML | IWCA | WN | 87026¶ | ML | IWCA | WN | 87035¶ | I | ICCA | WN |
| 87009 | ML | IPSA | WN | 87018 | I | IWCA | WN | 87027 | I | IWCA | WN | | | | |

## CLASS 87/1 AC ELECTRIC BR 4850hp. Bo-Bo

(Electric Train Heating. Index 66 or 95 on stock with 600 amp wiring. Maximum speed 110mph.
Multiple working with electric locomotives fitted with 36way jumper cables).

| | | | |
|---|---|---|---|
| 87101 | | FGLC | CE |

## CLASS 89/0 AC ELECTRIC Brush (at BREL) 5380hp. Co-Co

(Electric Train Heating. Index 95. Maximum speed 125mph).

| | | | |
|---|---|---|---|
| 89001 | Iw | IECA | BN |

## CLASS 90 AC ELECTRIC BREL 4850hp. Bo-Bo

(Electric Train Heating. Index 95. Maximum speed 110mph. TDM fitted).

| | | | | | | | | | | | | | | | |
|---|---|---|---|---|---|---|---|---|---|---|---|---|---|---|---|
| 90001 | Iw | IPSA | WN | 90014 | Iw | IWCA | WN | 90027 | ML | FDQC | CE | 90040 | Fg | FDQC | CE |
| 90002 | Iw | IWCA | WN | 90015 | Iw | IPSA | WN | 90028 | ML | FDQC | CE | 90041 | Fg | FDQC | CE |
| 90003 | Iw | IPSA | WN | 90016 | Iw | RXLE | CE | 90029 | ML | FDQC | CE | 90042 | Fg | FDQC | CE |
| 90004 | Iw | IPSA | WN | 90017 | Iw | RXLE | CE | 90030 | ML | FDQC | CE | 90043 | Fg | FDQC | CE |
| 90005 | Iw | IPSA | WN | 90018 | Iw | RXLE | CE | 90031 | ML | FDQC | CE | 90044 | Fg | FDYX | |
| 90006 | Iw | IWCA | WN | 90019 | Iw | RXLE | CE | 90032 | ML | FDQC | CE | 90045 | Fg | FDYX | |
| 90007 | Iw | IWCA | WN | 90020 | Iw | RXLE | CE | 90033 | ML | FDQC | CE | 90046 | Fg | FDYX | |
| 90008 | Iw | IPSA | WN | 90021 | Iw | FDQC | CE | 90034 | ML | FDQC | CE | 90047 | Fg | FDYX | |
| 90009 | Iw | IPSA | WN | 90022 | Iw | FDQC | CE | 90035 | ML | FDQC | CE | 90048 | Fg | FDYX | |
| 90010 | Iw | IWCA | WN | 90023 | Iw | FDQC | CE | 90036 | ML | FDQC | CE | 90049 | Fg | FDYX | |
| 90011 | Iw | IPSA | WN | 90024 | Iw | FDQC | CE | 90037 | Fg | FDQC | CE | 90050 | Fg | FDYX | |
| 90012 | Iw | IPSA | WN | 90025 | Iw | FDQC | CE | 90038 | Fg | FDQC | CE | | | | |
| 90013 | Iw | IPSA | WN | 90026 | ML | FDQC | CE | 90039 | Fg | FDQC | CE | | | | |

## CLASS 91 AC ELECTRIC GEC (at BREL) 6350hp. Bo-Bo

(Electric Train Heating. Index 95. Maximum speed 140mph. All TDM fitted).

| | | | | | | | | | | | | | | | |
|---|---|---|---|---|---|---|---|---|---|---|---|---|---|---|---|
| 91001 | Iw | IECA | BN | 91010 | Iw | IECA | BN | 91019 | Iw | IECA | | 91028 | Iw | IECA | |
| 91002 | Iw | IECA | BN | 91011 | Iw | IECA | BN | 91020 | Iw | IECA | | 91029 | Iw | IECA | |
| 91003 | Iw | IECA | BN | 91012 | Iw | IECA | BN | 91021 | Iw | IECA | | 91030 | Iw | IECA | |
| 91004 | Iw | IECA | BN | 91013 | Iw | IECA | BN | 91022 | Iw | IECA | | 91031 | Iw | IECA | |
| 91005 | Iw | IECA | BN | 91014 | Iw | IECA | | 91023 | Iw | IECA | | 91032 | Iw | IECA | |
| 91006 | Iw | IECA | BN | 91015 | Iw | IECA | | 91024 | Iw | IECA | | 91033 | Iw | IECA | |
| 91007 | Iw | IECA | BN | 91016 | Iw | IECA | | 91025 | Iw | IECA | | 91034 | Iw | IECA | |
| 91008 | Iw | IECA | BN | 91017 | Iw | IECA | | 91026 | Iw | IECA | | 91035 | Iw | IECA | |
| 91009 | Iw | IECA | BN | 91018 | Iw | IECA | | 91027 | Iw | IECA | | | | | |

## CLASS 92

Proposed new locomotive for Railfreight. Orders scheduled to be placed mid-1990.

## CLASS 93

Proposed new locomotive for 'InterCity 250' to operate with Mk 5 coaching stock.

## DEPARTMENTAL SERVICE SPECIAL PURPOSE VEHICLES.

### CLASS 97/2 — ETHEL BR 1250hp. — 2-2

(Electric Train Heating mobile generator. Index 54. Not self propelled).

| | | | | | | | |
|---|---|---|---|---|---|---|---|
| 97251 | I | ICHA | CL | 97252 | I | ICHA | OC |

### CLASS 97/4 — TYPE 4 BR 2500hp. — 1Co-Co1

| | | | | | | | |
|---|---|---|---|---|---|---|---|
| 97403 | ★ | DRTC | HQ | 97404 | | DRTC | HQ |

### CLASS 97/0 — SHUNTERS Ruston & Hornsby 165hp. — 0-6-0

| | | | | | | | | |
|---|---|---|---|---|---|---|---|---|
| 97651 | DCWA | CF(@GL) | 97653 | DCWA | CF(@RR) | 97654 | DCWA | RG. |

### CLASS 97/0 — SHUNTER BR 400hp. — 0-6-0

| | | |
|---|---|---|
| 97806 | DOPA | CF(@Sudbrook). |

### CLASS 97/7 — BATTERY ELECTRIC BR 740hp. — Bo-Bo

| | | | | | | | | | |
|---|---|---|---|---|---|---|---|---|---|
| 97701 | DCMA | HQ(@BD). | 97704 | DCEA | HQ(@HE). | 97707 | N | DCEA | HQ(@HE). |
| 97702 | DCMA | HQ(@BD). | 97705 | DCEA | HQ(@HE). | 97708 | N | DCEA | HQ(@HE). |
| 97703 | DCEA | HQ(@HE). | 97706 | DCEA | HQ(@HE). | | | | |

### ZZB — MOBILE LOAD BANK — North British — 22

(Not Self propelled)

| | | |
|---|---|---|
| ADB968021 | DRTC | HQ |

### ZZR — TRACTION TRAINING LOCOMOTIVES — Bo-Bo

| | | | | | | | | |
|---|---|---|---|---|---|---|---|---|
| ADB968027 | DMEA | HO. | 20188 | NGEA | IL | 25206 | DBMS | ZF |

The Mobile Load Bank, ADB968021, has to test all newly AC electrified lines before use. The former Class 84 locomotive is seen at York on 17 September hauled by Class 31/4 No 31461 in BR General grey livery (ZG).

# DIESEL MULTIPLE UNITS
# FIRST GENERATION VEHICLES.

## Class 119 Gloucester RC&W — DMBC.DQ3.02
**Seats: 1st 18, Std 16.** — **Livery: N.**

| | | | | | | | | | | | | | | | |
|---|---|---|---|---|---|---|---|---|---|---|---|---|---|---|---|
| 51060 | | NSB | RG | 51065 | | NSB | RG | 51073 | | NSB | RG | 51076 | | NSB | RG |
| 51062 | | NWR | RG | 51066 | | NSB | RG | 51074 | | NSB | RG | 51079 | | NSB | RG |

## Class 119 Gloucester RC&W — DMS(L).DP2.03
**Seats: 68** — **Livery: N**

| | | | | | | | | | | | | | | | |
|---|---|---|---|---|---|---|---|---|---|---|---|---|---|---|---|
| 51086 | | NSB | RG | 51090 | | NWR | RG | 51099 | | NSB | RG | 51104 | | NSB | RG |
| 51088 | | NSB | RG | 51094 | | NSB | RG | 51103 | | NSB | RG | 51107 | | NSB | RG |

## Class 116 BR Derby — DMBS.DQ2.30
**Seats: 65**

| | | | | | | | | | | | | | | | |
|---|---|---|---|---|---|---|---|---|---|---|---|---|---|---|---|
| 51128 | | PCF | CF | 51131 | | PTS | TS | 51134 | | PCF | CF | 51138 | | PTS | TS |
| 51129 | | PTS | TS | 51132 | | PCF | CF | 51135 | | PCF | CF | 51139 | | PCF | CF |
| 51130 | | PTS | TS | 51133 | | PCF | CF | 51136 | | PCF | CF | 51140 | | PCF | CF |

## Class 116 BR Derby — DMS.DP2.20
**Seats: 89**

| | | | | | | | | | | | | | | | |
|---|---|---|---|---|---|---|---|---|---|---|---|---|---|---|---|
| 51141 | | PCF | CF | 51144 | | PTS | TS | 51147 | | PCF | CF | 51151 | | PTS | TS |
| 51142 | | PTS | TS | 51145 | | PCF | CF | 51148 | | PCF | CF | 51152 | | PCF | CF |
| 51143 | | PTS | TS | 51146 | | PTS | TS | 51149 | | PTS | TS | 51153 | | PCF | CF |

## Class 101 Metro-Cammell — DMBS.DQ2.02/DQ2.32†
**Seats: 49† or 52**

| | | | | | | | | | | | | | | | |
|---|---|---|---|---|---|---|---|---|---|---|---|---|---|---|---|
| 51175 | | PNL | NL | 51190† | N | NNE | CA | 51215 | N | NNE | CA | 51231 | | PLA | LA |
| 51177 | | PCH | CH | 51191 | | PNL | NL | 51218 | | PNC | NC | 51234 | | PLA | LA |
| 51178 | | PNL | NL | 51192 | | PNC | NC | 51219 | | PLA | LA | 51241 | | PLA | LA |
| 51179 | | PLA | LA | 51194 | | PNL | NL | 51220 | N | NWR | OO | 51244 | | PHA | HA |
| 51180 | | PNL | NL | 51201 | | PNC | NC | 51221 | N | NWR | OO | 51245 | | PCH | CH |
| 51181 | | PLA | LA | 51205 | | PLA | LA | 51222 | N | NNE | CA | 51246 | | PLA | LA |
| 51182 | | PHA | HA | 51207 | N | NNE | CA | 51223 | | PLA | LA | 51247 | | PNC | NC |
| 51184 | | PCH | CH | 51208 | N | NNE | CA | 51224 | PS | PED | ED | 51249 | PS | PED | ED |
| 51185 | | PNC | NC | 51210 | | PCH | CH | 51225 | N | NWR | OO | 51252 | | PNC | NC |
| 51187 | | PNC | NC | 51211† | N | NNE | CA | 51226† | N | NSB | RG | 51253 | | PNL | NL |
| 51188 | | PNL | NL | 51212 | N | NWR | OO | 51228 | | PHA | HA | | | | |
| 51189 | | PNC | NC | 51213 | | PNC | NC | 51230 | | PNC | NC | | | | |

## Class 118 Birmingham RC&W — DMBS.DQ2.20.
**Seats: 65**

| | | | | | | | | | | | | | | | |
|---|---|---|---|---|---|---|---|---|---|---|---|---|---|---|---|
| 51306 | | PTS | TS | 51314 | | PTS | TS | 51315 | | PCF | CF | 51316 | | PTS | TS |

## Class 118 Birmingham RC&W — DMS.DP2.21.
**Seats: 89**

| | | | | | | | | | | | | | | | |
|---|---|---|---|---|---|---|---|---|---|---|---|---|---|---|---|
| 51319 | N | NWR | OO | 51329 | | PTS | TS | 51330 | | PCF | CF | 51331 | | PTS | TS |
| 51321 | | PTS | TS | | | | | | | | | | | | |

## Class 117 Pressed Steel Co. — DMBS.DQ2.20.
**Seats: 65**

| | | | | | | | | | | | | | | | |
|---|---|---|---|---|---|---|---|---|---|---|---|---|---|---|---|
| 51332 | N | NWR | RG | 51340 | N | NWR | RG | 51348 | | PTS | TS | 51356 | N | NWR | RG |
| 51333 | N | NWR | RG | 51341 | N | NWR | RG | 51349 | N | NWR | RG | 51358 | N | NWR | RG |
| 51334 | | PTS | TS | 51342 | N | NWR | RG | 51350 | N | NWR | RG | 51359 | N | NWR | RG |
| 51335 | N | NWR | RG | 51343 | N | NWR | RG | 51351 | N | NWR | RG | 51360 | | PTS | TS |
| 51336 | N | NWR | RG | 51344 | N | NWR | RG | 51352 | | PTS | TS | 51361 | N | NWR | RG |
| 51337 | N | NWR | RG | 51345 | N | NWR | RG | 51353 | | PTS | TS | 51362 | N | NWR | RG |
| 51338 | | PTS | TS | 51346 | N | NWR | RG | 51354 | N | NWR | RG | 51363 | N | NWR | RG |
| 51339 | | PTS | TS | 51347 | N | NWR | RG | 51355 | N | NWR | RG | 51364 | | PTS | TS |

| | | | |
|---|---|---|---|
| 51365 | | PTS | TS |
| 51366 | N | NWR | RG |
| 51367 | N | NWR | RG |
| 51368 | ★ | PTS | TS |
| 51369 | | PTS | TS |
| 51370 | | PTS | TS |
| 51371 | | PTS | TS |
| 51372 | | PTS | TS |
| 51373 | | PTS | TS |

## Class 117 Pressed Steel Co. — DMS.DP2.21.

**Seats: 89**

| | | | |
|---|---|---|---|
| 51374 | N | NWR | RG |
| 51375 | N | NWR | RG |
| 51376 | | PTS | TS |
| 51377 | N | NWR | RG |
| 51378 | N | NWR | RG |
| 51379 | N | NWR | RG |
| 51380 | | PTS | TS |
| 51381 | N | NWR | RG |
| 51382 | | PTS | TS |
| 51383 | N | NWR | RG |
| 51384 | N | NWR | RG |
| 51385 | N | NWR | RG |
| 51386 | N | NWR | RG |
| 51387 | N | NWR | RG |
| 51388 | N | NWR | RG |
| 51389 | N | NWR | RG |
| 51390 | | PTS | TS |
| 51391 | N | NWR | RG |
| 51392 | N | NWR | RG |
| 51393 | N | NWR | RG |
| 51394 | | PTS | TS |
| 51395 | | PTS | TS |
| 51396 | N | NWR | RG |
| 51397 | N | NWR | RG |
| 51398 | N | NWR | RG |
| 51399 | N | NWR | RG |
| 51400 | N | NWR | RG |
| 51401 | N | NWR | RG |
| 51402 | | PTS | TS |
| 51404 | N | NWR | RG |
| 51405 | N | NWR | RG |
| 51406 | | PTS | TS |
| 51407 | | PTS | TS |
| 51408 | N | NWR | RG |
| 51409 | N | NWR | RG |
| 51410 | ★ | PTS | TS |
| 51411 | | PTS | TS |
| 51412 | | PTS | TS |
| 51413 | | PTS | TS |
| 51414 | | PTS | TS |
| 51415 | | PTS | TS |

## Class 108 BR Derby — DMBS.DQ2.13.

**Seats: 52**

| | | | |
|---|---|---|---|
| 51416 | | PBR | BR |
| 51417 | | PCF | CF |
| 51418 | | PCH | CH |
| 51419 | | PCF | CF |
| 51420 | | PNL | NL |
| 51421 | | PLO | LO |
| 51422 | | PLO | LO |
| 51424 | | PLO | LO |

## Class 101 Metro-Cammell — DMBS.DQ2.02/DQ2.32†

**Seats: 49† or 52**

| | | | |
|---|---|---|---|
| 51425† | N | NSB | RG |
| 51426 | | PCH | CH |
| 51427 | | PNC | NC |
| 51428 | | PNC | NC |
| 51429 | | PNC | NC |
| 51431† | N | NSB | RG |
| 51432† | N | NSB | RG |
| 51434† | | NSB | RG |
| 51435 | | PLA | LA |
| 51437† | N | NSB | RG |
| 51438 | N | NNE | CA |
| 51442 | | PNC | NC |
| 51443 | N | NWR | OO |
| 51444 | N | NNE | CA |
| 51445 | N | NNE | CA |
| 51462 | | PCH | CH |
| 51463 | | PNL | NL |

## Class 101 Metro-Cammell — DMC(L)*f*/DMS(L).DP3.17*f*/DP2.10.

**Seats: 1st 12 Std 46*f*/Std 65**

| | | | |
|---|---|---|---|
| 51496 | | PTS | TS |
| 51498*f* | N | NSB | RG |
| 51499*f* | N | NSB | RG |
| 51500 | | PLA | LA |
| 51501*f* | N | NSB | RG |
| 51503*f* | | NSB | RG |
| 51504*f* | N | NSB | RG |
| 51505 | | PTS | TS |
| 51506 | | PNC | NC |
| 51508 | | PNC | NC |
| 51509 | | PTS | TS |
| 51511 | | PTS | TS |
| 51512 | | PLA | LA |
| 51513 | | PTS | TS |
| 51530 | | PLA | LA |
| 51531 | | PNC | NC |
| 51533 | | PTS | TS |

## Class 108 BR Derby — DMC(L)*f*/DMS(L).DP3.11*f*/DP2.26/DP2.—‡

**Seats: 1st 12 Std 52*f*/Std 64/71‡.**

| | | | |
|---|---|---|---|
| 51561‡ | | PLE | LE |
| 51562 | | PLE | LE |
| 51563 | | PLE | LE |
| 51565 | | PLE | LE |
| 51566 | | PCH | CH |
| 51567 | | PLE | LE |
| 51568 | | PCH | CH |
| 51569 | | PCH | CH |
| 51570 | | PLA | LA |
| 51571*f* | N | NMY | BY |
| 51572*f* | N | NMY | BY |

## Class 115 BR Derby — DMBS.DQ2.18/DQ2.33†

**Seats: 74† or 78**

| | | | |
|---|---|---|---|
| 51651† | N | NMY | BY |
| 51652† | N | NMY | BY |
| 51653 | N | NMY | BY |
| 51654† | N | NMY | BY |
| 51655 | N | NMY | BY |
| 51656† | N | NMY | BY |
| 51657† | N | NMY | BY |
| 51658 | N | NMY | BY |
| 51659 | N | NMY | BY |
| 51660 | N | NMY | BY |
| 51661† | N | NMY | BY |
| 51662† | | PTS | TS |
| 51663† | N | NMY | BY |
| 51664 | N | NMY | BY |
| 51665 | N | NMY | BY |
| 51666† | N | NMY | BY |
| 51667 | N | NMY | BY |
| 51668 | N | NMY | BY |
| 51669 | N | NMY | BY |
| 51670 | N | NMY | BY |
| 51671 | N | NMY | BY |
| 51673 | | NMY | BY |
| 51674 | N | NMY | BY |
| 51675 | N | NMY | BY |
| 51676† | N | NMY | BY |
| 51677 | N | NMY | BY |
| 51678 | N | NMY | BY |
| 51679† | N | NMY | BY |
| 51680 | N | NMY | BY |

## Class 101 Metro-Cammell — DMBS.DQ2.02

**Seats: 52.**

| | | | |
|---|---|---|---|
| 51800 | | PCH | CH |

## Class 101 Metro-Cammell — DMS.DP2.10.

**Seats: 65**

| | | | |
|---|---|---|---|
| 51803 | PS | PED | ED |
| 51808 | | PTS | TS |

## Class 115 BR Derby — DMBS.DQ2.18/DQ2.33†.

**Seats: 74† or 78**

| | | | |
|---|---|---|---|
| 51849† | N | NMY | BY |
| 51851† | | PTS | TS |
| 51852† | | PTS | TS |
| 51853† | | PTS | TS |
| 51854† | | PTS | TS |
| 51855† | N | NMY | BY |
| 51856† | | PTS | TS |
| 51857 | N | NMY | BY |
| 51858† | | PTS | TS |
| 51859† | | PTS | TS |
| 51860† | | PTS | TS |
| 51862† | | PTS | TS |
| 51863 | N | NMY | BY |
| 51865† | | PTS | TS |
| 51866† | N | NMY | BY |
| 51867† | | PTS | TS |
| 51868† | | PTS | TS |
| 51869† | | PTS | TS |
| 51870† | | PTS | TS |
| 51871 | N | NMY | BY |
| 51872 | | NMY | BY |
| 51873 | N | NMY | BY |
| 51874 | | NMY | BY |
| 51875 | N | NMY | BY |
| 51876† | | PTS | TS |
| 51877† | | PTS | TS |
| 51878† | N | NMY | BY |
| 51879 | N | NMY | BY |
| 51880† | | PTS | TS |
| 51883 | N | NMY | BY |
| 51884† | | PTS | TS |
| 51885 | N | NMY | BY |
| 51886 | N | NMY | BY |
| 51887 | N | NMY | BY |
| 51888 | N | NMY | BY |
| 51889 | N | NMY | BY |
| 51890 | | NMY | BY |
| 51891 | N | NMY | BY |
| 51892† | | PTS | TS |
| 51893† | N | NMY | BY |
| 51894 | N | NMY | BY |
| 51895† | N | NMY | BY |
| 51896 | N | NMY | BY |
| 51897† | | PTS | TS |
| 51899 | N | NMY | BY |
| 51900 | N | NMY | BY |

## Class 108 BR Derby — DMBS.DQ2.13.

**Seats: 52**

| | | | |
|---|---|---|---|
| 51901 | | PLO | LO |
| 51902 | | PCH | CH |
| 51903 | | PCH | CH |
| 51904 | | PCH | CH |
| 51905 | | PLO | LO |
| 51906 | | PLO | LO |
| 51907 | | PLO | LO |
| 51908 | | PLO | LO |
| 51909 | N | NNL | BY |
| 51911 | | PLO | LO |
| 51912 | N | NNL | BY |
| 51913 | | PLO | LO |
| 51914 | N | NNL | BY |
| 51916 | N | NNL | BY |
| 51917 | | PLO | LO |
| 51919 | | PLE | LE |
| 51920 | | PLO | LO |
| 51922 | | PLE | LE |
| 51924 | | PLE | LE |
| 51925 | | PLE | LE |
| 51926 | | PLE | LE |
| 51927 | | PCH | CH |
| 51928 | | PLE | LE |
| 51930 | | PLE | LE |
| 51931 | | PLE | LE |
| 51932 | | PLA | LA |
| 51933 | | PLA | LA |
| 51935 | | PCH | CH |
| 51936 | | PLA | LA |
| 51937 | | PCH | CH |
| 51938 | | PCH | CH |
| 51939 | | PLA | LA |
| 51940 | | PLA | LA |
| 51941 | | PCH | CH |
| 51942 | N | NNL | BY |
| 51943 | | PCH | CH |
| 51945 | | PCH | CH |
| 51947 | | PCH | CH |
| 51948 | | PCH | CH |
| 51950 | | PCH | CH |

## Class 107 BR Derby — DMBS.DQ2.11.

**Seats: 52**

| | | | |
|---|---|---|---|
| 51985 | | PED | ED |
| 51986 | PS | PED | ED |
| 51987 | PS | PED | ED |
| 51988 | | PED | ED |
| 51989 | PS | PED | ED |
| 51990 | PS | PED | ED |
| 51991 | | PHA | HA |
| 51992 | | PED | ED |
| 51993 | PS | PED | ED |
| 51994 | | PED | ED |
| 51997 | PS | PED | ED |
| 51998 | PS | PED | ED |
| 51999 | PS | PED | ED |
| 52000 | | PED | ED |
| 52001 | PS | PED | ED |
| 52004 | | PED | ED |
| 52005 | PS | PED | ED |
| 52006 | PS | PED | ED |
| 52007 | PS | PED | ED |
| 52008 | PS | PED | ED |
| 52010 | PS | PED | ED |

## Class 107 BR Derby — DMS(L).DP2.15.

**Seats: 65**

| | | | |
|---|---|---|---|
| 52011 | | PED | ED |
| 52012 | PS | PED | ED |
| 52013 | | PED | ED |
| 52015 | PS | PED | ED |
| 52016 | | PED | ED |
| 52018 | PS | PED | ED |
| 52020 | PS | PED | ED |
| 52021 | PS | PED | ED |
| 52023 | PS | PED | ED |
| 52024 | PS | PED | ED |
| 52025 | PS | PED | ED |
| 52026 | | PED | ED |
| 52028 | | PED | ED |
| 52029 | PS | PED | ED |
| 52030 | PS | PED | ED |
| 52031 | PS | PED | ED |
| 52033 | PS | PED | ED |
| 52034 | PS | PED | ED |
| 52035 | | PHA | HA |
| 52036 | | PED | ED |

## Class 108 BR Derby — DMS(L).DP2.27/DP2.—†.

**Seats: 65 or 71†**

| | | | |
|---|---|---|---|
| 52038 | | PLE | LE |
| 52039 | | PCH | CH |
| 52041 | | PLE | LE |
| 52042 | | PCH | CH |
| 52044 | | PLE | LE |
| 52045† | | PLE | LE |
| 52046 | | PLE | LE |
| 52047 | | PLA | LA |
| 52048 | | PLE | LE |
| 52049 | | PCH | CH |
| 52050 | | PCH | CH |
| 52051 | | PLA | LA |
| 52053 | | PLA | LA |
| 52054 | | PLA | LA |
| 52055 | | PLE | LE |
| 52056 | | PCH | CH |
| 52057 | | PLA | LA |
| 52058 | | PCH | CH |
| 52059 | | PLA | LA |
| 52060 | | PCH | CH |
| 52061 | | PLE | LE |
| 52062 | | PCH | CH |
| 52063 | | PLA | LA |
| 52064 | | PCH | CH |
| 52065 | | PCH | CH |

## Class 114 BR Derby

**DMBS.DQ2.17**

**Seats: 45**

| | | | |
|---|---|---|---|
| 53002 | | PTS | TS |
| 53005 | | PTS | TS |
| 53006 | | PTS | TS |
| 53019 | | PTS | TS |
| 53021 | | PTS | TS |
| 53036 | | PTS | TS |
| 53044 | | PTS | TS |

## Class 116 BR Derby

**DMBS.DQ2.30**

**Seats: 65**

| | | | |
|---|---|---|---|
| 53050 | | PTS | TS |
| 53053 | | PTS | TS |
| 53054 | | PTS | TS |
| 53055 | | PTS | TS |
| 53056 | | PTS | TS |
| 53058 | | PTS | TS |
| 53060 | | PTS | TS |
| 53061 | | PTS | TS |
| 53071 | | PTS | TS |
| 53073 | | PTS | TS |
| 53079 | | PTS | TS |
| 53082 | | PTS | TS |
| 53083 | N | NGB | OO |
| 53090 | | PTS | TS |

## Class 116 BR Derby

**DMS.DP2.20**

**Seats: 89**

| | | | |
|---|---|---|---|
| 53092 | | PTS | TS |
| 53093 | | PTS | TS |
| 53101 | | PTS | TS |
| 53102 | | PTS | TS |
| 53106 | | PTS | TS |
| 53114 | | PTS | TS |
| 53116 | | PTS | TS |
| 53124 | | PTS | TS |
| 53132 | | PTS | TS |

## Class 101 Metro-Cammell

**DMS(L).DP2.12.**

**Seats: 57**

| | | | |
|---|---|---|---|
| 53139 | | PNC | NC |
| 53146 | PS | PED | ED |
| 53149 | | PNC | NC |

## Class 101 Metro-Cammell

**DMBC‡/DMBS.DQ3.–‡/DQ2.02.**

**Seats: 1st 16 Std 33‡/Std 52**

| | | | |
|---|---|---|---|
| 53155‡ | N | NWR | OO |
| 53157 | | PLA | LA |

## Class 101 Metro-Cammell

**DMS(L).DP2.14.**

**Seats: 65**

| | | | |
|---|---|---|---|
| 53158 | PS | PCH | CH |
| 53160 | PS | PCH | CH |
| 53163 | | PLA | LA |

## Class 101 Metro-Cammell

**DMBS.DQ2.02.**

**Seats: 52**

| | | | |
|---|---|---|---|
| 53164 | | PNL | NL |
| 53165 | | PLA | LA |

## Class 101 Metro-Cammell

**DMS(L).DP2.14.**

**Seats: 65**

| | | | |
|---|---|---|---|
| 53168 | | PNC | NC |
| 53170 | | PNC | NC |
| 53171 | | PTS | TS |
| 53176 | | PHA | HA |
| 53177 | | PNC | NC |
| 53180 | | PNC | NC |
| 53181 | | PNC | NC |
| 53185 | PS | PCH | CH |
| 53189 | | PLA | LA |
| 53193 | | PNC | NC |
| 53194 | PS | PCH | CH |

## Class 101 Metro-Cammell

**DMBS.DQ2.02.**

**Seats: 52**

| | | | |
|---|---|---|---|
| 53198 | | PCH | CH |
| 53200 | | PLA | LA |
| 53201 | | PNC | NC |
| 53202 | | PNC | NC |
| 53203 | | PNL | NL |
| 53204 | | PNL | NL |
| 53207 | N | NNE | CA |
| 53208 | | PNC | NC |
| 53211 | | PCH | CH |
| 53212 | | PLA | LA |
| 53216 | | PCH | CH |
| 53223 | | PLA | LA |
| 53224 | | PCH | CH |
| 53228 | | PNC | NC |
| 53231 | | PNC | NC |

## Class 101 Metro-Cammell

**DMS(L).DP2.13.**

**Seats: 52**

| | | | |
|---|---|---|---|
| 53238 | | PNC | NC |
| 53239 | | PHA | HA |
| 53241 | PS | PED | ED |
| 53242 | | PTS | TS |
| 53243 | | PHA | HA |
| 53244 | | PTS | TS |
| 53245 | | PTS | TS |

## Class 101 Metro-Cammell

**DMBS.DQ2.03†/DQ2.02.**

**Seats: 44† or 52**

| | | | | | | | | | | | | | | | |
|---|---|---|---|---|---|---|---|---|---|---|---|---|---|---|---|
| 53247† | | PLA | LA | 53250 | | PCH | CH | 53253 | | PCH | CH | 53256 | | PLA | LA |
| 53248† | | PLA | LA | | | | | | | | | | | | |

## Class 101 Metro-Cammell

**DMC(L)¶/DMS(L).DP3.17¶/DP2.10.**

**Seats: 1st 12 Std 46¶/Std 65**

| | | | | | | | | | | | | | | | |
|---|---|---|---|---|---|---|---|---|---|---|---|---|---|---|---|
| 53260 | | PLA | LA | 53266 | | PNC | NC | 53268 | | PTS | TS | 53269 | | PTS | TS |
| 53265¶ | N | NNE | CA | 53267 | | PNC | NC | | | | | | | | |

## Class 101 Metro-Cammell

**DMBS.DQ2.02/DQ2.32†.**

**Seats: 49† or 52**

| | | | | | | | | | | | | | | | |
|---|---|---|---|---|---|---|---|---|---|---|---|---|---|---|---|
| 53291 | | PCH | CH | 53296 | N | NNE | CA | 53310† | | NSB | RG | 53314† | | NSB | RG |
| 53293 | | PNC | NC | 53305 | | PNC | NC | 53311† | | NSB | RG | 53315 | | PLA | LA |
| 53294 | | PCH | CH | 53308† | N | NSB | RG | 53312† | | NSB | RG | | | | |

## Class 101 Metro-Cammell

**DMC(L)¶/DMS(L).DP3.17¶/DP2.10.**

**Seats: 1st 12 Std 46¶/Std 65**

| | | | | | | | | | | | | | | | |
|---|---|---|---|---|---|---|---|---|---|---|---|---|---|---|---|
| 53321 | | PNC | NC | 53326¶ | | NSB | RG | 53330 | | PLA | LA | 53332¶ | | NSB | RG |
| 53322¶ | | NSB | RG | 53327¶ | | NSB | RG | 53331¶ | N | NSB | RG | 53333¶ | N | NNE | CA |

## Class 104 Birmingham RC&W

**DMBS.DQ2.05.**

**Seats: 52**

| | | | | | | | | | | | | | | | |
|---|---|---|---|---|---|---|---|---|---|---|---|---|---|---|---|
| 53429 | N | NGB | OO | 53447 | B | PCH | CH | 53455 | N | NGB | OO | 53477 | N | NGB | OO |
| 53437 | N | NGB | OO | 53451 | B | PCH | CH | 53470 | N | NGB | OO | 53479 | N | NGB | OO |
| 53442 | B | PCH | CH | | | | | | | | | | | | |

## Class 104 Birmingham RC&W

**DMS(L).DP2.09.**

**Seats: 66**

Livery: B

| | | | | | | | | | | | | | | | |
|---|---|---|---|---|---|---|---|---|---|---|---|---|---|---|---|
| 53494 | | PCH | CH | 53516 | | PCH | CH | 53529 | | PCH | CH | 53531 | | PCH | CH |
| 53512 | | PCH | CH | 53517 | | PCH | CH | | | | | | | | |

## Class 104 Birmingham RC&W

**DMBS.DQ2.05.**

**Seats: 52**

| | | | | | | | | | | | | | | | |
|---|---|---|---|---|---|---|---|---|---|---|---|---|---|---|---|
| 53534 | | PCH | CH | 53536 | B | PCH | CH. | 53539 | N | NGB | OO | 53540 | N | NGB | OO |

## Class 108 BR Derby

**DMBS.DQ2.12.**

**Seats: 52**

| | | | | | | | | | | | | | | | |
|---|---|---|---|---|---|---|---|---|---|---|---|---|---|---|---|
| 53599 | N | NMY | BY | 53616 | | PBR | BR | 53621 | | PCF | CF | 53627 | | PCF | CF |
| 53602 | | PBR | BR | 53617 | | PCF | CF | 53622 | | PCF | CF | 53628 | N | NNL | BY |
| 53608 | | PBR | BR | 53618 | | PBR | BR | 53624 | | PCF | CF | 53629 | | PCF | CF |
| 53612 | | PBR | BR | 53619 | | PBR | BR | 53625 | | PLE | LE | | | | |
| 53614 | | PBR | BR | 53620 | | PCF | CF | 53626 | | PNL | NL | | | | |

## Class 108 BR Derby

**DMS(L).DP2.19/DP2.—†**

**Seats: 62 or 71†**

| | | | | | | | | | | | | | | | |
|---|---|---|---|---|---|---|---|---|---|---|---|---|---|---|---|
| 53630 | | PCH | CH | 53634 | | PCH | CH | 53638† | | PLA | LA | 53643 | | PLE | LE |
| 53631 | | PLE | LE | 53635 | | PCF | CF | 53639 | | PLA | LA | 53644 | | PNL | NL |
| 53632 | | PBR | BR | 53636 | | PNL | NL | 53641 | | PNL | NL | 53645 | | PCH | CH |
| 53633 | | PLE | LE | 53637 | | PLA | LA | 53642 | | PLA | LA | 53646 | | PLA | LA |

## Class 101 Metro-Cammell

**DMC(L)¶/DMS(L).DP3.17¶/DP2.10.**

**Seats: 1st 12 Std 46¶/Std 65**

| | | | | | | | |
|---|---|---|---|---|---|---|---|
| 53746 | | PTS | TS | 53751¶ | N | NSB | RG |

## Class 116 BR Derby **DMBS.DQ2.30**
**Seats: 65**

| | | | | | | | | | | | | | | | |
|---|---|---|---|---|---|---|---|---|---|---|---|---|---|---|---|
| 53818 | | PTS | TS | 53827 | | PTS | TS | 53849 | | PTS | TS | 53863 | | PTS | TS |
| 53820 | N | NGB | OO | 53837 | | PTS | TS | 53850 | | PTS | TS | 53865 | | PTS | TS |
| 53822 | | PTS | TS | 53838 | | PTS | TS | 53853 | | PTS | TS | | | | |
| 53826 | | PTS | TS | 53844 | | PTS | TS | 53854 | | PTS | TS | | | | |

## Class 116 BR Derby **DMS.DP2.20**
**Seats: 89**

| | | | | | | | | | | | | | | | |
|---|---|---|---|---|---|---|---|---|---|---|---|---|---|---|---|
| 53873 | | PTS | TS | 53886 | | PTS | TS | 53894 | | PTS | TS | 53916 | | PTS | TS |
| 53878 | | PTS | TS | 53890 | | PTS | TS | 53897 | | PTS | TS | 53919 | | PTS | TS |
| 53880 | | PTS | TS | 53891 | | PTS | TS | 53902 | | PTS | TS | 53921 | | PTS | TS |
| 53881 | | PTS | TS | 53893 | | PTS | TS | 53907 | | PTS | TS | | | | |

## Class 108 BR Derby **DMBS.DQ2.12.**
**Seats: 52**

| | | | | | | | | | | | | | | | |
|---|---|---|---|---|---|---|---|---|---|---|---|---|---|---|---|
| 53924 | | PLO | LO | 53940 | | PNL | NL | 53955 | | PHT | HT | 53971 | | PNL | NL |
| 53925 | | PCH | CH | 53941 | | PCF | CF | 53956 | | PHT | HT | 53973 | | PHT | HT |
| 53926 | | PLE | LE | 53942 | | PLE | LE | 53957 | | PHT | HT | 53974 | | PNL | NL |
| 53927 | | PLO | LO | 53943 | | PNL | NL | 53958 | | PHT | HT | 53975 | | PLO | LO |
| 53928 | | PLE | LE | 53944 | | PNL | NL | 53959 | | PHT | HT | 53976 | | PLO | LO |
| 53929 | | PLO | LO | 53945 | | PLE | LE | 53960 | | PHT | HT | 53977 | | PCH | CH |
| 53930 | | PCH | CH | 53947 | | PLE | LE | 53962 | | PHT | HT | 53978 | | PLO | LO |
| 53931 | | PLO | LO | 53948 | | PBR | BR | 53963 | | PHT | HT | 53980 | | PLO | LO |
| 53932 | | PCH | CH | 53949 | | PNL | NL | 53964 | ★ | PHT | HT | 53981 | | PLO | LO |
| 53933 | | PCH | CH | 53950 | | PHT | HT | 53965 | | PNL | NL | 53982 | | PLO | LO |
| 53934 | | PCH | CH | 53951 | | PHT | HT | 53966 | | PNL | NL | 53983 | | PLO | LO |
| 53935 | | PLE | LE | 53952 | | PHT | HT | 53968 | | PNL | NL | 53986 | | PNL | NL |
| 53938 | | PLO | LO | 53953 | | PHT | HT | 53969 | | PNL | NL | 53987 | | PNL | NL |
| 53939 | | PLE | LE | 53954 | | PHT | HT | 53970 | | PLO | LO | | | | |

## Class 114 BR Derby **DTS(L).DS2.—**
**Seats: 74** (Official code DS3.13)

| | | | | | | | | | | | | | | | |
|---|---|---|---|---|---|---|---|---|---|---|---|---|---|---|---|
| 54006 | | PTS | TS | 54027 | | PTS | TS | 54043 | | PTS | TS | 54047 | | PTS | TS |
| 54010 | | PTS | TS | 54039 | | PTS | TS | | | | | | | | |
| 54012 | | PTS | TS | | | | | | | | | | | | |

## Class 101 Metro-Cammell **DTC(L)¶/DTS(L).DS3.02¶/DS2.06.**
**Seats: 1st 12 Std 53¶/Std 65.**

| | | | | | | | | | | | | | | | |
|---|---|---|---|---|---|---|---|---|---|---|---|---|---|---|---|
| 54050 | | PNC | NC | 54061 | | PNL | NL | 54068¶ | N | NNE | CA | 54081 | N | NNE | CA |
| 54055 | | PNC | NC | 54062 | | PNC | NC | 54070¶ | N | NWR | OO | 54085 | | PNL | NL |
| 54056 | | PNL | NL | 54065 | | PNC | NC | 54073 | | PNC | NC | 54091 | | PNL | NL |
| 54060 | | PNC | NC | | | | | | | | | | | | |

## Class 108 BR Derby **DTC(L)¶/DTS(L).DS3.10¶/DS2.07.**
**Seats: 1st 12 Std 53¶/Std 65**

| | | | | | | | | | | | | | | | |
|---|---|---|---|---|---|---|---|---|---|---|---|---|---|---|---|
| 54194¶ | N | NNL | BY | 54203 | | PCF | CF | 54207 | | PCF | CF | 54210 | | PCF | CF |
| 54197 | | PBR | BR | 54204 | | PBR | BR | 54208 | | PBR | BR | 54212 | | PCF | CF |
| 54201 | | PCF | CF | 54205 | | PCF | CF | 54209 | | PBR | BR | 54214 | | PLO | LO |

## Class 101 Metro-Cammell **DTC(L)¶/DTS(L).DS3.—¶/DS2.10.**
**Seats: 1st 12 Std 42¶/57**

| | | | | | | | |
|---|---|---|---|---|---|---|---|
| 54218 | | PNC | NC | 54220¶ | N | NNE | CA |

## Class 108 BR Derby **DTC(L)¶/DTS(L).DS3.10¶/DS2.07.**
**Seats: 1st 12 Std 53¶/Std 65**

| | | | | | | | | | | | | | | | |
|---|---|---|---|---|---|---|---|---|---|---|---|---|---|---|---|
| 54221 | | PNL | NL | 54225 | | PLO | LO | 54231 | | PLO | LO | 54238 | | PHT | HT |
| 54222¶ | N | NMY | BY | 54227 | | PHT | HT | 54232 | | PLO | LO | 54239 | | PHT | HT |
| 54223¶ | N | NMY | BY | 54228¶ | N | NMY | BY | 54235 | | PHT | HT | 54240 | | PHT | HT |
| 54224¶ | N | NMY | BY | 54230 | | PBR | BR | 54236 | | PHT | HT | 54241 | | PHT | HT |

| | | | | | | | | | | | |
|---|---|---|---|---|---|---|---|---|---|---|---|
| 54242 | PHT | HT | 54252 | PNL | NL | 54263 | PHT | HT | 54272 | PLO | LO |
| 54243 | PHT | HT | 54253 | PLO | LO | 54264 | PLO | LO | 54273 | PCF | CF |
| 54244 | PHT | HT | 54256 | PLO | LO | 54265 | PHT | HT | 54274¶ N | NMY | BY |
| 54245 | PHT | HT | 54257¶ N | NMY | BY | 54266 | PLO | LO | 54275 | PLO | LO |
| 54246 | PLO | LO | 54258 | PLO | LO | 54267 | PCF | CF | 54276 | PLO | LO |
| 54247 ★ | PHT | HT | 54259¶ N | NMY | BY | 54268 | PBR | BR | 54277 | PLO | LO |
| 54248 | PNL | NL | 54260 | PLO | LO | 54269 | PLO | LO | 54278 | PLO | LO |
| 54249 | PNL | NL | 54261 | PLO | LO | 54270 | PNL | NL | 54279¶ N | NNL | BY |
| 54251 | PNL | NL | 54262 | PHT | HT | 54271¶ N | NNL | BY | | | |

## Class 121 Pressed Steel — DTS.DS2.01/DS2.—†.

**Seats: 89†/91 Livery: N**

| | | | | | | | | | | | |
|---|---|---|---|---|---|---|---|---|---|---|---|
| 54280 | NWR | OO | 54284 | NWR | OO | 54287† | NWR | OO | 54289† | NWR | OO |
| 54283 | NWR | OO | | | | | | | | | |

## Class 101 Metro-Cammell — DTC(L)¶/DTS(L).DS3.02¶/DS2.06.

**Seats: 1st 12 Std 53¶/Std 65**

| | | | | | | | | | | | |
|---|---|---|---|---|---|---|---|---|---|---|---|
| 54332 | PNC | NC | 54362¶ N | NNE | CA | 54380 | PNC | NC | 54399 | PNC | NC |
| 54340 | PCH | CH | 54363¶ N | NNL | BY | 54381¶ N | NMY | BY | 54402¶ N | NNE | CA |
| 54343 | PNC | NC | 54365 | PNL | NL | 54382¶ N | NNE | CA | 54405¶ N | NNE | CA |
| 54346 | PNL | NL | 54368 | PNC | NC | 54385¶ N | NWR | OO | 54408 | PNL | NL |
| 54347 | PNC | NC | 54369 | PNC | NC | 54387 | PNC | NC | | | |
| 54352 | PNC | NC | 54371¶ N | NWR | OO | 54388 | PNC | NC | | | |
| 54354 | PNC | NC | 54372¶ N | NWR | OO | 54393 | PNC | NC | | | |
| 54358¶ N | NNL | BY | 54379 | PNC | NC | 54396¶ N | NWR | OO | | | |

## Class 108 BR Derby — DTC(L)¶/DTS(L).DS3.11¶/DS2.—.

**Seats: 1st 12 Std 53¶/Std 65**

| | | | | | | | | | | | |
|---|---|---|---|---|---|---|---|---|---|---|---|
| 54484 | PLO | LO | 54492 | PBR | BR | 54497 | PLO | LO | 54503 | PNL | NL |
| 54488 | PLO | LO | 54493¶ N | NNL | BY | 54498 | PCF | CF | 54504 | PNL | NL |
| 54489 | PLO | LO | 54494 | PBR | BR | 54499¶ N | NMY | BY | | | |
| 54490 | PLO | LO | 54495¶ N | NMY | BY | 54500¶ N | NMY | BY | | | |
| 54491¶ | NMY | BY | 54496 | PLO | LO | 54501 | PLO | LO | | | |

## Class 114/1 BR Derby — DTLV(L)DS5.02.

**(Converted from Class 114/0 at RTC Derby, BR Ilford Depot and BRML Doncaster).**
**Seats: 0 for public use.**

**Livery: R**

| | | | | | | | | | | | |
|---|---|---|---|---|---|---|---|---|---|---|---|
| 54900 | RPXN | CA | 54902 | RPXN | CA | 54903 | RPXN | CA | 54904 | RPXN | CA |
| 54901 | RPXN | CA | | | | | | | | | |

## Class 122 Gloucester RC&W — DMBS.DX2.02.

**Seats: 65**

| | | | | | | | | | | | |
|---|---|---|---|---|---|---|---|---|---|---|---|
| 55000 | PLA | LA | 55004 | PLAH | LA | 55006 | PLA | LA | 55011 | PLAH | LA |
| 55003 | PLA | LA | 55005 | PLA | LA | 55009 | PLA | LA | 55012 | PLA | LA |

## Class 121 Pressed Steel — DMBS.DX2.01.

**Seats: 65**

| | | | | | | | | | | | |
|---|---|---|---|---|---|---|---|---|---|---|---|
| 55020 N | NWR | OO | 55024 N | NWR | OO | 55028 N | NWR | OO | 55032 | PTS | TS |
| 55021 N | NWR | OO | 55025 N | NWR | OO | 55029 N | NWR | OO | 55033 ★ | PTS | TS |
| 55022 N | NWR | OO | 55026 | PLA | LA | 55030 N | NWR | OO | 55034 | PTS | TS |
| 55023 N | NWR | OO | 55027 N | NWR | OO | 55031 N | NWR | OO | | | |

## Class 114/1 BR Derby — DMLV.DQ5.02

**Seats: 0 for public use.**

**Livery: R**

| | | | | | | | | | | | |
|---|---|---|---|---|---|---|---|---|---|---|---|
| 55928 | RPXN | CA | 55930 | RPXN | CA | 55931 | RPXN | CA | 55932 | RPXN | CA |
| 55929 | RPXN | CA | | | | | | | | | |

## Class 128 Gloucester RC&W — DMLV.DX5.01

Seats: 0 for public use. Livery: R

| | | | | | | | | | | | |
|---|---|---|---|---|---|---|---|---|---|---|---|
| 55991 | RPXN | CA | 55993 | RPXN | CA | 55994 | RPXN | CA | 55995 | RPXN | CA |
| 55992 | RPXN | CA | | | | | | | | | |

## Class 116 BR Derby — TS.DT2.09.

Seats: 98

| | | |
|---|---|---|
| 59032 | PTS | TS |

## Class 101 Metro-Cammell — TS(L).DT2.01.

Seats: 61

| | | |
|---|---|---|
| 59042 | PCH | CH |

## Class 101 Metro-Cammell — TBS(L).DU2.02.

Seats: 45

| | | |
|---|---|---|
| 59055 | PNC | NC |

## Class 101 Metro-Cammell — TS(L).DT2.01.

Seats: 61

| | | | | | |
|---|---|---|---|---|---|
| 59061 | PHA | HA | 59072 N | NNE | CA |

## Class 101 Metro-Cammell — TBS(L).DU2.03.

Seats: 53

| | | | | | | | | |
|---|---|---|---|---|---|---|---|---|
| 59077 | PNC | NC | 59080 | PNC | NC | 59084 | PNC | NC |
| 59079 | PNC | NC | | | | | | |

## Class 101 Metro-Cammell — TS(L).DT2.01/DT2.28†.

Seats: 58†/61

| | | | | | | | | |
|---|---|---|---|---|---|---|---|---|
| 59086 | PHA | HA | 59090 PS | PED | ED | 59091† | NSB | RG |

## Class 101 Metro-Cammell — TBS(L).DU2.02.

Seats: 45

| | | | | | | | | |
|---|---|---|---|---|---|---|---|---|
| 59092 | PNC | NC | 59093 | PLA | LA | 59095 | PNC | NC |

## Class 101 Metro-Cammell — TC(L)¶/TS(L).DT3.01¶/DT2.02$/DT2.20/DT2.28†.

Seats: 1st 12 Std 46¶/58†/61/71$.

| | | | | | | | | | | | |
|---|---|---|---|---|---|---|---|---|---|---|---|
| 59107$ | PCH | CH | 59115¶ N | NNE | CA | 59124 | PHA | HA | 59130 | PLA | LA |
| 59110† | NSB | RG | 59117† | NSB | RG | 59125† N | NSB | RG | | | |
| 59111† N | NNE | CA | 59118 | PLA | LA | 59128† N | NSB | RG | | | |

## Class 104 Birmingham RC&W — TC(L).DT3.02.

Seats: 1st 12 Std 54 Livery: N

| | | |
|---|---|---|
| 59163 | NWR | RG |

## Class 104 Birmingham RC&W — TS(L).DT2.03.

Seats: 69

| | | |
|---|---|---|
| 59206 N | NMY | BY |

## Class 104 BR Derby — TBS(L).DU2.01.

**Seats: 50**

| | | | | | | | | | | | |
|---|---|---|---|---|---|---|---|---|---|---|---|
| 59245 | PCF | CF | 59248 | PCF | CF | 59249 | PNL | NL | 59250 | PNL | NL |
| 59246 | PNL | NL | | | | | | | | | |

## Class 101 Metro-Cammell — TS(L).DT2.02/DT2.28†.

**Seats: 58†/71**

| | | | | | | | | |
|---|---|---|---|---|---|---|---|---|
| 59302 | PCH | CH | 59303 | PCH | CH | 59306† N | NSB | RG |

## Class 116 BR Derby — TS.DT2.15†/DT2.19.

**Seats: 88/102†**

| | | | | | | | | | | | |
|---|---|---|---|---|---|---|---|---|---|---|---|
| 59335 | PTS | TS | 59344 | PTS | TS | 59353 | PTS | TS | 59367† | PTS | TS |

## Class 108 BR Derby — TS(L).DT2.05/DT2.06†.

**Seats: 68**

| | | | | | | | | | | | |
|---|---|---|---|---|---|---|---|---|---|---|---|
| 59380 | PLE | LE | 59383 | PCF | CF | 59386† | PLA | LA | 59389† | PCH | CH |
| 59381 | PLE | LE | 59384 | PLE | LE | 59387† | PNL | NL | 59390† | PCH | CH |
| 59382 | PLE | LE | 59385 | PCF | CF | 59388† | PCH | CH | | | |

## Class 119 Gloucester RC&W — TS(L).DT2.16.

**Seats: 60 Livery: N**

| | | | | | | | | | | | |
|---|---|---|---|---|---|---|---|---|---|---|---|
| 59416 | NSB | RG | 59421 | NSB | RG | 59425 | NSB | RG | 59435 | NSB | RG |
| 59419 | NSB | RG | 59424 | NSB | RG | 59430 | NSB | RG | 59437 | NSB | RG |

## Class 116 BR Derby — TS.DT2.19.

**Seats: 88**

| | | | | | | | | | | | |
|---|---|---|---|---|---|---|---|---|---|---|---|
| 59442 | PTS | TS | 59445 | PTS | TS | 59446 | PTS | TS | 59448 | PTS | TS |
| 59444 | PTS | TS | | | | | | | | | |

## Class 118 Birmingham RC&W — TS(L).DT2.30.

**Seats: 70**

| | | | | | | | | |
|---|---|---|---|---|---|---|---|---|
| 59473 | PTS | TS | 59481 | PTS | TS | 59483 | PTS | TS |

## Class 117 Pressed Steel Co. — TC(L)¶/TS(L).DT3.05¶/DT2.—.

**Seats: 1st 22 Std 48¶/Std 70**

| | | | | | | | | | | | |
|---|---|---|---|---|---|---|---|---|---|---|---|
| 59484¶ N | NWR | RG | 59494¶ N | NWR | RG | 59504 | PTS | TS | 59514¶ N | NWR | RG |
| 59485¶ N | NWR | RG | 59495¶ N | NWR | RG | 59505 | PTS | TS | 59515¶ N | NWR | RG |
| 59486 | PTS | TS | 59496¶ N | NWR | RG | 59506¶ N | NWR | RG | 59516 | PTS | TS |
| 59487¶ N | NWR | RG | 59497¶ N | NWR | RG | 59507¶ N | NWR | RG | 59517 | PTS | TS |
| 59488¶ N | NWR | RG | 59498¶ N | NWR | RG | 59508¶ N | NWR | RG | 59518¶ N | NWR | RG |
| 59489¶ N | NWR | RG | 59499¶ N | NWR | RG | 59509 | PTS | TS | 59519¶ N | NWR | RG |
| 59490 | PTS | TS | 59500 | PTS | TS | 59510¶ N | NWR | RG | 59520 ★ | PTS | TS |
| 59491¶ N | NWR | RG | 59501¶ N | NWR | RG | 59511¶ N | NWR | RG | 59521 | PTS | TS |
| 59492 | PTS | TS | 59502¶ N | NWR | RG | 59512 | PTS | TS | 59522 | PTS | TS |
| 59493¶ N | NWR | RG | 59503¶ N | NWR | RG | 59513¶ N | NWR | RG | | | |

## Class 101 Metro-Cammell — TS(L).DT2.20/DT2.28†.

**Seats: 58†/65**

| | | | | | | | | | | | |
|---|---|---|---|---|---|---|---|---|---|---|---|
| 59525 | PCH | CH | 59536 | PNC | NC | 59542 PS | PED | ED | 59570† N | NSB | RG |
| 59526† N | NSB | RG | 59539 | PLE | LE | 59543† N | NSB | RG | | | |
| 59530† N | NSB | RG | 59540† | NSB | RG | 59561 | PLA | LA | | | |

## Class 127 BR Derby — TS(L).DT2.26.

**Seats: 86**

| | | | | | | | | | | | |
|---|---|---|---|---|---|---|---|---|---|---|---|
| 59589 | PTS | TS | 59591 | PTS | TS | 59593 | PTS | TS | 59595 | PTS | TS |
| 59590 | PTS | TS | 59592 | PTS | TS | 59594 | PTS | TS | 59596 | PTS | TS |

| | | | |
|---|---|---|---|
| 59597 | | PTS | TS |
| 59598 | | PTS | TS |
| 59600 | | PTS | TS |
| 59602 | | PTS | TS |
| 59603 | | PTS | TS |
| 59604 | | PTS | TS |
| 59606 | | PTS | TS |
| 59607 | | PTS | TS |
| 59608 | | PTS | TS |
| 59609 | | PTS | TS |
| 59610 | | PTS | TS |
| 59611 | | PTS | TS |
| 59612 | | PTS | TS |
| 59613 | | PTS | TS |
| 59614 | | PTS | TS |
| 59615 | | PTS | TS |
| 59616 | | PTS | TS |
| 59617 | | PTS | TS |

## Class 127 BR Derby — TS.DT2.29.

**Seats: 98**

| | | | |
|---|---|---|---|
| 59625 | | PTS | TS |
| 59629 | | PTS | TS |
| 59632 | | PTS | TS |
| 59641 | | PTS | TS |
| 59643 | | PTS | TS |
| 59648 | | PTS | TS |

## Class 115 BR Derby TC(L)¶/TS‡$/TS(L)†.DT3.03¶/DT2.08‡/DT2.29$/DT2.—†.

**Seats: 1st 30 Std 40¶/106/98$/66†.**

| | | | |
|---|---|---|---|
| 59651‡ | | NMY | BY |
| 59652‡ | N | NMY | BY |
| 59654‡ | N | NMY | BY |
| 59655‡ | N | NMY | BY |
| 59656‡ | N | NMY | BY |
| 59657‡ | N | NMY | BY |
| 59658$ | | PTS | TS |
| 59659‡ | N | NMY | BY |
| 59660‡ | | NMY | BY |
| 59661$ | | PTS | TS |
| 59662‡ | N | NMY | BY |
| 59663‡ | N | NMY | BY |
| 59664¶ | N | NMY | BY |
| 59665¶ | N | NMY | BY |
| 59667¶ | N | NMY | BY |
| 59668† | | PTS | TS |
| 59669¶ | N | NMY | BY |
| 59670† | | PTS | TS |
| 59671¶ | N | NMY | BY |
| 59672† | | PTS | TS |
| 59673† | | PTS | TS |
| 59674† | | PTS | TS |
| 59675¶ | | NMY | BY |
| 59676¶ | N | NMY | BY |
| 59677† | | PTS | TS |
| 59678¶ | | NMY | BY |

## Class 101 Metro-Cammell — TS(L).DT2.20.

**Seats: 65**

| | | | |
|---|---|---|---|
| 59688 | | PCH | CH |

## Class 110 Birmingham RC&W — TS(L).DT2.07.

**Seats: 72**

| | | | |
|---|---|---|---|
| 59694 | | PNL | NL |
| 59701 | | PNL | NL |

## Class 115 BR Derby TC(L)¶/TS‡$/TS(L)†.DT3.03¶/DT2.08‡/DT2.27/DT2.29$/DT2.—†

**Seats: 1st 30 Std 40¶/106‡/98$/70/66†.**

| | | | |
|---|---|---|---|
| 59713$ | | PTS | TS |
| 59719† | | PTS | TS |
| 59720† | | PTS | TS |
| 59721† | | PTS | TS |
| 59722† | | PTS | TS |
| 59723† | | PTS | TS |
| 59724† | | PTS | TS |
| 59726$ | | PTS | TS |
| 59727‡ | N | NMY | BY |
| 59728‡ | N | NMY | BY |
| 59729‡ | N | NMY | BY |
| 59731‡ | | NMY | BY |
| 59732‡ | N | NMY | BY |
| 59733‡ | N | NMY | BY |
| 59734$ | N | NMY | BY |
| 59735$ | N | NMY | BY |
| 59736‡ | N | NMY | BY |
| 59737‡ | N | NMY | BY |
| 59738‡ | | NMY | BY |
| 59740‡ | | NMY | BY |
| 59741$ | | PTS | TS |
| 59743$ | | PTS | TS |
| 59745 | | PTS | TS |
| 59746¶ | | NMY | BY |
| 59747¶ | | NMY | BY |
| 59749¶ | N | NMY | BY |
| 59750¶ | N | NMY | BY |
| 59751 | | PTS | TS |
| 59752¶ | N | NMY | BY |
| 59753† | | PTS | TS |
| 59754¶ | N | NMY | BY |
| 59755¶ | N | NMY | BY |
| 59756† | | PTS | TS |
| 59757† | | PTS | TS |
| 59758¶ | | NMY | BY |
| 59759¶ | N | NMY | BY |
| 59760† | | PTS | TS |
| 59761¶ | N | NMY | BY |
| 59762¶ | N | NMY | BY |
| 59763¶ | N | NMY | BY |
| 59764¶ | N | NMY | BY |

## Class 107 BR Derby — TS(L).DT2.04.

**Seats: 71**

| | | | |
|---|---|---|---|
| 59782 | PS | PED | ED |
| 59783 | PS | PED | ED |
| 59784 | PS | PED | ED |
| 59785 | | PED | ED |
| 59786 | | PED | ED |
| 59789 | | PHA | HA |
| 59790 | PS | PED | ED |
| 59791 | | PED | ED |
| 59792 | PS | PED | ED |
| 59793 | PS | PED | ED |
| 59795 | PS | PED | ED |
| 59796 | PS | PED | ED |
| 59797 | | PED | ED |
| 59800 | | PED | ED |
| 59801 | PS | PED | ED |
| 59802 | PS | PED | ED |
| 59803 | PS | PED | ED |
| 59804 | | PED | ED |
| 59805 | | PED | ED |
| 59806 | PS | PED | ED |
| 59807 | PS | PED | ED |

# NEW GENERATION DIESEL MULTIPLE-UNITS

**THIS STOCK IS LISTED ONLY BY UNIT NUMBERS. VEHICLE NUMBER INFORMATION IS IN ACCORDANCE WITH THAT PUBLISHED EARLY IN 1989 EXCEPT AS SHOWN ON PAGES 96**

## Class 140 BR Derby/Leyland — DMS(L) + DMS.DP2.22 + DP2.23

**Seats: 50 + 52** — **Livery: Blue and grey**

| | | |
|---|---|---|
| 140001 | PXXH | HO |

## Classes 141/1 & 141/8† BREL Derby/Leyland National — DMS + DMS(L)DP.28 + DP2.29

**Class 141/8 experimental Voith transmission.**
**Vehicle 55524 of unit 141104 condemned.**
**Seats: 50 + 44** — **Livery PY**

| | | | | | | | | | | | |
|---|---|---|---|---|---|---|---|---|---|---|---|
| 141101 | PNL | NL | 141106 | PNL | NL | 141111 | PNL | NL | 141116 | PNL | NL |
| 141102 | PNL | NL | 141107 | PNL | NL | 141112 | PNL | NL | 141117 | PNL | NL |
| 141103 | PNL | NL | 141108 | PNL | NL | 141113† | PNL | NL | 141118 | PNL | NL |
| 55504 | PNLH | NL | 141109 | PNL | NL | 141114 | PNL | NL | 141119 | PNL | NL |
| 141105 | PNL | NL | 141110 | PNL | NL | 141115 | PNL | NL | 141120 | PNL | NL |

## Classes 142/2† & 142/5 BREL Derby/Leyland National — DMS + DMS(L).DP2.28 + DP2.29

**Seats: 62 + 59.** — **PACER** — **Livery: PB unless shown.**
**(Note: Fourth digit of unit number is to be revised to match class number. Class 142/2 units to be modified with Voith transmission to Class 142/5.)**

| | | | | | | | | | | | | | | | |
|---|---|---|---|---|---|---|---|---|---|---|---|---|---|---|---|
| 142001† | PM | PNH | NH | 142525 | PW | PHT | HT | 142049 | | PNH | NH | 142073 | | PNL | NL |
| 142002† | PM | PNH | NH | 142026 | PW | PNH | NH | 142050 | | PHT | HT | 142074 | | PNL | NL |
| 142003† | PM | PNH | NH | 142027 | PW | PNH | NH | 142051 | | PNH | NH | 142075† | | PNL | NL |
| 142004† | PM | PNH | NH | 142028† | | PNH | NH | 142052 | | PNH | NH | 142076† | | PNL | NL |
| 142005† | PM | PNH | NH | 142029 | | PNH | NH | 142053† | | PNH | NH | 142077† | | PNL | NL |
| 142006† | PM | PNH | NH | 142030† | | PNH | NH | 142054† | | PNH | NH | 142078† | | PNL | NL |
| 142007† | PM | PNH | NH | 142031† | | PNH | NH | 142055† | | PNH | NH | 142079 | | PNL | NL |
| 142008† | PM | PNH | NH | 142032† | | PNH | NH | 142056† | | PNH | NH | 142080 | | PNL | NL |
| 142009† | PM | PNH | NH | 142033† | | PNH | NH | 142057† | | PNH | NH | 142081 | | PNL | NL |
| 142010† | PM | PNH | NH | 142034 | | PNH | NH | 142058† | | PNH | NH | 142082 | | PNL | NL |
| 142011† | PM | PNH | NH | 142035 | | PNH | NH | 142059† | | PNH | NH | 142083 | | PNL | NL |
| 142012† | PM | PNH | NH | 142036 | | PNH | NH | 142060 | | PNH | NH | 142084 | | PNL | NL |
| 142013† | PM | PNH | NH | 142037 | | PNH | NH | 142061 | | PNH | NH | 142085 | | PNL | NL |
| 142014† | PM | PNH | NH | 142038 | | PNH | NH | 142062 | | PNL | NL | 142086 | | PNL | NL |
| 142015 | PW | PNL | NL | 142039 | | PNH | NH | 142063 | | PNL | NL | 142087 | | PNL | NL |
| 142516 | PW | PHT | HT | 142040 | | PNH | NH | 142064 | | PNH | NH | 142088 | | PNL | NL |
| 142017 | PW | PNL | NL | 142041 | | PNH | NH | 142065 | | PNL | NL | 142089 | | PNL | NL |
| 142518 | PW | PHT | HT | 142042 | | PNH | NH | 142066 | | PNL | NL | 142090 | | PNL | NL |
| 142519 | PW | PHT | HT | 142043 | | PNH | NH | 142067 | | PNL | NL | 142091 | | PNL | NL |
| 142520 | PW | PHT | HT | 142044 | | PNH | NH | 142068 | | PNL | NL | 142092 | | PNL | NL |
| 142521 | PW | PHT | HT | 142045 | | PNH | NH | 142069 | | PNH | NH | 142093 | | PNL | NL |
| 142522 | PW | PHT | HT | 142046 | | PNH | NH | 142070 | | PNL | NH | 142094 | | PNL | NL |
| 142023 | PW | PNL | NL | 142047 | | PNH | NH | 142071 | | PNH | NL | 142095 | | PNL | NL |
| 142024 | PW | PNL | NL | 142048 | | PNH | NH | 142072 | | PNL | NL | 142096 | | PNL | NL |

## Classes 143/3† & 143/6 W.Alexander/A.Barclay — DMS + DMS(L).DP2.36 + DP2.37

**Seats: 62 + 60.** — **PACER** — **Livery PT unless shown**
**(Class 143/3 units to be modified with Voith tranmission to Class 143/6)**

| | | | | | | | | | | | | |
|---|---|---|---|---|---|---|---|---|---|---|---|---|
| 143601 | PHT | HT | 143608 | PHT | HT | 143614 | PHT | HT | 143320† | PB | PHT | HT |
| 143602 | PHT | HT | 143609 | PHT | HT | 143615 | PHT | HT | 143321† | PB | PHT | HT |
| 143603 | PHT | HT | 143610 | PHT | HT | 143616 | PHT | HT | 143322† | PB | PHT | HT |
| 143604 | PHT | HT | 143611 | PHT | HT | 143617 | PHT | HT | 143323† | PB | PHT | HT, |
| 143605 | PHT | HT | 143612 | PHT | HT | 143618 | PHT | HT | 143324† | PB | PHT | HT |
| 143606 | PHT | HT | 143613 | PHT | HT | 143619 | PHT | HT | 143325† | PB | PHT | HT |
| 143607 | PHT | HT | | | | | | | | | | |

## Classes 144/4 & 144/7† BREL Derby/W.Alexander
## DMS + MS★ + DMS(L).DP2.40 + DR2.05★ + DP2.37

**Seats: 62 + 73★ + 60** **PACER** **Livery PY**

**(Class 144/4 units to be modified with Voith transmission to Class 144/7)**

| | | | | | | | | | | | |
|---|---|---|---|---|---|---|---|---|---|---|---|
| 144001 | PNL | NL | 144007 | PNL | NL | 144013† | PNL | NL | 144019★ | PNL | NL |
| 144002 | PNL | NL | 144008 | PNL | NL | 144014★ | PNL | NL | 144020★ | PNL | NL |
| 144003 | PNL | NL | 144009† | PNL | NL | 144015★ | PNL | NL | 144021★ | PNL | NL |
| 144004 | PNL | NL | 144010† | PNL | NL | 144016★ | PNL | NL | 144022★ | PNL | NL |
| 144005 | PNL | NL | 144011† | PNL | NL | 144017★ | PNL | NL | 144023★ | PNL | NL |
| 144006 | PNL | NL | 144012† | PNL | NL | 144018★ | PNL | NL | | | |

## CLASS 150/0 BREL York DMS(L) + MS + DMS. DP2.30 + DR2.02 + DP2.31

**Seats:75 + 84 + 79** **SPRINTER** **Livery: PB**

| | | |
|---|---|---|
| 150001 | PTS | TS |

## CLASS 150/1 BREL York DMS(L) + DMS.DP2.38 + DP2.39

**Seats: 68 + 70 (Due reseating 1990)** **SPRINTER** **Livery: PB**

**(★ Some units formed as three car with addition of Class 150/2 DMS(L) or DMS– see Depot Allocation Summary pages following this section)**

| | | | | | | | | | | | |
|---|---|---|---|---|---|---|---|---|---|---|---|
| 150101 | PDY | DY | 150114 | PDY | DY | 150127 | PDY | DY | 150140 | PDY | DY |
| 150102 | PDY | DY | 150115 | PDY | DY | 150128 | PDY | DY | 150141★ | PTS | TS |
| 150103 | PDY | DY | 150116 | PDY | DY | 150129 | PDY | DY | 150142 | PDY | DY |
| 150104 | PDY | DY | 150117 | PDY | DY | 150130 | PDY | DY | 150143 | PDY | DY |
| 150105 | PDY | DY | 150118 | PDY | DY | 150131 | PDY | DY | 150144★ | PTS | TS |
| 150106 | PDY | DY | 150119 | PDY | DY | 150132 | PDY | DY | 150145★ | PTS | TS |
| 150107 | PDY | DY | 150120 | PDY | DY | 150133 | PDY | DY | 150146★ | PTS | TS |
| 150108 | PDY | DY | 150121 | PDY | DY | 150134 | PDY | DY | 150147 | PDY | DY |
| 150109 | PDY | DY | 150122 | PDY | DY | 150135 | PDY | DY | 150148★ | PTS | TS |
| 150110 | PDY | DY | 150123 | PDY | DY | 150136 | PDY | DY | 150149★ | PTS | TS |
| 150111 | PDY | DY | 150124 | PDY | DY | 150137 | PDY | DY | 150150 | PDY | DY |
| 150112 | PDY | DY | 150125 | PDY | DY | 150138 | PDY | DY | | | |
| 150113 | PDY | DY | 150126 | PDY | DY | 150139 | PDY | DY | | | |

## CLASS 150/2 BREL York DMS(L) + DMS.DP2.42 + DP2.43

**Seats: 73 + 76/70 + 73†** **SPRINTER** **Livery: PB unless shown.**

**(★ Some units formed as three car with addition of Class 150/2 DMS(L) or DMS– see Depot Allocation Summary pages following this section. $DMS vehicle formed in three-car set, DMS(L) vehicle withdrawn)**

| | | | | | | | | | | | | |
|---|---|---|---|---|---|---|---|---|---|---|---|---|
| 150201 | PN | PNH | NH | 150223 | PNH | NH | 150245 | PHA | HA | 150267 | PCF | CF |
| 150202† | | PNH | NH | 150224† | PNH | NH | 150246† | PCF | CF | 150268 | PCF | CF |
| 150203 | PN | PNH | NH | 150225 | PNH | NH | 150247 | PCF | CF | 150269 | PCF | CF |
| 150204† | | PNH | NH | 150226† | PNH | NH | 150248† | PHA | HA | 150270 | PCF | CF |
| 150205★ | | PTS | TS | 150227 | PNH | NH | 150249 | PCF | CF | 150271 | PCF | CF |
| 150206† | | PNH | NH | 150228† | PHA | HA | 150250† | PHA | HA | 150272 | PCF | CF |
| 150207 | PN | PNH | NH | 150229 | PDY | DY | 150251 | PCF | CF | 150273 | PCF | CF |
| 150208 | | PHA | HA | 150230† | PNL | NL | 150252† | PHA | HA | 150274 | PCF | CF |
| 57209$★ | | PNH | NH | 150231 | PNH | NH | 150253★ | PTS | TS | 150275 | PCF | CF |
| 150210† | | PNH | NH | 150232† | PNL | NL | 150254† | PCF | CF | 150276 | PCF | CF |
| 150211 | PN | PNH | NH | 150233 | PNH | NH | 150255 | PHA | HA | 150277 | PCF | CF |
| 57212†$ | | PNH | NH | 150234† | PNL | NL | 150256† | PHA | HA | 150278 | PCF | CF |
| 150213 | PN | PNH | NH | 150235 | PNH | NH | 150257 | PHA | HA | 150279 | PCF | CF |
| 150214†★ | | PNH | NH | 150236† | PNL | NL | 150258† | PHA | HA | 150280 | PCF | CF |
| 150215 | PN | PNH | NH | 150237 | PNH | NH | 150259 | PHA | HA | 150281 | PCF | CF |
| 150216†★ | | PNH | NH | 150238† | PNL | NL | 150260† | PHA | HA | 150282 | PCF | CF |
| 150217 | PN | PNH | NH | 150239 | PNH | NH | 150261 | PCF | CF | 150283 | PHA | HA |
| 150218†★ | | PNH | NH | 150240† | PNL | NL | 150262† | PHA | HA | 150284 | PHA | HA |
| 150219 | | PNH | NH | 150241★ | PTS | TS | 150263 | PCF | CF | 150285 | PHA | HA |
| 150220† | | PNH | NH | 150242† | PNL | NL | 150264 | PHA | HA | | | |
| 150221 | | PNH | NH | 150243 | PNL | NL | 150265 | PCF | CF | | | |
| 150222† | | PNH | NH | 150244† | PHA | HA | 150266 | PCF | CF | | | |

## CLASS 151 Metro-Cammell DMS + MS + DMS(L).DP2.33 + DR2.04 + DP2.32

**Seats: 80 + 84 + 68** **SPRINTER** **Livery: PB**

| | | | | | |
|---|---|---|---|---|---|
| 151003 | PXXH | DY | 151004 | PXXH | DY |

## CLASS 153 Leyland Bus DMS(L).DP2.—

**Proposed single car modification from Class 155 units 155301-35. for service on lightly used Provincial Sector routes. Subject to tender.**

## CLASS 154 BREL York DMS + MS + DMS(L).DP2.47 + DR2.06 + DP2.46

**Seats: 60 + 72 + 58** **SPRINTER** **Livery: PB**

| | | |
|---|---|---|
| 154002 | PDY | DY |

## CLASSES 155/0 & 155/1† Leyland Bus DMS + DMS(L)DP2.49 + DP2.48

**Seats: 80 + 80** **SUPER SPRINTER** **Livery: PB unless shown**

| | | | | | | | | | | | | |
|---|---|---|---|---|---|---|---|---|---|---|---|---|
| 155301 | PCF | CF | 155312 | PCF | CF | 155323 | PCF | CF | 155334 | | PCF | CF |
| 155302 | PCF | CF | 155313 | PCF | CF | 155324 | PCF | CF | 155335 | | PCF | CF |
| 155303 | PCF | CF | 155314 | PCF | CF | 155325 | PCF | CF | 155341† | PY | PNL | NL |
| 155304 | PCF | CF | 155315 | PCF | CF | 155326 | PCF | CF | 155342† | PY | PNL | NL |
| 155305 | PCF | CF | 155316 | PCF | CF | 155327 | PCF | CF | 155343† | PY | PNL | NL |
| 155306 | PCF | CF | 155317 | PCF | CF | 155328 | PCF | CF | 155344† | PY | PNL | NL |
| 155307 | PCF | CF | 155318 | PCF | CF | 155329 | PCF | CF | 155345† | PY | PNL | NL |
| 155308 | PCF | CF | 155319 | PCF | CF | 155330 | PCF | CF | 155346† | PY | PNL | NL |
| 155309 | PCF | CF | 155320 | PCF | CF | 155331 | PCF | CF | 155347† | PY | PNL | NL |
| 155310 | PCF | CF | 155321 | PCF | CF | 155332 | PCF | CF | | | | |
| 155311 | PCF | CF | 155322 | PCF | CF | 155333 | PCF | CF | | | | |

## CLASS 156 Metro-Cammell DMS(L) + DMS.DP2.44 + DP2.45

**Seats: 79 + 84** **SUPER SPRINTER** **Livery: PB unless shown**

| | | | | | | | | | | | | |
|---|---|---|---|---|---|---|---|---|---|---|---|---|
| 156401 | PNC | NC | 156430 | PCK | CK | 156459 | PNL | NL | 156488 | | PNL | NL |
| 156402 | PNC | NC | 156431 | PCK | CK | 156460 | PNL | NL | 156489 | | PNL | NL |
| 156403 | PNC | NC | 156432 | PCK | CK | 156461 | PHA | HA | 156490 | | PNL | NL |
| 156404 | PNC | NC | 156433 | PCK | CK | 156462 | PHA | HA | 156491 | | PNL | NL |
| 156405 | PNC | NC | 156434 | PCK | CK | 156463 | PNL | NL | 156492 | | PHA | HA |
| 156406 | PNC | NC | 156435 | PCK | CK | 156464 | PHA | HA | 156493 | | PHA | HA |
| 156407 | PNC | NC | 156436 | PCK | CK | 156465 | PHA | HA | 156494 | | PHA | HA |
| 156408 | PNC | NC | 156437 | PCK | CK | 156466 | PHA | HA | 156495 | | PHA | HA |
| 156409 | PNC | NC | 156438 | PNL | NL | 156467 | PNL | NL | 156496 | | PHA | HA |
| 156410 | PNC | NC | 156439 | PCK | CK | 156468 | PHA | HA | 156497 | | PNL | NL |
| 156411 | PNC | NC | 156440 | PNC | NC | 156469 | PNL | NL | 156498 | | PNL | NL |
| 156412 | PNC | NC | 156441 | PNL | NL | 156470 | PHA | HA | 156499 | | PHA | HA |
| 156413 | PNC | NC | 156442 | PCK | CK | 156471 | PNL | NL | 156500 | | PHA | HA |
| 156414 | PNC | NC | 156443 | PNL | NL | 156472 | PHA | HA | 156501 | PS | PCK | CK |
| 156415 | PNC | NC | 156444 | PNL | NL | 156473 | PHA | HA | 156502 | PS | PCK | CK |
| 156416 | PNC | NC | 156445 | PHA | HA | 156474 | PHA | HA | 156503 | PS | PHA | HA |
| 156417 | PNC | NC | 156446 | PIS | IS | 156475 | PNL | NL | 156504 | PS | PHA | HA |
| 156418 | PNC | NC | 156447 | PHA | HA | 156476 | PHA | HA | 156505 | PS | PHA | HA |
| 156419 | PNC | NC | 156448 | PNL | NL | 156477 | PHA | HA | 156506 | PS | PCK | CK |
| 156420 | PNC | NC | 156449 | PHA | HA | 156478 | PHA | HA | 156507 | PS | PCK | CK |
| 156421 | PNC | NC | 156450 | PHA | HA | 156479 | PNL | NL | 156508 | PS | PCK | CK |
| 156422 | PNC | NC | 156451 | PNL | NL | 156480 | PNL | NL | 156509 | PS | PCK | CK |
| 156423 | PNC | NC | 156452 | PNC | NC | 156481 | PNL | NL | 156510 | PS | PCK | CK |
| 156424 | PNC | NC | 156453 | PHA | HA | 156482 | PNL | NL | 156511 | PS | PCK | CK |
| 156425 | PNC | NC | 156454 | PNL | NL | 156483 | PHA | HA | 156512 | PS | PCK | CK |
| 156426 | PNC | NC | 156455 | PHA | HA | 156484 | PNL | NL | 156513 | PS | PCK | CK |
| 156427 | PNC | NC | 156456 | PHA | HA | 156485 | PHA | HA | 156514 | PS | PCK | CK |
| 156428 | PNC | NC | 156457 | PIS | IS | 156486 | PHA | HA | | | | |
| 156429 | PNC | NC | 156458 | PIS | IS | 156487 | PNL | NL | | | | |

## CLASS 158 BREL Derby DMS(L) + MS(L)‡ + DMS(L).DP2.51 + DR2.07‡ + DP2.52

**Seats: 70 + 70‡ + 68** **EXPRESS** **Livery: PE unless shown**

**(‡ 39 units to be formed as three-car with addition of MS(L) vehicle)**

| | | | | | | | | | | | |
|---|---|---|---|---|---|---|---|---|---|---|---|
| 158701 | PHA | HA | 158708 | PHA | HA | 158715 | PHA | HA | 158722 | PHA | HA |
| 158702 | PHA | HA | 158709 | PHA | HA | 158716 | PHA | HA | 158723 | PHA | HA |
| 158703 | PHA | HA | 158710 | PHA | HA | 158717 | PHA | HA | 158724 | PHA | HA |
| 158704 | PHA | HA | 158711 | PHA | HA | 158718 | PHA | HA | 158725 | PHA | HA |
| 158705 | PHA | HA | 158712 | PHA | HA | 158719 | PHA | HA | 158726 | PHA | HA |
| 158706 | PHA | HA | 158713 | PHA | HA | 158720 | PHA | HA | 158727 | PHA | HA |
| 158707 | PHA | HA | 158714 | PHA | HA | 158721 | PHA | HA | 158728 | PHA | HA |

| | | |
|---|---|---|
| 158729 | PHA | HA |
| 158730 | PHA | HA |
| 158731 | PHA | HA |
| 158732 | | |
| 158733 | | |
| 158734 | | |
| 158735 | | |
| 158736 | | |
| 158737 | | |
| 158738 | | |
| 158739 | | |
| 158740 | | |
| 158741 | | |
| 158742 | | |
| 158743 | | |
| 158744 | | |
| 158745 | | |
| 158746 | | |
| 158747 | | |
| 158748 | | |
| 158749 | | |
| 158750 | | |
| 158751 | | |
| 158752 | | |
| 158753 | | |
| 158754 | | |
| 158755 | | |
| 158756 | | |
| 158757 | | |
| 158758 | | |
| 158759 | | |
| 158760 | | |
| 158761 | | |
| 158762 | | |
| 158763 | | |
| 158764 | | |
| 158765 | | |
| 158766 | | |
| 158767 | | |
| 158768 | | |
| 158769 | | |
| 158770 | | |
| 158771 | | |
| 158772 | | |
| 158773 | | |
| 158774 | | |
| 158775 | | |
| 158776 | | |
| 158777 | | |
| 158778 | | |
| 158779 | | |
| 158780 | | |
| 158781 | | |
| 158782 | | |
| 158783 | | |
| 158784 | | |
| 158785 | | |
| 158786 | | |
| 158787 | | |
| 158788 | | |
| 158789 | | |
| 158790 | | |
| 158791 | | |
| 158792 | | |
| 158793 | | |
| 158794 | | |
| 158795 | | |
| 158796 | | |
| 158797 | | |
| 158798 | | |
| 158799 | | |
| 158800 | | |
| 158801‡ | | |
| 158802‡ | | |
| 158803‡ | | |
| 158804‡ | | |
| 158805‡ | | |
| 158806‡ | | |
| 158807‡ | | |
| 158808‡ | | |
| 158809‡ | | |
| 158810‡ | | |
| 158811‡ | | |
| 158812‡ | | |
| 158813‡ | | |
| 158814 | | |
| 158815 | | |
| 158816 | | |
| 158817 | | |
| 158818 | | |
| 158819 | | |
| 158820 | | |
| 158821 | | |
| 158822 | | |
| 158823 | | |
| 158824 | | |
| 158825 | | |
| 158826 | | |
| 158827 | | |
| 158828 | | |
| 158829 | | |
| 158830 | | |
| 158831 | | |
| 158832 | | |
| 158833 | | |
| 158834 | | |
| 158835 | | |
| 158836 | | |
| 158837 | | |
| 158838 | | |
| 158839 | | |
| 158840 | | |
| 158841 | | |
| 158842 | | |
| 158843 | | |
| 158844 | | |
| 158845 | | |
| 158846 | | |
| 158847 | | |
| 158848 | | |
| 158849 | | |
| 158850 | | |
| 158851 | | |
| 158852 | | |
| 158853 | | |
| 158854 | | |
| 158855 | | |
| 158856 | | |
| 158857 | | |
| 158858 | | |
| 158859 | | |
| 158860 | | |
| 158861 | | |
| 158862 | | |
| 158863 | | |
| 158864 | | |
| 158865 | | |
| 158866 | | |
| 158867‡ | | |
| 158868‡ | | |
| 158869‡ | | |
| 158870‡ | | |
| 158871‡ | | |
| 158872‡ | | |
| 158873‡ | | |
| 158874‡ | | |
| 158875‡ | | |
| 158876‡ | | |
| 158877‡ | | |
| 158878‡ | | |
| 158879‡ | | |
| 158880‡ | | |
| 158881‡ | | |
| 158882‡ | | |
| 158883‡ | | |
| 158884‡ | | |
| 158885‡ | | |
| 158886‡ | | |
| 158887‡ | | |
| 158888‡ | | |
| 158889‡ | | |
| 158890‡ | | |
| 158891‡ | | |
| 158892‡ | | |
| 158893 | | |
| 158894 | | |
| 158895 | | |
| 158896 | | |
| 158897 | | |
| 158898 | | |
| 158899 | | |
| 158900 | | |
| 158901 | | |
| 158902 | | |
| 158903 | | |
| 158904 | | |

## CLASSES 165/0 & 165/1 BREL York
### DMC(L) + MS(L)‡ + DMS(L)DP2.53/DP2.55‡ + DR2.08‡ + DP2.54

**Seats: Two-car:1st 16 Std 72 + 98/Three-car 1st 24 Std 60 + 106 + 98**
**To be introduced from February 1991** NETWORKER TURBO **Livery: N**

| | | |
|---|---|---|
| 165001–165022 (2-car) | NMY | AL |
| 165023–165033 (3-car)‡ | NMY | AL |
| 165034–165039 (2-car) | NMY | AL |
| 165101–165117 (3-car)‡ | NWR | RG |
| 165118–165137 (2-car) | NWR | RG |

## DIESEL-ELECTRIC MULTIPLE-UNITS.

**THIS STOCK IS LISTED ONLY BY UNIT NUMBERS. VEHICLE NUMBER INFORMATION IS IN ACCORDANCE WITH THAT PUBLISHED EARLY IN 1989 EXCEPT AS SHOWN ON PAGE 96.**

### Class 205 (3H) BR Eastleigh DMBS + TS + DTC(L). DB2.03/DB2.04‡ + DH2.03 + DE3.01/DE3.02†/DE3.03‡

**Seats: 52 + 104 + 1st 13 Std 50/52 + 104 + 1st 19 Std 50†/ 42 + 104 + 1st 13 Std 62‡.**

| | | | | | | | | | | | | | | | |
|---|---|---|---|---|---|---|---|---|---|---|---|---|---|---|---|
| 205001 | N | NKC | SU | 205015† | N | NSX | SU | 205025 | N | NSX | SU | 205030‡ | N | NSS | EH |
| 205002 | N | NSX | SU | 205016† | N | NSX | SU | 205026 | N | NSX | SU | 205031‡ | | NSS | EH |
| 205008† | | NSX | SU | 205018† | N | NSX | SU | 205027‡ | | NSX | SU | 205032‡ | N | NSS | EH |
| 205009† | N | NSX | SU | 205023† | | NSX | SU | 205028‡ | N | NSS | EH | 205033‡ | | NSS | EH |
| 205012† | N | NSX | SU | 205024 | N | NSX | SU | 205029‡ | N | NSS | EH | | | | |

### Class 205/1 (3H) BR Eastleigh DMBS + TS + DTS(L). DB2.03 + DH2.03 + DE2.04.

**Seats: 52 + 104 + 76.**

| | | |
|---|---|---|
| 205101 | NKC | SU |

### Class 207 (3D) BR Eastleigh DMBS + TC(L) + DTS. DB2.05 + DH3.01 + DE2.01.

**Seats: 42 + 1st 24 Std 42 + 76.**

| | | | | | | | | | | | | | | | |
|---|---|---|---|---|---|---|---|---|---|---|---|---|---|---|---|
| 207001 | N | NSX | SU | 207004 | | NSX | SU | 207010 | | NSS | EH | 207017 | N | NSS | EH |
| 207002 | N | NSX | SU | 207005 | | NSS | EH | 207013 | N | NSS | EH | | | | |

The last 14 Super Sprinter units are painted in Strathclyde PTE orange livery (PS). The last, No 156514, is seen at Corkerhill (CK) in September 1989 immediately after delivery from Metro-Cammell. The compiler was privileged to travel on this special run from Birmingham to Glasgow via Shap and Beattock.

# DIESEL MULTIPLE-UNIT DEPOT ALLOCATION SUMMARY.

FORMATIONS FOR 1st GENERATION UNITS AND SEMI-PERMANENT REVISIONS ON MODERN UNITS.

## ANGLIA REGION

### CAMBRIDGE CA *(SECTOR NNE)*

| Set: | Vehicles: | | |
|---|---|---|---|
| L200 | 51215 | 54081 | |
| L220 | 51207 | 54405 | |
| L221 | 51208 | 54402 | |
| L222 | 51438 | 54382 | |
| L223 | 51444 | 54068 | |
| L224 | 51445 | 54362 | |
| L225 | 51222 | 54220 | |
| L700 | 53207 | 59115 | 53296 |
| L830 | 51190 | 59111 | 53333 |
| L831 | 51211 | 59072 | 53265 |

*(SECTOR RPXN Parcels units:)*

| | | |
|---|---|---|
| L928 | 55928 | 54903 |
| L929 | 55929 | 54904 |
| L930 | 55930 | 54900 |
| L931 | 55931 | 54901 |
| L932 | 55932 | 54902 |
| L991 | 55991 | |
| L992 | 55992 | |
| L993 | 55993 | |
| L994 | 55994 | |
| L995 | 55995 | |

### NORWICH NC *(SECTOR PNC).*

| | | | |
|---|---|---|---|
| 051 | 51218 | 54399 | |
| 053 | 51247 | 54387 | |
| 054 | 51230 | 54369 | |
| 055 | 51427 | 54368 | |
| 056 | 51429 | 54393 | |
| 058 | 51213 | 54380 | |
| 059 | 51442 | 54073 | |
| 063 | 51428 | 54218 | |
| 065 | 51189 | 54343 | |
| 066 | 51192 | 54354 | |
| 067 | 51187 | 54332 | |
| 068 | 53293 | 54379 | |
| 070 | 53202 | 54388 | |
| 072 | 51201 | 54347 | |
| 076 | 51252 | 54352 | |
| 078 | 53201 | 54065 | |
| 081 | 53231 | 54050 | |
| 085 | 51185 | 54062 | |
| 086 | 53228 | 54055 | |
| 088 | 53208 | 54060 | |
| 100 | 51508 | 59095 | 53181 |
| 101 | 51506 | 59055 | 53266 |
| 102 | 53168 | 59084 | 53193 |
| 103 | 53305 | 59536 | 53180 |
| 104 | 53321 | 59080 | 51531 |
| 106 | 53139 | 59092 | 53238 |
| 107 | 53177 | 59079 | 53267 |
| 108 | 53149 | 59077 | 53170 |

Class 156 units:

401 402 403 404 405 406 407 408 409
410 411 412 413 414 415 416 417 418
419 420 421 422 423 424 425 426 427
428 429 440 452

## EASTERN REGION.

### HEATON HT *(SECTOR PHT)*

| | | |
|---|---|---|
| 50 | 53950 | 54227 |
| 51 | 53951 | 54235 |
| 52 | 53952 | 54244 |
| 53 | 53953 | 54242 |
| 54 | 53954 | 54265 |
| 55 | 53955 | 54262 |
| 56 | 53956 | 54238 |
| 57 | 53957 | 54236 |
| 58 | 53958 | 54239 |
| 59 | 53959 | 54243 |
| 60 | 53960 | 54241 |
| 62 | 53962 | 54245 |
| 63 | 53963 | 54240 |
| 64 | 53964 | 54247 |
| 73 | 53973 | 54263 |

Class 142/5 units:

516 518 519 520 521 522 525 050

Class 143/3★ and 143/6 units:

320★ 321★ 322★ 323★ 324★ 325★
601 602 603 604 605 606 607 608 609
610 611 612 613 614 615 616 617 618
619

### Departmental Service units: *(SECTOR DMEX)*

| | | |
|---|---|---|
| Inspection Saloons: | DB975349 | DB975539 |
| Inspection Saloons: | DB975637 | DB975664 |
| Sandite unit: | DB977536 | DB977535 |

### NEVILLE HILL. NL *(SECTOR PNL)*

| | | | |
|---|---|---|---|
| 226 | 51188 | 54408 | |
| 232 | 53164 | 54365 | |
| 253 | 53940 | 54221 | |
| 254 | 53943 | 54346 | |
| 255 | 53944 | 54252 | |
| 256 | 53949 | 54056 | |
| 257 | 53965 | 54248 | |
| 258 | 53966 | 54249 | |
| 259 | 53968 | 54061 | |
| 260 | 53969 | 54091 | |
| 261 | 53971 | 54504 | |
| 262 | 53974 | 54503 | |
| 263 | 53986 | 54085 | |
| 264 | 53987 | 54270 | |
| 521 | 51194 | 59250 | 53641 |
| 523 | 53626 | 59246 | 53644 |
| 524 | 51178 | 59701 | 51180 |
| 528 | 51175 | 59694 | 53204 |
| 530 | 51463 | 59249 | 53636 |
| 552 | 51191 | 59387 | 51253 |
| 037 | 51420 | | |

Others spare:

53203 54251

Class 141/1 & 141/8★ units :

101 102 103 105 106 107 108 109 110
111 112 113★ 114 115 116 117 118 119
120

Spare Vehicle: 55504

Class 142/2★ & 142/5 units:

015 017 023 024 062 063 065 066 067
068 070 072 073 074 075★ 076★ 077★ 078★
079 080 081 082 083 084 085 086 087
088 089 090 091 092 093 094 095 096

Class 144/4 & 144/7★ units:
(2 car)001 002 003 004 005 006 007 008
009★ 010★ 011★ 012★ 013★
(3 car)014 015 016 017 018 019 020 021
022 023

Class 150/2 units:
230 232 234 236 238 240 242 243

Class 155/1 units:
341 342 343 344 345 346 347

Class 156 units:
438 441 443 444 448 451 454 459 460
463 467 469 475 476 479 480 481 482
484 487 488 489 490 491 497 498

**Departmental Service Unit.** *(SECTOR DMEX):*

Route Learner: 919 51174 51799

# LONDON MIDLAND REGION.

## BLETCHLEY BY

**Bucks/Beds units:** *(SECTOR NNL).*

Vehicles:
51909 54271
51912 54493
51914 54279
51916 54194
51942 54358
53628 54363

**Chiltern Lines units:** *(SECTOR NMY)*

L850: 51878 59206 51571
L851: 53599 59734 51572

Fixed formations not maintained. Two-car with gangways † or four-car
51651† 51652† 51653 51654† 51655 51656† 51657†
51658 51659 51660 51661† 51663 51664 51665
51666 51667 51668 51669 51670 51671 51673
51674 51675 51676† 51677 51678 51679† 51680
51849† 51855† 51857 51863 51866† 51871 51872
51873 51874 51875 51879 51883 51885 51886
51887 51888 51889 51890 51891 51893† 51894
51895† 51896 51899 51900
54222† 54223† 54224† 54228† 54257† 54259† 54274†
54381† 54491† 54495† 54499† 54500†
59651 59652 59654 59655 59656 59657 59659
59660 59662 59663 59664 59665 59667 59669
59671 59675 59676 59678 59727 59728 59729
59731 59732 59733 59735 59736 59737 59738
59740 59746 59747 59749 59750 59752 59754
59755 59758 59759 59761 59762 59763 59764

**Departmental Service Unit.** *(SECTOR DMEX)*

L119: ADB 975042 (Sandite).

## CHESTER CH *SECTOR PCH*

Set No: Vehicles:
CH347 53216 59303 53294
CH348 53253 59042 51210
CH350 51935 59388 51927
CH351 51418 59107 53977
CH352 51903 59390 51904
CH353 53934 59389 53204
CH354 51800 59525 53645
CH355 53291 59688 51177
CH356 53250 59302 53198
CH610 53447 53531
CH611 53451 53517
CH613 53536 53494
CH615 53534 51505
CH616 53442 53516
CH619 51937 52058 (Auto-Gear)
CH620 51943 51568
CH621 51902 52049
CH624 51948 52050
CH625 51938 52065
CH626 51941 52064
CH627 51945 52060
CH628 51947 53634
CH629 51950 52062
CH631 53925 52039
CH632 53930 52056
CH633 53932 51569
CH634 53933 51566
CH641 51245 53160
CH642 51426 53158
CH643 51462 53185
CH645 53224 53194
CH647 51184 53630
CH648 53211 52042

## CARLISLE CL

**Departmental Service Unit** *(SECTOR DMEX)*
Route Learner: TDB 975023

## DERBY DY *(SECTOR PDY)*

Class 150/1 units:
101 102 103 104 105 106 107 108 109
110 111 112 113 114 115 116 117 118
119 120 121 122 123 124 125 126 127
128 129 130 131 132 133 134 135 136
137 138 139 140 142 143 147 150
Class 151 units:
003 004 (Stored)
Class 154 unit:
002

## LONGSIGHT LO *(SECTOR PLO)*

LO252 53975 54258
LO253 51421 54275
LO254 51422 54277
LO255 51424 54232
LO256 51901 54231
LO257 53970 54264
LO260 51905 54488
LO261 51906 54496
LO262 51907 54490
LO263 51908 54501
LO264 51911 54489
LO265 51913 54497
LO266 51917 54272
LO267 51920 54276
LO268 53924 54278
LO269 53927 54214
LO270 53929 54269
LO271 53931 54260
LO272 53938 54484
LO273 53976 54225
LO274 53978 54261
LO275 53980 54256
LO276 53981 54253
LO277 53982 54246
LO278 53983 54266

## NEWTON HEATH NH *(SECTOR PNH)*

Class 142/0 and 142/5★ units:
001 002 003 004 005 006 007 008 009
010 011 012 013 014 026★ 027★ 028 029★
030 031 032 033 034★ 035★ 036★ 037★ 038★
039★ 040★ 041★ 042★ 043★ 044★ 045★ 046★ 047★
048★ 049★ 051★ 052 053 054 055 056 057
058 059 060★ 061★ 064★ 069★ 071★

Class 150/2 units (Three car set†):
201 202 203 204 206 207 210 211 213
214 215 216 217 218† 219 220 221 222
223 225 226 227 231‡ 233‡ 235‡ 237‡ 239‡

(† spare vehicle 57209 to three-car unit 231
Spare vehicle 57212 to three-car unit 233
unit 239 split: 52239 to 235, 57239 to 237)

## TYSELEY TS *(SECTOR PTS)*

T012 55032
T013 55033
T014 55034
T021 53021 54012
T022 53002 54047
T023 53036 54006
T024 53044 54043
T025 53005 54039
T026 53006 54010
T027 53019 54027
T031 53082 51496
T032 51131 51513
T033 53054 53245
T034 53056 53269
T035 53055 51808
T036 53865 53746
T037 53050 51533
T038 53863 53268
T039 53090 53171
T041 53826 51509
T042 53837 53244
T043 53838 51505
T044 53058 51511
T045 53061 53242
T301 51353 59505 51395
T302 51360 59512 51402
T303 51364 59516 51406
T304 51365 59517 51407
T305 51368 59520 51410
T306 51369 59521 51411
T307 51370 59522 51412
T308 51371 59509 51413
T309 51372 59490 51414
T310 51373 59486 51415
T311 51334 59500 51376
T312 51338 59504 51380
T313 51339 59492 51382
T314 51348 59677 51390
T315 51352 59745 51394
T316 51306 59473 51321
T317 51314 59481 51329
T318 51316 59483 51331
T319 51129 59756 51149
T320 51138 59720 53890
T321 53854 59723 53907
T322 53071 59760 53880
T323 53818 59670 53093
T324 53053 59672 53101
T325 53060 59757 51142
T326 53822 59668 53881
T328 53073 59724 53132
T329 53853 59751 53102
T334 53079 59596 53850
T335 53844 59674 53827
T336 53849 59721 51130
T401 51662 59610 59743 53886
T402 51851 59658 59614 51146
T403 51852 59641 59616 53106
T404 51853 59604 59445 53919
T405 51854 59615 59726 51143
T406 51856 59606 59592 53893
T407 51858 59594 59442 53916
T408 51859 59593 59632 53114
T409 51860 59600 59367 53894
T410 51862 59602 59713 53124
T411 51865 59597 59625 53873
T412 51867 59590 59446 53116
T414 51869 59661 59613 51144
T415 51870 59589 59353 53921
T416 51876 59609 59648 53891
T417 51877 59335 59603 53897
T418 51880 59598 59643 53902
T419 51884 59629 59608 51151
T420 51892 59607 59448 53092
T421 51897 59741 59612 53878

Spare: 51868 53838 59032 59344 59444
59591 59595 59611 59617 59673 59719
59722 59753

Class 150/0 unit:
001

Class 150/1 units:
141 145 146 148 149

Class 150/2 units:
(205) (241) (253)
Three-car unit formations:
001 as built
141 + 52205
144 + 57253
145 + 57205
146 + 52253
148 + 57241
149 + 52241

# SCOTRAIL

## HAYMARKET HA *(SECTOR PHA)*

101306 51228 59086 53243
101318 51244 59061 53176
101350 51182 59124 53239
107731 51991 59789 52035

Class 150/2 units:
208 228 244 245 248 250 252 255 256
257 258 259 260 262 264 283 284 285

Class 156 units:
436 445 447 449 450 453 455 456 462
465 476 483 485 492 493 494 495 496
499 500 503 504 505

Class 158 units:
702 704 705
*(to be delivered 701/03/06-31)*

## CORKERHILL CK *(SECTOR PCK)*

Class 156 units:
(GSW route):
430 431 432 433 434 435 436 437 439
442
(Strathclyde):
501 502 506 507 508 509 510 511 512
513 514

## EASTFIELD ED *(SECTOR PED)*

101304 51224 59090 53241
101321 51249 59542 53146
107725 51985 59797 52028
107726 51986 59803 52018
107727 51987 59793 52020
107728 51988 59786 52013
107729 51989 59795 52023
107730 51990 59802 51803
107732 51992 59800 52026
107733 51993 59790 52012
107734 51994 59791 52011
107736 51997 59784 52025

| | | | |
|---|---|---|---|
| 107737 | 51998 | 59782 | 52021 |
| 107738 | 51999 | 59796 | 52030 |
| 107739 | 52000 | 59785 | 52036 |
| 107740 | 52001 | 59783 | 52024 |
| 107743 | 52004 | 59805 | 52016 |
| 107744 | 52005 | 59804 | 52031 |
| 107745 | 52006 | 59801 | 52015 |
| 107746 | 52007 | 59806 | 52033 |
| 107747 | 52008 | 59792 | 52029 |
| 107749 | 52010 | 59807 | 52034 |

### Departmental Service units *(SECTOR DMEX):*

Training & Sandite units:

| | | |
|---|---|---|
| 101302 | ADB 977651 | ADB 977652 |
| 101336 | ADB 977607 | ADB 977608 |

## SOUTHERN REGION

### EASTLEIGH EH *(SECTOR NSS)*

Class 205/0 units:
025 026 027 028 029 030 031 032 033

Class 207 units:
005 010 013 017

### SELHURST SU *(SECTOR NSX or NKC‡)*

Class 205/0 units:
001‡ 002 008 009 012 015 016 018 023 024

Class 205/1 unit:
101

Class 207 units:
001 002 004

## WESTERN REGION:

### OLD OAK COMMON OO
*(SECTOR NWR or NSB†)*

| | | |
|---|---|---|
| L120 | 55020 | |
| L121 | 55021 | |
| L122 | 55022 | |
| L123 | 55023 | |
| L124 | 55024 | |
| L125 | 55025 | |
| L127 | 55027 | |
| L128 | 55028 | |
| L129 | 55029 | |
| L130 | 55030 | |
| L131 | 55031 | |
| L201 | 51212 | 54070 |
| L202 | 51225 | 54372 |
| L204 | 51220 | 54371 |
| L205 | 51443 | 54385 |
| L207 | 51221 | 54396 |
| L210 | 53083 | 54289 |
| L211 | 53155 | 54287 |
| L280 | 54280 | |
| L283 | 54283 | |
| L284 | 54284 | |

*(SECTOR NGB):*

| | | |
|---|---|---|
| L701 | 53437 | 53479 |
| L702 | 53455 | 53539 |
| L703 | 53429 | 53470 |
| L704 | 53477 | 53540 |
| L705 | 51319 | 53820 |

### Departmental Service vehicles
*(SECTOR DMEX):*

Training unit L135 TDB975659
Sandite trailer L281 ADB977615

### READING RG *(SECTOR NWR)*

| | | | |
|---|---|---|---|
| L400 | 51332 | 59484 | 51374 |
| L401 | 51333 | 59485 | 51375 |
| L402 | 51335 | 59487 | 51377 |
| L403 | 51336 | 59488 | 51378 |
| L404 | 51337 | 59489 | 51379 |
| L405 | 51340 | 59491 | 51381 |
| L406 | 51341 | 59493 | 51383 |
| L407 | 51342 | 59494 | 51384 |
| L408 | 51343 | 59495 | 51385 |
| L409 | 51344 | 59496 | 51386 |
| L410 | 51345 | 59497 | 51387 |
| L411 | 51346 | 59498 | 51388 |
| L412 | 51347 | 59499 | 51389 |
| L413 | 51349 | 59501 | 51391 |
| L414 | 51350 | 59502 | 51392 |
| L415 | 51351 | 59503 | 51393 |
| L417 | 51354 | 59506 | 51396 |
| L418 | 51355 | 59507 | 51397 |
| L419 | 51356 | 59508 | 51398 |
| L420 | 51358 | 59510 | 51400 |
| L421 | 51359 | 59511 | 51401 |
| L423 | 51361 | 59513 | 51399 |
| L424 | 51362 | 59514 | 51404 |
| L425 | 51363 | 59515 | 51405 |
| L428 | 51366 | 59518 | 51408 |
| L429 | 51367 | 59519 | 51409 |

Spare: 59163

*(SECTOR NSB or NWR†)*

| | | | |
|---|---|---|---|
| L575 | 51060 | 59419 | 51088 |
| L576† | 51062 | 59421 | 51090 |
| L579 | 51065 | 59424 | 51103 |
| L580 | 51066 | 59425 | 51094 |
| L588 | 51079 | 59437 | 51107 |
| L594 | 51073 | 59435 | 51104 |
| L595 | 51074 | 59430 | 51086 |
| L596 | 51076 | 59416 | 51099 |
| L832 | 51226 | 59570 | 51499 |
| L833 | 51425 | 59543 | 51504 |
| L834 | 51431 | 59526 | 51501 |
| L835 | 51432 | 59530 | 51498 |
| L836 | 51434 | 59540 | 51503 |
| L837 | 51437 | 59128 | 53751 |
| L838 | 53308 | 59125 | 53331 |
| L839 | 53310 | 59306 | 53326 |
| L840 | 53311 | 59117 | 53322 |
| L841 | 53312 | 59091 | 53332 |
| L842 | 53314 | 59101 | 53327 |

Spare: 59072 (for L831)

### Departmental Service unit *(SECTOR DMEX)*

Ultrasonic Test Train: DB977391 DB999602 DB977392

### BRISTOL BR *(SECTOR PBR)*

| | | |
|---|---|---|
| B398 | 51416 | 53632 |
| B960 | 53602 | 54197 |
| B961 | 53608 | 54208 |
| B962 | 53612 | 54492 |
| B963 | 53948 | 54268 |
| B964 | 53614 | 54204 |
| B965 | 53616 | 54209 |
| B966 | 53618 | 54494 |
| B967 | 53619 | 54230 |

### LAIRA LA *(SECTOR PLA)*

| | |
|---|---|
| P100 | 55000 |
| P103 | 55003 |
| P104† | 55004 |
| P105 | 55005 |

| | | | | |
|---|---|---|---|---|
| P106 | 55006 | | | |
| P109 | 55009 | | | |
| P111† | 55011 | | | |
| P112 | 55012 | | | |
| P126 | 55026 | | | |
| P825 | 53165 | 59118 | 51246 | |
| P826 | 53223 | 59561 | 51219 | |
| P827 | 53212 | 59130 | 51223 | |
| P828 | 51936 | 59386 | 52051 | |
| P829 | 51500 | 59093 | 53157 | |
| P860 | 51181 | 51530 | | |
| P861 | 51205 | 51512 | | |
| P862 | 51179 | 51570 | | |
| P863 | 51234 | 53163 | | |
| P864 | 51241 | 53260 | | |
| P865 | 51231 | 53189 | | |
| P870 | 53200 | 53638 | | |
| P871 | 53256 | 53639 | | |
| P872 | 53247 | 53646 | | |
| P873 | 53248 | 53637 | | |
| P874 | 53315 | 53330 | | |
| P954 | 51932 | 52047 | | |
| P955 | 51933 | 52054 | | |
| P956 | 51939 | 52063 | | |
| P957 | 51940 | 52057 | | |
| tba | 51435 | 52053 | 52059 | 53642 |

†: out of traffic at Tyseley.

*(SECTOR DMEX)*
Sandite trailer: P286 TDB977466

## CARDIFF CF *(SECTOR PCF)*

| | | | | |
|---|---|---|---|---|
| C391 | 51141 | 51128 | | |
| C392 | 51134 | 51147 | | |
| C393 | 51135 | 51148 | | |
| C394 | 51139 | 51152 | | |
| C395 | 51140 | 51153 | | |
| C399 | 53635 | 53617 | | |
| C472 | 51315 | 51330 | | |
| C968 | 53620 | 54203 | | |
| C969 | 53621 | 54201 | | |
| C970 | 53622 | 54207 | | |
| C971 | 53941 | 54205 | | |
| C972 | 53627 | 54210 | | |
| C973 | 53629 | 54267 | | |
| C975 | 53624 | 54498 | | |
| C976 | 51417 | 54212 | | |
| C977 | 51419 | 54273 | | |
| tba | 51132 | 51133 | 51136 | 51145 |
| Spare: | 59245 | 59248 | 59383 | 59385 |

Class 150/2 units:

| | | | | | | | | |
|---|---|---|---|---|---|---|---|---|
| 246 | 247 | 249 | 251 | 254 | 261 | 263 | 265 | 266 |
| 267 | 268 | 269 | 270 | 271 | 272 | 273 | 274 | 275 |
| 276 | 277 | 278 | 279 | 280 | 281 | 282 | | |

Class 155/0 units

| | | | | | | | | |
|---|---|---|---|---|---|---|---|---|
| 301 | 302 | 303 | 304 | 305 | 306 | 307 | 308 | 309 |
| 310 | 311 | 312 | 313 | 314 | 315 | 316 | 317 | 318 |
| 319 | 320 | 321 | 322 | 323 | 324 | 325 | 326 | 327 |
| 328 | 329 | 330 | 331 | 332 | 333 | 334 | 335 | |

## Departmental Service unit *(SECTOR DMEX)*

Sandite trailer: C285 TDB977486.

## LANDORE LE *(SECTOR PLE)*

| | | | |
|---|---|---|---|
| S939 | 51926 | 53631 | |
| S940 | 51919 | 52048 | |
| S941 | 51922 | 51562 | |
| S942 | 51928 | 59382 | 52044 |
| S943 | 51930 | 51561 | |
| S944 | 51931 | 52055 | |
| S945 | 51925 | 59380 | 53643 |
| S946 | 53939 | 52046 | |
| S947 | 53942 | 51567 | |
| S948 | 53928 | 51565 | |
| S949 | 53945 | 51563 | |
| S950 | 53926 | 59381 | 52061 |
| S951 | 53935 | 52041 | |
| S952 | 53625 | 52045 | |
| S958 | 51924 | 59384 | 52038 |
| S959 | 53947 | 53633 | |

Spare: 59539

New Class 158 'Express' DMU No 158704 is seen at Swindon Servicing Depot in April. This class has had serious production problems and the first series will be over a year late when they enter service on the Edinburgh–Glasgow route, hopefully this summer.

# ELECTRIC MULTIPLE-UNITS : 25kV AC OVERHEAD.

**THIS STOCK IS LISTED ONLY BY UNIT NUMBERS. VEHICLE NUMBER INFORMATION IS IN ACCORDANCE WITH THAT PUBLISHED EARLY IN 1989 EXCEPT AS SHOWN ON PAGE 96.**

## Class 302/0 BR Doncaster & York BDTS(L) + MBS + TC(L) + DTS†/BDTC(L) + MBS + TS(L) + DTS.

**EF2.01 + ED2.05 + EH3.02 + EE2.05†/EF3.03 + ED2.16 + EH2.23 + EE2.19/ EF2.01 + DE2.17 + EH3.02.**
**Seats: 80 + 96 + 1st 19 Std 60 + 108†/1st 24 Std 52 + 76 + 86 + 88/80 + 82 + 1st 19 Std 60**

| | | |
|---|---|---|
| 302201 | NTS | EM |
| 302202 | NTS | EM |
| 302203 | NTS | EM |
| 302204 | NTS | EM |
| 302205 | NTS | EM |
| 302206 | NTS | EM |
| 302207 | NTS | EM |
| 302208 | NTS | EM |
| 302209 | NTS | EM |
| 302210 | NTS | EM |
| 302211 | NTS | EM |
| 302212 N | NTS | EM |
| 302213 | NTS | EM |
| 302214 | NTS | EM |
| 302215 | NTS | EM |
| 302216 | NTS | EM |
| 302217 N | NTS | EM |
| 302218 N | NTS | EM |
| 302219 | NTS | EM |
| 302220 | NTS | EM |
| 302221 | NTS | EM |
| 302222 | NTS | EM |
| 302223 | NTS | EM |
| 302224 | NTS | EM |
| 302225 | NTS | EM |
| 302226 | NTS | EM |
| 302227 | NTS | EM |
| 302228 | NTS | EM |
| 302229 | NTS | EM |
| 302230 | NTS | EM |
| 302234† | NNE | EM |
| 302252† | NNE | EM |
| 302261† | NNE | EM |
| 302262† | NNE | EM |
| 302274† | NNE | EM |
| 302283† | NNE | EM |

## Class 302/1 BR Doncaster & York BDLV + MLV + DTLV

**(Modified BR Ilford Depot).EF5.01 + ED5.01 + EE5.01.**
**Seats: 0 for public use. Livery: R.**

| | | |
|---|---|---|
| 302990 | RPMA | IL |
| 302991 | RPMA | IL |
| 302992 | RPMA | IL |

## Classes 303/0† & 303/1 Pressed Steel DTS + MBS + BDTS.

**ED2.01 + EE2.06 + EF2.02†/ED2.20 + EE2.41 + EF2.17.**
**Seats: 70 + 83 + 83/48 + 56 + 56.**

| | | | |
|---|---|---|---|
| 303001 | PS | PGW | GW |
| 303003 | PS | PGW | GW |
| 303004 | PS | PGW | GW |
| 303006 | PS | PGW | GW |
| 303008 | PS | PGW | GW |
| 303009 | PS | PGW | GW |
| 303010 | PS | PGW | GW |
| 303011 | PS | PGW | GW |
| 303012 | PS | PGW | GW |
| 303013 | PS | PGW | GW |
| 303014 | PS | PGW | GW |
| 303016 | PS | PGW | GW |
| 303019 | PS | PGW | GW |
| 303020 | PS | PGW | GW |
| 303021 | PS | PGW | GW |
| 303023 | PS | PGW | GW |
| 303024 | PS | PGW | GW |
| 303025 | PS | PGW | GW |
| 303027 | PS | PGW | GW |
| 303028 | PS | PGW | GW |
| 303029 | PS | PGW | GW |
| 303032 | PS | PGW | GW |
| 303033 | PS | PGW | GW |
| 303034 | PS | PGW | GW |
| 303037 | PS | PGW | GW |
| 303038 | PS | PGW | GW |
| 303039† | PS | PGW | GW |
| 303040 | PS | PGW | GW |
| 303043 | PS | PGW | GW |
| 303045 | PS | PGW | GW |
| 303046 | PS | PGW | GW |
| 303047 | PS | PGW | GW |
| 303048† | PS | PGW | GW |
| 303049† | PM | PXXH | HQ |
| 303052† | PS | PGW | GW |
| 303054 | PS | PGW | GW |
| 303055 | PS | PGW | GW |
| 303056 | PS | PGW | GW |
| 303058 | PS | PGW | GW |
| 303060† | PM | PXXH | HQ |
| 303061 | PS | PGW | GW |
| 303062† | PS | PGW | GW |
| 303063† | PS | PGW | GW |
| 303065 | PS | PGW | GW |
| 303066† | PM | PXXH | HQ |
| 303069† | PS | PGW | GW |
| 303070 | PS | PGW | GW |
| 303072† | PS | PGW | GW |
| 303073 | PS | PGW | GW |
| 303075† | PS | PGW | GW |
| 303076† | PS | PGW | GW |
| 303077 | PS | PGW | GW |
| 303079 | PS | PGW | GW |
| 303080 | PS | PGW | GW |
| 303082 | PM | PXXH | HQ |
| 303083 | PS | PGW | GW |
| 303085 | PS | PGW | GW |
| 303087 | PS | PGW | GW |
| 303088 | PS | PGW | GW |
| 303089 | PS | PGW | GW |
| 303090 | PS | PGW | GW |
| 303091 | PS | PGW | GW |

## Class 304 BR Wolverton DTBS + MBS + BDTS

**EG2.02 + ED2.15 + EF2.33/EG2.03 + ED2.03 + EF2.04†.**
**Seats: 82 + 82 + 80/82 + 72 + 80.**

| | | |
|---|---|---|
| 304001 | PLG | LG |
| 304002 | PLG | LG |
| 304003 | PLG | LG |
| 304004 | PLG | LG |
| 304005 | PLG | LG |
| 304006 | PLG | LG |
| 304007 | PLG | LG |
| 304008 | PLG | LG |
| 304009 | PLG | LG |
| 304010 | PLG | LG |
| 304011 | PLG | LG |
| 304012 | PLG | LG |
| 304013 | PLG | LG |
| 304014 | PLG | LG |
| 304015 | PLG | LG |
| 304016† | PLG | LG |
| 304017† | PLG | LG |
| 304019† | PLG | LG |
| 304020† | PLG | LG |
| 304021† | PLG | LG |
| 304023† | PLG | LG |
| 304024† | PLG | LG |
| 304027† | PLG | LG |
| 304028† | PLG | LG |
| 304029† | PLG | LG |
| 304030† | PLG | LG |
| 304032† | PLG | LG |
| 304033† | PLG | LG |
| 304034† | PLG | LG |
| 304035† | PLG | LG |
| 304036† | PLG | LG |
| 304037† | PLG | LG |
| 304039† | PLG | LG |
| 304040† | PLG | LG |
| 304041† | PLG | LG |
| 304042† | PLG | LG |
| 304043† | PLG | LG |
| 304045† | PLG | LG |

## Class 305/1 BR York **BDTS + MBS + DTS**

**EF2.05/EF2.01† + ED2.04 + EE2.09.**
**Seats: 92/80† + 82 + 92.**

| | | | | | | | | | | | | | | | |
|---|---|---|---|---|---|---|---|---|---|---|---|---|---|---|---|
| 305401 | | NNE | IL | 305407 | | NNE | IL | 305413 | | NNE | IL | 305419 | | NNE | IL |
| 305402 | | NNE | IL | 305408 | | NNE | IL | 305414† | | NNE | IL | 305420 | | NNE | IL |
| 305403 | | NNE | IL | 305409 | | NNE | IL | 305415 | | NNE | IL | 305421 | | NNE | IL |
| 305404 | | NNE | IL | 305410 | | NNE | IL | 305416 | | NNE | IL | 305422 | | NNE | IL |
| 305405 | | NNE | IL | 305411 | | NNE | IL | 305417 | | NNE | IL | | | | |
| 305406 | | NNE | IL | 305412 | | NNE | IL | 305418 | | NNE | IL | | | | |

## Class 305/2 BR Doncaster **DTS + TS(L) + MBS + BDTC(L).**

**EE2.20 + EH2.23 + ED2.16 + EF3.04..**
**Seats: 88 + 86 + 76 + 1st 24 Std 52.**

| | | | | | | | | | | | | | | | |
|---|---|---|---|---|---|---|---|---|---|---|---|---|---|---|---|
| 305501 | N | NTS | EM | 305506 | N | NTS | EM | 305511 | N | NTS | EM | 305517 | N | NTS | EM |
| 305502 | N | NTS | EM | 305507 | | NTS | EM | 305513 | N | NTS | EM | 305518 | N | NTS | EM |
| 305503 | | NTS | EM | 305508 | N | NTS | EM | 305514 | N | NTS | EM | 305519 | N | NTS | EM |
| 305504 | | NTS | EM | 305509 | N | NTS | EM | 305515 | N | NTS | EM | | | | |
| 305505 | N | NTS | EM | 305510 | N | NTS | EM | 305516 | N | NTS | EM | | | | |

## Class 305/3 BR York **BDTS + MBS + TC(L) + DTS**

**EF2.05 + ED2.04 + EH3.— + EE2.09.**
**Seats: 92 + 82 + 1st 19 Std 59 + 92.**

| | | | | | | | | | | | | | | | |
|---|---|---|---|---|---|---|---|---|---|---|---|---|---|---|---|
| 305521 | | NTS | EM | 305523 | | NTS | EM | 305525 | | NTS | EM | 305527 | | NTS | EM |
| 305522 | | NTS | EM | 305524 | | NTS | EM | 305526 | | NTS | EM | 305528 | | NTS | EM |

## Class 306 Metro-Cammell & Birmingham RC&W **DMS + TBS + DTS**

**EA2.03 + EJ2.01 + EE2.11.**
**Seats: 62 + 46 + 60. Special hire duties only. Livery: BR Green**

| | | | |
|---|---|---|---|
| 306017 | | NXX | IL |

## Class 307 BR Eastleigh **BDBS + MS + TS(L) + DTC(L)**

**EO2.02 + EC2.04 + EH2.22 + EE3.07**
**Seats: 66 + 98 + 86 + 1st 24 Std 52.**

| | | | | | | | | | | | | | | | |
|---|---|---|---|---|---|---|---|---|---|---|---|---|---|---|---|
| 307102 | N | PNL | NL | 307110 | | RPMB | HQ | 307117 | N | NGE | IL | 307126 | | RPMB | HQ |
| 307103 | | RPMB | HQ | 307111 | N | PNL | NL | 307118 | | PNLD | NL | 307127 | | NGE | IL |
| 307104 | | NGE | IL | 307112 | | NGE | IL | 307120 | N | PNL | NL | 307128 | | NGE | IL |
| 307105 | N | PNL | NL | 307113 | | NGE | IL | 307122 | N | PNL | NL | 307129 | | NGE | IL |
| 307107 | | RPMB | HQ | 307114 | | NGE | IL | 307123 | | RPMB | HQ | 307130 | N | PNL | NL |
| 307108 | | NGE | IL | 307115 | | NGE | IL | 307124 | | NGE | IL | 307131 | | RPMB | HQ |
| 307109 | | NGE | IL | 307116 | | PNLD | NL | 307125 | | RPMB | HQ | 307132 | N | NGE | IL |

## Class 308/1 BR Doncaster **BDTC(L)/BDTS(L)‡ + MBS + TS(L) + DTS**

**EF3.04/EF2.01‡ + ED2.16 + EH2.23 + EE2.20.**
**Seats: 1st 24 Std 52/Std 80‡ + 76 + 86 + 88.**

| | | | | | | | | | | | | | | | |
|---|---|---|---|---|---|---|---|---|---|---|---|---|---|---|---|
| 308133 | | NTS | EM | 308142 | | NTS | EM | 308151 | | NTS | EM | 308160 | N | NTS | EM |
| 308134 | | NTS | EM | 308143 | | NTS | EM | 308152 | N | NTS | EM | 308161 | | NTS | EM |
| 308135 | N | NTS | EM | 308144‡ | | NTS | EM | 308153 | | NTS | EM | 308162 | N | NTS | EM |
| 308136 | N | NTS | EM | 308145 | | NTS | EM | 308154 | | NTS | EM | 308163 | N | NTS | EM |
| 308137 | | NTS | EM | 308146 | | NTS | EM | 308155 | N | NTS | EM | 308164 | N | NTS | EM |
| 308138 | N | NTS | EM | 308147 | | NTS | EM | 308156 | N | NTS | EM | 308165 | | NTS | EM |
| 308139 | | NTS | EM | 308148 | | NTS | EM | 308157 | N | NTS | EM | | | | |
| 308140 | N | NTS | EM | 308149 | N | NTS | EM | 308158 | | NTS | EM | | | | |
| 308141 | | NTS | EM | 308150 | | NTS | EM | 308159 | N | NTS | EM | | | | |

## Classes 309/1 & 309/3†‡ BR York **DMBS + TC(L) + TS(L) + BDTS/BDTC(L) + MBS + TS + DTS(L)†‡.**

**EB2.07 + EH3.09 + EH2.27 + EF2.16/EF3.05 + ED2.18 + EH2.28(EH2.29‡) + EE2.29†.**
**Seats: 48 + 1st 24 Std 28 + 64 + 60/1st 18 Std 32 + 48 + 68 + 56‡. Livery: N**

| | | | | | | | | | | | | | | | |
|---|---|---|---|---|---|---|---|---|---|---|---|---|---|---|---|
| 309601 | | NGE | CC | 309604 | | NGE | CC | 309607 | | NGE | CC | 309612† | | NGE | CC |
| 309602 | | NGE | CC | 309605 | | NGE | CC | 309608 | | NGE | CC | 309613† | | NGE | CC |
| 309603 | | NGE | CC | 309606 | | NGE | CC | 309611† | | NGE | CC | 309614† | | NGE | CC |

| | | | | | | | | | | |
|---|---|---|---|---|---|---|---|---|---|---|
| 309615† | NGE | CC | 309618† | NGE | CC | 309623‡ | NGE | CC | 309626‡ | NGE | CC |
| 309616† | NGE | CC | 309621‡ | NGE | CC | 309624‡ | NGE | CC | 309627‡ | NGE | CC |
| 309617† | NGE | CC | 309622‡ | NGE | CC | 309625‡ | NGE | CC | | | |

## Class 310/0 BR Derby — BDTS + MBS + TS + DTC

**EF2.10 + ED2.10 + EH2.08 + EE3.06$/EF2.11 + ED2.19 + EH2.32 + EE3.06†/ EF2.11 + ED2.19 + EH2.32 + EE3.06/EF2.14 + ED2.19 + EH2.32 + EE3.06‡.**
**Seats: 68 + 70 + 100 + 1st 25 Std 43$/80 + 70 + 100 + 1st 25 Std 43†/ 80 + 70 + 98 + 1st 25 Std 43/75 + 70 + 98 + 1st 25 Std 43.**

| | | | | | | | | | | | | | | | |
|---|---|---|---|---|---|---|---|---|---|---|---|---|---|---|---|
| 310046 | N | NNE | EM | 310060 | N | NNE | EM | 310075 | N | NNE | EM | 310087 | N | NTS | EM |
| 310047 | N | NNE | EM | 310061 | N | NNE | EM | 310077 | N | NNE | EM | 310088 | N | NTS | EM |
| 310049 | N | NNE | EM | 310064 | N | NNE | EM | 310079 | N | NNE | EM | 310089 | N | NTS | EM |
| 310050 | N | NNE | EM | 310065 | N | NNE | EM | 310080 | N | NTS | EM | 310091 | N | NTS | EM |
| 310051 | N | NNE | EM | 310066$ | N | NNE | EM | 310081 | N | NTS | EM | 310092 | N | NTS | EM |
| 310052 | N | NNE | EM | 310067 | N | NNE | EM | 310082 | N | NTS | EM | 310093 | N | NTS | EM |
| 310056 | N | NNE | EM | 310068 | N | NNE | EM | 310083 | N | NTS | EM | 310094‡ | N | NTS | EM |
| 310057 | N | NNE | EM | 310069 | N | NNE | EM | 310084 | N | NTS | EM | 310095 | N | NTS | EM |
| 310058 | N | NNE | EM | 310070 | N | NNE | EM | 310085 | N | NTS | EM | | | | |
| 310059 | N | NNE | EM | 310074 | N | NNE | EM | 310086† | N | NTS | EM | | | | |

## Class 310/1 BR Derby — BDTS + MBS + TS + DTS

**EF2.11 + ED2.19 + EH2.32 + EE2.37.**
**Seats: 80 + 70 + 98 + 75. Livery: PB (Midline)**

| | | | | | | | | | | | |
|---|---|---|---|---|---|---|---|---|---|---|---|
| 310101 | PBY | BY | 310104 | PBY | BY | 310107 | PBY | BY | 310110 | PBY | BY |
| 310102 | PBY | BY | 310105 | PBY | BY | 310108 | PBY | BY | 310111 | PBY | BY |
| 310103 | PBY | BY | 310106 | PBY | BY | 310109 | PBY | BY | | | |

## Class 311 Cravens — DTS + MBS + BDTS

**EE2.14 + ED2.11 + EF2.12.**
**Seats: 83 + 70 + 83.**

| | | | | | | | | | | | | | | | |
|---|---|---|---|---|---|---|---|---|---|---|---|---|---|---|---|
| 311098 | PS | PGW | GW | 311103 | | PGW | GW | 311107 | | PGW | GW | 311110 | | PGW | GW |
| 311099 | | PGW | GW | 311104 | | PGW | GW | 311108 | | PGW | GW | | | | |
| 311102 | | PGW | GW | 311105 | PS | PGW | GW | 311109 | PS | PGW | GW | | | | |

## Class 312/0 BREL York — BDTS(L) + MBS + TS + DTC

**EF2.13 + ED2.12/ED2.14 + EH2.09 + EE3.05.**
**Seats: 84 + 68 + 98 + 1st 25 Std 47. Livery: N**

| | | | | | | | | | | | |
|---|---|---|---|---|---|---|---|---|---|---|---|
| 312701 | NGE | CC | 312709 | NGE | CC | 312717 | NGE | CC | 312725 | NGE | CC |
| 312702 | NGE | CC | 312710 | NGE | CC | 312718 | NGE | CC | 312726 | NGE | CC |
| 312703 | NGE | CC | 312711 | NGE | CC | 312719 | NGE | CC | 312727 | NGE | CC |
| 312704 | NGE | CC | 312712 | NGE | CC | 312720 | NGE | CC | 312728 | NGE | CC |
| 312705 | NGE | CC | 312713 | NGE | CC | 312721 | NGE | CC | 312729 | NGE | CC |
| 312706 | NGE | CC | 312714 | NGE | CC | 312722 | NGE | CC | 312730 | NGE | CC |
| 312707 | NGE | CC | 312715 | NGE | CC | 312723 | NGE | CC | | | |
| 312708 | NGE | CC | 312716 | NGE | CC | 312724 | NGE | CC | | | |

## Class 312/1 BREL York — BDTS(L) + MBS + TS + DTC

**EF2.13 + ED2.13 + EH2.19 + EE3.05.**
**Seats: 84 + 68 + 98+ 1st 25 Std 47. Livery: N**

| | | | | | | | | | | | |
|---|---|---|---|---|---|---|---|---|---|---|---|
| 312781 | NGE | CC | 312786 | NGE | CC | 312791 | NGE | CC | 312796 | NGE | CC |
| 312782 | NGE | CC | 312787 | NGE | CC | 312792 | NGE | CC | 312797 | NGE | CC |
| 312783 | NGE | CC | 312788 | NGE | CC | 312793 | NGE | CC | 312798 | NGE | CC |
| 312784 | NGE | CC | 312789 | NGE | CC | 312794 | NGE | CC | 312799 | NGE | CC |
| 312785 | NGE | CC | 312790 | NGE | CC | 312795 | NGE | CC | | | |

## Classes 313/0 & 313/1† BREL York 25kV AC & 750V DC — DMS + TS(P) + BDMS.

**EA2.04 + EH2.11 + EI2.01.**
**Seats: 74 + 84 + 74.(* TS(P) temporarily removed, able to run on DC only)**

| | | | | | | | | | | | | | | | |
|---|---|---|---|---|---|---|---|---|---|---|---|---|---|---|---|
| 313001† | N | NNW | BY | 313006† | N | NNW | BY | 313011† | N | NNW | BY | 313016† | N | NNL | BY |
| 313002† | N | NNL | BY | 313007† | N | NNW | BY | 313012† | N | NNW | BY | 313017† | N | NNL | BY |
| 313003† | N | NNW | BY | 313008† | N | NNW | BY | 313013† | N | NNW | BY | 313018† | N | NNL | BY |
| 313004† | N | NNW | BY | 313009† | N | NNW | BY | 313014† | N | NNW | BY | 313019 | N | NGN | HE |
| 313005† | N | NNW | BY | 313010† | N | NNW | BY | 313015† | N | NNL | BY | 313020 | N | NGN | HE |

| | | | | | | | | | | | | | | | |
|---|---|---|---|---|---|---|---|---|---|---|---|---|---|---|---|
| 313021† | N | NNL | BY | 313032 | N | NGN | HE | 313043 | | NGN | HE | 313054 | | NGN | HE |
| 313022† | N | NNL | BY | 313033 | N | NGN | HE | 313044 | N | NGN | HE | 313055 | | NGN | HE |
| 313023† | N | NNL | BY | 313034* | | NXXH | BY | 313045 | N | NGN | HE | 313056 | | NGN | HE |
| 313024 | N | NGN | HE | 313035 | N | NGN | HE | 313046 | N | NGN | HE | 313057 | N | NGN | HE |
| 313025 | | NGN | HE | 313036 | N | NGN | HE | 313047 | N | NGN | HE | 313058 | | NGN | HE |
| 313026 | | NGN | HE | 313037 | N | NGN | HE | 313048 | N | NGN | HE | 313059 | | NGN | HE |
| 313027 | N | NGN | HE | 313038 | N | NGN | HE | 313049 | N | NGN | HE | 313060 | N | NGN | HE |
| 313028 | N | NGN | HE | 313039 | N | NGN | HE | 313050 | | NGN | HE | 313061 | | NGN | HE |
| 313029 | N | NGN | HE | 313040 | N | NGN | HE | 313051 | N | NGN | HE | 313062 | N | NGN | HE |
| 313030 | N | NGN | HE | 313041 | N | NGN | HE | 313052 | | NGN | HE | 313063 | | NGN | HE |
| 313031 | N | NGN | HE | 313042 | | NGN | HE | 313053 | | NGN | HE | 313064 | | NGN | HE |

## Class 314 BREL York — DMS + TS(P) + DMS.

**EA2.06 + EH2.11 + EA2.06.**
**Seats: 68 + 76 + 68. Livery: PS**

| | | | | | | | | | | | |
|---|---|---|---|---|---|---|---|---|---|---|---|
| 314201 | PGW | GW | 314205 | PGW | GW | 314209 | PGW | GW | 314213 | PGW | GW |
| 314202 | PGW | GW | 314206 | PGW | GW | 314210 | PGW | GW | 314214 | PGW | GW |
| 314203 | PGW | GW | 314207 | PGW | GW | 314211 | PGW | GW | 314215 | PGW | GW |
| 314204 | PGW | GW | 314208 | PGW | GW | 314212 | PGW | GW | 314216 | PGW | GW |

## Class 315 BREL York — DMS + TS + TS(P) + DMS

**EA2.07 + EH2.16 + EH2.17 + EA2.07.**
**Seats: 74 + 86 + 84 + 74.**

| | | | | | | | | | | | | | | | |
|---|---|---|---|---|---|---|---|---|---|---|---|---|---|---|---|
| 315801 | N | NGE | IL | 315817 | N | NGE | IL | 315833 | N | NGE | IL | 315849 | N | NNE | IL |
| 315802 | N | NGE | IL | 315818 | N | NGE | IL | 315834 | N | NGE | IL | 315850 | N | NNE | IL |
| 315803 | N | NGE | IL | 315819 | N | NGE | IL | 315835 | N | NGE | IL | 315851 | N | NNE | IL |
| 315804 | N | NGE | IL | 315820 | N | NGE | IL | 315836 | N | NGE | IL | 315852 | N | NNE | IL |
| 315805 | | NGE | IL | 315821 | N | NGE | IL | 315837 | N | NGE | IL | 315853 | N | NNE | IL |
| 315806 | N | NGE | IL | 315822 | | NGE | IL | 315838 | N | NGE | IL | 315854 | N | NNE | IL |
| 315807 | | NGE | IL | 315823 | N | NGE | IL | 315839 | N | NGE | IL | 315855 | N | NNE | IL |
| 315808 | N | NGE | IL | 315824 | N | NGE | IL | 315840 | N | NGE | IL | 315856 | N | NNE | IL |
| 315809 | | NGE | IL | 315825 | N | NGE | IL | 315841 | N | NGE | IL | 315857 | N | NNE | IL |
| 315810 | N | NGE | IL | 315826 | N | NGE | IL | 315842 | N | NGE | IL | 315858 | N | NNE | IL |
| 315811 | N | NGE | IL | 315827 | N | NGE | IL | 315843 | N | NGE | IL | 315859 | N | NNE | IL |
| 315812 | N | NGE | IL | 315828 | N | NGE | IL | 315844 | N | NGE | IL | 315860 | N | NNE | IL |
| 315813 | | NGE | IL | 315829 | N | NGE | IL | 315845 | N | NGE | IL | 315861 | N | NNE | IL |
| 315814 | N | NGE | IL | 315830 | N | NGE | IL | 315846 | N | NGE | IL | | | | |
| 315815 | N | NGE | IL | 315831 | N | NGE | IL | 315847 | N | NGE | IL | | | | |
| 315816 | N | NGE | IL | 315832 | N | NGE | IL | 315848 | N | NNE | IL | | | | |

## Class 317/0 BREL Derby and York — DTS + MS + TC(L)/TS(L)† + DTS

**EE2.16 + EC2.02 + EH3.07/EH2.—† + EE2.35.**
**Seats: 74 + 79 + 1st 22 Std 46/68† + 70. Livery: N**

| | | | | | | | | | | | |
|---|---|---|---|---|---|---|---|---|---|---|---|
| 317301 | NGN | HE | 317310† | NML | HE | 317319† | NML | HE | 317328 | NGN | HE |
| 317302 | NGN | HE | 317311† | NML | HE | 317320† | NML | HE | 317329 | NGN | HE |
| 317303 | NGN | HE | 317312† | NML | HE | 317321† | NML | HE | 317330 | NGN | HE |
| 317304 | NGN | HE | 317313† | NML | HE | 317322† | NML | HE | 317331 | NGN | HE |
| 317305 | NGN | HE | 317314† | NML | HE | 317323† | NML | HE | 317332 | NGN | HE |
| 317306 | NGN | HE | 317315† | NGN | HE | 317324† | NML | HE | 317333 | NGN | HE |
| 317307 | NGN | HE | 317316† | NGN | HE | 317325† | NML | HE | 317334 | NGN | HE |
| 317308† | NML | HE | 317317† | NML | HE | 317326† | NML | HE | | | |
| 317309† | NML | HE | 317318† | NML | HE | 317327† | NML | HE | | | |

## Class 317/1 BREL Derby and York — DTS + MS + TC(L) + DTS

**EE2.16 + EC2.02/EC2.08 + EH3.08 + EE2.17/EE2.32/EE2.35†.**
**Seats: 74 + 79 + 1st 22 Std 46 + 70. Livery: N**

| | | | | | | | | | | | |
|---|---|---|---|---|---|---|---|---|---|---|---|
| 317335† | NGN | HE | 317339 | NGN | HE | 317343 | NGN | HE | 317347 | NGN | HE |
| 317336† | NGN | HE | 317340 | NGN | HE | 317344 | NGN | HE | 317348 | NGN | HE |
| 317337 | NGN | HE | 317341 | NGN | HE | 317345 | NGN | HE | | | |
| 317338 | NGN | HE | 317342 | NGN | HE | 317346 | NGN | HE | | | |

## Class 317/2 BREL Derby and York — DTS + MS + TC(L) + DTS

**EE2.24 + EC2.05 + EH3.08 + EE2.25.**
**Seats: 74 + 79 + 1st 22 Std 46 + 74.**

| | | | | | | | | | | | | | | | |
|---|---|---|---|---|---|---|---|---|---|---|---|---|---|---|---|
| 317349 | N | NGN | HE | 317351 | N | NGN | HE | 317353 | | NGN | HE | 317355 | N | NGN | HE |
| 317350 | N | NGN | HE | 317352 | | NGN | HE | 317354 | N | NGN | HE | 317356 | N | NGN | HE |

| | | | |
|---|---|---|---|
| 317357 | | NGN | HE |
| 317358 | N | NGN | HE |
| 317359 | N | NGN | HE |
| 317360 | N | NGN | HE |
| 317361 | N | NGN | HE |
| 317362 | N | NGN | HE |
| 317363 | N | NGN | HE |
| 317364 | N | NGN | HE |
| 317365 | N | NGN | HE |
| 317366 | N | NNE | HE |
| 317367 | N | NNE | HE |
| 317368 | N | NNE | HE |
| 317369 | N | NNE | HE |
| 317370 | N | NNE | HE |
| 317371 | N | NNE | HE |
| 317372 | N | NNE | HE |

## Class 318 BREL Derby and York DTS(L) + MS + DTS

**EE2.27 + EC2.07 + EE2.28.**
**Seats: 66 + 79 + 71. Livery: PS**

| | | |
|---|---|---|
| 318250 | PGW | GW |
| 318251 | PGW | GW |
| 318252 | PGW | GW |
| 318253 | PGW | GW |
| 318254 | PGW | GW |
| 318255 | PGW | GW |
| 318256 | PGW | GW |
| 318257 | PGW | GW |
| 318258 | PGW | GW |
| 318259 | PGW | GW |
| 318260 | PGW | GW |
| 318261 | PGW | GW |
| 318262 | PGW | GW |
| 318263 | PGW | GW |
| 318264 | PGW | GW |
| 318265 | PGW | GW |
| 318266 | PGW | GW |
| 318267 | PGW | GW |
| 318268 | PGW | GW |
| 318269 | PGW | GW |
| 318270 | PGW | GW |

## Class 319/0 BREL York 25kV AC & 750V DC. BDTS + MS + TS(L) + DTS

**EE2.34 + EC2.09 + EH2.34 + EE2.33.**
**Seats: 78 (+ 8 tip up) + 76 + 76 + 81. Livery: N**

| | | |
|---|---|---|
| 319001 | NML | SU |
| 319002 | NSX | SU |
| 319003 | NSX | SU |
| 319004 | NSX | SU |
| 319005 | NSX | SU |
| 319006 | NSX | SU |
| 319007 | NSX | SU |
| 319008 | NSX | SU |
| 319009 | NSX | SU |
| 319010 | NSX | SU |
| 319011 | NSX | SU |
| 319012 | NSX | SU |
| 319013 | NML | SU |
| 319014 | NML | SU |
| 319015 | NML | SU |
| 319016 | NML | SU |
| 319017 | NML | SU |
| 319018 | NML | SU |
| 319019 | NML | SU |
| 319020 | NML | SU |
| 319021 | NML | SU |
| 319022 | NML | SU |
| 319023 | NML | SU |
| 319024 | NML | SU |
| 319025 | NML | SU |
| 319026 | NML | SU |
| 319027 | NML | SU |
| 319028 | NML | SU |
| 319029 | NML | SU |
| 319030 | NML | SU |
| 319031 | NML | SU |
| 319032 | NML | SU |
| 319033 | NML | SU |
| 319034 | NML | SU |
| 319035 | NML | SU |
| 319036 | NML | SU |
| 319037 | NML | SU |
| 319038 | NML | SU |
| 319039 | NML | SU |
| 319040 | NML | SU |
| 319041 | NML | SU |
| 319042 | NML | SU |
| 319043 | NML | SU |
| 319044 | NML | SU |
| 319045 | NML | SU |
| 319046 | NML | SU |
| 319047 | NML | SU |
| 319048 | NML | SU |
| 319049 | NML | SU |
| 319050 | NML | SU |
| 319051 | NML | SU |
| 319052 | NML | SU |
| 319053 | NML | SU |
| 319054 | NML | SU |
| 319055 | NML | SU |
| 319056 | NML | SU |
| 319057 | NML | SU |
| 319058 | NML | SU |
| 319059 | NML | SU |
| 319060 | NML | SU |

## Class 319/1 BREL York 25kV AC & 750V DC. BDTC + MS + TS(L) + DTS

**EE3.10 + EC2.14 + EH2.38 + EE2.40.**
**Seats: 1st 28 Std 37 + 79 + 74 + 78. THAMESLINK. Livery: N**

| | | | |
|---|---|---|---|
| 319161 | 319168 | 319175 | 319182 |
| 319162 | 319169 | 319176 | 319183 |
| 319163 | 319170 | 319177 | 319184 |
| 319164 | 319171 | 319178 | 319185 |
| 319165 | 319172 | 319179 | 319186 |
| 319166 | 319173 | 319180 | |
| 319167 | 319174 | 319181 | |

## Class 320 BREL York DTS(L) + MS + DTS

**EE2.38 + EC2.12 + EE2.39.**
**Seats: 77 + 76 + 77. Livery: PS**

| | | |
|---|---|---|
| 320301 | PGW | GW |
| 320302 | PGW | GW |
| 320303 | PGW | GW |
| 320304 | PGW | GW |
| 320305 | PGW | GW |
| 320306 | PGW | GW |
| 320307 | PGW | GW |
| 320308 | PGW | GW |
| 320309 | PGW | GW |
| 320310 | PGW | GW |
| 320311 | PGW | GW |
| 320312 | PGW | GW |
| 320313 | PGW | GW |
| 320314 | PGW | GW |
| 320315 | PGW | GW |
| 320316 | PGW | GW |
| 320317 | PGW | GW |
| 320318 | PGW | GW |
| 320319 | PGW | GW |
| 320320 | PGW | GW |
| 320321 | PGW | GW |
| 320322 | PGW | GW |

## Class 321/3 BREL York BDTS + MS + TS(L) + DTC

**EE2.36 + EC2.10 + EE3.08 + EH2.35**
**Seats:78 + 79 + 74 + 1st 16 Std 56. Livery: N**

| | | |
|---|---|---|
| 321301 | NGE | IL |
| 321302 | NGE | IL |
| 321303 | NGE | IL |
| 321304 | NGE | IL |
| 321305 | NGE | IL |
| 321306 | NGE | IL |
| 321307 | NGE | IL |
| 321308 | NGE | IL |
| 321309 | NGE | IL |
| 321310 | NGE | IL |
| 321311 | NGE | IL |
| 321312 | NGE | IL |
| 321313 | NGE | IL |
| 321314 | NGE | IL |
| 321315 | NGE | IL |
| 321316 | NGE | IL |
| 321317 | NGE | IL |
| 321318 | NGE | IL |
| 321319 | NGE | IL |
| 321320 | NGE | IL |
| 321321 | NGE | IL |
| 321322 | NGE | IL |
| 321323 | NGE | IL |
| 321324 | NNE | IL |
| 321325 | NNE | IL |
| 321326 | NGE | IL |
| 321327 | NGE | IL |
| 321328 | NGE | IL |

| | | | | | | | | | | | |
|---|---|---|---|---|---|---|---|---|---|---|---|
| 321329 | NGE | IL | 321339 | NNE | IL | 321349 | NGE | IL | 321359 | NGE | IL |
| 321330 | NGE | IL | 321340 | NNE | IL | 321350 | NGE | IL | 321360 | NGE | IL |
| 321331 | NGE | IL | 321341 | NNE | IL | 321351 | NGE | IL | 321361 | NGE | IL |
| 321332 | NGE | IL | 321342 | NNE | IL | 321352 | NGE | IL | 321362 | NGE | IL |
| 321333 | NGE | IL | 321343 | NNE | IL | 321353 | NGE | IL | 321363 | NGE | IL |
| 321334 | NGE | IL | 321344 | NNE | IL | 321354 | NGE | IL | 321364 | NGE | IL |
| 321335 | NGE | IL | 321345 | NNE | IL | 321355 | NGE | IL | 321365 | NGE | IL |
| 321336 | NGE | IL | 321346 | NNE | IL | 321356 | NGE | IL | 321366 | NGE | IL |
| 321337 | NGE | IL | 321347 | NGE | IL | 321357 | NGE | IL | | | |
| 321338 | NGE | IL | 321348 | NGE | IL | 321358 | NGE | IL | | | |

## Class 321/4 BREL York — BDTS + MS + TS(L) + DTC

**EE2.36 + EC2.10 + EH2.35 + EE3.09.**
**Seats: 78 + 79 + 74 + 1st 28 Std 40. Livery: N**

| | | | | | | | | | | | |
|---|---|---|---|---|---|---|---|---|---|---|---|
| 321401 | NNW | BY | 321413 | NNW | BY | 321425 | NNW | BY | 321437 | NNW | BY |
| 321402 | NNW | BY | 321414 | NNW | BY | 321426 | NNW | BY | 321438 | NNW | BY |
| 321403 | NNW | BY | 321415 | NNW | BY | 321427 | NNW | BY | 321439 | NNW | BY |
| 321404 | NNW | BY | 321416 | NNW | BY | 321428 | NNW | BY | 321440 | NNW | BY |
| 321405 | NNW | BY | 321417 | NNW | BY | 321429 | NNW | BY | 321441 | NNW | BY |
| 321406 | NNW | BY | 321418 | NNW | BY | 321430 | NNW | BY | 321442 | NNW | BY |
| 321407 | NNW | BY | 321419 | NNW | BY | 321431 | NNW | BY | 321443 | NNW | BY |
| 321408 | NNW | BY | 321420 | NNW | BY | 321432 | NNW | BY | 321444 | NNW | BY |
| 321409 | NNW | BY | 321421 | NNW | BY | 321433 | NNW | BY | 321445 | NNW | BY |
| 321410 | NNW | BY | 321422 | NNW | BY | 321434 | NNW | BY | 321446 | NNW | BY |
| 321411 | NNW | BY | 321423 | NNW | BY | 321435 | NNW | BY | 321447 | NNW | BY |
| 321412 | NNW | BY | 321424 | NNW | BY | 321436 | NNW | BY | 321448 | NNW | BY |

## Class 322 BREL York — BDTS + MS + TS(L) + DTC

**EE2.41 + EC2.15 + EH2.39 + EE3.13 .**
**Seats: 65 + 70 + 60 + 1st 35 Std 22. STANSTED EXPRESS. Livery: BA**

| | | | | | | | | | | | |
|---|---|---|---|---|---|---|---|---|---|---|---|
| 322481 | NNE | IL | 322483 | NNE | IL | 322484 | NNE | IL | 322485 | NNE | IL |
| 322482 | NNE | IL | | | | | | | | | |

## Class 323.

**Proposed new units for Provincial Sector services. Eighteen three-car for Birmingham Cross-City line electrification. Extra units to be purchased to replace Class 304 units and possibly for West Yorkshire PTE services.**

Looking very different from its days in passenger service, Parcels Sector EMU No 302991 stands at Ilford Depot (IL) in red livery with yellow piping (R). Surplus Class 307 units may be similarly converted this year.

# ELECTRIC MULTIPLE-UNITS: 750V DC THIRD RAIL.

**THIS STOCK IS LISTED ONLY BY UNIT NUMBERS. VEHICLE NUMBER INFORMATION IS IN ACCORDANCE WITH THAT PUBLISHED EARLY IN 1989 EXCEPT AS SHOWN ON PAGE 96.**

**NSE SOUTHERN REGION PASSENGER UNITS SECTOR CODES:**

| Depot: | Pool. | | | | | | | | | | |
|---|---|---|---|---|---|---|---|---|---|---|---|
| BI | NSX | GI | NKS | RY | NSS | SL | IVG | WC | NSB/NSS | HQ | Stored |
| EH | NSS | RE | NKC | SG | NKS | SU | NSL | WD | NSB | | |

## Class 421/1 (4–CIG) BR York DTC(L) + MBS + TS + DTC(L)

**EE3.64 + ED2.60 + EH2.75 + EE3.63.**
**Seats: 1st 18 Std 36 + 56 + 72 + 1st 24 Std 28.**
**(† both DTCs EE3.64 1st 18 Std 36). Livery: N**

| | | | | | | | | | | | |
|---|---|---|---|---|---|---|---|---|---|---|---|
| 1100 | BI | 1110† | BI | 1114 | BI | 1118 | BI | 1123 | BI | 1127 | BI |
| 1105 | BI | 1111 | BI | 1116 | BI | | | | | | |

## Class 421/2 (4–CIG) BREL York DTC(L) + MBS + TS + DTC(L)

**EE3.64 + ED2.60 + EH2.75 + EE3.63.**
**Seats: 1st 18 Std 36 + 56 + 72 + 1st 24 Std 28.**

| | | | | | | | | | | | | | | | | | |
|---|---|---|---|---|---|---|---|---|---|---|---|---|---|---|---|---|---|
| 1201 | N | BI | 1213 | N | WD | 1224 | N | WD | 1257 | N | BI | 1272 | | BI | 1292 | N | BI |
| 1202 | N | BI | 1214 | N | WD | 1225 | N | WD | 1258 | N | BI | 1274 | | BI | 1293 | N | BI |
| 1203 | N | BI | 1215 | N | WD | 1226 | N | WD | 1259 | N | BI | 1275 | N | BI | 1294 | N | BI |
| 1204 | N | BI | 1216 | N | WD | 1243 | | WD | 1260 | N | BI | 1277 | N | BI | 1295 | N | BI |
| 1205 | N | BI | 1217 | N | WD | 1245 | N | WD | 1261 | N | BI | 1281 | N | BI | | | |
| 1206 | N | BI | 1218 | N | WD | 1246 | N | WD | 1262 | N | BI | 1285 | N | BI | | | |
| 1208 | N | WD | 1219 | N | WD | 1247 | N | WD | 1263 | | BI | 1286 | N | BI | | | |
| 1209 | N | WD | 1220 | N | WD | 1249 | N | WD | 1266 | N | BI | 1287 | N | BI | | | |
| 1210 | N | WD | 1221 | N | WD | 1253 | N | WD | 1268 | N | BI | 1288 | N | BI | | | |
| 1211 | N | WD | 1222 | N | WD | 1255 | N | BI | 1270 | N | BI | 1289 | N | BI | | | |
| 1212 | N | WD | 1223 | N | WD | 1256 | N | BI | 1271 | N | BI | 1291 | N | BI | | | |

## Class 421/5 (4-CIG) BREL York DTC(L) + MBS + TS + DTC(L)

**EE3.64 + ED2.60 + EH2.75 + EE3.63.**
**Seats: 1st 18 Std 36 + 56 + 72 + 1st 18 Std 36. GREYHOUNDS. Livery: N**

| | | | | | | | | | | | |
|---|---|---|---|---|---|---|---|---|---|---|---|
| 1301 | EH | 1304 | EH | 1307 | EH | 1310 | EH | 1313 | EH | 1316 | EH |
| 1302 | EH | 1305 | EH | 1308 | EH | 1311 | EH | 1314 | EH | | |
| 1303 | EH | 1306 | EH | 1309 | EH | 1312 | EH | 1315 | EH | | |

## Class 411/4 (4-CEP) BR Eastleigh DMS + TBC(L) + TS(L) + DMS

**EA2.63 + EJ3.61 + EH2.82/EH2.84† + EA2.63★/EA2.64 + EJ3.61 + EH2.82/EH2.84† + EA2.64**
**Seats: 64 + 1st 24 Std 6 + 64 + 64.**

| | | | | | | | | | | | | | | | | | |
|---|---|---|---|---|---|---|---|---|---|---|---|---|---|---|---|---|---|
| 1501★ | N | RE | 1517 | L | RE | 1533† | N | RE | 1549 | L | RE | 1565 | L | RE | 1581 | L | RE |
| 1502★ | L | RE | 1518 | L | RE | 1534† | N | RE | 1550 | L | RE | 1566 | L | RE | 1582† | L | RE |
| 1503★ | L | RE | 1519 | L | RE | 1535† | L | RE | 1551 | L | RE | 1567 | L | RE | 1583 | L | RE |
| 1504★† | L | RE | 1520 | L | RE | 1536† | L | RE | 1552 | L | RE | 1568 | L | RE | 1584 | L | RE |
| 1505★ | N | RE | 1521 | L | RE | 1537 | L | RE | 1553 | L | RE | 1569 | L | RE | 1585 | L | RE |
| 1506 | N | RE | 1522 | L | RE | 1538 | N | RE | 1554 | L | RE | 1570 | L | RE | 1586 | L | RE |
| 1507 | N | RE | 1523 | L | RE | 1539† | L | RE | 1555 | L | RE | 1571† | N | RE | 1587† | L | RE |
| 1508 | N | RE | 1524 | L | RE | 1540 | N | RE | 1556 | L | RE | 1572 | L | RE | 1588 | L | RE |
| 1509 | N | RE | 1525 | L | RE | 1541† | N | RE | 1557 | L | RE | 1573 | L | RE | 1589 | L | RE |
| 1510 | N | RE | 1526 | L | RE | 1542† | L | RE | 1558 | L | RE | 1574† | L | RE | 1590 | L | RE |
| 1511 | N | RE | 1527 | L | RE | 1543 | L | RE | 1559 | L | RE | 1575 | L | RE | 1591 | L | RE |
| 1512 | N | RE | 1528 | L | RE | 1544 | L | RE | 1560 | N | RE | 1576 | L | RE | 1592 | L | RE |
| 1513 | N | RE | 1529 | L | RE | 1545 | N | RE | 1561 | N | RE | 1577 | L | RE | 1593 | L | RE |
| 1514 | N | RE | 1530 | L | RE | 1546 | L | RE | 1562 | N | RE | 1578 | L | RE | 1594 | L | RE |
| 1515 | N | RE | 1531 | L | RE | 1547 | L | RE | 1563 | L | RE | 1579 | L | RE | 1595 | L | RE |
| 1516 | N | RE | 1532† | N | RE | 1548 | L | RE | 1564 | L | RE | 1580 | N | RE | 1596 | N | RE |

| | | | | | | | | | | | | | | | | | |
|---|---|---|---|---|---|---|---|---|---|---|---|---|---|---|---|---|---|
| 1597 | L | RE | 1602 | L | RE | 1606 | N | RE | 1610 | L | RE | 1614 | L | RE | 1618 | L | RE |
| 1598 | N | RE | 1603 | N | RE | 1607 | N | RE | 1611 | L | RE | 1615 | L | RE | 1619 | L | RE |
| 1599 | L | RE | 1604 | N | RE | 1608 | N | RE | 1612 | L | RE | 1616 | L | RE | 1620 | N | RE |
| 1600 | N | RE | 1605 | N | RE | 1609 | L | RE | 1613 | L | RE | 1617 | L | RE | 1621 | N | RE |
| 1601 | N | RE | | | | | | | | | | | | | | | |

## Class 421/3 (4-CIG) BR York DTC(L) + MBS + TS + DTC(L)

**EE3.64 + ED2.60 + EH2.75 + EE3.63.**
**Seats: 1st 18 Std 36 + 56 + 72 + 1st 18 Std 36. Livery: N**

| | | | | | | | | | | | |
|---|---|---|---|---|---|---|---|---|---|---|---|
| 1701 | BI | 1707 | BI | 1713 | BI | 1719 | BI | 1725 | BI | 1731 | BI |
| 1702 | BI | 1708 | BI | 1714 | BI | 1720 | BI | 1726 | BI | 1732 | BI |
| 1703 | BI | 1709 | BI | 1715 | BI | 1721 | BI | 1727 | BI | | |
| 1704 | BI | 1710 | BI | 1716 | BI | 1722 | BI | 1728 | BI | | |
| 1705 | BI | 1711 | BI | 1717 | BI | 1723 | BI | 1729 | BI | | |
| 1706 | BI | 1712 | BI | 1718 | BI | 1724 | BI | 1730 | BI | | |

## Class 421/6 (4-CIG) BR/BREL York DTC(L) + MBS + TS + DTC(L)

**EE3.64 + ED2.60 + EH2.75 + EE3.63.**
**Seats: 1st 18 Std 36 + 56 + 72 + 1st 24 Std 28. Livery: N**

| | | | | | | | | | | | |
|---|---|---|---|---|---|---|---|---|---|---|---|
| 1751 | BI | 1753 | BI | 1755 | BI | 1757 | BI | 1759 | BI | 1761 | BI |
| 1752 | BI | 1754 | BI | 1756 | BI | 1758 | BI | 1760 | BI | 1762 | BI |

## Class 421/4 (4-CIG) BREL York DTC(L) + MBS + TS + DTC(L)

**EE3.64 + ED2.61 + EH2.75 + EE3.63.**
**Seats: 1st 18 Std 36 + 56 + 72 + 1st 18 Std 36. Livery: N**

| | | | | | | | | | | | |
|---|---|---|---|---|---|---|---|---|---|---|---|
| 1801 | BI | 1805 | BI | 1808 | BI | 1811 | BI | 1831 | BI | 1833 | BI |
| 1803 | BI | 1806 | BI | 1809 | BI | 1812 | BI | 1832 | BI | | |
| 1804 | BI | 1807 | BI | 1810 | BI | 1813 | BI | | | | |

## Class 431 (6-REP) BR York DMS + TBS(L) + TC(L) + TC(L) + TBS(L) + DTS

**EA2.60 + EJ2.60 + EH3.62 + EH3.62 + EJ2.60 + EE2.66.**
**Seats: 64 + 32 + 1st 36 Std 8 + 1st 36 Std 8 + 32 + 64. Livery: N**

| | | | | | | | | | | | |
|---|---|---|---|---|---|---|---|---|---|---|---|
| 1901 | | 1902 | BM | 1903 | BM | 1904 | BM | 1905 | BM | 1906 | BM |

## Class 422/2 (4-BIG) BR York DTC(L) + MBS + TBRS + DTC(L)

**EE3.64 + ED2.60 + EN2.60 + EE3.63.**
**Seats: 1st 18 Std 36 + 56 + 40 + 1st 24 Std 28.**

| | | | | | | | | | | | | | | | | | |
|---|---|---|---|---|---|---|---|---|---|---|---|---|---|---|---|---|---|
| 2203 | N | BI | 2205 | | BI | 2206 | | BI | 2208 | N | BI | 2209 | N | BI | 2210 | N | BI |
| 2204 | | BI | | | | | | | | | | | | | | | |

## Class 422/3 (4-BIG) BREL/BR York DTC(L) + MBS + TBRS + DTC(L)

**EE3.64 + ED2.60 + EN2.60 + EE3.63.**
**Seats: 1st 18 Std 36 + 56 + 40 + 1st 24 Std 28. Livery: N**

| | | | | | | | | | | | |
|---|---|---|---|---|---|---|---|---|---|---|---|
| 2251 | BI | 2253 | BI | 2255 | BI | 2257 | BI | 2259 | BI | 2261 | BI |
| 2252 | BI | 2254 | BI | 2256 | BI | 2258 | BI | 2260 | BI | 2262 | BI |

## Class 412/3 (4-BEP) BR Eastleigh DMS + TBC(L) + TRBS(L) + DMS

**EA2.64 + EJ3.61 + EN2.61 + EA2.64.**
**Seats: 64 + 1st 24 Std 6 + 33 + 64. Livery: N**

| | | | | | | | | | | | |
|---|---|---|---|---|---|---|---|---|---|---|---|
| 2301 | EH | 2303 | EH | 2304 | EH | 2305 | EH | 2306 | EH | 2307 | EH |
| 2302 | EH | | | | | | | | | | |

## Class 442 (5-WES) BREL Derby DTF(L) + TS(L) + MBLS + TS(L) + DTS(L)

**EE1.60 + EH2.88 + ED2.65 + EH2.89 + EE2.73.**
**Seats: 1st 50 + 80 + 14 + 78 + 78. Livery: N**

| | | | | | | | | | | | |
|---|---|---|---|---|---|---|---|---|---|---|---|
| 2401 | BM | 2405 | BM | 2409 | BM | 2413 | BM | 2417 | BM | 2421 | BM |
| 2402 | BM | 2406 | BM | 2410 | BM | 2414 | BM | 2418 | BM | 2422 | BM |
| 2403 | BM | 2407 | BM | 2411 | BM | 2415 | BM | 2419 | BM | 2423 | BM |
| 2404 | BM | 2408 | BM | 2412 | BM | 2416 | BM | 2420 | BM | 2424 | BM |

## Class 423/0 (4-VEP) BR Derby & York DTC(L) + MBS + TS + DTC(L)

**EE3.65 + ED2.62 + EH2.78 + EE3.66+/EE3.66 + ED2.62 + EH2.78 + EE3.66$/EE3.68 + ED2.63 + EH2.76 + EE3.71‡/EE3.68 + ED2.63 + EH2.83 + EE3.68†/EE3.71 + ED2.61 + EH2.76 + EE3.71●**
**Seats: 1st 18 Std 46† + 58 + 98 + 1st 18 Std 46†‡●/1st 24 Std 34 + 58 + 90 + 1st 24 Std 34+. Livery: N**

| | | | | | | | | | | | |
|---|---|---|---|---|---|---|---|---|---|---|---|
| 3001● | EH | 3020● | EH | 3092$ | BI | 3144† | WD | 3163† | RE | 3180† | RE |
| 3002● | EH | 3026● | BM | 3093$ | BI | 3147† | BI | 3164† | RE | 3181† | RE |
| 3003● | EH | 3030● | EH | 3094$ | BI | 3148† | BI | 3165† | RE | 3182† | RE |
| 3006● | EH | 3032● | EH | 3095$ | BI | 3149† | BI | 3166† | RE | 3183† | RE |
| 3007● | EH | 3034● | EH | 3096$ | BI | 3152† | BI | 3167† | RE | 3184† | RE |
| 3008● | EH | 3035● | EH | 3097$ | BI | 3153† | WD | 3169† | RE | 3185† | RE |
| 3009● | EH | 3037● | EH | 3098+ | BI | 3154† | WD | 3170† | RE | 3186† | RE |
| 3010● | EH | 3046● | EH | 3099$ | BI | 3155† | WD | 3171† | RE | 3187† | RE |
| 3012● | EH | 3068† | EH | 3113† | BI | 3156† | WD | 3172† | RE | 3188† | RE |
| 3013● | EH | 3069† | WD | 3120† | BI | 3157† | WD | 3173† | RE | 3189† | RE |
| 3014● | EH | 3075† | WD | 3121† | BI | 3158† | WD | 3175† | RE | 3190† | RE |
| 3015● | EH | 3077† | WD | 3125† | BI | 3159† | WD | 3176† | RE | 3191† | RE |
| 3017● | EH | 3078† | WD | 3134† | BI | 3160† | WD | 3177† | RE | 3192† | RE |
| 3018● | EH | 3080† | BI | 3139† | BI | 3161† | RE | 3178† | RE | 3193† | RE |
| 3019● | EH | 3088$ | BI | 3140 | BI | 3162† | RE | 3179† | RE | 3194† | RE |

## Class 413/2 (4-CAP) BR Eastleigh DTC(L)/DTS(L)† + MBS + MLS + DTS(L)

**EE3.61/EE2.–† + EB2.69 + EB2.69 + EE2.21.**
**Seats: 1st 19 Std 50/Std 76 + 84 + 84 + 69.**

| | | | | | | | | | | | | | | | | | |
|---|---|---|---|---|---|---|---|---|---|---|---|---|---|---|---|---|---|
| 3201† | N | GI | 3204† | N | GI | 3206† | N | GI | 3208† | N | GI | 3210 | | HQ | 3212 | | GI |
| 3202† | N | GI | 3205† | N | GI | 3207† | N | GI | 3209† | N | GI | 3211† | N | GI | 3213 | | GI |
| 3203† | N | GI | | | | | | | | | | | | | | | |

## Class 413/3 (4-CAP) BR Eastleigh DTC(L)/DTS(L)† + MBS + MLS + DTS(L)

**EE3.62/EE2.–† + EB2.70 + EB2.70 + EE2.22.**
**Seats: 1st 19 Std 50/Std 76 + 84 + 84 + 69.**

| | | | | | | | | | | | | | | | | | |
|---|---|---|---|---|---|---|---|---|---|---|---|---|---|---|---|---|---|
| 3301† | N | GI | 3303† | N | GI | 3305† | N | GI | 3307† | | GI | 3309 | | HQ | 3311 | N | GI |
| 3302† | N | GI | 3304† | N | GI | 3306† | N | GI | 3308† | N | HQ | 3310 | | GI | | | |

## Class 423/1 (4-VEP) BR Derby & York DTC(L) + MBS + TS + DTC(L)

**EE3.73 + ED2.66 + EH2.91 + EE3.73.**
**Seats: 1st 18 Std 46 + 76 + 98 + 1st 18 Std 46. Livery: N**

| | | | | | | | | | | | |
|---|---|---|---|---|---|---|---|---|---|---|---|
| 3404 | EH | 3438 | BI | 3459 | WD | 3479 | WD | 3499 | RE | 3519 | |
| 3405 | EH | 3439 | BI | 3460 | BI | 3480 | WD | 3500 | RE | 3520 | |
| 3411 | EH | 3440 | BI | 3461 | BI | 3481 | WD | 3501 | BI | 3521 | |
| 3416 | EH | 3442 | BI | 3462 | BI | 3482 | WD | 3502 | BI | 3522 | |
| 3421 | RE | 3443 | BI | 3463 | BI | 3483 | WD | 3503 | BI | 3523 | |
| 3422 | RE | 3444 | BI | 3464 | BI | 3484 | WD | 3504 | BI | 3524 | |
| 3423 | RE | 3445 | RE | 3465 | BI | 3485 | WD | 3505 | BI | 3525 | |
| 3424 | RE | 3446 | RE | 3466 | WD | 3486 | WD | 3506 | BI | 3526 | |
| 3425 | WD | 3447 | RE | 3467 | WD | 3487 | WD | 3507 | BI | 3527 | |
| 3426 | WD | 3448 | RE | 3468 | WD | 3488 | WD | 3508 | WD | 3528 | |
| 3427 | WD | 3449 | RE | 3469 | WD | 3489 | WD | 3509 | WD | 3529 | |
| 3428 | WD | 3450 | RE | 3470 | WD | 3490 | WD | 3510 | WD | 3530 | |
| 3429 | WD | 3451 | RE | 3471 | RE | 3491 | RE | 3511 | WD | 3531 | |
| 3430 | WD | 3452 | RE | 3472 | RE | 3492 | RE | 3512 | BI | 3532 | |
| 3431 | WD | 3453 | RE | 3473 | RE | 3493 | RE | 3513 | BI | 3533 | |
| 3432 | WD | 3454 | RE | 3474 | RE | 3494 | RE | 3514 | BI | 3534 | |
| 3433 | WD | 3455 | WD | 3475 | RE | 3495 | RE | 3515 | BI | 3535 | |
| 3434 | WD | 3456 | WD | 3476 | RE | 3496 | RE | 3516 | WD | 3536 | |
| 3435 | BI | 3457 | WD | 3477 | RE | 3497 | RE | 3517 | BI | 3537 | |
| 3436 | BI | 3458 | WD | 3478 | BI | 3498 | RE | 3518 | | 3538 | |
| 3437 | BI | | | | | | | | | | |

## Class 414/2 (2-HAP) BR Eastleigh — DMBS + DTC(L)

**EE2.69 + EE3.61.**
**Seats: 84 + 1st 19 Std 50.**

| | | |
|---|---|---|
| 4201 | | WD |

## Class 414/3 (2-HAP) BR Eastleigh — DMBS + DTC(L)

**EE2.70 + EE3.62.**
**Seats: 84 + 1st 19 Std 50.**

| | | | | | | | | | | | | | | | | | |
|---|---|---|---|---|---|---|---|---|---|---|---|---|---|---|---|---|---|
| 4301 | | WD | 4305 | | WD | 4309 | N | WD | 4313 | N | WD | 4317 | N | WD | 4321 | N | WD |
| 4302 | N | WD | 4306 | N | WD | 4310 | | WD | 4314 | N | WD | 4318 | N | WD | 4322 | N | WD |
| 4303 | N | WD | 4307 | N | WD | 4311 | N | WD | 4315 | N | WD | 4319 | N | WD | | | |
| 4304 | N | WD | 4308 | N | WD | 4312 | | WD | 4316 | | WD | 4320 | | WD | | | |

## Classes 465/0 and 465/2 4-car NETWORKER 1

**BREL York (units 465001-50) and Metro-Cammell (units 465201-50) for delivery in 1991. Additional units to be ordered. Allocation SG, Livery N.**

## Class 415/1 (4-EPB) BR Eastleigh — DMBS + TS + TS + DMBS

**EB2.66 + EH2.70 + EH2.70 + EB2.66/EB2.67 + EH2.70 + EH2.70 + EB2.67‡/EB2.69 + EH2.70 + EH2.70 + EB2.66†/EB2.69 + EH2.70 + EH2.70 + EB2.69$.**
**Seats: 82 + 102 + 102 + 82†/84 + 102 + 102 + 82/84 + 102 + 102 + 84‡.**

| | | | | | | | | | | | |
|---|---|---|---|---|---|---|---|---|---|---|---|
| 5104 | SG | 5145 | SG | 5169† | SG | 5196 | SG | 5230 | SG | 5269 | SG |
| 5107 | HQ | 5146 | SG | 5170 | SG | 5201 | SG | 5231 | SG | 5270 | SG |
| 5113 | SG | 5148 | SG | 5173 | SG | 5202 | SG | 5232 | SG | 5271 | SG |
| 5114 | SG | 5150 | SG | 5174 | SG | 5209 | SG | 5240 | SG | 5272 | SG |
| 5115 | SG | 5153 | SG | 5176 | SG | 5210 | SG | 5242 | SG | 5273 | SG |
| 5121 | SG | 5154 | SG | 5177 | SG | 5213 | SG | 5243 | SG | 5274 | HQ |
| 5124 | SG | 5155 | SG | 5182 | SG | 5217 | SG | 5248 | SG | 5275 | SG |
| 5126 | SG | 5156 | SG | 5185 | SG | 5220 | SG | 5261$ | SG | 5276 | SG |
| 5131 | SG | 5157 | SG | 5189 | SG | 5222 | SG | 5264‡ | SG | 5277 | SG |
| 5133 | SG | 5159 | SG | 5190 | SG | 5223 | SG | 5265 | SG | | |
| 5134† | SG | 5160 | SG | 5191 | HQ | 5226 | SG | 5266 | SG | | |
| 5138 | SG | 5166 | HQ | 5194 | SG | 5228 | HQ | 5267 | SG | | |
| 5139 | SG | 5168 | SG | 5195 | SG | 5229 | SG | 5268 | SG | | |

## Class 415/4 (4-EPB) BR Eastleigh — DMBS + TS + TS + DMBS

**EB2.77 + EH2.79 + EH2.79 + EB2.77★/EB2.77 + EH2.81 + EH2.79 + EB2.77‡/ EB2.77 + EH2.80 + EH2.80 + EB2.77$/EB2.77 + EH2.81 + EH2.81 + EB2.77†/ EB2.77 + EH2.80 + EH2.81 + EB2.77/EB2.78 + EH2.80 + EH2.81 + EB2.78+.**
**Seats: 82 + 102 + 102 + 82.**

| | | | | | | | | | | | | | | | | | |
|---|---|---|---|---|---|---|---|---|---|---|---|---|---|---|---|---|---|
| 5401† | | SU | 5418 | | SU | 5434 | | SU | 5450★ | | SG | 5466$ | | SG | 5482$ | | SG |
| 5402‡ | | SU | 5419 | N | SU | 5435 | | SU | 5451★ | | SG | 5467$ | | SG | 5483$ | | SG |
| 5403$ | | SU | 5420 | N | SU | 5436 | | SU | 5452★ | | SG | 5468$ | | SG | 5484$ | | SG |
| 5404+ | | SU | 5421 | N | SU | 5437 | | SU | 5453★ | | SG | 5469$ | | SG | 5485$ | N | SG |
| 5405 | N | SU | 5422 | N | SU | 5438 | | SU | 5454★ | N | SG | 5470$ | | SG | 5486 | N | SG |
| 5406 | | SU | 5423 | | SU | 5439 | | SU | 5455$ | | SG | 5471$ | | SG | 5487 | N | SG |
| 5407 | N | SU | 5424 | N | SU | 5440 | | SU | 5456$ | | SG | 5472$ | | SG | 5488 | N | SG |
| 5408 | N | SU | 5425‡ | N | SU | 5441 | | SU | 5457 | | SG | 5473$ | | SG | 5489 | N | SG |
| 5409 | N | SU | 5426 | N | SU | 5442 | | SG | 5458 | | SG | 5474$ | | SG | 5490† | N | SG |
| 5410 | N | SU | 5427 | | SU | 5443 | | SG | 5459 | | SG | 5475$ | | SG | 5491† | N | SG |
| 5411 | N | SU | 5428 | N | SU | 5444 | | SG | 5460 | | SG | 5476$ | | SG | 5492† | N | SG |
| 5412‡ | | SU | 5429 | | SU | 5445 | | SG | 5461 | | SG | 5477$ | | SG | 5493† | N | SG |
| 5413 | | SU | 5430 | | SU | 5446‡ | | SG | 5462 | | SG | 5478$ | | SG | 5494† | N | SG |
| 5414 | | SU | 5431 | | SU | 5447‡ | | SG | 5463 | | SG | 5479$ | | SG | 5495† | N | SG |
| 5415 | | SU | 5432 | N | SU | 5448‡ | | SG | 5464$ | | SG | 5480$ | | SG | 5496† | N | SG |
| 5416 | N | SU | 5433 | N | SU | 5449† | | SG | 5465$ | | SG | 5481$ | | SG | 5497† | N | SG |
| 5417 | N | SU | | | | | | | | | | | | | | | |

## Class 415/5 (4-EPB{COM}) BR Eastleigh — DMBS + TS + TS + DMBS

**EB2.66 + EH2.67 + EH2.68 + EB2.66†/EB2.66 + EH2.68 + EH2.68 + EB2.66**
**Seats: 82 + 108 + 120 + 82/82 + 120 + 120 + 82†.**

| | | | | | | | | | | | |
|---|---|---|---|---|---|---|---|---|---|---|---|
| 5501 | SG | 5510† | SG | 5516 | SG | 5520 | SG | 5524 | SG | 5528 | SG |
| 5502 | SG | 5513 | SG | 5517 | SG | 5521 | SG | 5525 | SG | 5529 | SG |
| 5503 | SG | 5514 | SG | 5518 | SG | 5522 | SG | 5526 | SG | 5531† | SG |
| 5508 | SG | 5515 | SG | 5519 | SG | 5523 | SG | 5527 | SG | | |

## Class 415/6 (4-EPB) BR Eastleigh — DMBS + TS + TS + DMBS

**EB2.71 + EH2.71 + EH2.71 + EB2.72.**
**Seats: 84 + 112 + 112 + 84.**

| | | | | | | | | | | | | | | | | | |
|---|---|---|---|---|---|---|---|---|---|---|---|---|---|---|---|---|---|
| 5601 | | SG | 5605 | | SG | 5611 | N | SG | 5614 | N | SG | 5617 | N | SG | 5620 | N | SG |
| 5602 | N | SG | 5606 | N | SG | 5612 | N | SG | 5615 | N | SG | 5618 | N | SG | 5621 | N | SG |
| 5603 | | SG | 5610 | N | SG | 5613 | N | SG | 5616 | N | SG | 5619 | N | SG | 5622 | N | SG |
| 5604 | | SG | | | | | | | | | | | | | | | |

## Class 415/7 (4-EPB Express) BR Eastleigh — DMBS + TS + TS + DMBS

**EB2.71 + EH2.71 + EH2.71 + EB2.72.**
**Seats: 84 + 112 + 112 + 84. Livery: N**

| | | | | | | | | | | | |
|---|---|---|---|---|---|---|---|---|---|---|---|
| 5623 | SG | 5624 | SG | 5625 | SG | 5626 | SG | 5627 | SG | 5628 | SG |

## Class 455/7 BREL York — DTS + MS + TS + DTS

**EE2.18 + EC2.03 + EH2.19 + EE2.18.**
**Seats: 74 + 84 + 86 + 74.**

| | | | | | | | | | | | | | | | | | |
|---|---|---|---|---|---|---|---|---|---|---|---|---|---|---|---|---|---|
| 5701 | N | WD | 5709 | N | WD | 5716 | N | WD | 5723 | N | WD | 5730 | N | WD | 5737 | | WD |
| 5702 | N | WD | 5710 | N | WD | 5717 | N | WD | 5724 | | WD | 5731 | N | WD | 5738 | | WD |
| 5703 | N | WD | 5711 | N | WD | 5718 | N | WD | 5725 | N | WD | 5732 | N | WD | 5739 | | WD |
| 5704 | N | WD | 5712 | N | WD | 5719 | N | WD | 5726 | N | WD | 5733 | | WD | 5740 | N | WD |
| 5705 | N | WD | 5713 | N | WD | 5720 | N | WD | 5727 | N | WD | 5734 | | WD | 5741 | N | WD |
| 5706 | N | WD | 5714 | N | WD | 5721 | N | WD | 5728 | | WD | 5735 | | WD | 5742 | N | WD |
| 5707 | N | WD | 5715 | N | WD | 5722 | N | WD | 5729 | | WD | 5736 | | WD | 5743 | | WD |
| 5708 | N | WD | | | | | | | | | | | | | | | |

## Class 455/8 BREL York — DTS + MS + TS + DTS

**EE2.18 + EC2.03 + EH2.21 + EE2.18.**
**Seats: 74 + 84 + 84 + 74. Livery: N**

| | | | | | | | | | | | |
|---|---|---|---|---|---|---|---|---|---|---|---|
| 5801 | SU | 5814 | SU | 5827 | SU | 5840 | WD | 5853 | WD | 5866 | WD |
| 5802 | SU | 5815 | SU | 5828 | SU | 5841 | WD | 5854 | WD | 5867 | WD |
| 5803 | SU | 5816 | SU | 5829 | SU | 5842 | WD | 5855 | WD | 5868 | WD |
| 5804 | SU | 5817 | SU | 5830 | SU | 5843 | WD | 5856 | WD | 5869 | WD |
| 5805 | SU | 5818 | SU | 5831 | SU | 5844 | WD | 5857 | WD | 5870 | WD |
| 5806 | SU | 5819 | SU | 5832 | SU | 5845 | WD | 5858 | WD | 5871 | WD |
| 5807 | SU | 5820 | SU | 5833 | SU | 5846 | WD | 5859 | WD | 5872 | WD |
| 5808 | SU | 5821 | SU | 5834 | SU | 5847 | WD | 5860 | WD | 5873 | WD |
| 5809 | SU | 5822 | SU | 5835 | SU | 5848 | WD | 5861 | WD | 5874 | WD |
| 5810 | SU | 5823 | SU | 5836 | SU | 5849 | WD | 5862 | WD | | |
| 5811 | SU | 5824 | SU | 5837 | SU | 5850 | SU | 5863 | WD | | |
| 5812 | SU | 5825 | SU | 5838 | WD | 5851 | WD | 5864 | WD | | |
| 5813 | SU | 5826 | SU | 5839 | WD | 5852 | WD | 5865 | WD | | |

## Class 455/9 BREL York — DTS + MS + TS + DTS/DTS + MS + MS + DTS†

**EE2.26 + EC2.06 + EH2.24 + EE2.26/EE2.26 + EC2.06 + EC2.11 + EE2.26†**
**Seats: 74 + 84 + 84 + 74. Livery: N**

| | | | | | | | | | | | |
|---|---|---|---|---|---|---|---|---|---|---|---|
| 5901 | WD | 5905 | WD | 5909 | WD | 5912 | WD | 5915 | WD | 5918 | WD |
| 5902 | WD | 5906 | WD | 5910 | WD | 5913 | WD | 5916 | WD | 5919 | WD |
| 5903 | WD | 5907 | WD | 5911 | WD | 5914 | WD | 5917 | WD | 5920† | WD |
| 5904 | WD | 5908 | WD | | | | | | | | |

## Class 456/0 BREL York

**DMS + BDTS(L)**

**EA2.67 + EE2.76.**
**Seats: 79 + 51. To be introduced 1990. Sector NSL. Livery: N**

| | | | | | |
|---|---|---|---|---|---|
| 6001 | 6005 | 6009 | 6013 | 6017 | 6021 |
| 6002 | 6006 | 6010 | 6014 | 6018 | 6022 |
| 6003 | 6007 | 6011 | 6015 | 6019 | 6023 |
| 6004 | 6008 | 6012 | 6016 | 6020 | 6024 |

## Class 416/2 (2-EPB) BR Eastleigh

**DMBS + DTS**

**EB2.69 + EE2.64/EB2.79 + EE2.64†/EB2.79 + EE2.75‡.**
**Seats: 84 + 102/82 + 102/82 + 94‡.**

| | | | | | | | | | | | |
|---|---|---|---|---|---|---|---|---|---|---|---|
| 6202 | SG | 6222 | SG | 6235† | SG | 6245 | SG | 6260 | SG | 6270 | SG |
| 6203 | SG | 6223 | SG | 6236† | SG | 6247 | SG | 6261 | SG | 6271 | SG |
| 6205 | SG | 6224 | SG | 6237† | SG | 6249 | SG | 6262 | SG | 6272 | SG |
| 6207 | SG | 6225 | SG | 6238‡ | SG | 6251 | SG | 6263 | SG | 6273 | SG |
| 6212 | SG | 6226 | SG | 6239 | SG | 6253 | SG | 6264 | SG | 6274 | SG |
| 6213 | SG | 6227 | SG | 6240‡ | SG | 6255 | SG | 6265 | SG | 6275 | SG |
| 6217 | SG | 6229† | SG | 6241 | SG | 6256 | SG | 6267 | SG | 6276 | SG |
| 6218 | SG | 6230† | SG | 6243 | SG | 6257 | SG | 6268 | SG | 6277 | SG |
| 6221 | SG | 6231† | SG | 6244 | SG | 6259 | SG | 6269 | SG | 6278 | SG |

## Class 416/3 (2-EPB) BR Eastleigh

**DMBS + DTS**

**EB2.77 + EE2.69.**
**Seats: 82 + 92.**

| | | | | | | | | | | | | | | | | | |
|---|---|---|---|---|---|---|---|---|---|---|---|---|---|---|---|---|---|
| 6301 | | SU | 6307 | | SU | 6313 | N | SU | 6319 | N | SU | 6325 | | SU | 6331 | | SU |
| 6302 | | SU | 6308 | N | SU | 6314 | N | SU | 6320 | N | SU | 6326 | | SU | 6332 | | SU |
| 6303 | | SU | 6309 | N | SU | 6315 | N | SU | 6321 | N | SU | 6327 | | SU | 6333 | | SU |
| 6304 | | SU | 6310 | N | SU | 6316 | N | SU | 6322 | | SU | 6328 | | SU | 6334 | | SU |
| 6305 | | SU | 6311 | N | SU | 6317 | N | SU | 6323 | N | SU | 6329 | | SU | | | |
| 6306 | | SU | 6312 | N | SU | 6318 | N | SU | 6324 | | SU | 6330 | | SU | | | |

## Class 416/4 (2-EPB) BR Eastleigh

**MBS + DTS**

**EB2.81 + EE2.74/EB2.80 + EE2.71†**
**Seats: 79 + 90/82 + 92.**

| | | | | | | | | | | | | | | | | | |
|---|---|---|---|---|---|---|---|---|---|---|---|---|---|---|---|---|---|
| 6401 | | SG | 6404 | | SG | 6407 | N | SG | 6410† | N | SG | 6413† | N | SG | 6416† | N | SG |
| 6402 | N | SG | 6405 | N | SG | 6408 | N | SG | 6411† | N | SG | 6414† | | SG | 6417† | N | SG |
| 6403 | N | SG | 6406 | | SG | 6409 | N | SG | 6412† | N | SG | 6415† | N | SG | 6418† | N | SG |

## Class 438/0 (4-TC) BR York

**DTS + TC(L) + TBS(L) + DTS**

**EE2.66 + EH3.62 + EJ2.60 + EE2.66.**
**Seats: 64 + 1st 36 Std 8 + 32 + 64.**

| | | | | | | | | | | | | | | | | | |
|---|---|---|---|---|---|---|---|---|---|---|---|---|---|---|---|---|---|
| 8001 | N | BM | 8010 | N | BM | 8012 | N | BM | 8014 | | BM | 8015 | N | BM | 8017 | N | BM |

## Class 488/2 BREL Derby and Eastleigh

**TFH(L) + TSH(L)**

**EP1.01 + EP2.02.**
**Seats: 1st 41 + Std 48. Livery: IG**

| | | | | | | | | | | | |
|---|---|---|---|---|---|---|---|---|---|---|---|
| 8201 | SL | 8203 | SL | 8205 | SL | 8207 | SL | 8209 | SL | 8210 | SL |
| 8202 | SL | 8204 | SL | 8206 | SL | 8208 | SL | | | | |

## Class 488/3 BREL Derby and Eastleigh

**TSH(L) + TS(L) + TSH(L)**

**EP2.01 + EH2.90 + EP2.02.**
**Seats: 48 + 48 + 48. Livery: IG**

| | | | | | | | | | | | |
|---|---|---|---|---|---|---|---|---|---|---|---|
| 8302 | SL | 8305 | SL | 8308 | SL | 8311 | SL | 8314 | SL | 8317 | SL |
| 8303 | SL | 8306 | SL | 8309 | SL | 8312 | SL | 8315 | SL | 8318 | SL |
| 8304 | SL | 8307 | SL | 8310 | SL | 8313 | SL | 8316 | SL | 8319 | SL |

## Class 419 BR Eastleigh — DMLV
**EX5.60.**

| | | | | | | | | | | | | | | | |
|---|---|---|---|---|---|---|---|---|---|---|---|---|---|---|---|
| 9001 | N | RPMD | RE | 9004 | N | RPMD | RE | 9007 | L | RPMD | RE | 9010 | L | NBT | RE |
| 9002 | N | RPMD | RE | 9005 | L | RPMD | RE | 9008 | N | RPMD | RE | | | | |
| 9003 | L | RPMD | RE | 9006 | L | NBT | RE | 9009 | R | RPMD | RE | | | | |

## Class 489 BREL Eastleigh — DMLV
**EB5.01. RAILAIR Luggage Van. Livery: IG**

| | | | | | | | | | | | |
|---|---|---|---|---|---|---|---|---|---|---|---|
| 9101 | SL | 9103 | SL | 9105 | SL | 9107 | SL | 9109 | SL | 9110 | SL |
| 9102 | SL | 9104 | SL | 9106 | SL | 9108 | SL | | | | |

## Class 482 BREL Derby — MS
**20 vehicles for Waterloo & City line for delivery during 1991. Livery: N**

## Class 483 Metro-Cammell 1938 London Transport stock.
**Rebuilt BRML Eastleigh 1989. DMS + DMS.**
**EA2.65 + EA2.66.**
**Seats: 42 + 42. Livery: N**

| | | | | | | | | | | | |
|---|---|---|---|---|---|---|---|---|---|---|---|
| 001 | RY | 003 | RY | 005 | RY | 006 | RY | 007 | RY | 008 | RY |
| 002 | RY | 004 | RY | | | | | | | | |

## Class 485 (VEC) Metro-Cammell 1935 London Transport stock.
**Rebuilt BR Eastleigh 1967. Formations variable, individual vehicles listed.**
**DMBS EB2.61 + DTS**
**EE2.60 + TS EH2.61.**
**Seats: 26 + 38 + 42. Livery: N**

DMBS:

| | | | | | | | | | |
|---|---|---|---|---|---|---|---|---|---|
| 1 | RY | 5 | RY | 7 | RY | 8 | RY | 10 | RY |
| 2 | RY | | | | | | | | |

DTS:

| | | | | | | | | | |
|---|---|---|---|---|---|---|---|---|---|
| 26 | RY | 27 | RY | 28 | RY | 31 | RY | 34 | RY |

TS:

| | | | |
|---|---|---|---|
| 44 | RY | 49 | RY |

## CLASS 487 English Electric — DMBS + TS
**EB2.60 + EH2.60.**
**No fixed formations. Normal operation DMBS + TS + TS + TS + DMBS. Seats 40 + 52. Livery: N**

DMBS:

| | | | | | | | | | | | |
|---|---|---|---|---|---|---|---|---|---|---|---|
| 51 | WC | 54 | WC | 57 | WC | 59 | WC | 61 | WC | 62 | WC |
| 53 | WC | 56 | WC | 58 | WC | 60 | WC | | | | |

TS:

| | | | | | | | | | | | |
|---|---|---|---|---|---|---|---|---|---|---|---|
| 72 | WC | 74 | WC | 76 | WC | 78 | WC | 83 | WC | 85 | WC |
| 73 | WC | 75 | WC | 77 | WC | 80 | WC | 84 | WC | 86 | WC |

## Class 504 BR Wolverton — DMBS + DTS
**EB2.04 + EE2.15**
**Seats: 84 + 94.1200V DC BURY LINE UNITS. Livery: PM.**

| | | | | | | | | | | | |
|---|---|---|---|---|---|---|---|---|---|---|---|
| 504444 | PBQ | BQ | 504450 | PBQ | BQ | 504454 | PBQ | BQ | 504458 | PBQ | BQ |
| 504445 | PBQ | BQ | 504451 | PBQ | BQ | 504455 | PBQ | BQ | 504459 | PBQ | BQ |
| 504446 | PBQ | BQ | 504452 | PBQ | BQ | 504456 | PBQ | BQ | 504460 | PBQ | BQ |
| 504447 | PBQ | BQ | 504453 | PBQ | BQ | 504457 | PBQ | BQ | 504461 | PBQ | BQ |
| 504449 | PBQ | BQ | | | | | | | | | |

## Class 507 BREL York — BDMS + TS + DMS
**EI2.02 + EH2.05 + EA2.01**
**Seats: 74 + 86 + 74.**

| | | | | | | | | | | | |
|---|---|---|---|---|---|---|---|---|---|---|---|
| 507001 | PHR | HR | 507004 | PHR | HR | 507007 | PHR | HR | 507010 | PHR | HR |
| 507002 | PHRH | HR | 507005 | PHR | HR | 507008 | PHR | HR | 507011 | PHR | HR |
| 507003 | PHR | HR | 507006 | PHR | HR | 507009 | PHR | HR | 507012 | PHR | HR |

| | | | | | | | | | | | |
|---|---|---|---|---|---|---|---|---|---|---|---|
| 507013 | PHR | HR | 507019 | PHR | HR | 507024 | PHR | HR | 507029 | PHR | HR |
| 507014 | PHR | HR | 507020 | PHR | HR | 507025 | PHR | HR | 507030 | PHR | HR |
| 507015 | PHR | HR | 507021 | PHR | HR | 507026 | PHR | HR | 507031 | PHR | HR |
| 507016 | PHR | HR | 507022 | PHR | HR | 507027 | PHR | HR | 507032 | PHR | HR |
| 507017 | PHR | HR | 507023 | PHR | HR | 507028 | PHR | HR | 507033 | PHR | HR |
| 507018 | PHR | HR | | | | | | | | | |

## Class 508 BREL York — BDMS + TS + DMS

**EI2.03 + EH2.18 + EA2.08**
**Seats: 74 + 82 + 74.**

| | | | | | | | | | | | |
|---|---|---|---|---|---|---|---|---|---|---|---|
| 508101 | PBD | BD | 508113 | PBD | BD | 508124 | PBD | BD | 508135 | PBD | BD |
| 508102 | PBD | BD | 508114 | PBD | BD | 508125 | PBD | BD | 508136 | PBD | BD |
| 508103 | PBD | BD | 508115 | PBD | BD | 508126 | PBD | BD | 508137 | PBD | BD |
| 508104 | PBD | BD | 508116 | PBD | BD | 508127 | PBD | BD | 508138 | PBD | BD |
| 508105 | PBD | BD | 508117 | PBD | BD | 508128 | PBD | BD | 508139 | PBD | BD |
| 508106 | PBD | BD | 508118 | PBD | BD | 508129 | PBD | BD | 508140 | PBD | BD |
| 508107 | PBD | BD | 508119 | PBD | BD | 508130 | PBD | BD | 508141 | PBD | BD |
| 508108 | PBD | BD | 508120 | PBD | BD | 508131 | PBD | BD | 508142 | PBD | BD |
| 508109 | PBD | BD | 508121 | PBD | BD | 508132 | PBD | BD | 508143 | PBD | BD |
| 508110 | PBD | BD | 508122 | PBD | BD | 508133 | PBD | BD | | | |
| 508112 | PBD | BD | 508123 | PBD | BD | 508134 | PBD | BD | | | |

Few departmental units are purpose built, generally they are conversions from Capital stock. The last 'exception' was the Track Recording Unit DB999600/01 built in 1987 by BREL York (ZR) to the Class 150/1 design. It is seen here south of York.

# DEPARTMENTAL MULTIPLE UNIT STOCK.

**DIESEL:**

| Veh Nos: | Use: | Dep. |
|---|---|---|
| RRB975010 | Test coach Iris | HQ |
| TDB975023 | Route learning and Sandite car | CL |
| TDB975025 | SR General Manager's saloon | SL |
| ADB975042 (L119) | Sandite spray | BY |
| DB975349 + DB975539 | RCE Inspection saloon | HT |
| RDB975386 | RTC Tilt testing | HQ |
| TDB975540 (T121) | Route learning | TS |
| TDB975659 (L135) | Route learning car | OO |
| RDB975964 | Stores van | HQ |
| ADB977048 | Sandite spray | BX |
| ADB977342 | RTC Carriage wash | HQ |
| ADB977376 + ADB977377 + ADB977378 ({951}066) | Sandite train | SU |
| DB977391 + DB999602 + DB977392 | Track assessment train | RG |
| TDB977466 (P286) | Sandite spray | CF |
| TDB977486 (C285) | Sandite spray | LA |
| TDB977535 + TDB977536 | Sandite spray | HT |
| ADB977607 + ADB977608 (101336) | Route learning & Sandite | ED |
| ADB977615 (L281) | Sandite spray | OO |
| ADB977651 + ADB977652 (101302) | Route learning & Sandite | ED |
| RDB999507 | RTC Track recorder | HQ |
| DB999600 + DB999601 | RTC Track recorder | HQ |
| 51174 + 51799 (NL919) | Route learning | NL |

**ELECTRIC:**

| | | |
|---|---|---|
| ADB975032 | R & D Test Car Mars | HQ |
| ADB975586 + ADB975587 (004) | Rail cleaning unit | EH |
| ADB975588 + ADB975589 (005) | Rail cleaning unit | WD |
| ADB975590 + ADB975591 (006) | Rail cleaning unit | WD |
| ADB975592 + ADB975593 (007) | Rail cleaning unit | GI |
| ADB975594 + ADB975595 (003) | Rail cleaning unit | SU |
| ADB975596 + ADB975597 (008) | Rail cleaning unit | GI |
| ADB975598 + ADB975599 (009) | Rail cleaning unit | BI |
| ADB975600 + ADB975601 (010) | Rail cleaning unit | BI |
| ADB975602 + ADB975603 (011) | Rail cleaning unit | RE |
| ADB975604 + ADB975605 (012) | Rail cleaning unit | EH |
| ADB975896 + ADB975897 (013) | Rail cleaning unit | RE |
| ADB977068 + ADB977069 (019) | Stores unit | SG |
| ADB977290 + ADB977291 (018) | Stores unit | SG |
| ADB977296 + ADB977297 (050) | RSD Test unit | SH |
| ADB977304 + ADB977305 (021) | Traction shunting unit | WD |
| DB977335 + DB977336 | RTC Track recording train | HQ |
| ADB977345 + ADB977346 (001) | Rail cleaning unit | BD |
| ADB977347 + ADB977348 (002) | Rail cleaning unit | BD |
| ADB977349 + ADB977350 (003) | Rail cleaning unit | BD |
| ADB977362 | De-icing coach | BI |
| ADB977363 | De-icing coach | EH |
| ADB977364 | De-icing coach | RE |
| ADB977365 + ADB977368 (001) | Rail cleaning unit | SU |
| ADB977366 + ADB977367 (002) | Rail cleaning unit | BM |
| ADB977385 + ADB977386 (148) | Rail cleaning unit | WN |
| ADB977505 + ADB977506 (053) | RSD Test unit | SH |
| ADB977507 + ADB977508 (054) | RSD Test unit | SH |
| ADB977531 + ADB977532 (015) | Sandite unit | SU |
| ADB977533 + ADB977534 (016) | Sandite unit | SU |
| ADB977559 + ADB977560 (062) | Carriage cleaning fluid carrier | SU |
| ADB977566 + ADB977567 (017) | Stores unit | SU |
| ADB977598 + ADB977599 + ADB977600 (996) | Rail cleaning unit | IL |
| ADB977601 + ADB977602 + ADB977603 (997) | Rail cleaning unit | IL |
| ADB977604 + ADB977605 + ADB977606 (998) | Rail cleaning unit | IL |
| ADB977609 + ADB977610 (022) | Rail cleaning unit | WD |
| ADB977639 + ADB977640 + ADB977641 (305935) | Mobile Classroom | HQ |
| ADB977578 | Sandite spray | HE |
| ADB977579 | Sandite spray | SU |
| ADB977684 + ADB977685 + ADB977686 + ADB977687 (8007) | R&D Channel Tunnel test train | SL |
| 61389 + 70302 + 61388 (1500) | De-icing unit | RE |

## PFK BR Derby — AP1Z

**Pullman Parlour with Kitchen Mk2.** — AP1.01 Seats: 1st 18. Livery: IP

| | | | | | |
|---|---|---|---|---|---|
| 504 | ICHV | EN | 506 | ICHV | EN |

## PFP BR Derby — AQ1Z

**Pullman Parlour Mk2.** — AQ1.01 Seats: 1st 36 Livery: IP

| | | | | | | | | | | | |
|---|---|---|---|---|---|---|---|---|---|---|---|
| 546 | ICHV | EN | 549 | ICHV | EN | 551 | ICHV | EN | 553 | ICHV | EN |
| 548 | ICHV | EN | 550 | ICHV | EN | 552 | ICHV | EN | | | |

## PFB BR Derby — AR1Z

**Pullman Brake Mk2** — AR1.01 Seats: 1st 30 Livery: IP

| | | |
|---|---|---|
| 586 | ICHV | EN |

## RFO BR Derby — AJ1F

**Restaurant Lounge First Mk2f** — AJ1.04 Seats: 1st 26 Livery: I

| | | | | | | | | | | | |
|---|---|---|---|---|---|---|---|---|---|---|---|
| 1200 | ICC | PC | 1206 | ICC | PC | 1212 | ICC | PC | 1218 | ICC | PC |
| 1201 | ICC | PC | 1207 | ICC | PC | 1213 | ICC | PC | 1219 | ICC | PC |
| 1202 | ICC | PC | 1208 | ICC | PC | 1214 | ICC | EC | 1220 | ICC | PC |
| 1203 | ICC | PC | 1209 | ICC | PC | 1215 | ICC | EC | 1221 | ICC | OY |
| 1204 | ICC | EC | 1210 | ICC | PC | 1216 | ICC | PC | | | |
| 1205 | ICC | PC | 1211 | ICC | PC | 1217 | ICC | PC | | | |

## RBR Pressed Steel — AJ41

**Restaurant Buffet with Kitchen Mk1** — AJ4.03/AJ4.17† Seats: 23/22 loose chairs (unclassified)

| | | | | | | | | | | | | | | | |
|---|---|---|---|---|---|---|---|---|---|---|---|---|---|---|---|
| 1644 | I | ICHV | OM | 1655 | I | IWC | EN | 1673 | | ICC | MA | 1691 | I | IAN | NC |
| 1645 | I | ICHV | OM | 1657† | I | ICC | MA | 1674 | I | ICHV | BN | 1692 | I | IAN | NC |
| 1646 | I | ICHV | OM | 1658† | I | ICC | DY | 1675 | I | ICHV | BN | 1693 | I | ICHV | BN |
| 1647 | I | IAN | NC | 1659 | I | ICHV | BN | 1678 | I | ICHV | OM | 1694 | | ICC | MA |
| 1648 | I | ICC | PC | 1663 | I | IWC | EN | 1679 | I | ICHV | BN | 1695 | | ICC | MA |
| 1649 | I | ICC | DY | 1665 | | IXXZ | HQ | 1680 | | ICC | MA | 1696 | I | IAN | NC |
| 1650 | I | ICC | PC | 1666 | I | IANL | NC | 1683 | I | IAN | NC | 1697 | I | IAN | NC |
| 1651 | I | ICC | MA | 1667 | I | ICHV | BN | 1684 | | IWC | EN | 1698 | I | ICHV | BN |
| 1652 | I | ICC | MA | 1670 | | ICC | PC | 1686 | I | IAN | NC | 1699 | I | IAN | NC |
| 1653† | I | ICC | DY | 1671 | I | IAN | NC | 1688 | I | ICC | MA | | | | |
| 1654 | | ICC | MA | 1672 | I | ICHV | BN | 1689 | I | IAN | NC | | | | |

## RMB BR Wolverton/York AN21

**Restaurant Miniature Buffet (Open Std) Mk1** — AN2.02†/AN2.03/AN2.08$ Seats: 44

| | | | | | | | | | | | | | | | |
|---|---|---|---|---|---|---|---|---|---|---|---|---|---|---|---|
| 1805†# | I | IWC | EN | 1848† | I | IWR | OM | 1864 | | IWC | WB | 1876 | I | IWC | EN |
| 1813 | I | IWR | OM | 1850$ | N | NWR | OM | 1865 | N | NWR | OM | 1878 | | IWR | OM |
| 1816 | | IWR | OM | 1853 | I | IWR | OM | 1867 | I | IWR | OM | 1879 | I | IWR | OM |
| 1832 | I | IWR | OM | 1854 | I | IWR | OM | 1869 | I | IWR | OM | 1880 | | IWC | WB |
| 1833 | I | ICC | MA | 1857 | | ICH | BN | 1870 | I | IWR | OM | 1882 | I | IWR | OM |
| 1842$ | N | NWR | OM | 1860 | I | IWC | WB | 1871$ | N | NWR | OM | | | | |
| 1845† | | ICHS | OY | 1863 | | IWC | WB | 1875 | I | IWR | OM | | | | |

## RBR BR Ashford/Swindon — AJ41

**Restaurant Buffet with Kitchen Mk1** — AJ4.14/AJ4.18† Seats: 23/22† loose chairs (unclassified)

| | | | | | | | | | | | | | | | |
|---|---|---|---|---|---|---|---|---|---|---|---|---|---|---|---|
| 1923 | I | ICC | MA | 1948 | I | ICC | MA | 1961 | | ICC | PC | 1971 | I | ICC | EC |
| 1944 | | ICC | PC | 1953 | I | ICHL | OM | 1962 | | ICC | DY | 1972 | | ICC | DY |
| 1945 | | ICC | MA | 1954 | | ICC | PC | 1966 | I | ICC | MA | 1973† | I | ICC | DY |
| 1946 | | ICC | MA | 1956 | | ICC | DY | 1969 | I | ICC | MA | 1981 | I | ICC | DY |
| 1947 | I | ICC | PC | 1959† | I | ICC | DY | 1970 | | ICC | PC | 1984 | | ICC | MA |

## SLSC BR Derby & Cathays — AU51

**Sleeper Staff Coach** — AU5.01 Accomodation: 5 twin-bed berths and seated kitchen area. Livery:I

| | | | | | |
|---|---|---|---|---|---|
| 2833 | ICHV | BN | 2834 | ICHV | BN |

## ROYAL TRAIN COACHES

**Some vehicles to standard BR Design: Mk2c(‡) or Mk3a(†).**
**All Pool ICH based ZN. Livery: Maroon**

| | | |
|---|---|---|
| 2900 | AT5.01 | Saloon |
| 2901 | AT5.03 | Saloon |
| 2903† | AT5.25 | Saloon |
| 2904† | AT5.26 | Saloon |
| 2905 | AT5.27 | Sleeper Power Brake |
| 2906 | AT5.28 | Sleeper |
| 2907 | AT5.17 | Restaurant & Kitchen |
| 2914† | AT5.31 | Sleeper |
| 2915† | AT5.31 | Sleeper |
| 2916† | AT5.37 | Dining and Royal Household |
| 2917† | AT5.32 | Household Staff Diner |
| 2918† | AT5.38 | Lounge Sleeper |
| 2919† | AT5.32 | Saloon, Diner & Sleeper |
| 2920‡ | AT5.36 | Generator |
| 2921‡ | AT5.- | Escort Vehicle |
| 2922† | AT5.34 | Sleeper |
| 2923† | AT5.35 | Sleeper & Lounge |

## FO BR Swindon and BRCW†. AD11

**Open First Mk1.**

**AD1.03 Seats: 42 Livery: I**

| | | |
|---|---|---|
| 3096† | ICHH | CL |
| 3097† | ICHV | BN |
| 3098† | ICHV | BN |
| 3100† | ICHV | BN |
| 3107 | ICHV | BN |
| 3111 | ICHV | BN |
| 3114 | ICHV | BN |
| 3115 | ICHV | BN |
| 3118 | ICHV | BN |
| 3119 | ICHV | BN |
| 3120 | ICHV | BN |
| 3121 | ICHV | BN |
| 3123 | ICHV | BN |
| 3124 | ICHV | BN |
| 3127 | ICHV | BN |
| 3131 | ICHV | BN |
| 3132 | ICHV | BN |
| 3133 | ICHV | BN |
| 3134 | ICHV | BN |
| 3136 | ICHV | BN |
| 3140 | ICHV | BN |
| 3141 | ICHV | CL |
| 3143 | ICHV | BN |
| 3144 | ICHV | BN |
| 3146 | ICHV | BN |
| 3147 | ICHV | BN |
| 3148 | ICHV | BN |
| 3149 | ICHV | BN |
| 3150 | ICHV | BN |

## FO BR Derby AD1D

**Open First Mk2d**

**AD1.03 Seats: 42 Livery: I**

| | | |
|---|---|---|
| 3172 | IAN | NC |
| 3174 | IAN | NC |
| 3178 | ICHV | OM |
| 3181 | ICHV | BN |
| 3182 | IAN | NC |
| 3186 | IAN | NC |
| 3187 | ICHV | OM |
| 3188 | IAN | NC |
| 3192 | ICHM | MA |
| 3202 | ICHM | MA |

## FO BR Derby AD11

**Open First Mk2e**

**AD1.06 Seats: 41† or 42**

| | | | |
|---|---|---|---|
| 3221† | I | IAN | NC |
| 3222 | | ICHM | MA |
| 3223 | | ICHV | OM |
| 3224 | I | ICC | MA |
| 3225 | I | ICHM | MA |
| 3226 | I | ICHV | OM |
| 3227 | I | ICHV | OM |
| 3228 | I | ICC | MA |
| 3229 | I | ICC | MA |
| 3230 | I | ICHV | OM |
| 3231 | I | ICC | MA |
| 3232† | I | IAN | NC |
| 3233 | I | ICHM | MA |
| 3234 | I | IAN | NC |
| 3235 | I | ICC | MA |
| 3236 | I | ICC | DY |
| 3237 | I | ICHM | MA |
| 3238 | I | ICC | DY |
| 3239 | I | PEC | EC |
| 3240 | I | ICC | DY |
| 3241 | I | ICC | MA |
| 3242† | I | IAN | NC |
| 3244† | I | IAN | NC |
| 3245† | Ps | PEC | EC |
| 3246 | I | IAN | NC |
| 3247 | Ps | PEC | EC |
| 3248 | Ps | PEC | EC |
| 3249 | I | IAN | NC |
| 3250† | I | IAN | NC |
| 3251† | I | IAN | NC |
| 3252† | I | IAN | NC |
| 3253 | | IML | DY |
| 3254 | I | ICHV | OM |
| 3255 | I | ICC | DY |
| 3256† | I | IAN | NC |
| 3257† | I | IAN | NC |
| 3258 | I | IAN | NC |
| 3259† | I | IAN | NC |
| 3260 | I | ICHV | OM |
| 3261† | I | IAN | NC |
| 3262 | I | IAN | NC |
| 3263 | I | ICHV | OM |
| 3264 | I | ICHV | OM |
| 3265 | Ps | PEC | EC |
| 3266 | I | IAN | NC |
| 3267 | I | IML | DY |
| 3268 | I | ICHM | MA |
| 3269 | I | ICC | DY |
| 3270 | | ICHM | MA |
| 3271 | I | ICC | MA |
| 3272 | | ICHM | MA |
| 3273 | I | PEC | EC |
| 3274 | I | ICH | OM |
| 3275 | | ICHM | MA |

## FO BR Derby AD1F

**Open First Mk2f**

**AD1.07 Seats: 39† or 42**

| | | | |
|---|---|---|---|
| 3277 | I | IWCR | EN |
| 3278 | I | IWCR | MA |
| 3279 | I | IWC | EN |
| 3280 | | IWC | EN |
| 3284 | I | PEC | EC |
| 3285 | I | IWC | OY |
| 3290 | I | IWCR | EN |
| 3292 | I | IWCR | OY |
| 3293 | I | IWCR | MA |
| 3295 | I | IWCR | OY |
| 3296 | | IWC | WB |
| 3299 | I | IWCR | OY |
| 3300 | I | IWC | OY |
| 3303 | I | IWCR | WB |
| 3304 | I | IWCR | OY |
| 3309 | | IWC | MA |
| 3312 | I | IWCR | MA |
| 3313 | I | IWCR | OY |
| 3314 | I | IWCR | WB |
| 3318 | I | IWCR | EN |
| 3322 | | IWC | EN |
| 3325 | I | IWCR | OY |
| 3326 | I | IWC | OY |
| 3330 | I | IWCR | OY |
| 3331 | I | IWCR | EN |
| 3333 | I | IWCR | OY |
| 3334 | I | IWCR | EN |
| 3336 | I | IWCR | PC |
| 3337 | I | IWCR | OY |
| 3338 | I | IWCR | EN |
| 3340 | I | IWCR | OY |
| 3344 | I | IWCR | PC |
| 3345 | I | IWCR | OY |
| 3348 | I | IWCR | OY |
| 3350 | I | IWCR | OY |
| 3351 | I | IWCR | OY |

## TSO BR Derby — AC2B

Tourist Open Standard Mk2b — AC2.07. Seats: 62

| | | | | | | | | | | | | | | | |
|---|---|---|---|---|---|---|---|---|---|---|---|---|---|---|---|
| 5434 | | PLL | LL | 5450 | N | NSS | LA | 5466 | | IWC | WB | 5482 | N | NSS | LA |
| 5435 | N | NSS | LA | 5451 | N | NSS | LA | 5467 | | ICC | PC | 5483 | | PCL | CL |
| 5436 | N | NSS | LA | 5452 | N | NWR | OM | 5468 | N | NSS | LA | 5484 | N | NSS | EH |
| 5437 | | PNL | NL | 5453 | Pb | PLL | LL | 5470 | N | NSS | LA | 5486 | | IWC | WB |
| 5438 | N | ICC | MA | 5454 | N | NSS | LA | 5471 | N | NSS | EH | 5487 | | IML | DY |
| 5439 | N | NSS | EH | 5455 | N | NSS | LA | 5472 | N | NSS | LA | 5488 | | PEC | EC |
| 5440 | | PCL | CL | 5456 | N | NSS | LA | 5473 | | PLL | LL | 5489 | | PCL | CL |
| 5442 | N | NSS | LA | 5457 | N | NSS | LA | 5474 | N | NSS | LA | 5490 | N | NSS | EH |
| 5443 | N | NSS | EH | 5458 | N | NSS | EH | 5475 | N | NSS | LA | 5491 | N | NWR | OM |
| 5444 | N | NSS | LA | 5459 | | IWC | WB | 5476 | | IWC | WB | 5492 | N | NSS | LA |
| 5445 | | PEC | EC | 5461 | | IWC | WB | 5477 | | IWC | WB | 5493 | N | NSS | LA |
| 5446 | N | NSS | LA | 5462 | N | NSS | LA | 5478 | | IWC | WB | 5494 | N | NSS | LA |
| 5447 | N | NSS | LA | 5463 | PP | PHT | HT | 5479 | PP | PHT | HT | 5495 | N | NSS | LA |
| 5448 | N | NSS | LA | 5464 | N | NSS | LA | 5480 | N | NSS | LA | 5496 | | IWC | WB |
| 5449 | N | NSS | LA | 5465 | N | NSS | LA | 5481 | N | NSS | LA | 5497 | N | NSS | LA |

## TSO BR Derby — AC2C

Tourist Open Standard Mk2c — AC2.08. Seats: 62

| | | | | | | | | | | | | | | | |
|---|---|---|---|---|---|---|---|---|---|---|---|---|---|---|---|
| 5500 | | IWC | WB | 5527 | | ICC | MA | 5557 | | ICC | PC | 5591 | | IWC | WB |
| 5501 | | IWC | WB | 5529 | | ICC | MA | 5560 | | ICC | PC | 5594 | | ICC | MA |
| 5502 | | IWC | WB | 5530 | | IWC | WB | 5561 | | ICC | PC | 5595 | | IWC | WB |
| 5505 | | ICC | PC | 5532 | | ICC | PC | 5565 | | IWC | WB | 5596 | | ICC | PC |
| 5508 | | IWC | WB | 5533 | | IWC | WB | 5566 | | ICC | PC | 5597 | | ICC | MA |
| 5509 | | ICC | PC | 5536 | | ICC | MA | 5569 | | IWC | WB | 5600 | | IWC | WB |
| 5512 | | IWC | WB | 5539 | | ICC | PC | 5572 | | IWC | WB | 5601 | | IWC | WB |
| 5515 | | IWC | WB | 5540 | | ICC | MA | 5574 | | ICC | MA | 5604 | | ICC | MA |
| 5517 | | IWC | WB | 5541 | | ICC | MA | 5576 | | ICC | MA | 5605 | | IWC | WB |
| 5519 | | ICC | MA | 5542 | | IWC | WB | 5581 | | ICC | MA | 5607 | | IWC | WB |
| 5520 | PP | PHT | HT | 5546 | | ICC | MA | 5582 | | IWC | WB | 5609 | | ICC | MA |
| 5522 | | ICC | PC | 5548 | | ICC | PC | 5584 | | IWC | WB | 5610 | | IWC | WB |
| 5523 | N | NSS | LA | 5549 | | IWC | WB | 5585 | | IWC | WB | 5613 | | ICC | MA |
| 5524 | | IWC | WB | 5550 | | ICC | MA | 5586 | | ICC | PC | 5614 | PP | PHT | HT |
| 5525 | N | NSS | LA | 5552 | | IWC | WB | 5589 | | ICC | MA | 5615 | | IWC | WB |
| 5526 | | IWC | WB | 5554 | | ICC | PC | 5590 | | IWC | WB | | | | |

## TSO BR Derby — AC2D

Tourist Open Standard Mk2d — AC2.09. Seats: 64

| | | | | | | | | | | | | | | | |
|---|---|---|---|---|---|---|---|---|---|---|---|---|---|---|---|
| 5616 | I | ICC | DY | 5648 | I | ICC | DY | 5680 | I | ICC | DY | 5714 | I | IWR | OM |
| 5617 | I | ICC | DY | 5650 | I | IANR | NC | 5681 | I | ICC | DY | 5715 | I | IANR | NC |
| 5618 | I | IANR | NC | 5651 | I | IANR | NC | 5682 | I | ICCR | PC | 5716 | Ps | ICC | DY |
| 5619 | I | IANR | NC | 5652 | I | IANR | NC | 5684 | I | ICC | DY | 5717 | I | ICC | DY |
| 5620 | I | ICCR | PC | 5653 | I | ICCR | PC | 5685 | I | ICCR | PC | 5718 | I | IWR | OM |
| 5621 | I | IWR | OM | 5654 | I | IANR | NC | 5686 | I | IANR | NC | 5719 | I | ICC | DY |
| 5623 | I | ICCR | PC | 5657 | I | IANR | NC | 5687 | I | ICC | MA | 5722 | I | ICC | DY |
| 5624 | I | IANR | NC | 5658 | I | IANR | NC | 5689 | I | PEC | EC | 5723 | I | IANR | NC |
| 5625 | I | IAN | NC | 5659 | I | ICCR | PC | 5690 | I | IANR | NC | 5724 | I | IANR | NC |
| 5626 | I | ICCR | PC | 5660 | I | ICC | DY | 5692 | I | IANR | NC | 5726 | I | ICCR | PC |
| 5628 | I | IANR | NC | 5661 | I | ICC | DY | 5693 | I | IANR | NC | 5727 | I | ICC | MA |
| 5629 | I | IANR | NC | 5662 | I | ICCR | PC | 5694 | Ps | ICC | DY | 5728 | I | IANR | NC |
| 5630 | I | ICC | MA | 5663 | Ps | PEC | EC | 5695 | I | IANR | NC | 5729 | I | IWR | OM |
| 5631 | I | ICCR | PC | 5665 | I | IANR | NC | 5699 | I | ICC | MA | 5730 | I | IANR | NC |
| 5632 | I | IANR | NC | 5666 | I | ICC | DY | 5700 | I | ICCR | PC | 5731 | I | IWR | OM |
| 5633 | I | ICC | DY | 5667 | | ICC | DY | 5701 | I | ICC | DY | 5732 | I | IWR | OM |
| 5634 | I | ICCR | PC | 5668 | I | IWR | OM | 5703 | I | IANR | NC | 5734 | I | ICC | DY |
| 5636 | I | ICCR | PC | 5669 | I | IANR | NC | 5704 | I | ICC | MA | 5735 | I | IANR | NC |
| 5637 | | ICC | DY | 5670 | I | ICC | DY | 5705 | I | IAN | NC | 5737 | I | IANR | NC |
| 5638 | I | ICCR | PC | 5671 | I | ICCR | PC | 5706 | I | ICC | DY | 5738 | I | ICC | DY |
| 5639 | I | ICC | DY | 5672 | I | IAN | NC | 5707 | I | ICC | DY | 5739 | I | ICC | DY |
| 5640 | I | ICC | DY | 5673 | I | ICCR | PC | 5708 | I | ICC | DY | 5740 | I | ICCR | PC |
| 5642 | | ICC | DY | 5674 | I | ICC | DY | 5709 | | ICC | MA | 5742 | I | ICC | DY |
| 5643 | I | ICCR | DY | 5675 | I | ICC | DY | 5710 | I | IANR | NC | 5743 | I | IANR | NC |
| 5645 | I | ICC | MA | 5676 | I | IANR | NC | 5711 | I | ICCR | PC | | | | |
| 5646 | I | IANR | NC | 5678 | I | ICC | DY | 5712 | I | IWR | OM | | | | |
| 5647 | | ICC | DY | 5679 | I | IANR | NC | 5713 | I | IWR | OM | | | | |

## TSO BR Derby

**Tourist Open Standard Mk2e**

# AC2E

**AC2.10. Seats: 64 Livery: I**

| | | | | | | | | | | | |
|---|---|---|---|---|---|---|---|---|---|---|---|
| 5744 | ICC | PC | 5784 | ICCR | PC | 5828 | ICC | MA | 5868 | ICCR | PC |
| 5745 | ICC | PC | 5785 | ICC | PC | 5829 | ICC | MA | 5869 | ICCR | PC |
| 5746 | ICCR | PC | 5786 | ICC | MA | 5830 | ICC | PC | 5870 | ICC | PC |
| 5747 | ICC | PC | 5787 | ICC | MA | 5831 | ICC | PC | 5871 | ICC | PC |
| 5748 | ICCR | PC | 5788 | ICC | PC | 5832 | ICC | PC | 5872 | IWR | LA |
| 5749 | ICC | PC | 5789 | ICCR | PC | 5833 | ICC | MA | 5873 | ICC | MA |
| 5750 | IWR | LA | 5790 | ICC | PC | 5834 | ICC | MA | 5874 | ICC | PC |
| 5751 | ICCR | PC | 5791 | ICCR | PC | 5835 | ICC | MA | 5875 | ICC | PC |
| 5752 | ICC | PC | 5792 | ICCR | PC | 5836 | ICC | PC | 5876 | ICCR | PC |
| 5753 | ICC | PC | 5793 | ICCR | PC | 5837 | ICC | MA | 5877 | ICC | MA |
| 5754 | ICCR | PC | 5794 | ICCR | PC | 5838 | ICC | PC | 5878 | ICC | MA |
| 5755 | ICC | PC | 5795 | ICC | PC | 5839 | ICC | MA | 5879 | IWR | LA |
| 5756 | IWR | LA | 5796 | ICCR | PC | 5840 | ICC | MA | 5880 | ICC | PC |
| 5757 | ICC | PC | 5797 | ICCR | PC | 5841 | ICC | PC | 5881 | IWR | LA |
| 5758 | ICC | PC | 5798 | ICC | PC | 5842 | ICC | MA | 5882 | ICC | PC |
| 5759 | ICC | PC | 5799 | IWR | LA | 5843 | ICCR | PC | 5883 | ICC | PC |
| 5760 | ICCR | PC | 5800 | ICC | MA | 5844 | ICC | PC | 5884 | ICC | PC |
| 5761 | ICC | PC | 5801 | ICCR | PC | 5845 | ICC | MA | 5885 | ICC | PC |
| 5762 | ICC | PC | 5802 | ICC | PC | 5846 | ICC | PC | 5886 | ICC | PC |
| 5763 | ICC | PC | 5803 | ICCR | PC | 5847 | ICCR | PC | 5887 | ICCR | PC |
| 5764 | ICC | PC | 5804 | ICC | PC | 5848 | ICC | PC | 5888 | ICCR | PC |
| 5765 | ICC | MA | 5809 | ICC | PC | 5849 | ICC | PC | 5889 | ICCR | PC |
| 5766 | ICC | PC | 5810 | ICC | PC | 5850 | ICC | PC | 5890 | ICC | PC |
| 5767 | ICC | MA | 5811 | ICC | MA | 5851 | ICC | PC | 5891 | ICC | PC |
| 5768 | ICC | PC | 5812 | ICCR | PC | 5852 | ICC | PC | 5892 | ICCR | PC |
| 5769 | ICCR | PC | 5813 | ICC | PC | 5853 | ICC | PC | 5893 | ICCR | PC |
| 5770 | ICC | PC | 5814 | ICCR | PC | 5854 | ICC | MA | 5894 | ICC | PC |
| 5771 | ICC | PC | 5815 | IWR | LA | 5855 | IWR | LA | 5895 | ICC | PC |
| 5772 | ICCR | PC | 5816 | ICCR | PC | 5856 | ICC | MA | 5896 | ICCR | PC |
| 5773 | ICC | PC | 5817 | ICC | PC | 5857 | ICC | MA | 5897 | ICCR | PC |
| 5774 | ICC | PC | 5818 | ICC | PC | 5858 | ICC | PC | 5898 | ICC | PC |
| 5775 | ICC | PC | 5819 | ICC | PC | 5859 | ICC | PC | 5899 | ICCR | PC |
| 5776 | ICCR | PC | 5820 | ICC | MA | 5860 | ICC | PC | 5900 | ICCR | PC |
| 5777 | ICC | PC | 5821 | ICCR | PC | 5861 | ICC | PC | 5901 | ICC | PC |
| 5778 | ICCR | PC | 5822 | ICC | PC | 5862 | ICC | MA | 5902 | ICC | PC |
| 5779 | ICC | PC | 5823 | ICC | MA | 5863 | ICC | PC | 5903 | ICC | PC |
| 5780 | ICCR | PC | 5824 | ICCR | PC | 5864 | ICC | MA | 5904 | ICC | PC |
| 5781 | ICC | PC | 5825 | ICCR | PC | 5865 | ICCR | PC | 5905 | ICCR | PC |
| 5782 | ICC | MA | 5826 | ICCR | PC | 5866 | ICC | PC | 5906 | ICCR | PC |
| 5783 | ICC | MA | 5827 | ICC | PC | 5867 | ICC | MA | 5907 | ICC | PC |

## TSO BR Derby

**Tourist Open Standard Mk2f**

# AC2F

**AC2.11/AC2.15†. Seats: 62† or 64**

| | | | | | | | | | | | | | | | |
|---|---|---|---|---|---|---|---|---|---|---|---|---|---|---|---|
| 5908 | I | IWCR | OY | 5937 | I | IWC | OY | 5966 | I | IANR | NC | 6000 | I | IWCR | OY |
| 5910† | I | IWCR | OY | 5939 | I | IWCR | OY | 5967 | | IWC | EN | 6001 | I | IWCR | OY |
| 5911 | I | IWCR | OY | 5940† | I | IWC | MA | 5968 | I | PEC | EC | 6002 | I | IWCR | OY |
| 5912 | I | IWCR | OY | 5941 | I | IWCR | OY | 5969† | I | IWCR | OY | 6005 | I | IWC | EN |
| 5913 | I | IWCR | OY | 5943† | I | IWCR | OY | 5971 | I | IWCR | WB | 6006 | I | IWCR | OY |
| 5914 | I | IWCR | OY | 5944† | I | IWCR | OY | 5973 | I | IANR | NC | 6008 | I | IWCR | OY |
| 5915 | I | IWCR | OY | 5945† | I | IWCR | MA | 5975 | I | IWC | WB | 6009 | I | IWCR | OY |
| 5916† | | IWC | PC | 5946 | I | IWCR | OY | 5976 | I | IWC | OY | 6010 | | IWC | WB |
| 5917 | I | IANR | NC | 5947 | | IWC | EN | 5977 | I | IWCR | OY | 6011 | I | IWC | WB |
| 5918† | I | IWC | EN | 5948† | I | IWCR | OY | 5978 | I | IWC | WB | 6012 | I | IWCR | OY |
| 5919 | I | IWCR | OY | 5949† | I | IWCR | OY | 5980 | I | IWCR | OY | 6013 | I | IANR | NC |
| 5920 | I | IWCR | OY | 5950 | I | IANR | NC | 5981 | I | IWCR | OY | 6014 | I | IWC | WB |
| 5921 | I | IANR | NC | 5951 | | IWC | WB | 5983 | I | IWC | OY | 6015 | I | IWC | OY |
| 5922 | I | IANR | NC | 5952 | | IWC | WB | 5984 | I | IWCR | OY | 6016 | I | IWCR | OY |
| 5924 | | IWC | WB | 5953 | I | IWCR | MA | 5985 | I | IWCR | OY | 6018 | I | IWCR | PC |
| 5925 | I | IWC | WB | 5954 | I | IANR | NC | 5986 | I | IWCR | OY | 6021 | I | IANR | NC |
| 5926 | I | IWC | MA | 5955 | I | IWCR | OY | 5987 | I | IWCR | OY | 6022† | I | IWCR | OY |
| 5927 | I | IANR | NC | 5956 | I | IANR | NC | 5988† | I | IWCR | OY | 6024 | I | IWCR | OY |
| 5928 | I | IANR | NC | 5957 | I | IANR | NC | 5989† | | IWC | EN | 6025 | I | IWCR | MA |
| 5929 | I | PEC | EC | 5958 | I | IWCR | OY | 5991 | I | IWC | EN | 6026 | I | IWCR | OY |
| 5930 | I | IWCR | OY | 5959 | I | PEC | EC | 5993† | I | IWC | WB | 6027† | I | IWCR | OY |
| 5931† | I | IWCR | MA | 5960 | I | IANR | NC | 5994 | I | IWC | MA | 6028 | I | IWCR | EN |
| 5932 | I | IWCR | MA | 5961 | I | IANR | NC | 5995 | | IWC | WB | 6029 | I | IWCR | OY |
| 5933 | I | IWCR | OY | 5962 | I | IWCR | EN | 5996 | I | IWCR | OY | 6030 | I | IWCR | OY |
| 5934 | I | IWCR | MA | 5963 | I | IWC | OY | 5997 | I | IWCR | OY | 6031 | I | IWCR | OY |
| 5935 | | IWC | WB | 5964 | I | PEC | EC | 5998 | I | IANR | NC | 6034 | I | IWCR | OY |
| 5936 | I | IANR | NC | 5965 | I | IWCR | EN | 5999 | I | IANR | NC | 6035† | I | IWCR | OY |

| | | | | | | | | | | | | | | | |
|---|---|---|---|---|---|---|---|---|---|---|---|---|---|---|---|
| 6036 | I | IANR | NC | 6065 | I | IWC | OY | 6124 | I | IWCR | OY | 6160 | I | PEC | EC |
| 6037 | I | IWCR | OY | 6066 | I | IWCR | OY | 6134 | I | IWCR | OY | 6161 | I | IWCR | OY |
| 6038 | I | IWCR | OY | 6067 | I | IWCR | OY | 6135 | I | IWCR | EN | 6162 | I | IWCR | OY |
| 6041 | I | IWCR | OY | 6073 | | IWC | WB | 6136 | I | IANR | NC | 6163 | I | IWC | PC |
| 6042 | I | IWCR | EN | 6100 | I | IWC | MA | 6137 | I | IWC | OY | 6164 | I | IWCR | OY |
| 6043 | I | IWC | MA | 6101 | I | IWCR | OY | 6138 | I | IWCR | WB | 6165 | I | IWCR | OY |
| 6045† | I | IWCR | OY | 6102 | I | IWCR | MA | 6139 | I | PEC | EC | 6166 | I | IANR | NC |
| 6046 | I | IWCR | OY | 6103 | I | IANR | NC | 6141† | I | IWCR | OY | 6167 | I | PEC | EC |
| 6047 | I | IWC | WB | 6104 | I | IWCR | OY | 6142 | I | IWC | WB | 6168 | I | IWCR | EN |
| 6049 | I | IWC | OY | 6105 | I | IWCR | OY | 6144 | I | IWC | PC | 6170 | I | IWCR | OY |
| 6050 | I | IWC | WB | 6106 | I | IWCR | MA | 6145 | I | IWC | OY | 6171 | I | IWCR | OY |
| 6051 | I | IWCR | OY | 6107 | I | IWCR | OY | 6146 | I | IWCR | OY | 6172 | I | IWCR | EN |
| 6052† | I | IWCR | OY | 6110† | I | IWCR | EN | 6147 | I | IWCR | OY | 6173 | I | IWCR | OY |
| 6053 | I | IANR | NC | 6111 | I | IWC | OY | 6148 | I | IWC | WB | 6174 | I | IANR | NC |
| 6054 | I | IWCR | OY | 6112 | | IWC | WB | 6149† | I | IWCR | OY | 6175 | I | IWCR | OY |
| 6055 | I | IWCR | OY | 6113 | I | IANR | NC | 6150 | I | IWCR | EN | 6176† | I | IWCR | OY |
| 6056 | I | IWC | OY | 6115 | I | IWCR | OY | 6151 | I | IWC | EN | 6177 | I | IWCR | EN |
| 6057 | I | IWCR | OY | 6116 | I | IWCR | OY | 6152 | I | IWC | WB | 6178† | I | IWCR | OY |
| 6059 | I | IWCR | WB | 6117 | I | IWCR | OY | 6153 | I | IWC | PC | 6179 | I | IWCR | OY |
| 6060 | I | IWC | OY | 6119 | I | IWCR | EN | 6154 | I | IWCR | EN | 6180 | I | IWCR | PC |
| 6061 | I | IWC | WB | 6120 | I | IWCR | OY | 6155 | | IWC | EN | 6181 | I | IWCR | WB |
| 6062 | I | IWCR | OY | 6121 | I | IWCR | OY | 6157 | I | IANR | NC | 6182 | I | IWCR | EN |
| 6063 | I | IWCR | OY | 6122 | I | IWCR | OY | 6158 | I | IWC | OY | 6183 | I | IWCR | OY |
| 6064 | I | IWCR | OY | 6123 | I | IANR | NC | 6159 | I | IWC | WB | 6184 | I | IWC | WB |

## SO BR Derby

**AD2D**

**Open Standard Mk2d**

**AC2.17. Seats: 58 Livery: I**

| | | | | | | | | | | | |
|---|---|---|---|---|---|---|---|---|---|---|---|
| 6200 | IWC | MA | 6209 | IWC | OY | 6218 | IWR | OM | 6227 | IWC | EN |
| 6201 | IWC | OY | 6210 | IWC | EN | 6219 | IWC | EN | 6228 | IWC | OY |
| 6202 | IWC | MA | 6211 | IWC | MA | 6220 | IWC | MA | 6229 | IWC | MA |
| 6203 | IWC | OY | 6212 | IWC | EN | 6221 | IWC | MA | 6230 | IWC | MA |
| 6204 | IWR | OM | 6213 | IWC | EN | 6222 | IWC | MA | 6231 | IWR | OM |
| 6205 | IWC | MA | 6214 | IWC | OY | 6223 | IWC | EN | 6232 | IWC | MA |
| 6206 | IWR | OM | 6215 | IWC | EN | 6224 | IWC | MA | 6233 | IWC | EN |
| 6207 | IWR | OM | 6216 | IWC | OY | 6225 | IWC | MA | 6234 | IWC | MA |
| 6208 | IWC | MA | 6217 | IWC | OY | 6226 | IWC | OY | 6235 | IWC | OY |

## SALOON Metro-Cammell

**AD4**

**Open Standard Observation Saloon**

**AD4.01 Seats: 42 unclassified. Livery: PC**

| | | |
|---|---|---|
| 6300 | PIS | IS |

## GENERATOR BR Derby

**HSGV**

**InterCity 125 Generator Van**

**GX5.01 Seats: 0 Livery: I**

| | | |
|---|---|---|
| 6310 | IEC | BN |

## SALOON

**AZ5**

**General Manager's Saloon**

**AZ5.01 Seats: 12 loose chairs, unclassified. Livery: I**

| | | |
|---|---|---|
| 6320 | ICHV | BN |

## HSBV

**GS5**

**INTERCITY 125 BARRIER COACHES.**

**GS5.02†/GS5.03$/GS5.04‡/GS5.05#/GS5.07★/GS5.—**

**(For movements of empty stock without Class 43 power cars.**
**Some vehicles not yet renumbered from Departmental stock 'ADB' series).**

| | | | | | | | | | | | | | | | |
|---|---|---|---|---|---|---|---|---|---|---|---|---|---|---|---|
| 6330$ | | IWRG | OM | 6335 | | IEC | EC | 6339$ | | IWR | PM | 6343 | | IEC | NL |
| 6332 | | IEC | HT | 6336 | | IEC | BN | 6340‡ | | IWRG | OM | 6344 | Iw | IECG | HT |
| 6333 | | IEC | EC | 6337 | | IEC | BN | 6341# | | IWR | PM | | | | |
| 6334★ | | IECG | NL | 6338★ | I | IWRG | PM | 6342# | | IWRG | LA | | | | |

Above: Two rarely photographed coaches are Mk1 Sleeper Support Coaches. They are used to provide dormitory and kitchen facilities for staff on the InterCity Luxury Charter sleeper touring services from London to Scotland or the West of England. No 2833 is seen at Bounds Green T & RSMD (BN).
Below: Mk4 AJ1.05 RFM Restaurant First (Modular catering) coach No 10301 stands at Leeds City station between duties to King's Cross.

## BARRIER

## GS5

**INTERCITY 225 BARRIER COACHES.GS5.–**
**(For movements of empty stock without Class 91 locomotives.**
**Some vehicles not yet renumbered from withdrawn stock).**

| | | | | | | | | | | | | | | | |
|---|---|---|---|---|---|---|---|---|---|---|---|---|---|---|---|
| 6350 | | IEC | BN | 6353 | | IEC | BN | 6356 | | | | 6359 | | | |
| 6351 | | IEC | BN | 6354 | | | | 6357 | | | | | | | |
| 6352 | | IEC | BN | 6355 | | | | 6358 | | | | | | | |

## SO BR Derby

## AD2C

**Open Standard Mk2c**

**AD2.05 Seats: 42**

| | | | | | | | | | | | | | | | |
|---|---|---|---|---|---|---|---|---|---|---|---|---|---|---|---|
| 6400 | | PLL | LL | 6405 | | IXXZ | HQ | 6414 | | PLL | LL | 6415 | | PLL | LL |

## TSOT BR Derby

## AG2C

**Micro-Buffet (Open Standard) Mk2c**

**AG2.01 Seats: 55**

| | | | | | | | | | | | | | | | |
|---|---|---|---|---|---|---|---|---|---|---|---|---|---|---|---|
| 6500 | N | NSS | LA | 6510 | | PIS | IS | 6518 | | PIS | IS | 6526 | | PLL | LL |
| 6501 | N | NSS | LA | 6511 | | IML | DY | 6519 | | PIS | IS | 6527 | N | NSS | LA |
| 6502 | N | NSS | LA | 6513 | N | NSS | LA | 6520 | | IML | DY | 6528 | | PLL | LL |
| 6503 | N | NSS | LA | 6514 | | PIS | IS | 6521 | N | NSS | LA | 6529 | | PLL | LL |
| 6506 | | ICC | MA | 6515 | | PNL | NL | 6522 | N | NSS | LA | | | | |
| 6508 | | ICC | MA | 6516 | | IWC | WB | 6523 | | ICC | MA | | | | |
| 6509 | | IML | DY | 6517 | N | NSS | LA | 6524 | | ICC | MA | | | | |

## TSOT BR Derby

## AG2D

**Micro-Buffet (Open Standard) Mk2d**

**AG2.02 Seats: 55**

| | | | | | | | | | | | | | | | |
|---|---|---|---|---|---|---|---|---|---|---|---|---|---|---|---|
| 6600 | I | ICC | EC | 6605 | Ps | PEC | EC | 6613 | Ps | PEC | EC | 6618 | I | ICC | EC |
| 6601 | Ps | PEC | EC | 6607 | | PEC | EC | 6614 | Ps | PEC | EC | 6619 | Ps | PEC | EC |
| 6603 | | PIS | IS | 6608 | I | ICC | EC | 6616 | I | IAN | NC | | | | |
| 6604 | Ps | PEC | EC | 6609 | I | IAN | NC | 6617 | I | IAN | NC | | | | |

## RMBT BR Derby

## AN2D

**Restaurant-Micro-Buffet Mk2d**

**AN2.07 Seats: 47 Livery: I**

| | | | | | | | | | | | | | | | |
|---|---|---|---|---|---|---|---|---|---|---|---|---|---|---|---|
| 6652 | | ICC | MA | 6661 | | IWR | LA | 6662 | | IWR | LA | 6665 | | IWC | WB |
| 6660 | | IWR | LA | | | | | | | | | | | | |

## RLB BR Derby

## AN1F

**Restaurant Lounge Buffet, First Mk2f**

**AN1.01 Seats: 26 loose chairs. Livery: I**

| | | | | | | | | | | | | | | | |
|---|---|---|---|---|---|---|---|---|---|---|---|---|---|---|---|
| 6700 | | IWC | EC | 6703 | | IWC | EC | 6705 | | IWC | EC | 6707 | | IWC | EC |
| 6701 | | IWC | EC | 6704 | | IWC | EC | 6706 | | IWC | EC | 6708 | | IWC | EC |
| 6702 | | IWC | EC | | | | | | | | | | | | |

## TSO BR Derby

## AC2F

**Tourist Open Standard Mk2f**

**AC2.24. Seats: 74 Livery: I**

| | | | | | | | | | | | | | | | |
|---|---|---|---|---|---|---|---|---|---|---|---|---|---|---|---|
| 6800 | | IEC | BN | 6808 | | IEC | BN | 6816 | | IEC | BN | 6824 | | IEC | BN |
| 6801 | | IEC | BN | 6809 | | IEC | BN | 6817 | | IEC | BN | 6825 | | IML | DY |
| 6802 | | IEC | BN | 6810 | | IML | DY | 6818 | | IEC | BN | 6826 | | IML | DY |
| 6803 | | IEC | BN | 6811 | | IML | DY | 6819 | | IEC | BN | 6827 | | IML | DY |
| 6804 | | IEC | BN | 6812 | | IML | DY | 6820 | | IEC | BN | 6828 | | IML | DY |
| 6805 | | IEC | BN | 6813 | | IML | DY | 6821 | | IEC | BN | 6829 | | IML | DY |
| 6806 | | IEC | BN | 6814 | | IML | DY | 6822 | | IEC | BN | | | | |
| 6807 | | IEC | BN | 6815 | | IEC | BN | 6823 | | IEC | BN | | | | |

## CK BR Derby — AA31
**Corridor Composite Mk1** — AA3.01/AA3.02† Seats: 1st 24 Std 18/1st 24 Std 24. Livery: N

| | | | | | | | | | | | |
|---|---|---|---|---|---|---|---|---|---|---|---|
| 7153 | NWR | OM | 7167 | NWR | OM | 7190 | NWR | OM | 7219† | NWR | OM |
| 7156 | NWR | OM | 7168 | NWR | OM | 7195 | NWR | OM | 7232 | NWR | OM |
| 7158 | NWR | OM | 7172 | NWR | OM | 7212† | NWR | OM | 7235 | NWR | OM |
| 7165 | NWR | OM | 7188 | NWR | OM | 7213† | NWR | OM | 7237 | NWR | OM |
| 7166 | NWR | OM | | | | | | | | | |

## CK BR Derby — AA3C
**Corridor Composite Mk2c** — AA3.04 Seats: 1st 24 Std 18

| | | | | | | | | | | | |
|---|---|---|---|---|---|---|---|---|---|---|---|
| 7550 | PIS | IS | 7553 | PIS | IS | 7558 | PIS | IS | 7561 | PIS | IS |
| 7551 | PIS | IS | | | | | | | | | |

## BSOT BR Derby — AH21
**Brake Open Standard, Micro-Buffet Mk1** — AH2.01†/AH2.02. Seats: 31

| | | | | | |
|---|---|---|---|---|---|
| 9007 | ICHS | FW | 9016† | IXXZ | HQ |

## BSOT BR Derby — AH2Z
**Brake Open Standard, Micro-Buffet Mk2** — AH2.03†/AH2.04. Seats: 27 or 31

| | | | | | | | | | | | |
|---|---|---|---|---|---|---|---|---|---|---|---|
| 9100† | PIS | IS | 9102 | PNL | NL | 9104 | PCL | CL | 9105 | PPC | PC |
| 9101† | PIS | IS | 9103 | PCL | CL | | | | | | |

## BSO BR Derby — AE2Z
**Brake Open Standard Mk2** — AE2,03. Seats: 31

| | | | | | | | | | | | | | | | |
|---|---|---|---|---|---|---|---|---|---|---|---|---|---|---|---|
| 9382 | N | NWR | OM | 9388 | PC | PIS | IS | 9393 | | PIS | IS | 9409 | N | NWR | OM |
| 9384 | N | NWR | OM | 9390 | N | NWR | OM | 9394 | | PNL | NL | 9410 | | PNL | NL |
| 9385 | | PNL | NL | 9391 | N | NWR | OM | 9396 | N | NWR | OM | 9412 | | PIS | IS |
| 9386 | | PNL | NL | 9392 | | PNL | NL | 9397 | | PIS | IS | 9414 | PC | PIS | IS |

## BSO BR Derby — AE2A
**Brake Open Standard Mk2a** — AE2,04. Seats: 31

| | | | | | | | | | | | | | | | |
|---|---|---|---|---|---|---|---|---|---|---|---|---|---|---|---|
| 9417 | | PLL | LL | 9422 | N | PLL | LL | 9427 | | IWR | OM | 9434 | | PIS | IS |
| 9418 | | PEC | EC | 9423 | | PIS | IS | 9428 | | PDY | DY | 9435 | | PLL | LL |
| 9419 | | PLL | LL | 9424 | | PIS | IS | 9429 | | IAND | NC | 9436 | | PCL | CL |
| 9420 | | PLL | LL | 9425 | | PLL | LL | 9431 | | PIS | IS | 9437 | | PCL | CL |
| 9421 | | IML | DY | 9426 | | PLL | LL | 9432 | | IAND | NC | 9438 | I | IWR | OM |

## BSO BR Derby — AE2C
**Brake Open Standard Mk2c** — AE2,05. Seats: 31

| | | | | | | | | | | | | | | | |
|---|---|---|---|---|---|---|---|---|---|---|---|---|---|---|---|
| 9439 | | IWC | WB | 9449 | | PEC | EC | 9459 | I | IWR | OM | 9469 | | ICHM | MA |
| 9440 | | PCL | CL | 9450 | | IWC | WB | 9460 | | PIS | IS | 9471 | | IWC | WB |
| 9441 | | ICHM | MA | 9451 | | PIS | IS | 9461 | | IML | DY | 9472 | | ICHM | MA |
| 9442 | | PLL | LL | 9452 | | PLL | LL | 9462 | | PCL | CL | 9473 | | IWC | WB |
| 9443 | | IML | DY | 9453 | | IWC | WB | 9463 | | PIS | IS | 9474 | | ICC | MA |
| 9444 | | PIS | IS | 9454 | | ICC | MA | 9464 | | ICC | MA | 9475 | | IWC | WB |
| 9445 | | PIS | IS | 9455 | | IAND | NC | 9465 | I | IWR | OM | 9476 | | ICC | PC |
| 9446 | | PIS | IS | 9456 | | ICHM | MA | 9466 | | IML | DY | 9477 | | IAND | NC |
| 9447 | | IML | DY | 9457 | | ICHM | MA | 9467 | | ICC | MA | 9478 | | ICC | PC |
| 9448 | | PCL | CL | 9458 | | PCL | CL | 9468 | | IWC | WB | | | | |

## BSO BR Derby — AE2D
**Brake Open Standard Mk2d** — AE2,06. Seats: 31 Livery I

| | | | | | | | | | | | | | | | |
|---|---|---|---|---|---|---|---|---|---|---|---|---|---|---|---|
| 9479 | | IAN | NC | 9483 | | IAN | NC | 9487 | | IAN | NC | 9492 | | IAN | NC |
| 9480 | | ICC | PC | 9484 | | ICC | PC | 9488 | | IAN | NC | 9493 | | IAN | NC |
| 9481 | | IWR | OM | 9485 | | IAN | NC | 9489 | | IAN | NC | 9494 | I | IAN | NC |
| 9482 | | IWR | OM | 9486 | | IAN | NC | 9490 | | ICC | PC | 9495 | I | IAN | NC |

## BSO BR Derby **AE2E**

**Brake Open Standard Mk2e**

**AE2,07. Seats: 32**

| | | | |
|---|---|---|---|
| 9496 | I | IWC | EN |
| 9497 | I | IWC | WB |
| 9498 | I | IWR | LA |
| 9499 | | IWR | LA |
| 9500 | I | IWC | OY |
| 9501 | I | IWR | OM |
| 9502 | I | IWC | WB |
| 9503 | I | IWR | OM |
| 9504 | I | ICC | PC |
| 9505 | I | IWC | EN |
| 9506 | I | IWR | LA |
| 9507 | I | IWC | EN |
| 9508 | I | IWR | OM |
| 9509 | | ICC | PC |

## BSO BR Derby **AE2F**

**Brake Open Standard Mk2f**

**AE2,08. Seats: 31 Livery: I**

| | | |
|---|---|---|
| 9513 | IWC | WB |
| 9516 | IWCR | OY |
| 9520 | IWCR | WB |
| 9521 | IWC | OY |
| 9522 | IWCR | WB |
| 9523 | IWC | WB |
| 9524 | IWC | WB |
| 9525 | IWC | OY |
| 9526 | IWCR | WB |
| 9527 | IWCR | WB |
| 9529 | IWCR | WB |
| 9531 | IWC | WB |
| 9533 | IWC | WB |
| 9537 | IWC | WB |
| 9538 | IWC | WB |
| 9539 | IWCR | OY |

## DBSO BR Derby & Glasgow **AF2F**

**Driving Brake Open Standard Mk2f (InterCity fleet TDM fitted)**

**AF2,01. Seats: 32**

| | | | |
|---|---|---|---|
| 9701 | Ps | PEC | EC |
| 9702 | I | IAN | NC |
| 9703 | I | IAN | NC |
| 9704 | Ps | PEC | EC |
| 9705 | Ps | PEC | EC |
| 9707 | Ps | PEC | EC |
| 9708 | Ps | PEC | EC |
| 9709 | Ps | PEC | EC |
| 9710 | Ps | PEC | EC |
| 9711 | Ps | PEC | EC |
| 9712 | Ps | PEC | EC |
| 9713 | Ps | PEC | EC |
| 9714 | I | IAN | NC |

## RFM BR Derby **AJ1G**

**Restaurant First Modular Mk3a**

**AJ1.01†/AJ1.03 Seats: 22 or 24 Livery: I**

| | | |
|---|---|---|
| 10200† | IWC | WB |
| 10201† | IWC | WB |
| 10202 | IWC | MA |
| 10203 | IWC | WB |
| 10204 | IWC | OY |
| 10205 | IWC | OY |
| 10206 | IWC | OY |
| 10207 | IWC | OY |
| 10208 | IWC | WB |
| 10209 | IWC | OY |
| 10210 | IWC | WB |
| 10211 | IWC | WB |
| 10212 | IWC | WB |
| 10213 | IWC | WB |
| 10214 | IWC | OY |
| 10215 | IWC | WB |
| 10216 | IWC | EN |
| 10217 | IWC | MA |
| 10218 | IWC | EN |
| 10219 | IWC | OY |
| 10220 | IWC | OY |
| 10221 | IWC | WB |
| 10222 | IWC | OY |
| 10223 | IWC | WB |
| 10224 | IWC | WB |
| 10225 | IWC | EN |
| 10226 | IWC | WB |
| 10227 | IWC | WB |
| 10228 | IWC | OY |
| 10229 | IWC | MA |
| 10230 | IWC | WB |
| 10231 | IWC | WB |
| 10232 | IWC | OY |
| 10233 | IWC | EN |
| 10234 | IWC | OY |
| 10235 | IWC | WB |
| 10236 | IWC | WB |
| 10237 | IWC | WB |
| 10238 | IWC | WB |
| 10240 | IWC | OY |
| 10241 | IWC | WB |
| 10242 | IWC | WB |
| 10245 | IWC | WB |
| 10246 | IWC | MA |
| 10247 | IWC | PC |
| 10248 | IWC | WB |
| 10249 | IWC | OY |
| 10250 | IWC | OY |
| 10251 | IWC | PC |
| 10252 | IWC | WB |
| 10253 | IWC | WB |
| 10254 | IWC | WB |
| 10255 | IWC | OY |
| 10256 | IWC | WB |
| 10257 | IWC | WB |
| 10258 | IWC | WB |
| 10259 | IWC | WB |
| 10260 | IWC | WB |

## RFM Metro-Cammell **AJ1H**

**Restaurant First Modular Mk4**

**AJ1.05 Seats: 20 Livery: I**

| | | |
|---|---|---|
| 10300 | IEC | BN |
| 10301 | IEC | BN |
| 10302 | IEC | BN |
| 10303 | IEC | BN |
| 10304 | IEC | BN |
| 10305 | IEC | BN |
| 10306 | IEC | BN |
| 10307 | IEC | BN |
| 10308 | IEC | BN |
| 10309 | IEC | BN |
| 10310 | IEC | BN |
| 10311 | IEC | |
| 10312 | IEC | |
| 10313 | IEC | |
| 10314 | IEC | |
| 10315 | IEC | |
| 10316 | IEC | |
| 10317 | IEC | |
| 10318 | IEC | |
| 10319 | IEC | |
| 10320 | IEC | |
| 10321 | IEC | |
| 10322 | IEC | |
| 10323 | IEC | |
| 10324 | IEC | |
| 10325 | IEC | |
| 10326 | IEC | |
| 10327 | IEC | |
| 10328 | IEC | |
| 10329 | IEC | |
| 10330 | IEC | BN |
| 10331 | IEC | |
| 10332 | IEC | |
| 10333 | IEC | |

## SLEP BR Derby **AU4G**

**Sleeper with Pantry (either class) Mk3a**

**AU4.01 Berths: 1st 12 or Std 24 (†Refurbished for 1st Class use only)**

| | | | |
|---|---|---|---|
| 10500 | I | ICHV | BN |
| 10501† | I | IWCR | EC |
| 10502 | I | IWC | EC |
| 10503 | I | ICHV | BN |
| 10504 | I | IWC | EC |
| 10506 | I | IWC | WB |
| 10507 | I | IWC | WB |
| 10508† | I | IWCR | EC |
| 10509 | | IXXH | HQ |
| 10510† | I | IWCR | EC |
| 10511 | | IXXH | HQ |
| 10512 | | IWC | EC |
| 10513† | I | IWCR | EC |
| 10514 | I | ICHV | BN |
| 10515† | I | IWCR | EC |
| 10516† | I | IWCR | EC |
| 10517 | | IXXH | HQ |
| 10518 | | IXXH | HQ |
| 10519† | I | IWCR | EC |
| 10520 | I | IWC | EC |
| 10521 | | IXXH | HQ |
| 10522† | I | IWCR | EC |
| 10523† | I | IWCR | EC |
| 10525 | | IXXH | HQ |
| 10526† | I | IWCR | EC |
| 10527 | I | IWC | EC |
| 10529 | I | IWC | EC |
| 10530† | I | IWCR | EC |
| 10531 | I | IWC | EC |
| 10532 | I | ICC | EC |
| 10533 | I | IWC | EC |
| 10534 | I | ICC | EC |
| 10535 | I | ICC | EC |
| 10536 | I | IWC | EC |
| 10537 | I | ICC | EC |
| 10538 | I | IWC | EC |
| 10539 | I | IWC | EC |
| 10540 | I | IWC | EC |
| 10541 | I | IWC | EC |
| 10542 | I | IWC | EC |
| 10543 | I | IWC | EC |
| 10544 | I | IWC | EC |
| 10545 | I | ICC | EC |
| 10546 | | IWC | EC |

| | | | |
|---|---|---|---|
| 10547† | I | IWCR | EC |
| 10548† | I | IWCR | EC |
| 10549 | I | IWC | EC |
| 10550 | I | IWC | EC |
| 10551 | I | IWC | EC |
| 10552 | | IXXH | HQ |
| 10553 | I | IWC | WB |
| 10554 | I | ICC | EC |
| 10555 | I | IWC | EC |
| 10556 | I | IWR | LA |
| 10557 | I | IWC | EC |
| 10558† | I | IWR | LA |
| 10559 | I | IWC | EC |
| 10560 | I | IWC | EC |
| 10561† | I | IWCR | EC |
| 10562† | I | IWCR | EC |
| 10563 | I | IWC | EC |
| 10564† | I | IWR | LA |
| 10565 | I | IWC | EC |
| 10566 | I | IWC | EC |
| 10567 | I | IWC | WB |
| 10568 | I | IWC | EC |
| 10569 | I | IWC | WB |
| 10570 | | IWR | LA |
| 10571 | I | IWC | WB |
| 10572 | I | IWC | WB |
| 10573 | I | IWC | EC |
| 10574 | I | ICHV | BN |
| 10575 | I | ICHV | BN |
| 10576 | | IWCD | WB |
| 10577 | | IWCD | WB |
| 10578 | I | IWC | EC |
| 10579 | I | IWC | EC |
| 10580 | I | IWC | WB |
| 10581 | | IWCD | WB |
| 10582 | I | IWC | EC |
| 10583 | I | IWC | EC |
| 10584† | I | IWCR | EC |
| 10585 | I | IWR | LA |
| 10586 | I | IWR | LA |
| 10587 | I | IWR | LA |
| 10588 | I | IWR | LA |
| 10589 | | IWC | EC |
| 10590 | I | IWC | EC |
| 10591 | I | IWC | WB |
| 10592 | I | ICC | EC |
| 10593 | I | IWC | EC |
| 10594 | I | IWR | LA |
| 10595 | | IWCD | WB |
| 10596† | I | IWCR | EC |
| 10597 | I | IWC | EC |
| 10598† | I | IWCR | EC |
| 10599 | I | IWC | WB |
| 10600 | I | IWC | EC |
| 10601 | I | IWC | WB |
| 10602 | | IWC | EC |
| 10603 | I | IWR | LA |
| 10604 | I | IWC | EC |
| 10605† | I | IWCR | EC |
| 10606 | I | IWC | EC |
| 10607† | I | IWCR | EC |
| 10608 | | IXXH | HQ |
| 10609 | | IWCD | WB |
| 10610† | I | IWCR | EC |
| 10611 | | IXXH | HQ |
| 10612 | | IWC | EC |
| 10613† | I | IWCR | EC |
| 10614† | I | IWCR | EC |
| 10615 | | IWCD | WB |
| 10616 | | ICC | EC |
| 10617 | | ICC | EC |
| 10618 | | IXXH | HQ |
| 10619 | | IXXH | HQ |

## SLE BR Derby — AS4G

**Sleeper, either class. Mk3a**

**AS4.04 Berths: 1st 13 or Std 26 († Refurbished for 1st Class use only)**

| | | | |
|---|---|---|---|
| 10646 | I | ICHV | BN |
| 10647† | I | IWCR | EC |
| 10648† | I | IWCR | EC |
| 10649† | I | IWCR | EC |
| 10650† | I | IWCR | EC |
| 10651† | I | IWCR | EC |
| 10653† | I | IWCR | EC |
| 10654† | I | IWCR | EC |
| 10655† | I | IWCR | EC |
| 10656 | I | IWC | EC |
| 10657† | I | IWCR | EC |
| 10658 | I | IWC | EC |
| 10660 | I | IWC | EC |
| 10661 | I | ICHV | BN |
| 10662 | | ICHV | BN |
| 10663 | I | ICC | EC |
| 10665 | | IWC | EC |
| 10666 | I | ICC | EC |
| 10668 | I | IWC | WB |
| 10670 | I | IWC | EC |
| 10671 | I | ICC | EC |
| 10672 | I | ICC | EC |
| 10673 | | IWC | EC |
| 10674 | I | ICC | EC |
| 10675 | I | IWC | EC |
| 10678 | | IWC | EC |
| 10679 | | IWC | EC |
| 10680† | I | IWCR | EC |
| 10682 | I | IWC | EC |
| 10683 | I | IWC | EC |
| 10684 | I | ICC | EC |
| 10685 | I | IWC | EC |
| 10686 | I | IWC | WB |
| 10687 | I | IWC | EC |
| 10688 | I | ICC | EC |
| 10689† | I | IWCR | EC |
| 10690 | I | IWC | EC |
| 10691 | | IWC | EC |
| 10692† | I | IWCR | EC |
| 10693 | I | IWC | EC |
| 10696 | I | IWC | EC |
| 10697 | I | IWC | EC |
| 10699† | I | IWCR | EC |
| 10700 | | IWC | EC |
| 10701 | I | IWC | WB |
| 10702 | I | IWC | EC |
| 10703 | I | IWC | EC |
| 10704 | I | IWC | EC |
| 10705 | I | IWC | EC |
| 10706 | I | IWC | EC |
| 10707 | I | IWC | EC |
| 10708† | I | IWCR | EC |
| 10709† | I | IWCR | EC |
| 10710† | I | IWCR | EC |
| 10711 | I | IWC | EC |
| 10712† | I | IWCR | EC |
| 10713 | I | IWC | EC |
| 10714† | I | IWCR | EC |
| 10715 | I | IWC | EC |
| 10716† | I | IWCR | EC |
| 10717† | I | IWCR | EC |
| 10718 | I | IWCR | EC |
| 10719† | I | IWCR | EC |
| 10720 | I | IWC | EC |
| 10722† | I | IWCR | EC |
| 10723† | I | IWCR | EC |
| 10724 | I | ICHV | BN |
| 10725 | I | ICHV | BN |
| 10726 | I | ICHV | BN |
| 10727 | I | ICHV | BN |
| 10728 | | ICHV | BN |
| 10729 | I | ICHV | BN |
| 10730† | I | IWCR | EC |
| 10731† | I | IWCR | EC |
| 10732† | I | IWCR | EC |

## FO BR Derby — AD1G

**Open First Mk3a**

**AD1.08 Seats 48 Livery: I**

| | | |
|---|---|---|
| 11005 | IWC | WB |
| 11006 | IWC | WB |
| 11007 | IWC | WB |
| 11011 | IWC | WB |
| 11013 | IWC | WB |
| 11016 | IWC | WB |
| 11017 | IWC | WB |
| 11018 | IWC | WB |
| 11019 | IWC | WB |
| 11020 | IWC | WB |
| 11021 | IWC | WB |
| 11023 | IWC | WB |
| 11024 | IWC | WB |
| 11026 | IWC | WB |
| 11027 | IWC | WB |
| 11028 | IWC | WB |
| 11029 | IWC | WB |
| 11030 | IWC | WB |
| 11031 | IWC | WB |
| 11033 | IWC | WB |
| 11036 | IWC | WB |
| 11037 | IWC | WB |
| 11038 | IWC | WB |
| 11039 | IWC | WB |
| 11040 | IWC | WB |
| 11042 | IWC | WB |
| 11044 | IWC | WB |
| 11045 | IWC | WB |
| 11046 | IWC | WB |
| 11048 | IWC | WB |
| 11052 | IWC | WB |
| 11054 | IWC | WB |
| 11055 | IWC | WB |
| 11058 | IWC | WB |
| 11060 | IWC | WB |

## FO BR Derby — AD1H

**Open First Mk3b**

**AD1.10 Seats 48**

| | | | |
|---|---|---|---|
| 11064 | I | IWC | WB |
| 11065 | I | IWC | WB |
| 11066 | I | IWC | WB |
| 11067 | I | IWC | WB |
| 11068 | I | IWC | WB |
| 11069 | I | IWC | WB |
| 11070 | I | IWC | WB |
| 11071 | I | IWC | WB |
| 11072 | I | IWC | WB |
| 11073 | IP | IWC | WB |
| 11074 | IP | IWC | WB |
| 11075 | I | IWC | WB |
| 11076 | IP | IWC | WB |
| 11077 | IP | IWC | WB |
| 11078 | I | IWC | WB |
| 11079 | IP | IWC | WB |
| 11080 | IP | IWC | WB |
| 11081 | IP | IWC | WB |
| 11082 | IP | IWC | WB |
| 11083 | IP | IWC | WB |
| 11084 | IP | IWC | WB |
| 11085 | IP | IWC | WB |
| 11086 | IP | IWC | WB |
| 11087 | IP | IWC | WB |
| 11088 | IP | IWC | WB |
| 11089 | IP | IWC | WB |
| 11090 | IP | IWC | WB |
| 11091 | I | IWC | WB |
| 11092 | IP | IWC | WB |
| 11093 | IP | IWC | WB |
| 11094 | IP | IWC | WB |
| 11095 | I | IWC | WB |
| 11096 | I | IWC | WB |
| 11097 | I | IWC | WB |
| 11098 | I | IWC | WB |
| 11099 | I | IWC | WB |
| 11100 | I | IWC | WB |
| 11101 | I | IWC | WB |

## FO Metro-Cammell — AD1H

Open First or Pullman Mk4 — AD1.11 Seats 46 Livery: I

| | | | | | | | | | | | |
|---|---|---|---|---|---|---|---|---|---|---|---|
| 11200 | IEC | BN | 11218 | IEC | BN | 11236 | IEC | | 11254 | IEC | |
| 11201 | IEC | BN | 11219 | IEC | BN | 11237 | IEC | | 11255 | IEC | |
| 11202 | IEC | BN | 11220 | IEC | | 11238 | IEC | | 11256 | IEC | BN |
| 11203 | IEC | BN | 11221 | IEC | | 11239 | IEC | | 11257 | IEC | BN |
| 11204 | IEC | BN | 11222 | IEC | | 11240 | IEC | | 11258 | IEC | |
| 11205 | IEC | BN | 11223 | IEC | | 11241 | IEC | | 11259 | IEC | |
| 11206 | IEC | BN | 11224 | IEC | | 11242 | IEC | | 11260 | IEC | |
| 11207 | IEC | BN | 11225 | IEC | | 11243 | IEC | | 11261 | IEC | |
| 11208 | IEC | BN | 11226 | IEC | | 11244 | IEC | | 11262 | IEC | |
| 11209 | IEC | BN | 11227 | IEC | | 11245 | IEC | | 11263 | IEC | |
| 11210 | IEC | BN | 11228 | IEC | | 11246 | IEC | | 11264 | IEC | |
| 11211 | IEC | BN | 11229 | IEC | | 11247 | IEC | | 11265 | IEC | |
| 11212 | IEC | BN | 11230 | IEC | | 11248 | IEC | | 11266 | IEC | |
| 11213 | IEC | BN | 11231 | IEC | | 11249 | IEC | | 11267 | IEC | |
| 11214 | IEC | BN | 11232 | IEC | | 11250 | IEC | | 11268 | IEC | |
| 11215 | IEC | BN | 11233 | IEC | | 11251 | IEC | | | | |
| 11216 | IEC | BN | 11234 | IEC | | 11252 | IEC | | | | |
| 11217 | IEC | BN | 11235 | IEC | | 11253 | IEC | | | | |

## TSO BR Derby — AC2G

Tourist Open Standard Mk3a — AC2.12$/AC2.13/AC2.16†/AC2.22# Seats 70#/72$/74†/76.

| | | | | | | | | | | | | | | | |
|---|---|---|---|---|---|---|---|---|---|---|---|---|---|---|---|
| 12004$ | I | IWC | WB | 12048 | I | IWC | WB | 12090$ | I | IWC | WB | 12131 | I | IWC | WB |
| 12005 | I | IWC | WB | 12049 | I | IWC | WB | 12091$ | I | IWC | WB | 12132 | I | IWC | WB |
| 12007 | I | IWC | WB | 12050 | I | IWC | WB | 12092 | I | IWC | WB | 12133 | I | IWC | WB |
| 12008 | I | IWC | WB | 12051 | I | IWC | WB | 12093 | I | IWC | WB | 12134 | I | IWC | WB |
| 12009 | I | IWC | WB | 12052 | I | IWC | WB | 12094 | I | IWC | WB | 12135$ | I | IWC | WB |
| 12010 | I | PEC | EC | 12053 | I | IWC | WB | 12095 | I | IWC | WB | 12136 | I | IWC | WB |
| 12011 | I | IWC | WB | 12054† | I | IWC | WB | 12096 | I | IWC | WB | 12137 | I | IWC | WB |
| 12012$ | I | IWC | WB | 12055 | I | PEC | EC | 12097 | I | IWC | WB | 12138$ | I | IWC | WB |
| 12013 | I | IWC | WB | 12056 | I | IWC | WB | 12098 | I | IWC | WB | 12139 | I | IWC | WB |
| 12014 | I | IWC | WB | 12057 | I | IWC | WB | 12099 | I | IWC | WB | 12140† | I | IWC | WB |
| 12015 | I | IWC | WB | 12058 | I | IWC | WB | 12100† | I | IWC | WB | 12141 | I | IWC | WB |
| 12016$ | I | IWC | WB | 12059† | I | IWC | WB | 12101† | I | IWC | WB | 12142† | I | IWC | WB |
| 12017 | I | IWC | WB | 12060 | I | IWC | WB | 12102$ | I | IWC | WB | 12143 | I | IWC | WB |
| 12019$ | I | IWC | WB | 12061$ | I | IWC | WB | 12103# | I | IWC | WB | 12144# | I | IWC | WB |
| 12020$ | I | IWC | WB | 12062 | I | IWC | WB | 12104$ | I | IWC | WB | 12145$ | I | IWC | WB |
| 12021$ | I | IWC | WB | 12063 | I | IWC | WB | 12105# | I | IWC | WB | 12146 | I | IWC | WB |
| 12022 | I | IWC | WB | 12064 | I | IWC | WB | 12106 | I | IWC | WB | 12147 | I | IWC | WB |
| 12023 | I | IWC | WB | 12065 | I | IWC | WB | 12107 | I | IWC | WB | 12148 | I | IWC | WB |
| 12024 | I | IWC | WB | 12066 | I | IWC | WB | 12108# | I | IWC | WB | 12149 | I | IWC | WB |
| 12025 | I | IWC | WB | 12067 | I | IWC | WB | 12109† | I | IWC | WB | 12150 | I | IWC | WB |
| 12026$ | I | IWC | WB | 12068 | I | IWC | WB | 12110 | I | IWC | WB | 12151 | I | IWC | WB |
| 12027 | I | IWC | WB | 12069 | I | PEC | EC | 12111 | I | IWC | WB | 12152 | I | IWC | WB |
| 12028 | I | IWC | WB | 12070 | I | IWC | WB | 12112 | I | IWC | WB | 12153† | I | IWC | WB |
| 12029 | I | IWC | WB | 12071 | I | IWC | WB | 12113† | I | IWC | WB | 12154† | I | IWC | WB |
| 12030 | I | IWC | WB | 12072 | I | IWC | WB | 12114 | I | IWC | WB | 12155 | I | IWC | WB |
| 12031 | I | IWC | WB | 12073 | I | IWC | WB | 12115 | I | IWC | WB | 12156 | I | IWC | WB |
| 12032 | I | IWC | WB | 12075 | I | IWC | WB | 12116 | I | IWC | WB | 12157 | I | IWC | WB |
| 12033† | I | IWC | WB | 12076 | I | IWC | WB | 12117 | I | IWC | WB | 12158 | I | IWC | WB |
| 12034 | I | IWC | WB | 12077 | I | IWC | WB | 12118 | I | IWC | WB | 12159$ | I | IWC | WB |
| 12035 | I | IWC | WB | 12078 | I | IWC | WB | 12119 | I | IWC | WB | 12160# | I | IWC | WB |
| 12036† | I | IWC | WB | 12079$ | I | IWC | WB | 12120 | I | IWC | WB | 12161† | I | IWC | WB |
| 12037 | I | IWC | WB | 12080 | I | IWC | WB | 12121$ | I | IWC | WB | 12163 | I | IWC | WB |
| 12038 | I | IWC | WB | 12081 | I | IWC | WB | 12122 | I | IWC | WB | 12164 | I | IWC | WB |
| 12040 | I | IWC | WB | 12082 | I | IWC | WB | 12123 | I | IWC | WB | 12165$ | I | IWC | WB |
| 12041 | I | IWC | WB | 12083 | I | IWC | WB | 12124$ | I | IWC | WB | 12166 | I | IWC | WB |
| 12042† | I | IWC | WB | 12084 | I | IWC | WB | 12125 | I | IWC | WB | 12167 | I | IWC | WB |
| 12043 | I | PEC | EC | 12085† | I | IWC | WB | 12126 | I | IWC | WB | 12168 | I | IWC | WB |
| 12044$ | I | IWC | WB | 12086† | I | IWC | WB | 12127 | I | IWC | WB | 12169† | I | IWC | WB |
| 12045 | I | IWC | WB | 12087† | I | IWC | WB | 12128† | I | IWC | WB | 12170† | I | IWC | WB |
| 12046 | I | IWC | WB | 12088† | I | IWC | WB | 12129$ | I | IWC | WB | 12171† | I | IWC | WB |
| 12047† | I | IWC | WB | 12089 | I | IWC | WB | 12130 | I | IWC | WB | 12172† | I | IWC | WB |

## TSOE Metro-Cammell — AI2H

Tourist Standard Open-End coach — AI2.01 Seats: 74 Livery: I

| | | | | | | | | | | | |
|---|---|---|---|---|---|---|---|---|---|---|---|
| 12200 | IEC | BN | 12204 | IXXH | HQ | 12208 | IEC | BN | 12212 | IEC | |
| 12201 | IEC | BN | 12205 | IEC | BN | 12209 | IEC | BN | 12213 | IEC | |
| 12202 | IEC | BN | 12206 | IEC | BN | 12210 | IEC | | 12214 | IEC | |
| 12203 | IEC | BN | 12207 | IEC | BN | 12211 | IEC | | 12215 | IEC | |

| | | | | | | | | | | | |
|---|---|---|---|---|---|---|---|---|---|---|---|
| 12216 | IEC | | 12221 | IEC | | 12225 | IEC | | 12229 | IEC | |
| 12217 | IEC | | 12222 | IEC | | 12226 | IEC | | 12230 | IEC | |
| 12218 | IEC | | 12223 | IEC | | 12227 | IEC | | 12231 | IEC | |
| 12219 | IEC | | 12224 | IEC | | 12228 | IEC | BN | 12232 | IEC | BN |
| 12220 | IEC | | | | | | | | | | |

## TSOD Metro-Cammell — AL2H

**Tourist Standard Open-Disabled coach** — **AL2.01 Seats: 72 Livery: I**

| | | | | | | | | | | | |
|---|---|---|---|---|---|---|---|---|---|---|---|
| 12300 | IEC | BN | 12308 | IEC | BN | 12316 | IEC | | 12324 | IEC | |
| 12301 | IEC | BN | 12309 | IEC | | 12317 | IEC | | 12325 | IEC | |
| 12302 | IEC | BN | 12310 | IEC | | 12318 | IEC | | 12326 | IEC | |
| 12303 | IEC | BN | 12311 | IEC | | 12319 | IEC | | 12327 | IEC | BN |
| 12304 | IEC | BN | 12312 | IEC | | 12320 | IEC | | 12328 | IEC | |
| 12305 | IEC | BN | 12313 | IEC | | 12321 | IEC | | 12329 | IEC | |
| 12306 | IEC | BN | 12314 | IEC | | 12322 | IEC | | 12330 | IEC | |
| 12307 | IEC | BN | 12315 | IEC | | 12323 | IEC | | | | |

## TSO Metro-Cammell — AC2H

**Tourist Standard Open** — **AC2.14 Seats: 74 Livery: I**

| | | | | | | | | | | | |
|---|---|---|---|---|---|---|---|---|---|---|---|
| 12400 | IEC | BN | 12429 | IEC | | 12458 | IEC | | 12487 | IEC | |
| 12401 | IEC | BN | 12430 | IEC | | 12459 | IEC | | 12488 | IEC | |
| 12402 | IEC | BN | 12431 | IEC | | 12460 | IEC | | 12489 | IEC | |
| 12403 | IEC | BN | 12432 | IEC | | 12461 | IEC | | 12490 | IEC | |
| 12404 | IEC | BN | 12433 | IEC | | 12462 | IEC | | 12491 | IEC | |
| 12405 | | | 12434 | IEC | | 12463 | IEC | | 12492 | IEC | |
| 12406 | IEC | BN | 12435 | IEC | | 12464 | IEC | | 12493 | IEC | |
| 12407 | IEC | BN | 12436 | IEC | | 12465 | IEC | | 12494 | IEC | |
| 12408 | IEC | BN | 12437 | IEC | | 12466 | IEC | | 12495 | IEC | |
| 12409 | IEC | BN | 12438 | IEC | | 12467 | IEC | | 12496 | IEC | |
| 12410 | IEC | BN | 12439 | IEC | | 12468 | IEC | | 12497 | IEC | |
| 12411 | IEC | BN | 12440 | IEC | | 12469 | IEC | | 12498 | IEC | |
| 12412 | IEC | BN | 12441 | IEC | | 12470 | IEC | | 12499 | IEC | |
| 12413 | IEC | BN | 12442 | IEC | | 12471 | IEC | | 12500 | IEC | |
| 12414 | IEC | BN | 12443 | IEC | | 12472 | IEC | | 12501 | IEC | |
| 12415 | IEC | BN | 12444 | IEC | | 12473 | IEC | | 12502 | IEC | |
| 12416 | IEC | BN | 12445 | IEC | | 12474 | IEC | | 12503 | IEC | |
| 12417 | IEC | BN | 12446 | IEC | | 12475 | IEC | | 12504 | IEC | |
| 12418 | IEC | BN | 12447 | IEC | | 12476 | IEC | | 12505 | IEC | |
| 12419 | IEC | BN | 12448 | IEC | | 12477 | IEC | | 12506 | IEC | |
| 12420 | IEC | BN | 12449 | IEC | | 12478 | IEC | BN | 12507 | IEC | |
| 12421 | IEC | BN | 12450 | IEC | | 12479 | IEC | BN | 12508 | IEC | |
| 12422 | IEC | BN | 12451 | IEC | | 12480 | IEC | BN | 12509 | IEC | |
| 12423 | IEC | | 12452 | IEC | | 12481 | IEC | | 12510 | IEC | |
| 12424 | IEC | | 12453 | IEC | | 12482 | IEC | | 12511 | IEC | |
| 12425 | IEC | | 12454 | IEC | | 12483 | IEC | | 12512 | IEC | |
| 12426 | IEC | | 12455 | IEC | | 12484 | IEC | | 12513 | IEC | |
| 12427 | IEC | | 12456 | IEC | | 12485 | IEC | | 12514 | IEC | |
| 12428 | IEC | | 12457 | IEC | | 12486 | IEC | | 12515 | IEC | |

## FK BR Ashford/Swindon — AA11

**Corridor First Mk1** — **AA1.01 Seats: 42**

| | | | | | | | | | | | | | | | |
|---|---|---|---|---|---|---|---|---|---|---|---|---|---|---|---|
| 13225 | I | ICHV | BN | 13237 | I | IWR | OM | 13320 | | IXXH | HQ | 13331 | N | NWR | OM |
| 13227 | I | ICHV | BN | 13303 | | IXXH | HQ | 13321 | | IXXH | HQ | 13335 | N | NWR | OM |
| 13228 | I | ICHL | PH | 13306 | | IXXH | HQ | 13324 | N | NWR | OM | 13341 | I | IWR | OM |
| 13229 | I | ICHL | PH | 13308 | N | NWR | OM | 13325 | | IXXH | HQ | 13342 | I | ICHH | BN |
| 13230 | I | IWR | OM | 13314 | I | IWR | OM | 13326 | | IXXH | HQ | 13344 | | ICHL | PH |
| 13233 | | IXXH | HQ | 13316 | | IXXH | HQ | 13328 | N | NWR | OM | | | | |
| 13236 | I | IWR | OM | 13318 | I | ICHV | BN | 13329 | N | NWR | OM | | | | |

## FK BR Derby — AA1A

**Corridor First Mk2a** — **AA1.06 Seats: 42**

| | | | | | | | | | | | | | | | |
|---|---|---|---|---|---|---|---|---|---|---|---|---|---|---|---|
| 13435 | N | NWR | OM | 13444 | N | NWR | OM | 13456 | | PEC | EC | 13470 | N | NNE | CA |
| 13436 | N | NNE | CA | 13445 | PP | PLL | LL | 13459 | N | NSS | EH | 13472 | | PLL | LL |
| 13437 | N | NWR | OM | 13446 | N | NWR | OM | 13461 | | PEC | EC | 13473 | N | NSS | EH |
| 13440 | N | NWR | OM | 13447 | N | NNE | CA | 13462 | N | NSS | EH | 13474 | N | NNE | CA |
| 13441 | N | NWR | OM | 13450 | N | NNE | CA | 13463 | PP | PLL | LL | 13475 | N | NWR | OM |
| 13443 | N | NWR | OM | 13451 | PP | PLL | LL | 13467 | N | NSS | EH | | | | |

## FK BR Derby — AA1B
**Corridor First Mk2b** — AA1.07 Seats: 42

| | | | | | | | | | | | | | | | |
|---|---|---|---|---|---|---|---|---|---|---|---|---|---|---|---|
| 13479 | N | NSS | EH | 13488 | N | NWR | OM | 13499 | N | NSS | EH | 13507 | N | NSS | EH |
| 13482 | N | NSS | EH | 13493 | N | NWR | OM | 13502 | N | NSS | LA | 13513 | N | NSS | EH |

## FK BR Derby — AA1C
**Corridor First Mk2c** — AA1.08 Seats: 42

| | | | | | | | | | | | | | | | |
|---|---|---|---|---|---|---|---|---|---|---|---|---|---|---|---|
| 13514 | N | NSS | EH | 13519 | PP | PLL | LL | 13525 | N | NSS | EH | 13527 | PP | PLL | LL |
| 13516 | PP | PLL | LL | 13520 | PP | PLL | LL | 13526 | N | NSS | EH | 13532 | PP | PLL | LL |
| 13517 | N | NWR | OM | | | | | | | | | | | | |

## FK BR Ashford/Swindon — AA1D
**Corridor First Mk2d** — AA1.09 Seats: 42

| | | | | | | | | | | | | | | | |
|---|---|---|---|---|---|---|---|---|---|---|---|---|---|---|---|
| 13562 | I | PEC | EC | 13576 | | ICHM | MA | 13588 | I | IWR | OM | 13600 | | IEC | BN |
| 13563 | | IEC | BN | 13577 | I | IWR | OM | 13589 | I | IWR | OM | 13601 | I | ICC | PC |
| 13564 | I | IWR | OM | 13578 | I | ICC | PC | 13590 | I | ICHM | MA | 13602 | I | IWR | OM |
| 13565 | I | ICC | DY | 13579 | I | IWR | OM | 13591 | I | ICC | MA | 13603 | I | IWRL | OM |
| 13566 | I | ICC | MA | 13580 | I | ICC | MA | 13592 | I | ICC | MA | 13604 | I | IEC | BN |
| 13567 | I | IWR | OM | 13581 | I | ICC | MA | 13593 | I | ICC | DY | 13605 | | IEC | BN |
| 13568 | I | ICC | PC | 13582 | I | ICC | PC | 13594 | I | IWR | OM | 13606 | | IWR | OM |
| 13569 | I | ICC | PC | 13583 | I | IWR | OM | 13595 | I | IWR | OM | 13607 | I | IEC | BN |
| 13571 | I | ICC | PC | 13584 | I | IWR | OM | 13596 | I | ICC | PC | 13608 | | IEC | BN |
| 13572 | | PEC | EC | 13585 | I | IEC | BN | 13597 | | PEC | EC | 13609 | I | IXXH | BN |
| 13574 | I | IWRL | OM | 13586 | I | IWR | OM | 13598 | I | ICC | MA | 13610 | I | IWRL | OM |
| 13575 | | IEC | BN | 13587 | I | ICC | MA | 13599 | | IEC | BN | | | | |

## BFK BR Ashford/Swindon — AB11
**Brake Corridor First Mk1** — AB1.01 Seats: 24

| | | | | | | | | | | | |
|---|---|---|---|---|---|---|---|---|---|---|---|
| 17015 | I | ICHV | BN | 17021 | | ICHL | HQ | 17023 | I | ICHV | BN |

## BFK BR Derby — AB1Z
**Brake Corridor First Mk2** — AB1.02 Seats: 24

| | | | | | | | | | | | | | | | |
|---|---|---|---|---|---|---|---|---|---|---|---|---|---|---|---|
| 17037 | I | IWR | OM | 17042 | I | ICH | OM | 17047 | | IXXH | OY | 17052 | | ICHC | OY |
| 17039 | | PIS | IS | 17043 | | IXXH | OY | 17051 | | IWR | OM | 17054 | | ICHC | OY |
| 17040 | N | NWR | OM | | | | | | | | | | | | |

## BFK BR Ashford/Swindon — AB1A
**Brake Corridor First Mk2a** — AB1.03 Seats: 24

| | | | | | | | | | | | | | | | |
|---|---|---|---|---|---|---|---|---|---|---|---|---|---|---|---|
| 17056 | N | NSS | LA | 17069 | N | NSS | LA | 17081 | N | NSS | EH | 17096 | N | NSS | LA |
| 17057 | N | NSS | LA | 17070 | N | NSS | LA | 17082 | N | NSS | LA | 17097 | N | NSS | LA |
| 17058 | N | NWR | OM | 17072 | N | NSS | LA | 17085 | N | NWR | OM | 17098 | I | ICHD | OY |
| 17059 | | PIS | IS | 17073 | N | NSS | LA | 17086 | N | NSS | LA | 17099 | | PIS | IS |
| 17060 | N | NWR | OM | 17074 | N | NSS | LA | 17088 | N | NSS | LA | 17100 | I | ICHD | OY |
| 17062 | N | NWR | OM | 17075 | I | ICHD | OY | 17089 | N | NWR | OM | 17101 | | ICH | LL |
| 17063 | N | NSS | LA | 17076 | N | NSS | LA | 17090 | N | NWR | OM | 17102 | I | ICH | OY |
| 17064 | N | NWR | OM | 17077 | N | NSS | LA | 17091 | N | NWR | OM | 17103 | | ICHC | OY |
| 17066 | | ICHC | OY | 17079 | N | NSS | EH | 17092 | N | NWR | OM | | | | |
| 17068 | N | NWR | OM | 17080 | N | NSS | LA | 17093 | I | IEC | BN | | | | |

## BFK BR Ashford/Swindon — AB1C
**Brake Corridor First Mk2c** — AB1.05 Seats: 24

| | | | | | | | | | | | | | | | |
|---|---|---|---|---|---|---|---|---|---|---|---|---|---|---|---|
| 17113 | I | ICHD | OY | 17121 | N | NSS | LA | 17128 | | PIS | IS | 17135 | I | IAN | NC |
| 17114 | N | NSS | LA | 17122 | I | ICC | PC | 17129 | I | ICC | PC | 17136 | | IEC | BN |
| 17115 | N | NSS | LA | 17123 | | ICC | PC | 17130 | I | ICC | MA | 17137 | | IWCD | MA |
| 17117 | I | ICH | OM | 17124 | | ICC | MA | 17131 | | ICC | PC | 17138 | I | ICC | MA |
| 17118 | N | NWR | OM | 17125 | | ICC | PC | 17132 | N | NSS | LA | | | | |
| 17119 | | IXXH | PC | 17126 | I | ICC | MA | 17133 | N | NSS | EH | | | | |
| 17120 | N | NSS | LA | 17127 | | PIS | IS | 17134 | I | ICC | MA | | | | |

## BFK BR Derby — AB1D
**Brake Corridor First Mk2d** — AB1.06 Seats: 24

| | | | |
|---|---|---|---|
| 17139 | I | ICC | PC |
| 17140 | I | ICC | PC |
| 17141 | I | ICC | MA |
| 17142 | I | ICC | MA |
| 17143 | I | IAN | NC |
| 17144 | I | ICC | DY |
| 17145 | I | ICC | DY |
| 17146 | I | ICC | MA |
| 17147 | I | ICC | MA |
| 17148 | I | ICC | DY |
| 17149 | I | ICC | MA |
| 17150 | I | ICC | PC |
| 17151 | I | ICC | MA |
| 17152 | | ICC | PC |
| 17153 | I | IAN | NC |
| 17154 | I | IAN | NC |
| 17155 | I | ICC | MA |
| 17156 | I | ICC | MA |
| 17157 | I | ICC | MA |
| 17158 | I | IAN | NC |
| 17159 | I | IEC | BN |
| 17160 | I | ICC | PC |
| 17161 | I | IAN | NC |
| 17162 | I | ICC | PC |
| 17163 | I | ICC | PC |
| 17164 | I | ICC | MA |
| 17165 | I | ICC | MA |
| 17166 | I | ICC | PC |
| 17167 | I | ICC | PC |
| 17168 | I | ICC | MA |
| 17169 | I | ICC | PC |
| 17170 | I | ICC | PC |
| 17171 | I | ICC | PC |
| 17172 | I | ICCR | PC |

## BFO BR Derby — AE1H
**Brake Open First Mk3b** — AE1.01 Seats: 36 Livery: I

| | | | |
|---|---|---|---|
| 17173 | | IWC | WB |
| 17174 | | IWC | WB |
| 17175 | | IWC | WB |

## SK BR Derby & Wolverton — AA21
**Corridor Standard Mk1** — AA2.01†/AA2.02 Seats: 48† or 64

| | | | |
|---|---|---|---|
| 18284† | | PIS | IS |
| 18288† | | PIS | IS |
| 18597† | | PLL | LL |
| 18601 | N | PLL | LL |
| 18602 | N | NWR | OM |
| 18603 | N | PNL | NL |
| 18604 | N | PLL | LL |
| 18605 | N | NWR | OM |
| 18608 | N | PNL | NL |
| 18610 | | NXXZ | OM |
| 18611 | N | NWR | OM |
| 18616 | N | NWR | OM |
| 18622 | N | NWR | OM |
| 18627 | N | PNL | NL |
| 18704 | N | NWR | OM |
| 18706 | N | PLL | LL |
| 18709 | N | PNL | NL |
| 18711 | N | NWR | OM |
| 18712 | | PLL | LL |
| 18714 | N | PNL | NL |
| 18715 | N | NWR | OM |
| 18716 | | PLL | LL |
| 18717 | N | NWR | OM |
| 18727 | N | PLL | LL |
| 18728 | N | NWR | OM |
| 18729 | N | NWR | OM |
| 18730 | N | NWR | OM |
| 18743† | N | NWR | OM |
| 18749† | | PNL | NL |
| 18750† | | PLL | LL |
| 18752† | N | NWR | OM |
| 18756† | | ICHL | LL |
| 18769† | N | NWR | OM |
| 18771† | N | NWR | OM |
| 18774† | | PNL | NL |
| 18775 | N | NWR | OM |
| 18783† | | PLL | LL |
| 18784 | N | PNL | NL |
| 18788 | N | PLL | LL |
| 18789 | N | PLL | LL |
| 18792 | N | PLL | LL |
| 18794 | N | NWR | OM |
| 18805 | N | NWR | OM |
| 18806† | | ICHL | LL |
| 18809 | | PLL | LL |
| 18813† | | PNL | NL |
| 18814 | N | NWR | OM |
| 18818 | N | NWR | OM |
| 18819† | | ICHH | OM |
| 18835 | | PLL | LL |
| 18838† | | PNL | NL |
| 18849† | | PLL | LL |
| 18863† | N | NWR | OM |
| 18869† | N | NWR | OM |
| 18875† | N | PLL | LL |
| 18901† | | ICHH | OM |
| 18911 | | PCF | CF |
| 18921 | N | PLL | LL |
| 18925 | N | PLL | LL |
| 18931 | N | PLL | LL |
| 18933 | N | NWR | OM |
| 18935 | N | PNL | NL |
| 18936 | N | PNL | NL |
| 18937 | N | NWR | OM |
| 18938 | N | PLL | LL |
| 18940 | N | PLL | LL |
| 18941 | N | PLL | LL |
| 18943 | N | PLL | LL |
| 18945 | N | PLL | LL |
| 18951 | | NXXZ | OM |
| 18952 | N | NWR | OM |
| 18955 | N | PNL | NL |
| 18958 | N | PLL | LL |
| 18959 | N | PLL | LL |
| 18960 | N | PLL | LL |
| 18967 | N | NWR | OM |
| 18968 | N | PLL | LL |
| 18970 | N | PLL | LL |
| 18977† | | ICHH | OM |
| 18996† | | PNL | NL |
| 18997† | N | NWR | OM |
| 19011† | | ICHH | OM |
| 19012† | | PLL | LL |
| 19014† | | ICHL | HQ |
| 19022 | N | NWR | OM |

## SK BR Derby — AA2A
**Corridor Standard Mk2a** — AA2.09 Seats: 42

| | | | |
|---|---|---|---|
| 19452 | | PLL | LL |
| 19454 | | IXXZ | HQ |
| 19455 | | PLL | LL |
| 19458 | | PDY | DY |
| 19464 | | IXXZ | HQ |
| 19465 | | IEC | BN |

## SK BR Derby — AA2B
**Corridor Standard Mk2b** — AA2.07 Seats: 42

| | | | |
|---|---|---|---|
| 19478 | | IEC | BN |
| 19486 | | PLL | LL |

## SK BR Derby — AA2C
**Corridor Standard Mk2c** — AA2.08 Seats: 42

| | | | |
|---|---|---|---|
| 19522 | | PLL | LL |
| 19523 | | PLL | LL |
| 19529 | | PLL | LL |
| 19536 | | PLL | LL |
| 19545 | | PLL | LL |
| 19548 | | PLL | LL |
| 19549 | | PLL | LL |
| 19555 | | PLL | LL |
| 19556 | | PLL | LL |

## BCK BR Derby & Swindon — AB31
**Brake Corridor Composite Mk1** — AB3.01/AB3.02 Seats: 1st 12 Std 18/1st 12 Std 24

| | | | |
|---|---|---|---|
| 21241 | IT | ICHS | BN |
| 21242 | | ICHS | BN |
| 21246 | I | ICHV | BN |
| 21247 | | ICHL | HQ |
| 21265 | N | NSS | EH |
| 21266 | I | ICHV | BN |
| 21268 | I | ICH | BN |
| 21269 | | ICC | EC |
| 21274 | I | ICH | BN |

## SK BR Derby & Wolverton — AA21

**Corridor Standard Mk1** — **AA2.01†/AA2.02 Seats: 48† or 64**

| | | | | | | | | | | | |
|---|---|---|---|---|---|---|---|---|---|---|---|
| 24895† | | PPC | PC | 25008† | | ICHS | FW | 26125 | | ICHS | FW |

## BSK BR Wolverton/Gloucester RC&W — AB21

**Brake Corridor Standard Mk1** — **AB2.01/AB2.02 Seats: 24 or 32.**

| | | | | | | | | | | | | | | | |
|---|---|---|---|---|---|---|---|---|---|---|---|---|---|---|---|
| 34538 | | PLL | LL | 35333 | | PLL | LL | 35453 | | PLL | LL | 35471 | N | NWR | OM |
| 34668 | | PPC | PC | 35339 | N | NWR | OM | 35454 | | ICHS | LL | 35473 | | PLL | LL |
| 34681 | | PNL | NL | 35340 | | PLL | LL | 35455 | N | NWR | OM | 35474 | N | NWR | OM |
| 35284 | | PLA | LA | 35343 | | PLL | LL | 35457 | | PNL | NL | 35475 | N | PLL | LL |
| 35290 | N | NWR | OM | 35447 | N | NWR | OM | 35459 | | ICHL | LL | 35476 | | IXXZ | OM |
| 35306 | | PLL | LL | 35448 | | IXXH | OM | 35464 | N | NWR | OM | 35479 | N | NWR | OM |
| 35309 | N | NWR | OM | 35449 | | ICHL | OM | 35465 | N | ICHS | LL | 35482 | | PLA | LA |
| 35317 | N | NWR | OM | 35450 | | ICHL | OY | 35469 | | ICHS | OY | 35483 | | PIS | IS |
| 35329 | N | NWR | OM | 35452 | N | NWR | OM | 35470 | | PLL | LL | | | | |

## BSK BR Derby — AB2A

**Brake Corridor Standard Mk2a** — **AB2.04 Seats: 24 Livery: I**

| | | |
|---|---|---|
| 35500 | NWR | OM |

## INTERCITY 125 Mk3a COACHING STOCK BREL DERBY

### TRFB — GN1G.

**Trailer Restaurant First with Buffet.** — **GN1.01. Seats: 23 Livery: I**

| | | | | | | | | | | | |
|---|---|---|---|---|---|---|---|---|---|---|---|
| 40204 | IWR | PM | 40208 | IWR | PM | 40212 | IWR | LA | 40231 | ICC | LA |
| 40205 | IWR | PM | 40209 | IWR | PM | 40213 | IWR | PM | 40232 | IWR | PM |
| 40206 | IWR | PM | 40210 | IWR | PM | 40221 | IWR | LA | 40233 | ICC | LA |
| 40207 | IWR | PM | 40211 | IWR | PM | 40228 | IWR | LA | 40234 | | |

### TRSB — GK2H

**Trailer Restaurant Standard with Buffet.** — **GK2.02. Seats: 35.**

| | | | | | | | | | | | | | | | |
|---|---|---|---|---|---|---|---|---|---|---|---|---|---|---|---|
| 40401 | I | ICC | PM | 40417 | I | IWR | LA | 40424 | I | ICC | LA | 40434 | | ICC | LA |
| 40402 | I | ICC | PM | 40418 | I | IWR | LA | 40425 | I | ICC | PM | 40435 | I | IWR | PM |
| 40403 | I | ICC | PM | 40419 | I | IWR | LA | 40426 | I | ICC | LA | 40436 | I | IWR | LA |
| 40414 | I | ICC | LA | 40420 | I | ICC | PM | 40427 | I | ICC | LA | 40437 | I | IWR | PM |
| 40415 | I | ICC | LA | 40422 | I | IWR | LA | 40429 | I | ICC | LA | | | | |
| 40416 | I | IWR | LA | 40423 | I | IWR | LA | 40430 | I | ICC | LA | | | | |

### TRFK — GL1G

**Trailer Restaurant First with Kitchen (Pullman).** — **GL1.01. Seats: 24 Livery: IP**

| | | | | | | | | |
|---|---|---|---|---|---|---|---|---|
| 40501 | IEC | NL | 40505 | IEC | NL | 40511 | IEC | HT |

### TLUK — GM4G

**Trailer Lounge with Kitchen, unclassified.** — **GM4.01. Seats: 23 Livery: I**

| | | |
|---|---|---|
| 40513 | ICHV | BN |

### TRFM — GK1G

**Trailer Restaurant First, Modular catering.** — **GK1.02. Seats: 17 Livery: I**

| | | |
|---|---|---|
| 40619 | IML | NL |

### TRFB — GK1G

**Trailer Restaurant First with Buffet.** — **GK1.01. Seats: 23.**

| | | | | | | | | | | | | | | | |
|---|---|---|---|---|---|---|---|---|---|---|---|---|---|---|---|
| 40700 | I | IEC | NL | 40706 | I | IEC | BN | 40712 | I | IML | NL | 40718 | I | IEC | BN |
| 40701 | I | IEC | BN | 40707 | I | IEC | BN | 40713 | I | IEC | NL | 40720 | I | IEC | BN |
| 40702 | I | IEC | BN | 40708 | I | IEC | BN | 40714 | I | IEC | NL | 40721 | I | IEC | BN |
| 40703 | I | IEC | BN | 40709 | I | IML | NL | 40715 | I | IEC | BN | 40722 | I | IWR | LA |
| 40704 | I | IEC | BN | 40710 | I | IEC | BN | 40716 | I | IEC | BN | 40723 | I | IWR | LA |
| 40705 | I | IEC | BN | 40711 | I | IML | NL | 40717 | I | IEC | NL | 40724 | I | IWR | LA |

| | | | | | | | | | | | | | | | |
|---|---|---|---|---|---|---|---|---|---|---|---|---|---|---|---|
| 40725 | I | IWR | LA | 40734 | I | IEC | BN | 40742 | I | IEC | BN | 40750 | I | IML | NL |
| 40726 | I | IWR | LA | 40735 | I | IML | NL | 40743 | I | IEC | NL | 40751 | I | IEC | NL |
| 40727 | I | IWR | LA | 40736 | I | IEC | BN | 40744 | I | IWR | PM | 40752 | I | IWR | PM |
| 40728 | I | IEC | NL | 40737 | I | IML | NL | 40745 | I | IML | NL | 40753 | I | IEC | NL |
| 40729 | I | IEC | BN | 40738 | I | IML | NL | 40746 | I | IML | NL | 40754 | I | IEC | BN |
| 40730 | I | IEC | NL | 40739 | I | IEC | BN | 40747 | I | IWR | PM | 40755 | I | IWR | LA |
| 40731 | I | IWR | LA | 40740 | I | IEC | BN | 40748 | I | IML | NL | 40756 | I | IEC | BN |
| 40732 | I | IWR | LA | 40741 | IP | IEC | HT | 40749 | I | IML | NL | 40757 | I | IWR | LA |
| 40733 | I | IEC | BN | | | | | | | | | | | | |

## TF

## GH1G

**Trailer First**

**GH1.02. Seats: 48.**

(Seats removed on some coaches for wheelchair passengers, details not yet reported)

| | | | | | | | | | | | | | | | |
|---|---|---|---|---|---|---|---|---|---|---|---|---|---|---|---|
| 41003 | I | IWR | PM | 41046 | I | IEC | BN | 41093 | I | IEC | BN | 41136 | I | IWR | LA |
| 41004 | I | IWR | PM | 41047 | I | IWR | PM | 41094 | I | IEC | BN | 41137 | I | IWR | LA |
| 41005 | I | IWR | PM | 41048 | I | IWR | PM | 41095 | I | IEC | BN | 41138 | I | IWR | LA |
| 41006 | I | IWR | PM | 41049 | I | IWR | PM | 41096 | I | IEC | BN | 41139 | I | IWR | LA |
| 41007 | I | IWR | PM | 41050 | I | IWR | PM | 41097 | I | IML | NL | 41140 | I | IWR | LA |
| 41008 | I | IWR | PM | 41051 | I | IWR | LA | 41098 | I | IML | NL | 41141 | I | IWR | LA |
| 41009 | I | IWR | PM | 41052 | I | IWR | LA | 41099 | I | IML | NL | 41142 | I | IWR | LA |
| 41010 | I | IWR | PM | 41055 | I | IML | NL | 41100 | I | IML | NL | 41143 | I | IWR | LA |
| 41011 | I | IWR | PM | 41056 | I | IML | NL | 41101 | I | IML | NL | 41144 | I | IWR | LA |
| 41012 | I | IWR | PM | 41057 | I | IEC | BN | 41102 | I | IML | NL | 41145 | I | IWR | LA |
| 41013 | I | IWR | PM | 41058 | I | IEC | BN | 41103 | I | IEC | NL | 41146 | I | IWR | LA |
| 41014 | I | IWR | PM | 41059 | I | IEC | BN | 41104 | I | IEC | NL | 41147 | I | ICC | PM |
| 41015 | I | IWR | PM | 41060 | I | IEC | BN | 41105 | I | IEC | NL | 41148 | I | ICC | PM |
| 41016 | I | IWR | PM | 41061 | I | IEC | BN | 41106 | I | IEC | NL | 41149 | I | IEC | BN |
| 41017 | I | IWR | PM | 41062 | I | IEC | BN | 41107 | I | IEC | BN | 41150 | I | IEC | BN |
| 41018 | I | IWR | PM | 41063 | I | IEC | BN | 41108 | I | IEC | BN | 41151 | I | IEC | BN |
| 41019 | I | IWR | PM | 41064 | I | IEC | BN | 41109 | I | IEC | BN | 41152 | I | IEC | BN |
| 41020 | I | IWR | PM | 41065 | I | IML | NL | 41110 | I | IEC | BN | 41153 | I | IEC | HT |
| 41021 | I | IWR | PM | 41066 | I | IEC | HT | 41111 | I | IML | NL | 41154 | I | IEC | HT |
| 41022 | I | IWR | PM | 41067 | I | IEC | NL | 41112 | I | IML | NL | 41155 | I | IML | NL |
| 41023 | I | IWR | LA | 41068 | I | IEC | NL | 41113 | I | IEC | BN | 41156 | I | IML | NL |
| 41024 | I | IWR | LA | 41069 | I | IEC | NL | 41114 | I | IEC | BN | 41157 | I | IEC | NL |
| 41025 | I | IWR | LA | 41070 | I | IEC | NL | 41115 | I | IEC | BN | 41158 | I | IEC | NL |
| 41026 | I | IWR | LA | 41071 | I | IEC | NL | 41116 | I | IEC | BN | 41159 | I | ICC | PM |
| 41027 | I | IWR | LA | 41072 | I | IEC | NL | 41117 | I | IML | NL | 41160 | I | ICC | PM |
| 41028 | I | IWR | LA | 41075 | I | IEC | BN | 41118 | I | IEC | BN | 41161 | I | ICC | PM |
| 41029 | I | IWR | LA | 41076 | I | IEC | BN | 41119 | I | IEC | BN | 41162 | I | ICC | LA |
| 41030 | I | IWR | LA | 41077 | I | IEC | NL | 41120 | I | IEC | BN | 41163 | I | ICC | LA |
| 41031 | I | IWR | LA | 41078 | I | IEC | NL | 41121 | I | IWR | LA | 41164 | I | IWR | PM |
| 41032 | I | IWR | LA | 41079 | I | IEC | NL | 41122 | I | IWR | LA | 41165 | I | ICC | LA |
| 41033 | I | IWR | LA | 41080 | I | IEC | NL | 41123 | I | IWR | PM | 41166 | I | ICC | LA |
| 41034 | I | IWR | LA | 41081 | I | IEC | BN | 41124 | I | IWR | PM | 41167 | | ICC | LA |
| 41035 | I | IWR | LA | 41082 | I | IEC | BN | 41125 | I | IWR | LA | 41168 | I | ICC | LA |
| 41036 | I | IWR | LA | 41083 | I | IEC | BN | 41126 | I | IWR | LA | 41169 | | ICC | LA |
| 41037 | I | IWR | LA | 41084 | I | IEC | BN | 41127 | I | IWR | LA | 41170 | I | IEC | BN |
| 41038 | I | IWR | LA | 41085 | I | IEC | BN | 41128 | I | IWR | LA | 41171 | I | IEC | BN |
| 41039 | I | IML | NL | 41086 | I | IEC | BN | 41129 | I | IWR | LA | 41172 | I | IEC | BN |
| 41040 | I | IML | NL | 41087 | I | IEC | BN | 41130 | I | IWR | LA | 41173 | I | IEC | BN |
| 41041 | I | IEC | NL | 41088 | I | IEC | BN | 41131 | I | IWR | PM | 41174 | I | IEC | BN |
| 41042 | I | IWR | LA | 41089 | I | IEC | BN | 41132 | I | IWR | PM | 41175 | I | IML | NL |
| 41043 | I | IML | NL | 41090 | I | IEC | BN | 41133 | I | IWR | LA | 41176 | I | IML | NL |
| 41044 | I | IML | NL | 41091 | I | IEC | BN | 41134 | I | IWR | LA | | | | |
| 41045 | I | IML | NL | 41092 | I | IEC | BN | 41135 | I | IWR | LA | | | | |

## TS.

## GH2G.

**Trailer Standard.**

**GH2.02†/GH2.03. Seats: 72† or 76**

| | | | | | | | | | | | | | | | |
|---|---|---|---|---|---|---|---|---|---|---|---|---|---|---|---|
| 42003 | I | IWR | LA | 42016† | I | IWR | PM | 42029 | I | IWR | PM | 42042 | I | IWR | LA |
| 42004 | I | IWR | PM | 42017† | I | IWR | PM | 42030 | I | IWR | PM | 42043 | I | IWR | LA |
| 42005 | I | IWR | PM | 42018† | I | IWR | PM | 42031 | I | IWR | PM | 42044 | I | IWR | LA |
| 42006† | I | IWR | PM | 42019† | I | IWR | PM | 42032† | I | IWR | PM | 42045 | I | IWR | LA |
| 42007† | I | IWR | PM | 42020† | I | IWR | PM | 42033† | I | IWR | LA | 42046 | I | IWR | LA |
| 42008† | I | IWR | PM | 42021 | I | IWR | PM | 42034 | I | IWR | LA | 42047 | I | IWR | LA |
| 42009 | I | IWR | PM | 42022 | I | IWR | PM | 42035 | I | IWR | LA | 42048 | I | IWR | LA |
| 42010 | I | IWR | PM | 42023 | I | IWR | PM | 42036 | I | IWR | LA | 42049 | I | IWR | LA |
| 42011 | I | IWR | PM | 42024 | I | IWR | PM | 42037 | I | IWR | LA | 42050 | I | IWR | LA |
| 42012 | I | IWR | PM | 42025 | I | IWR | PM | 42038 | I | IWR | LA | 42051† | I | IWR | LA |
| 42013 | I | IWR | PM | 42026 | I | IWR | PM | 42039 | I | IWR | LA | 42052† | I | IWR | LA |
| 42014 | I | IWR | PM | 42027 | I | IWR | PM | 42040 | I | IWR | LA | 42053† | I | IWR | LA |
| 42015† | I | IWR | PM | 42028 | I | IWR | PM | 42041 | I | IWR | LA | 42054 | I | IWR | LA |

| | | | | | | | | | | | |
|---|---|---|---|---|---|---|---|---|---|---|---|
| 42055† I | IWR | LA | 42130 I | IEC | BN | 42205 I | IEC | HT | 42279 I | IWR | LA |
| 42056† I | IWR | LA | 42131 I | IEC | NL | 42206 I | IEC | NL | 42280 I | IWR | LA |
| 42057† I | IML | NL | 42132 I | IEC | NL | 42207 I | IEC | NL | 42281 I | IWR | LA |
| 42058† I | IML | NL | 42133 I | IEC | NL | 42208 I | IEC | NL | 42282 I | ICC | PM |
| 42059† I | IML | NL | 42134 I | IEC | BN | 42209 I | IEC | NL | 42283 I | IWR | LA |
| 42060† I | IWR | LA | 42135 I | IEC | NL | 42210 I | IEC | HT | 42284 I | IWR | LA |
| 42061† I | IWR | LA | 42136 I | IEC | NL | 42211 I | IEC | NL | 42285 I | IWR | LA |
| 42062† I | IML | NL | 42137 I | IEC | NL | 42212 I | IEC | NL | 42286† I | ICC | PM |
| 42063 I | IML | NL | 42138 I | IEC | BN | 42213 I | IEC | NL | 42287 I | IWR | LA |
| 42064 I | IML | NL | 42139 I | IEC | NL | 42214 I | IEC | NL | 42288 I | IWR | LA |
| 42065 I | IML | NL | 42140 I | IEC | NL | 42215 I | IML | NL | 42289 I | IWR | LA |
| 42066† I | IML | NL | 42141 I | IEC | NL | 42216 I | IWR | LA | 42290† I | ICC | PM |
| 42067† I | IML | NL | 42143 I | IWR | PM | 42217 I | IEC | BN | 42291 I | IWR | LA |
| 42068† I | IML | NL | 42144 I | IWR | PM | 42218 I | IEC | BN | 42292 I | IWR | LA |
| 42069† | IWR | PM | 42145 I | IWR | PM | 42219 I | IEC | BN | 42293 I | IWR | LA |
| 42070† | IWR | PM | 42146 I | IML | NL | 42220 I | IML | NL | 42294† I | ICC | PM |
| 42071† | IWR | PM | 42147 I | IEC | BN | 42221 I | IWR | LA | 42295 I | IWR | LA |
| 42072 I | IWR | PM | 42148 I | IEC | BN | 42222 I | IEC | BN | 42296 I | IWR | LA |
| 42073 I | IWR | PM | 42149 I | IEC | BN | 42223 I | IEC | BN | 42297 I | IWR | LA |
| 42074 I | IWR | PM | 42150 I | IML | NL | 42224 I | IEC | BN | 42298† I | ICC | PM |
| 42075 I | IWR | LA | 42151 I | IEC | NL | 42225 I | IML | NL | 42299 I | IWR | LA |
| 42076 I | IWR | LA | 42152 I | IEC | NL | 42226 I | IEC | BN | 42300 I | IWR | LA |
| 42077 I | IWR | LA | 42153 I | IEC | NL | 42227 I | IML | NL | 42301 I | IWR | LA |
| 42078 I | IWR | LA | 42154 I | IML | NL | 42228 I | IML | NL | 42302† I | ICC | PM |
| 42079† I | IWR | PM | 42155 I | IEC | NL | 42229 I | IML | NL | 42303† I | ICC | PM |
| 42080† I | IWR | PM | 42156 I | IEC | NL | 42230 I | IML | NL | 42304† I | ICC | PM |
| 42081† I | IML | NL | 42157 I | IEC | NL | 42231 I | IEC | BN | 42305† I | ICC | PM |
| 42082† I | IML | NL | 42158 I | IML | NL | 42232 I | IEC | BN | 42306 I | ICC | LA |
| 42083† I | IML | NL | 42159 I | IEC | BN | 42233 I | IEC | BN | 42307 I | ICC | LA |
| 42084† I | ICC | PM | 42160 I | IEC | BN | 42234 I | IEC | BN | 42308 I | ICC | LA |
| 42085† I | ICC | PM | 42161 I | IEC | BN | 42235 I | IML | NL | 42309 I | ICC | LA |
| 42086† I | ICC | PM | 42162 I | IEC | BN | 42236 I | IWR | PM | 42310† | ICC | LA |
| 42087† I | ICC | PM | 42163 I | IEC | BN | 42237 I | IEC | BN | 42311† | ICC | LA |
| 42088 I | ICC | LA | 42164 I | IEC | BN | 42238 I | IEC | BN | 42312† | ICC | LA |
| 42089 I | ICC | LA | 42165 I | IEC | BN | 42239 I | IEC | BN | 42313† | ICC | LA |
| 42090 I | ICC | LA | 42166 I | IEC | BN | 42240 I | IML | NL | 42314 I | ICC | LA |
| 42091 I | ICC | LA | 42167 I | IEC | BN | 42241 I | IEC | BN | 42315 I | ICC | LA |
| 42092 I | ICC | LA | 42168 I | IEC | BN | 42242 I | IEC | BN | 42316 I | ICC | LA |
| 42093 I | ICC | LA | 42169 I | IEC | BN | 42243 I | IEC | BN | 42317 I | ICC | LA |
| 42094 I | ICC | LA | 42170 I | IEC | BN | 42244 I | IEC | BN | 42318† | ICC | LA |
| 42095 I | ICC | LA | 42171 I | IEC | BN | 42245 I | IEC | NL | 42319† | ICC | LA |
| 42096† I | IWR | LA | 42172 I | IEC | BN | 42246 I | IEC | BN | 42320† | ICC | LA |
| 42097 I | IWR | LA | 42173 I | IEC | BN | 42247 I | IEC | BN | 42321† | ICC | LA |
| 42098 I | IWR | LA | 42174 I | IEC | BN | 42248 I | IEC | BN | 42322† I | ICC | LA |
| 42099 I | IWR | LA | 42175 I | IEC | BN | 42249 I | IEC | BN | 42323 I | IML | NL |
| 42100 I | IEC | NL | 42176 I | IEC | BN | 42250 I | IEC | NL | 42324 I | IEC | NL |
| 42101 I | IEC | BN | 42177 I | IEC | BN | 42251 I | IWR | LA | 42325 I | IWR | PM |
| 42102 I | IEC | BN | 42178 I | IEC | BN | 42252 I | IWR | LA | 42326 I | IEC | BN |
| 42103 I | IEC | BN | 42179 I | IEC | BN | 42253 I | IWR | LA | 42327 I | IEC | BN |
| 42104 I | IEC | BN | 42180 I | IEC | BN | 42254 I | ICC | PM | 42328 I | IEC | BN |
| 42105 I | IEC | BN | 42181 I | IEC | BN | 42255 I | IWR | PM | 42329 I | IEC | NL |
| 42106 I | IEC | BN | 42182 I | IEC | BN | 42256 I | IWR | PM | 42330 I | IEC | BN |
| 42107 I | IEC | BN | 42183 I | IEC | BN | 42257 I | IWR | PM | 42331 I | IEC | NL |
| 42108† I | ICC | LA | 42184 I | IEC | BN | 42258 I | ICC | PM | 42332 I | IWR | PM |
| 42109† I | ICC | LA | 42185 I | IEC | BN | 42259 I | IWR | LA | 42333 I | IWR | PM |
| 42110† I | ICC | LA | 42186 I | IEC | BN | 42260 I | IWR | LA | 42334 I | IEC | BN |
| 42111 I | IEC | BN | 42187 I | IEC | BN | 42261 I | IWR | LA | 42335 I | IEC | BN |
| 42112 I | IEC | BN | 42188 I | IEC | BN | 42262 I | ICC | PM | 42336 I | IEC | BN |
| 42113 I | IEC | BN | 42189 I | IEC | BN | 42263 I | IWR | PM | 42337 I | IEC | BN |
| 42115 I | IEC | BN | 42190 I | IEC | BN | 42264 I | IWR | LA | 42338 I | IEC | BN |
| 42116 I | IEC | BN | 42191 I | IML | NL | 42265 I | IWR | LA | 42339 I | IEC | NL |
| 42117 I | IEC | BN | 42192 I | IML | NL | 42266 I | ICC | PM | 42340 I | IML | NL |
| 42118 I | IWR | PM | 42193 I | IML | NL | 42267 I | IWR | LA | 42341 | IML | NL |
| 42119† I | IEC | BN | 42194 I | IEC | NL | 42268 I | IWR | LA | 42342 I | IWR | LA |
| 42120† I | IEC | BN | 42195 I | IML | NL | 42269 I | IWR | LA | 42343 I | IWR | LA |
| 42121† I | IEC | BN | 42196 I | IWR | LA | 42270 I | ICC | PM | 42344 I | IWR | LA |
| 42122 I | IEC | BN | 42197 I | IWR | LA | 42271 I | IWR | PM | 42345 I | IWR | LA |
| 42123 I | IEC | BN | 42198 I | IML | NL | 42272 I | IWR | PM | 42346 I | IWR | LA |
| 42124 I | IEC | BN | 42199 I | IML | NL | 42273† I | IWR | PM | 42347 I | IWR | LA |
| 42125 I | IEC | BN | 42200 I | IML | NL | 42274 I | ICC | PM | 42348 I | IWR | LA |
| 42126† I | IML | NL | 42201 I | IML | NL | 42275 I | IWR | LA | 42349 I | IWR | LA |
| 42127 I | IEC | BN | 42202 I | IML | NL | 42276 I | IWR | LA | 42350 I | IWR | |
| 42128 I | IEC | BN | 42203 I | IML | NL | 42277† I | IWR | LA | 42351 I | IWR | |
| 42129 I | IEC | BN | 42204 I | IML | NL | 42278 I | ICC | PM | | | |

## TGS. GJ2G.

**Trailer Guard Standard.** **GJ2.01†/GJ2.02/GJ2.03$/GJ2.04** Seats: 61/62$/63† **★Buffers for standard locomotive haulage**

| | | | |
|---|---|---|---|
| 44000 | I | ICC | PM |
| 44001 | I | IWR | PM |
| 44002 | I | IWR | PM |
| 44003† | I | IWR | PM |
| 44004 | I | IWR | PM |
| 44005† | I | IWR | PM |
| 44006 | I | IWR | PM |
| 44007 | I | IWR | PM |
| 44008 | I | IWR | PM |
| 44009 | I | IWR | PM |
| 44010 | I | IWR | PM |
| 44011 | I | IWR | LA |
| 44012 | I | IWR | LA |
| 44013 | I | IWR | LA |
| 44014 | I | IWR | LA |
| 44015 | I | IWR | LA |
| 44016 | I | IWR | LA |
| 44017† | I | IWR | LA |
| 44018† | I | IWR | LA |
| 44019 | I | IML | NL |
| 44020 | I | IWR | LA |
| 44021★ | I | IEC | BN |
| 44022† | I | IML | NL |
| 44023† | I | IWR | PM |
| 44024 | I | IWR | PM |
| 44025† | I | IWR | LA |
| 44026 | I | IWR | PM |
| 44027 | I | IML | NL |
| 44028 | I | IWR | LA |
| 44029† | I | IWR | PM |
| 44030 | I | IWR | LA |
| 44031 | I | IWR | PM |
| 44032 | I | IWR | LA |
| 44033† | I | IWR | PM |
| 44034 | I | IWR | LA |
| 44035 | I | IWR | LA |
| 44036 | I | IWR | LA |
| 44037$ | I | IWR | LA |
| 44038$ | I | IWR | LA |
| 44039 | I | IWR | LA |
| 44040 | I | IWR | LA |
| 44041 | I | IEC | BN |
| 44042 | I | IEC | BN |
| 44043 | I | IEC | BN |
| 44044† | I | IEC | BN |
| 44045 | I | IML | NL |
| 44046 | I | IEC | NL |
| 44047 | I | IEC | NL |
| 44048 | I | IEC | NL |
| 44049† | I | IWR | PM |
| 44050 | I | IEC | BN |
| 44051 | I | IEC | NL |
| 44052 | I | IEC | NL |
| 44053 | I | IEC | BN |
| 44054 | I | IEC | BN |
| 44055 | I | IEC | BN |
| 44056★ | I | IEC | BN |
| 44057 | I | IEC | BN |
| 44058★ | I | IEC | BN |
| 44059★ | I | IEC | BN |
| 44060 | I | IEC | BN |
| 44061 | I | IML | NL |
| 44062 | I | ICC | PM |
| 44063† | I | IML | NL |
| 44064 | I | IML | NL |
| 44065† | I | ICC | PM |
| 44066 | I | IEC | NL |
| 44067 | I | IEC | NL |
| 44068 | I | ICC | PM |
| 44069† | I | ICC | PM |
| 44070 | I | IEC | BN |
| 44071 | I | IML | NL |
| 44072 | I | ICC | LA |
| 44073† | I | IML | NL |
| 44074 | I | IEC | BN |
| 44075 | I | IEC | BN |
| 44076 | I | ICC | LA |
| 44077 | I | IEC | BN |
| 44078 | I | IEC | BN |
| 44079 | I | IEC | BN |
| 44080 | I | IEC | BN |
| 44081 | I | IWR | PM |
| 44083 | I | IEC | HT |
| 44084 | I | ICC | LA |
| 44085 | I | IML | NL |
| 44086 | I | IEC | NL |
| 44087 | I | ICC | LA |
| 44088 | I | ICC | LA |
| 44089★ | I | ICC | LA |
| 44090 | I | ICC | LA |
| 44091 | I | ICC | LA |
| 44093 | I | IEC | BN |
| 44094 | I | IML | NL |
| 44097★ | I | IEC | HT |
| 44098★ | I | IEC | BN |
| 44099 | I | IWR | LA |
| 44100 | I | IEC | EC |
| 44101★ | | IEC | BN |

## DGS. GF2G.

**Driving Trailer Guard Standard. To be converted from TGS with driving cab for InterCity Cross-Country services in 1991 operating with Class 43/2 power cars.**

44201-24.

# NON-PASSENGER CARRYING COACHING STOCK.

## RK Pressed Steel AK51

**Restaurant Kitchen Mk1**

**AK5.01 Seats: 0 Livery: I**

| | | |
|---|---|---|
| 80041 | ICHV | BN |

## BG BR Wolverton/Gloucester RC&W† NN5

**Riding and Toilet Van**

**NN5.03 Seats: 6 (staff only).**

| | | | |
|---|---|---|---|
| 80200 | | RPXG | OM |
| 80201 | | RPXG | DY |
| 80202 | | RPXG | OM |
| 80203† | | RPXG | DY |
| 80204 | R | RPXG | EN |
| 80205 | R | RPXG | HT |
| 80206 | R | RPXG | EN |
| 80207 | R | RPXG | EN |
| 80208 | R | RPXG | EN |
| 80209† | | RPXG | HT |
| 80210† | R | RPXG | HT |
| 80211 | R | RPXG | HT |
| 80212 | | RPXG | CA |
| 80213 | | RPXG | EN |
| 80214 | R | RPXG | HT |
| 80215† | R | RPXG | CA |
| 80216 | | RPXG | EN |
| 80217 | | RPXG | CA |
| 80218 | | RPXG | MA |
| 80219† | | RPXG | CA |
| 80220† | R | RPXG | HT |
| 80221 | R | RPXG | EN |
| 80222 | R | RPXG | EN |
| 80223 | | RPXG | CA |
| 80224 | | RPXG | OM |
| 80225 | | RPXG | OM |

## POS BR Wolverton/York† NS5

**Post Office Sorting Van.**

**NS5.01–NS5.06 & NS5.31 Seats: 6 (staff only). Livery: R**

(NS5.01)

| | | |
|---|---|---|
| 80300 | RPOM | MA |
| 80301 | RPOM | MA |
| 80302 | RPOM | MA |
| 80303 | RPOA | CA |
| 80304 | RPOA | CA |
| 80305 | RPOA | CA |

(NS5.02)

| | | |
|---|---|---|
| 80306 | RPOA | CA |
| 80307 | RPOA | CA |
| 80308 | RPOA | NC |

(NS5.01)

| | | |
|---|---|---|
| 80309 | RPOA | CA |
| 80310 | RPOE | HT |
| 80311 | RPOE | HT |
| 80312 | RPOE | HT |
| 80313 | RPOE | HT |
| 80314 | RPOE | HT |
| 80315 | RPOE | HT |
| 80316 | RPOA | NC |
| 80318 | RPOA | NC |

(NS5.04†)

| | | |
|---|---|---|
| 80319 | RPOA | CA |
| 80320 | RPOE | HT |
| 80321 | RPOZ | EC |
| 80322 | RPOE | HT |
| 80323 | RPOE | HT |
| 80324 | RPOE | HT |
| 80325 | RPOM | DY |
| 80326 | RPOM | DY |
| 80327 | RPOM | DY |

(NS5.05†)

| | | | | | | | | | | | |
|---|---|---|---|---|---|---|---|---|---|---|---|
| 80328 | RPOM | EN | 80331 | RPOE | HT | 80334 | RPOM | MA | 80337 | RPOE | HT |
| 80329 | RPOM | MA | 80332 | RPOE | HT | 80335 | RPOE | HT | 80338 | RPOM | EN |
| 80330 | RPOE | HT | 80333 | RPOE | HT | 80336 | RPOE | HT | | | |

(NS5.06†)

| | | | | | | | | | | | |
|---|---|---|---|---|---|---|---|---|---|---|---|
| 80339 | RPOM | EN | 80344 | RPOM | EN | 80348 | RPOM | EN | 80352 | RPOA | NC |
| 80340 | RPOM | MA | 80345 | RPOE | HT | 80349 | RPOM | DY | 80353 | RPOM | EN |
| 80341 | RPOM | EN | 80346 | RPOE | HT | 80350 | RPOA | NC | 80354 | RPOM | EN |
| 80342 | RPOM | EN | 80347 | RPOM | EN | 80351 | RPOM | DY | 80355 | RPOM | MA |
| 80343 | RPOM | MA | | | | | | | | | |

(NS5.03†)

| | | | | | | | | | | | |
|---|---|---|---|---|---|---|---|---|---|---|---|
| 80356 | RPOM | EN | 80363 | RPOE | HT | 80369 | RPOM | EN | 80375 | RPOM | MA |
| 80357 | RPOM | EN | 80364 | RPOE | HT | 80370 | RPOM | EN | 80376 | RPOM | EN |
| 80358 | RPOE | HT | 80365 | RPOE | HT | 80371 | RPOM | EN | 80377 | RPOM | EN |
| 80359 | RPOE | HT | 80366 | RPOM | EN | 80372 | RPOM | EN | 80378 | RPOM | EN |
| 80360 | RPOE | HT | 80367 | RPOM | EN | 80373 | RPOM | EN | 80379 | RPOW | OM |
| 80361 | RPOE | HT | 80368 | RPOM | EN | 80374 | RPOM | MA | 80380 | RPOM | MA |
| 80362 | RPOE | HT | | | | | | | | | |

(NS5.31)

| | | | | | | | | | | | |
|---|---|---|---|---|---|---|---|---|---|---|---|
| 80381 | RPOW | OM | 80385 | RPOW | OM | 80389 | RPOW | OM | 80393 | RPOW | OM |
| 80382 | RPOW | OM | 80386 | RPOW | OM | 80390 | RPOW | OM | 80394 | RPOW | OM |
| 80383 | RPOW | OM | 80387 | RPOW | OM | 80391 | RPOW | OM | 80395 | RPOM | MA |
| 80384 | RPOW | OM | 80388 | RPOW | OM | 80392 | RPOW | OM | | | |

## POS BR Wolverton/York† — NS5

**Post Office Stowage Van.** **NT5.01–NT5.05 & NT5.21 Seats: 0. Livery: R**

(NT5.02)

| | | | | | | | | |
|---|---|---|---|---|---|---|---|---|
| 80400 | RPOM | EN | 80401 | RPOM | EN | 80402 | RPOM | EN |

(NT5.03†)

| | | | | | | | | | | | |
|---|---|---|---|---|---|---|---|---|---|---|---|
| 80403 | RPOM | MA | 80404 | RPOM | MA | 80405 | RPOM | MA | 80406 | RPOM | MA |

(NT5.01†)

| | | | | | | | | | | | |
|---|---|---|---|---|---|---|---|---|---|---|---|
| 80407 | RPOA | CA | 80408 | RPOA | CA | 80409 | RPOW | OM | 80410 | RPOW | OM |

(NT5.03†)

| | | | | | | | | | | | |
|---|---|---|---|---|---|---|---|---|---|---|---|
| 80411 | RPOE | HT | 80412 | RPOM | MA | 80413 | RPOE | HT | 80414 | RPOM | MA |

(NT5.05†)

| | | | | | | | | | | | |
|---|---|---|---|---|---|---|---|---|---|---|---|
| 80415 | RPOM | EN | 80418 | RPOM | EN | 80421 | RPOE | HT | 80424 | RPOM | EN |
| 80416 | RPOM | EN | 80419 | RPOM | EN | 80422 | RPOE | HT | | | |
| 80417 | RPOM | EN | 80420 | RPOE | HT | 80423 | RPOW | OM | | | |

(NT5.04†)

| | | | | | | | | | | | |
|---|---|---|---|---|---|---|---|---|---|---|---|
| 80425 | RPOM | EN | 80427 | RPOE | HT | 80429 | RPOM | EN | 80430 | RPOM | EN |
| 80426 | RPOE | HT | 80428 | RPOM | EN | | | | | | |

(NT5.21)

| | | | | | | | | |
|---|---|---|---|---|---|---|---|---|
| 80431 | RPOM | DY | 80432 | RPOE | HT | 80433 | RPOE | HT |

(NT5.04)

| | | | | | | | | | | | |
|---|---|---|---|---|---|---|---|---|---|---|---|
| 80434 | RPOE | HT | 80435 | RPOW | OM | 80436 | RPOW | OM | 80437 | RPOW | OM |

(NT5.21)

| | | | | | |
|---|---|---|---|---|---|
| 80438 | RPOM | DY | 80439 | RPOM | DY |

## B.POT BR Wolverton/York† — NU5

**Post Office Brake Storage Van.** **NU5.01/NU5.02† Seats: 0 Livery: R**

| | | | | | | | | | | | |
|---|---|---|---|---|---|---|---|---|---|---|---|
| 80450 | RPOW | OM | 80453 | RPOW | OM | 80455 | RPOW | OM | 80457† | RPOM | EN |
| 80451 | RPOW | OM | 80454 | RPOW | OM | 80456† | RPOM | EN | 80458† | RPOM | EN |
| 80452 | RPOW | OM | | | | | | | | | |

## BG. — NC5†/ND5

**Gangwayed Brake** **NC.5.01/ND5.01**

(BR Derby)

| | | | | | | | | | | | |
|---|---|---|---|---|---|---|---|---|---|---|---|
| 80501 | RPXC | CA | 80514 | RPOM | EN | 80551 | RPXC | CA | 80565 | RPXC | CA |
| 80513† | RPPW | BJ | 80549 | RPXC | CA | 80554 | RPXC | CA | | | |

Above: The livery of the Royal Mail coaches is again being revised to show a post box/letter box effect on the coach side. No 80367 was the first so painted seen in the formation of a special train at the launch held on 20 March at Long Marston.
Below: New Metro-Cammell assembled Mk4 Driving Van Trailer No 82208 is seen at King's Cross at the time of the *Terence Cuneo* naming ceremony (see front cover).

(BR Wolverton)

| | | | | | | | | | | | | | | | |
|---|---|---|---|---|---|---|---|---|---|---|---|---|---|---|---|
| 80570 | | RPXC | CA | 80580 | | RPXC | CA | 80589 | | RPXC | CA | 80596 | | RPXC | CA |
| 80571 | Bg | RPXC | CA | 80582 | | RPXT | BJ | 80590 | | RPXC | CA | | | | |
| 80576 | | RPXT | BJ | 80583 | | RPXC | CA | 80592 | | RPXT | CA | | | | |

(BR York)

| | | | | | | | | | | | | | | | |
|---|---|---|---|---|---|---|---|---|---|---|---|---|---|---|---|
| 80608 | | RPXC | CA | 80646 | | RPXC | CA | 80654 | | RPXC | CA | 80668 | | RPXC | BJ |
| 80613† | | RPPA | CA | 80649† | | RPPA | CA | 80658 | | RPXC | CA | 80669 | | RPXT | CA |
| 80623 | | RPXC | CA | 80650 | | RPXC | CA | 80663 | | RPXT | BJ | 80670 | | RPXC | BJ |
| 80631† | | RPPA | CA | 80653 | | RPXC | CA | 80664 | | RPXC | CA | 80671 | | RPXC | CA |

(Metro-Cammell)

| | | | | | | | | | | | | | | | |
|---|---|---|---|---|---|---|---|---|---|---|---|---|---|---|---|
| 80680 | | RPXC | CA | 80695 | | RPPA | CA | 80701 | | RPXB | CA | 80710 | | RPXC | OM |
| 80682† | | RPPA | CA | 80699 | | RPXC | BJ | 80707 | | RPXC | OM | 80716 | | RPXC | CA |
| 80693 | | RPXC | HT | 80700 | | RPXB | CA | 80709 | | RPXC | OM | 80720† | | RPPW | BJ |

(Birmingham RC&W)

| | | | | | | | | | | | | | | | |
|---|---|---|---|---|---|---|---|---|---|---|---|---|---|---|---|
| 80728 | | RPXC | CA | 80748 | | RPXC | BJ | 80769 | | RPXC | BJ | 80789† | | RPPW | BJ |
| 80730 | | RPXC | CA | 80754 | | RPXC | CA | 80775† | | RPOM | EN | 80790 | R | RPXB | HT |
| 80736 | | RPXC | HT | 80763 | | RPXC | CA | 80780† | | RPPW | BJ | 80794 | | RPXC | CA |
| 80737 | | RPXB | CA | 80767† | | RPPW | BJ | 80781 | | RPXB | HT | 80795 | | RPXC | BJ |
| 80742 | | RPXC | HT | 80768† | | RPPW | BJ | 80782† | | RPPW | BJ | | | | |

(Cravens)

| | | | | | | | | | | | | | | | |
|---|---|---|---|---|---|---|---|---|---|---|---|---|---|---|---|
| 80804 | | RPXC | CA | 80810 | | RPXC | CA | 80831 | | RPXT | CA | 80837 | | RPXT | CA |
| 80805 | | RPXB | CA | 80820 | | RPXC | CA | 80834 | | RPXB | CA | 80843 | | RPXB | CA |
| 80806 | | RPXC | CA | 80824 | | RPXC | CA | 80835 | | RPXC | CA | | | | |

(Pressed Steel)

| | | | | | | | | | | | | | | | |
|---|---|---|---|---|---|---|---|---|---|---|---|---|---|---|---|
| 80859 | | RPXB | BJ | 80885 | | RPXB | CA | 80892 | | RPXB | BJ | 80945 | | RPXB | CA |
| 80861 | R | RPXB | PC | 80886 | | RPXB | BJ | 80893 | R | RPXB | CA | 80962 | | RPXB | CA |
| 80868 | R | RPXB | EC | 80889 | R | RPXB | EC | 80926 | | RPXB | HT | | | | |

(BR York)

| | | | | | | | | | | | | | | | |
|---|---|---|---|---|---|---|---|---|---|---|---|---|---|---|---|
| 80966† | | RPPA | CA | 80972 | | RPXT | CA | 80981 | | RPXT | CA | 80988 | | RPXB | HT |
| 80967 | | RPXC | CA | 80976 | | RPXC | CA | 80985 | | RPXC | CA | 80994 | | RPXC | CA |

## DVT BREL Derby — NZ5

**Driving Van Trailer Mk3** — **NZ5.02 Livery: Iw**

| | | | | | | | | | | | |
|---|---|---|---|---|---|---|---|---|---|---|---|
| 82101 | IWC | OY | 82114 | IWC | OY | 82127 | IWC | WB | 82140 | IWC | WB |
| 82102 | IWC | WB | 82115 | IWC | WB | 82128 | IWC | OY | 82141 | IWC | WB |
| 82103 | IWC | OY | 82116 | IWC | OY | 82129 | IWC | OY | 82142 | IWC | WB |
| 82104 | IWC | OY | 82117 | IWC | WB | 82130 | IWC | WB | 82143 | IWC | WB |
| 82105 | IWC | OY | 82118 | IWC | WB | 82131 | IWC | WB | 82144 | IWC | WB |
| 82106 | IWC | WB | 82119 | IWC | OY | 82132 | IWC | WB | 82145 | IWC | WB |
| 82107 | IWC | WB | 82120 | IWC | OY | 82133 | IWC | WB | 82146 | IWC | MA |
| 82108 | IWC | WB | 82121 | IWC | OY | 82134 | IWC | WB | 82147 | IWC | WB |
| 82109 | IWC | WB | 82122 | IWC | WB | 82135 | IWC | WB | 82148 | IWC | MA |
| 82110 | IWC | OY | 82123 | IWC | OY | 82136 | IWC | WB | 82149 | IWC | OY |
| 82111 | IWC | WB | 82124 | IWC | WB | 82137 | IWC | WB | 82150 | IWC | OY |
| 82112 | IWC | WB | 82125 | IWC | WB | 82138 | IWC | WB | 82151 | IWC | OY |
| 82113 | IWC | OY | 82126 | IWC | OY | 82139 | IWC | WB | 82152 | IWC | OY |

## DVT Metro-Cammell — NZ5

**Driving Van Trailer Mk4** — **NZ5.01**

| | | | | | | | | | | | | | | | |
|---|---|---|---|---|---|---|---|---|---|---|---|---|---|---|---|
| 82200 | Iw | IEC | BN | 82208 | I | IEC | BN | 82216 | I | IEC | | 82224 | I | IEC | |
| 82201 | Iw | IEC | BN | 82209 | I | IEC | BN | 82217 | I | IEC | | 82225 | I | IEC | |
| 82202 | Iw | IEC | BN | 82210 | I | IEC | BN | 82218 | I | IEC | | 82226 | I | IEC | |
| 82203 | Iw | IEC | BN | 82211 | I | IEC | | 82219 | I | IEC | | 82227 | I | IEC | |
| 82204 | Iw | IEC | BN | 82212 | I | IEC | BN | 82220 | I | IEC | | 82228 | I | IEC | |
| 82205 | Iw | IEC | BN | 82213 | I | IEC | | 82221 | I | IEC | | 82229 | I | IEC | |
| 82206 | Iw | IEC | BN | 82214 | I | IEC | | 82222 | I | IEC | | 82230 | I | IEC | |
| 82207 | Iw | IEC | BN | 82215 | I | IEC | | 82223 | I | IEC | | 82231 | I | IEC | |

## DVT Birmingham RC&W/RFS Industries — NZ5

**Driving Van Trailer** — **NZ5.03 (ex-Class 33/1 locomotive) Livery: ML**

| | | |
|---|---|---|
| 83301 | IXXH | SU |

## B.# & BG
**Brake & Gangwayed Brake**

## NB5#/NC5†/ND5
**NB5.01#/NC5.01†/ND5.01**

(BR York)

| | | | | | | | |
|---|---|---|---|---|---|---|---|
| 84010 | | RPXB | CA | 84012† | | RPPW | BJ |

(Cravens)

| | | | | | | | | | | | | | | | |
|---|---|---|---|---|---|---|---|---|---|---|---|---|---|---|---|
| 84015 | | RPXC | CA | 84026 | | RPXB | BJ | 84037 | | RPXC | CA | 84051 | | RPXB | CA |
| 84016 | | RPXC | CA | 84029† | | RPPW | BJ | 84041† | | RPPW | BJ | | | | |
| 84020 | | RPXC | BJ | 84036 | | RPXT | CA | 84044 | | RPXB | CA | | | | |

(Metro-Cammell)

| | | | | | | | | | | | | | | | |
|---|---|---|---|---|---|---|---|---|---|---|---|---|---|---|---|
| 84057 | | RPXC | BJ | 84104 | | RPXB | CA | 84133 | | RPXC | BJ | 84147 | | RPXC | CA |
| 84065 | | RPXC | CA | 84106 | | RPXC | CA | 84134 | | RPXB | CA | 84151 | | RPXC | CA |
| 84082 | | RPXC | CA | 84109 | | RPXC | CA | 84135† | | RPPW | BJ | 84159 | | RPXC | CA |
| 84086 | | RPXC | BJ | 84112† | | RPPW | BJ | 84137 | | RPXC | CA | 84160 | | RPXC | BJ |
| 84098 | | RPXC | CA | 84119† | | RPPA | CA | 84143 | | RPXC | CA | 84162 | | RPXC | CA |
| 84099 | | RPXB | CA | 84121 | | RPXT | OM | 84145 | | RPXC | CA | | | | |
| 84100† | | RPPA | CA | 84129† | | RPPA | CA | 84146 | | RPXC | CA | | | | |

(Cravens)

| | | | | | | | | | | | | | | | |
|---|---|---|---|---|---|---|---|---|---|---|---|---|---|---|---|
| 84181† | | RPOM | EN | 84191 | | RPXC | CA | 84195 | | RPXC | CA | 84202 | | RPXC | BJ |
| 84185 | | RPXC | BJ | 84193 | | RPXT | CA | 84197 | | RPXC | BJ | 84203 | | RPXC | HT |
| 84190 | | RPXC | OM | 84194 | | RPXC | CA | 84200 | | RPXB | BJ | 84204 | | RPXC | CA |

(Pressed Steel)

| | | | | | | | | | | | | | | | |
|---|---|---|---|---|---|---|---|---|---|---|---|---|---|---|---|
| 84211 | | RPXB | CA | 84302 | | RPXC | BJ | 84382# | | RPOM | EN | 84447 | | RPXC | BJ |
| 84212 | | RPXB | CA | 84313 | R | RPXB | CA | 84386 | | RPXC | BJ | 84456 | | RPXB | CA |
| 84215 | | RPXB | CA | 84318 | | RPXT | CA | 84387# | | RPOM | EN | 84458 | | RPXB | CA |
| 84217 | R | RPXB | HT | 84319 | | RPXC | BJ | 84388 | | RPXB | CA | 84461# | R | RPOM | EN |
| 84234 | R | RPXB | EC | 84320 | R | RPXB | PC | 84390 | | RPXC | CA | 84464 | | RPXC | BJ |
| 84239 | | RPXB | CA | 84322 | R | RPXB | PC | 84395 | | RPXB | BJ | 84467 | | RPOM | BJ |
| 84240 | | RPXB | CA | 84325 | | RPXB | CA | 84399 | | RPXB | CA | 84469 | | RPXB | BJ |
| 84242 | R | RPXB | PC | 84331 | | RPXT | BJ | 84402 | | RPXT | BJ | 84472 | | RPXB | CA |
| 84250 | R | RPXB | CA | 84339 | | RPXB | CA | 84404 | | RPXB | BJ | 84475 | | RPXB | BJ |
| 84251 | | RPXB | CA | 84342 | | RPXC | BJ | 84406 | | RPXC | BJ | 84477# | R | RPOM | EN |
| 84252 | R | RPXB | PC | 84344 | | RPXC | BJ | 84408 | | RPXC | BJ | 84499 | | RPXB | BJ |
| 84261 | | RPXB | BJ | 84346 | | RPXB | CA | 84415 | | RPXC | BJ | 84501 | R | RPXB | CA |
| 84262 | R | RPXB | CA | 84347 | | RPXC | BJ | 84416 | | RPXC | BJ | 84510 | R | RPXB | CA |
| 84273 | | RPXB | CA | 84350 | | RPXC | BJ | 84419 | | RPXB | BJ | 84512 | | RPXB | BJ |
| 84274 | | RPXB | CA | 84351 | | RPXB | CA | 84420 | R | RPXB | CA | 84515 | | RPXB | CA |
| 84279 | | RPXT | BJ | 84352 | | RPXB | CA | 84421 | | RPXC | BJ | 84519 | | RPXC | BJ |
| 84280 | | RPXB | CA | 84354 | R | RPXB | CA | 84422 | | RPXC | BJ | 84531 | | RPXB | CA |
| 84281 | | RPXB | BJ | 84356 | | RPXC | BJ | 84427 | | RPXB | CA | 84543 | | RPXT | BJ |
| 84286 | | RPXC | CA | 84361 | | RPXC | BJ | 84428 | | RPXC | BJ | 84547 | | RPXC | BJ |
| 84287 | | RPXC | BJ | 84363 | | RPXB | CA | 84430 | | RPXB | CA | 84552 | | RPXC | BJ |
| 84289 | | RPXB | CA | 84364 | | RPXC | BJ | 84434 | | RPXT | BJ | 84554 | | RPXT | BJ |
| 84290 | | RPXC | BJ | 84370 | | RPXB | CA | 84435 | | RPXC | BJ | 84558 | | RPXC | OM |
| 84296 | | RPXC | BJ | 84371 | | RPXC | BJ | 84436 | | RPXC | BJ | | | | |
| 84298 | | RPXC | BJ | 84373 | | RPXC | CA | 84439 | | RPXC | BJ | | | | |
| 84301 | | RPXC | BJ | 84380 | | RPXB | CA | 84445 | | RPXB | CA | | | | |

Gloucester RC & W.

| | | | | | | | | | | | |
|---|---|---|---|---|---|---|---|---|---|---|---|
| 84577 | | RPXB | HT | 84590 | | RPXB | CA | 84619 | | RPXC | BJ |

## BG.
**Gangwayed Brake. 100/110mph†**

## NE5/NH5†
**NE5.01/NH5.01†**

(Metro-Cammell)

| | | | |
|---|---|---|---|
| 92000 | I | RPXM | OY |

Pressed Steel

| | | | | | | | | | | | | | | | |
|---|---|---|---|---|---|---|---|---|---|---|---|---|---|---|---|
| 92001† | I | RPXM | WB | 92007 | I | RPXZ | EC | 92013 | I | RPXZ | EC | 92019 | I | RPXZ | EC |
| 92002 | I | RPXM | WB | 92008† | I | RPXM | WB | 92014 | I | RPXZ | EC | 92020 | | RPXZ | PC |
| 92003 | I | RPXM | WB | 92009 | I | RPXZ | EC | 92015 | I | RPXZ | EC | 92021 | | RPXZ | EC |
| 92004 | I | RPXM | WB | 92010 | | RPXZ | EC | 92016 | I | RPXZ | EC | 92022 | | RPXM | OY |
| 92005 | I | RPXM | WB | 92011† | I | RPXM | WB | 92017 | I | RPXZ | EC | | | | |
| 92006† | I | RPXM | WB | 92012 | I | RPXZ | PC | 92018 | | RPXZ | PC | | | | |

(BR York)

| | | | |
|---|---|---|---|
| 92023† | I | RPXM | WB |

(Cravens)

| | | | |
|---|---|---|---|
| 92025† | I | RPXM | WB |

(Metro-Cammell)

| | | | |
|---|---|---|---|
| 92026† | I | RPXM | WB |
| 92027† | I | RPXM | WB |
| 92028† | I | RPXM | WB |
| 92029† | I | RPXM | WB |
| 92031† | I | RPXM | WB |
| 92032† | I | RPXZ | EC |
| 92033† | I | RPXM | WB |
| 92034† | I | RPXM | WB |
| 92035† | I | RPXM | WB |
| 92036† | I | RPXM | WB |
| 92037† | I | RPXM | EN |
| 92038† | I | RPXM | EN |
| 92039† | I | RPXM | EN |

(Cravens)

| | | | |
|---|---|---|---|
| 92040 | I | RPXZ | PC |

(Pressed Steel)

| | | | |
|---|---|---|---|
| 92041 | | RPXM | WB |
| 92042 | R | RPXZ | PC |
| 92043 | R | RPXM | WB |
| 92044 | R | RPXH | HT |
| 92045 | | RPXZ | PC |
| 92046† | I | RPXM | EN |
| 92047 | | RPXZ | PC |
| 92048 | I | RPXM | EN |
| 92049 | | RPXZ | PC |
| 92050 | I | RPXZ | PC |
| 92051 | | RPXZ | EC |
| 92052 | R | RPXM | WB |
| 92053 | | RPXM | WB |
| 92054 | | RPXZ | PC |
| 92055 | I | RPXM | DY |
| 92056 | | RPXM | WB |
| 92057 | I | RPXM | OY |
| 92058 | Pb | RPXH | HT |
| 92059 | | RPXZ | PC |
| 92060 | | RPXM | MA |
| 92061 | I | RPXA | NC |
| 92062 | | RPXM | WB |
| 92063 | I | RPXZ | PC |
| 92064 | | RPXM | MA |
| 92065 | | RPXZ | EC |
| 92066 | | RPXM | WB |
| 92067 | | RPXZ | PC |
| 92068 | I | RPXZ | PC |
| 92069 | | RPXM | WB |
| 92070 | | RPXM | WB |
| 92071 | | RPXM | MA |
| 92072 | | RPXZ | EC |
| 92073 | | RPXZ | PC |
| 92074 | | RPXM | MA |
| 92075 | R | RPXM | EN |
| 92076 | | RPXM | EN |
| 92077 | | RPXW | LA |
| 92078 | | RPXM | MA |
| 92079 | | RPXZ | PC |
| 92081 | I | RPXM | MA |
| 92082 | R | RPXM | EN |
| 92083 | | RPXM | MA |
| 92084 | | RPXM | EN |
| 92086 | I | RPXA | NC |
| 92087 | I | RPXM | OY |
| 92088 | I | RPXA | NC |
| 92089 | Pb | RPXH | HT |
| 92090 | | RPXM | EN |
| 92091 | | RPXA | NC |
| 92092 | Pb | RPXH | HT |
| 92093 | | RPXW | LA |
| 92094 | I | RPXZ | PC |
| 92095 | R | RPXM | MA |
| 92096 | | RPXM | WB |
| 92097 | | RPXZ | PC |
| 92098† | I | RPXM | EN |
| 92099 | I | RPXM | OY |
| 92100 | | RPXW | LA |
| 92101 | | RPXM | EN |
| 92102 | | RPXM | EN |
| 92103 | | RPXW | BJ |
| 92104 | | RPXM | EN |
| 92105 | R | RPXM | EN |
| 92106 | | RPXA | NC |
| 92107 | | RPXA | CA |
| 92108 | R | RPXM | EN |
| 92109 | | RPXM | EN |
| 92110 | | RPXZ | EC |
| 92111† | I | RPXZ | PC |
| 92112 | R | RPXA | CA |
| 92113 | | RPXZ | EC |
| 92114† | I | RPXZ | PC |
| 92115 | | RPXM | WB |
| 92116 | I | RPXM | OY |
| 92117 | | RPXA | CA |
| 92118 | I | RPXM | EN |
| 92119 | R | RPXA | CA |
| 92120 | | RPXA | CA |
| 92121 | | RPXM | OY |
| 92122 | | RPXM | OY |
| 92123 | R | RPXM | EN |
| 92124 | R | RPXW | BJ |
| 92125 | | RPXM | OY |
| 92126 | I | RPXM | DY |
| 92127 | | RPXM | OY |
| 92129 | | RPXM | EN |
| 92130 | I | RPXZ | PC |
| 92131 | R | RPXM | MA |
| 92132 | R | RPXM | EN |
| 92133 | | RPXM | EN |
| 92134 | | RPXM | EN |
| 92135 | I | RPXM | EN |
| 92136 | | RPXW | LA |
| 92137 | Pb | RPXH | HT |
| 92138 | | RPXW | LA |
| 92139 | R | RPXM | MA |
| 92140 | | RPXM | MA |
| 92141 | | RPXM | EN |
| 92142 | | RPXM | MA |
| 92143 | | RPXZ | PC |
| 92144 | R | RPXZ | PC |
| 92145 | R | RPXM | EN |
| 92146† | I | RPXZ | PC |
| 92147 | | RPXZ | EC |
| 92148 | R | RPXM | EN |
| 92149 | | RPXA | NC |
| 92150 | R | RPXW | BJ |
| 92151 | I | RPXZ | PC |
| 92152 | | RPXZ | PC |
| 92153 | I | RPXM | OY |
| 92154 | | RPXA | CA |
| 92155 | I | RPXZ | PC |
| 92156 | | RPXM | OY |
| 92157 | I | RPXM | OY |
| 92158 | | RPXZ | PC |
| 92159 | I | RPXZ | PC |
| 92160 | R | RPXA | CA |
| 92161 | | RPXM | EN |
| 92162 | | RPXM | EN |
| 92163 | | RPXM | MA |
| 92164 | I | RPXZ | PC |
| 92165 | | RPXM | EN |
| 92166 | | RPXM | MA |
| 92167† | I | RPXZ | PC |
| 92168 | I | RPXZ | PC |
| 92169 | | RPXW | BJ |
| 92170 | | RPXW | BJ |
| 92171 | R | RPXA | CA |
| 92172 | I | RPXM | DY |
| 92173 | R | RPXA | CA |
| 92174† | I | RPXZ | PC |
| 92175 | I | RPXM | OY |
| 92176 | R | RPXW | BJ |
| 92177 | | RPXM | MA |

(Gloucester RC&W)

| | | | |
|---|---|---|---|
| 92178 | R | RPXW | BJ |
| 92179 | R | RPXA | CA |
| 92181 | | RPXW | BJ |
| 92182 | | RPXW | BJ |
| 92183 | I | RPXZ | PC |
| 92184 | | RPXM | EN |
| 92185 | I | IECG | BN |
| 92186 | | RPXM | OY |
| 92187 | R | RPXM | EN |
| 92188 | | RPXM | EN |
| 92189 | | RPXW | BJ |
| 92190 | | RPXM | EN |
| 92192 | | RPXW | BJ |
| 92193 | I | RPXZ | PC |
| 92194 | I | RPXM | DY |
| 92195 | | RPXM | EN |
| 92196 | I | RPXZ | PC |
| 92197 | I | RPXZ | PC |
| 92198 | | RPXM | MA |
| 92199 | R | RPXM | EN |
| 92200 | R | RPXA | CA |
| 92201 | | RPXW | BJ |
| 92202 | | RPXZ | PC |
| 92203 | I | RPXZ | PC |
| 92204 | Pb | RPXH | HT |
| 92205 | | RPXM | EN |
| 92206 | | RPXW | BJ |
| 92207 | R | RPXW | BJ |

The vehicles 92208-92383 represent conversions from the earlier series. All were converted by BREL at Wolverton (92208-38), Swindon (92239-57 & 92366-82), Glasgow (92308-39) or Derby (92340-65/83) except 92301-04 at RFS Industries, Doncaster. Original construction was by Pressed Steel unless indicated by the number as 'b' (Birmingham RC&W), 'c' (Cravens), 'm' (Metro-Cammell) or 'y' (BR York).

| | | | |
|---|---|---|---|
| 92208 | I | RPXW | BJ |
| 92209 | | RPXW | BJ |
| 92210 | | RPXW | BJ |
| 92211 | | RPXW | BJ |
| 92212 | R | RPXW | BJ |
| 92213 | | RPXW | BJ |
| 92214 | | RPXW | BJ |
| 92215 | | RPXW | BJ |
| 92216 | | RPXA | CA |
| 92217 | | RPXA | CA |
| 92218 | | RPXW | BJ |
| 92219 | | RPXA | CA |
| 92220 | R | RPXW | BJ |
| 92221 | R | RPXA | CA |
| 92222 | | RPXA | CA |
| 92223 | | RPXA | CA |
| 92224 | R | RPXW | BJ |
| 92225 | | RPXA | CA |
| 92226 | R | RPXM | EN |
| 92227 | | RPXW | BJ |
| 92228 | R | RPXW | BJ |
| 92229 | | RPXW | BJ |
| 92230 | | RPXW | BJ |
| 92231 | | RPXW | BJ |
| 92232 | | RPXW | BJ |
| 92233 | R | RPXW | BJ |
| 92234 | | RPXW | BJ |
| 92235 | | RPXW | BJ |
| 92236 | N | RPXW | OM |
| 92237b | | RPXA | NC |
| 92238 | | RPXW | BJ |
| 92239m | R | RPXW | BJ |
| 92240m | | RPXW | BJ |
| 92241 | | RPXW | BJ |
| 92242 | | RPXW | BJ |
| 92243 | | RPXW | BJ |
| 92244 | R | RPXW | BJ |
| 92245 | | RPXW | BJ |
| 92246 | R | RPXW | BJ |
| 92247 | | RPXH | HT |
| 92248 | R | RPXA | CA |
| 92249 | R | RPXW | BJ |
| 92250 | | RPXH | HT |
| 92251 | | RPXA | NC |
| 92252 | R | RPXW | BJ |
| 92253 | R | RPXA | CA |
| 92254 | R | RPXA | CA |
| 92255 | | RPXA | CA |
| 92256 | | RPXA | CA |
| 92257 | R | RPXA | NC |
| 92308b | | RPXW | BJ |
| 92309c | | RPXW | BJ |
| 92310m | R | RPXW | BJ |
| 92311 | | RPXW | BJ |
| 92312 | | RPXW | BJ |
| 92313 | | RPXH | HT |
| 92314b | | RPXA | CA |
| 92315c | R | RPXW | BJ |
| 92316y | Pb | RPXA | CA |
| 92317c | | RPXA | CA |
| 92318c | | RPXA | CA |
| 92319m | R | RPXM | EN |
| 92320m | | RPXH | HT |
| 92321 | R | RPXW | BJ |

| | | | |
|---|---|---|---|
| 92322b | | RPXW | BJ |
| 92323c | | RPXH | HT |
| 92324m | R | RPXM | EN |
| 92325b | | RPXA | CA |
| 92326 | | RPXA | CA |
| 92327c | | RPXA | CA |
| 92328y | R | RPXH | HT |
| 92329y | | RPXA | CA |
| 92330y | | RPXA | CA |
| 92331 | | RPXW | BJ |
| 92332c | | RPXA | CA |
| 92333y | | RPXA | CA |
| 92334y | | RPXA | CA |
| 92335y | | RPXA | CA |
| 92336c | | RPXW | BJ |
| 92337m | | RPXW | BJ |
| 92338 | | RPXW | BJ |
| 92339 | R | RPXW | BJ |
| 92340m | R | RPXW | OM |
| 92341 | | RPXW | BJ |
| 92342 | R | RPXW | BJ |
| 92343 | | RPXW | BJ |
| 92344m | | RPXW | BJ |
| 92345m | | RPXW | BJ |
| 92346m | | RPXW | BJ |
| 92347 | | RPXW | BJ |
| 92348m | | RPXA | CA |
| 92349m | R | RPXW | BJ |
| 92350c | | RPXW | BJ |
| 92351m | | RPXA | CA |
| 92352c | | RPXW | BJ |
| 92353 | | RPXH | HT |
| 92354 | N | RPXW | OM |
| 92355 | | RPXA | CA |
| 92356 | | RPXW | BJ |
| 92357m | | RPXW | BJ |
| 92358 | | RPXW | BJ |
| 92359 | | RPXW | BJ |
| 92360 | | RPXW | BJ |
| 92361 | R | RPXA | CA |
| 92362c | | RPXW | BJ |
| 92363 | | RPXW | BJ |
| 92364c | R | RPXA | CA |
| 92365m | | RPXW | BJ |
| 92366 | | RPXH | HT |
| 92367 | | RPXA | CA |
| 92368 | | RPXA | CA |
| 92369m | | RPXA | CA |
| 92370 | | RPXA | CA |
| 92371c | | RPXA | CA |
| 92372 | | RPXA | CA |
| 92373 | | RPXA | CA |
| 92374 | | RPXA | CA |
| 92375 | | RPXA | CA |
| 92376 | | RPXA | CA |
| 92377 | | RPXH | HT |
| 92379 | | RPXH | HT |
| 92380 | | RPXW | BJ |
| 92381 | | RPXA | CA |
| 92382 | | RPXA | CA |
| 92383 | | RPXA | CA |

## GUV. NK5†/NJ5.

**General Utility Van.** **NK5.01†/NJ5.01.**

(Pressed Steel)

| | | | |
|---|---|---|---|
| 93078† | | RPXD | BJ |
| 93079† | | RPXD | CA |
| 93081 | | RPXE | BJ |
| 93084 | | RPXE | BJ |
| 93086† | | RPXT | CA |
| 93090† | | RPXD | CA |
| 93091 | R | RPXE | CA |
| 93093† | | RPXT | CA |
| 93100† | | RPXD | CA |
| 93104 | R | RPOC | PY |
| 93105† | | RPXD | CA |
| 93107† | | RPXD | BJ |
| 93110 | | RPOC | PY |
| 93112 | | RPXE | CA |
| 93115† | | RPXD | CA |
| 93117† | | RPXD | CA |
| 93122 | R | RPOC | PY |
| 93126 | | RPOC | PY |
| 93131† | R | RPXD | BJ |
| 93134 | R | RPOC | PY |
| 93135† | | RPXD | BJ |
| 93138† | | RPXD | CA |
| 93140† | | RPXT | CA |
| 93141 | R | RPOC | PY |
| 93142 | | RPXE | CA |
| 93143 | | RPOC | PY |
| 93160 | | RPOC | PY |
| 93163† | | RPXD | BJ |
| 93165 | R | RPOC | PY |
| 93167 | | RPOC | PY |
| 93172 | R | RPOC | PY |
| 93174 | | RPOC | PY |
| 93176† | R | RPXD | CA |
| 93180† | | RPXD | CA |
| 93185† | | RPXD | CA |
| 93187† | | RPXD | CA |
| 93191† | | RPXD | CA |
| 93192 | | RPXE | CA |
| 93193† | | RPXX | CA |
| 93195† | | RPXD | CA |
| 93205 | | RPOC | PY |
| 93207 | | RPXD | CA |
| 93210 | | RPOC | PY |
| 93212 | | RPOC | PY |
| 93214† | | RPXD | CA |
| 93217† | | RPXD | CA |
| 93234† | | RPXT | CA |
| 93235 | | RPOC | PY |
| 93236 | | RPXD | BJ |
| 93241† | | RPXD | CA |
| 93249 | R | RPXE | CA |
| 93251 | | RPXD | BJ |
| 93253† | | RPXT | BJ |
| 93255 | | RPXE | BJ |
| 93257† | | RPXD | BJ |
| 93258 | | RPXD | CA |
| 93262 | | RPOC | PY |
| 93263 | R | RPOC | PY |
| 93265 | R | RPOC | PY |
| 93267 | R | RPXD | CA |
| 93269 | | RPXE | CA |
| 93272† | | RPXT | BJ |
| 93273† | | RPXD | CA |
| 93277 | | RPOC | PY |
| 93278 | | RPXD | BJ |
| 93284 | | RPXD | BJ |
| 93287† | | RPXT | BJ |
| 93291† | | RPXD | CA |
| 93292 | | RPXD | BJ |
| 93293 | | RPOC | PY |
| 93295† | | RPXD | CA |
| 93298† | | RPXT | CA |
| 93304† | | RPXD | CA |
| 93306† | | RPXD | CA |
| 93307† | | RPXD | CA |
| 93308† | | RPXT | CA |
| 93319† | | RPXD | CA |
| 93321† | | RPXD | CA |
| 93323 | R | RPXE | CA |
| 93325† | | RPXD | CA |
| 93329† | | RPXT | CA |
| 93330† | | RPXD | CA |
| 93336† | | RPXT | CA |
| 93338† | | RPXD | CA |
| 93339† | | RPXT | CA |
| 93343† | | RPXT | CA |
| 93345† | | RPXD | CA |
| 93347 | R | RPOC | PY |
| 93348† | | RPXD | CA |
| 93349 | | RPXD | CA |
| 93353 | | RPOC | PY |
| 93356 | | RPXT | BJ |
| 93359† | | RPXT | CA |
| 93362 | | RPOC | PY |
| 93367 | | RPXD | BJ |
| 93370 | R | RPXD | BJ |
| 93374† | | RPXD | BJ |
| 93375 | | RPXD | BJ |
| 93376 | | RPOC | PY |
| 93379 | R | RPXD | BJ |
| 93386† | | RPXD | BJ |
| 93388 | | RPXD | BJ |
| 93390† | | RPXT | BJ |
| 93391† | | RPXT | CA |
| 93393 | | RPXE | BJ |
| 93394 | | RPXD | BJ |
| 93395 | R | RPXE | CA |
| 93396 | | RPOC | PY |
| 93398† | | RPXD | CA |
| 93401 | | RPXD | BJ |
| 93406† | | RPXT | CA |
| 93407 | | RPXE | CA |
| 93411 | | RPXE | CA |
| 93412† | | RPXT | CA |
| 93413† | | RPXD | CA |
| 93416 | | RPXE | CA |
| 93417† | | RPXD | CA |
| 93419 | | RPXD | BJ |
| 93421† | | RPXT | BJ |
| 93426 | | RPXE | BJ |
| 93429 | | RPXE | BJ |
| 93431 | | RPXD | BJ |
| 93446 | | RPXD | BJ |
| 93450 | | RPXD | BJ |
| 93455† | | RPXD | CA |
| 93458† | | RPXD | CA |
| 93459† | | RPXD | CA |
| 93462 | | RPOC | PY |
| 93463† | | RPXD | CA |
| 93464† | | RPXD | CA |
| 93465† | | RPXX | CA |
| 93468 | | RPXE | CA |
| 93474 | R | RPXD | BJ |
| 93475† | | RPXD | BJ |
| 93476† | | RPXD | BJ |
| 93478 | | RPXD | BJ |
| 93479† | R | RPXD | CA |
| 93485 | | RPXE | CA |
| 93490 | | RPXD | BJ |
| 93495 | | RPXD | BJ |
| 93499 | | RPOC | PY |

(BR Doncaster)

| | | | |
|---|---|---|---|
| 93502† | | RPXT | CA |
| 93506† | | RPXT | BJ |
| 93508 | | RPXD | BJ |
| 93511 | R | RPXD | BJ |
| 93512† | | RPXD | BJ |
| 93514 | | RPXD | CA |
| 93515 | | RPXD | BJ |
| 93516† | | RPXD | BJ |
| 93518 | | RPXE | BJ |
| 93519† | | RPXD | BJ |

(BR York/St. Rollox Glasgow)

| | | | |
|---|---|---|---|
| 93521 | | RPXE | CA |
| 93523 | | RPOC | PY |
| 93525 | | RPXD | BJ |
| 93529 | | RPXD | CA |
| 93533† | | RPXD | CA |
| 93534 | | RPOC | PY |
| 93536 | | RPXD | BJ |
| 93538† | | RPXD | CA |
| 93539 | | RPOC | PY |
| 93541 | R | RPXD | CA |
| 93542† | | RPXT | CA |
| 93546† | | RPXD | CA |
| 93549† | | RPXD | CA |
| 93550† | | RPXD | CA |
| 93554† | | RPXD | BJ |
| 93556 | | RPXD | BJ |
| 93557 | | RPXD | BJ |
| 93560 | R | RPXD | BJ |
| 93562 | | RPXD | BJ |
| 93563 | | RPXD | BJ |
| 93571 | R | RPOC | PY |
| 93573† | | RPXD | CA |
| 93576 | | RPXE | CA |
| 93578 | | RPXE | BJ |
| 93579† | | RPXD | CA |
| 93581 | | RPXE | CA |
| 93585 | R | RPXD | CA |
| 93590 | | RPXE | CA |
| 93595† | | RPXD | BJ |
| 93596 | | RPXD | BJ |
| 93600 | | RPXE | BJ |
| 93601 | | RPXD | BJ |
| 93604 | | RPXE | BJ |
| 93606 | | RPOC | PY |
| 93607 | R | RPOC | PY |
| 93610 | | RPOC | PY |
| 93617 | | RPXD | CA |
| 93618 | | RPXD | CA |
| 93622 | | RPXD | BJ |
| 93623 | | RPXT | CA |
| 93624 | | RPXD | BJ |
| 93630 | | RPXD | BJ |
| 93631 | | RPXD | BJ |
| 93633 | | RPXD | BJ |

| | | |
|---|---|---|
| 93634† | RPXD | CA |
| 93635† | RPXD | CA |
| 93640† | RPXD | CA |
| 93643 R | RPXD | BJ |
| 93644† | RPXD | CA |
| 93648 | RPXE | BJ |
| 93652† | RPXT | CA |

Pressed Steel

| | | |
|---|---|---|
| 93656 | RPXD | BJ |
| 93660 R | RPXD | BJ |
| 93663† | RPXD | CA |
| 93664† | RPXD | CA |
| 93667† | RPXD | CA |
| 93668 | RPXE | BJ |
| 93673 R | RPXE | BJ |
| 93675 | RPXE | BJ |
| 93677 | RPXD | BJ |
| 93680† | RPXD | CA |
| 93681† | RPXD | BJ |
| 93683 | RPXD | CA |
| 93687† | RPXD | CA |
| 93692 | RPXE | BJ |
| 93694 N | NSS | EH |
| 93696† | RPXD | CA |
| 93701 | RPXD | BJ |
| 93706 | RPXD | BJ |
| 93710 | RPXD | BJ |
| 93711 | RPXD | BJ |
| 93713 R | RPXD | BJ |
| 93714 | RPXD | BJ |
| 93715 | RPXD | BJ |
| 93717 | RPXD | BJ |
| 93720 R | RPXD | BJ |
| 93722 R | RPXD | BJ |
| 93723 | RPXD | BJ |
| 93725 | RPXD | BJ |
| 93726 R | RPXD | BJ |
| 93727 | RPXD | BJ |
| 93728 | RPXD | BJ |
| 93762 | RPOC | PY |
| 93764 R | RPXE | BJ |
| 93765† | RPXT | BJ |
| 93767† | RPXD | CA |
| 93769† | RPXT | CA |
| 93775† | RPOC | PY |
| 93776† | RPXD | CA |
| 93779† | RPXD | CA |
| 93781† | RPXT | CA |
| 93788† | RPXD | CA |
| 93791† | RPXD | CA |
| 93792† | RPXD | CA |
| 93793† | RPXT | CA |
| 93795† | RPXT | CA |
| 93798 R | RPOC | PY |
| 93800† | RPXT | CA |
| 93801† | RPXD | CA |
| 93811 | RPXD | CA |
| 93815 | RPXD | CA |
| 93820 R | RPOC | PY |
| 93823† | RPXD | BJ |
| 93824† | RPXD | CA |
| 93829† | RPXD | CA |
| 93830 | RPXD | BJ |
| 93836 | RPOC | PY |
| 93844 | RPXE | BJ |
| 93846† | RPXD | BJ |
| 93847 R | RPXD | BJ |
| 93849 R | RPXD | BJ |
| 93852 N | NSS | EH |
| 93854 | RPXD | BJ |
| 93855 | RPXD | BJ |
| 93857 | RPXD | BJ |
| 93858 | RPXD | CA |
| 93859 | RPXD | BJ |
| 93860 | RPXE | BJ |
| 93863 | IXXZ | BJ |
| 93864 | RPXE | BJ |
| 93877† | RPXT | BJ |
| 93881 | RPXD | BJ |
| 93883† | RPXD | BJ |
| 93886 R | RPXD | CA |
| 93887 | RPXD | BJ |
| 93888† | RPXT | BJ |
| 93889 | RPXD | BJ |
| 93893 | RPXD | BJ |
| 93896† | RPXD | BJ |
| 93897 R | RPXE | BJ |
| 93901† | RPXD | BJ |
| 93904† | RPXD | BJ |
| 93905 R | RPXD | BJ |
| 93907† | RPXD | BJ |
| 93911† | RPXD | BJ |
| 93914 | RPXE | BJ |
| 93915 | RPXD | CA |
| 93919† | RPXD | BJ |
| 93922† | RPXD | CA |
| 93927† | RPXD | CA |
| 93930† | RPXT | BJ |
| 93931† | RPXD | BJ |
| 93932† | RPXD | BJ |
| 93935 R | RPXD | BJ |
| 93942 | RPXE | BJ |
| 93943† | RPXD | CA |
| 93948† | RPXD | BJ |
| 93950 | RPXD | BJ |
| 93952 | RPXD | BJ |
| 93955 | RPXD | BJ |
| 93956 | RPXA | CA |
| 93957† | RPXD | BJ |
| 93962 | RPXD | CA |
| 93969 R | RPXE | BJ |
| 93973 | RPXD | BJ |
| 93976† | RPXD | BJ |
| 93979 | RPXD | BJ |
| 93982 R | RPXD | BJ |

## PVG BR Doncaster/Wolverton†

**NL5**
**NL5.01**

**Gangwayed Newspaper Packing Van.**

| | | |
|---|---|---|
| 94001† | RPPW | BJ |
| 94002† R | RPPW | BJ |
| 94003† R | RPPW | BJ |
| 94004† | RPPW | BJ |
| 94005† R | RPPW | BJ |
| 94006† | RPPW | BJ |
| 94007† | RPPW | OM |
| 94008 | RPPW | OM |
| 94009 | RPPW | OM |
| 94010 | RPPW | OM |
| 94011 | RPPW | OM |
| 94012 R | RPPW | OM |
| 94013 | RPPE | HT |
| 94015 | RPPA | CA |
| 94016 | RPPA | CA |
| 94017 | RPPA | CA |
| 94018 | RPPE | HT |
| 94019 R | RPPW | OM |
| 94020 | RPPW | BJ |
| 94021 | RPPW | OM |
| 94022 | RPPE | HT |
| 94023 | RPPA | CA |
| 94024 | RPPA | CA |
| 94025 R | RPPW | OM |
| 94026 | RPPA | CA |
| 94027 | RPPW | BJ |
| 94028 | RPPW | BJ |
| 94029 | RPPW | BJ |
| 94030 | RPPW | OM |
| 94031 | RPPW | BJ |
| 94032 | RPPW | OM |
| 94033 | RPPA | CA |
| 94034 | RPPW | OM |

## PVG Pressed Steel/BR York & St. Rollox (Glasgow)$

**NM5**
**NM5.01†/NM5.02**

**Non-Gangwayed Newspaper Packing Van.**

| | | |
|---|---|---|
| 94050 | RPPA | CA |
| 94051† | RPPA | CA |
| 94052† | RPPA | CA |
| 94053† | RPPA | CA |
| 94056† | RPPA | CA |
| 94058$ | RPPA | CA |
| 94061 | RPPA | CA |
| 94062 | RPPA | CA |
| 94068 | RPPA | CA |
| 94071$ | RPPA | CA |
| 94076 | RPPA | CA |
| 94077 | RPPA | CA |
| 94078 | RPPA | CA |

## PVG

**NC5**
**NC5.01**

**Gangwayed Newspaper Packing Van.**
**Pressed Steel/Birmingham RC&W (b)/Cravens (c)/BR Derby (d)/Metro-Cammell (m)/BR York (y)**

| | | |
|---|---|---|
| 95200c | RPPA | CA |
| 95201 Bg | RPPW | BJ |
| 95202y | RPPA | CA |
| 95203y | RPAC | RE |
| 95204 | RPPA | CA |
| 95205y | RPPW | BJ |
| 95206d | RPPW | BJ |
| 95207d R | RPPW | BJ |
| 95208y | RPPW | BJ |
| 95209c | RPPA | CA |
| 95210b | RPPA | CA |
| 95211 R | RPPW | BJ |
| 95212c | RPPA | CA |
| 95213c | RPAC | RE |
| 95214 | RPPM | EN |
| 95215y | RPPW | BJ |
| 95216 | RPPW | BJ |
| 95217 | RPPM | EN |
| 95218m R | RPPW | BJ |
| 95219 | RPPM | EN |
| 95220m | RPPW | BJ |
| 95221m | RPPW | BJ |
| 95222b | RPPW | BJ |
| 95223 | RPPW | BJ |

## PVG.

**NM5.**
**NC5.01**

**Gangwayed Newspaper Van.**
**Pressed Steel/Cravens (c)/BR Derby (d)/Metro-Cammell (m)/BR York (y)**

| | | |
|---|---|---|
| 95300m | RPPA | CA |
| 95303y | RPPA | CA |
| 95304 R | RPPW | BJ |
| 95305 | RPPA | CA |
| 95307m | RPPA | CA |
| 95308m | RPPA | CA |
| 95310 | RPPW | BJ |
| 95312d | RPPA | CA |
| 95321d | RPPA | CA |
| 95329 | RPPA | CA |
| 95332c | RPPA | CA |

## GUV Pressed Steel

**NX5**

**General Utility Van-Motorail.**

**NX5.01**

| | | | | | | | | | | | | | | | |
|---|---|---|---|---|---|---|---|---|---|---|---|---|---|---|---|
| 96100 | | IWC | EN | 96138 | | ICC | EC | 96162 | Im | IWC | EN | 96178 | Im | IWC | EN |
| 96101 | | IWC | EN | 96139 | | ICC | EC | 96163 | Im | IWC | EN | 96179 | Im | IWC | EN |
| 96102 | Im | IWC | EN | 96140 | | ICC | EC | 96164 | Im | IWC | EN | 96180 | Im | IWC | EN |
| 96103 | | IWC | EN | 96141 | | ICC | EC | 96165 | Im | IWC | EC | 96181 | Im | IWC | EN |
| 96104 | | IWC | EN | 96150 | | IWC | EN | 96166 | Im | IWC | EN | 96182 | Im | IWC | EN |
| 96110 | | IWC | EN | 96151 | Im | IWC | EN | 96167 | Im | ICC | EC | 96185 | Bg | IXXH | EN |
| 96111 | Im | IWC | EN | 96152 | Bg | IWC | EN | 96168 | Im | IWC | EN | 96186 | | IXXH | EN |
| 96112 | | IWC | EN | 96153 | Im | IWC | EN | 96169 | Im | IWC | EN | 96187 | | IXXH | EN |
| 96130 | Im | IWC | EN | 96154 | Im | IWC | EN | 96170 | Bg | IWC | EN | 96188 | Im | IWC | EN |
| 96131 | | IWC | EN | 96155 | Bg | IWC | EN | 96171 | Im | IWC | EN | 96189 | Im | IWC | EN |
| 96132 | Im | IWC | EN | 96156 | Bg | IWC | EN | 96172 | Bg | IWC | EN | 96190 | Im | IWC | EN |
| 96133 | Im | ICC | EC | 96157 | | IWC | EN | 96173 | | IWC | EN | 96191 | Im | IWC | EN |
| 96134 | Im | ICC | EC | 96158 | | IWC | EN | 96174 | | IWC | EN | 96192 | Im | IWC | EN |
| 96135 | Im | ICC | EC | 96159 | Bg | IWC | EN | 96175 | Im | IWC | EN | 96193 | Im | IWC | EN |
| 96136 | Im | IXXH | EN | 96160 | | IWC | EN | 96176 | Bg | IWC | EN | 96194 | Im | IWC | EN |
| 96137 | | IXXH | EN | 96161 | | IWC | EN | 96177 | Im | IWC | EN | 96195 | Im | IWC | EN |

## Exhibition Van

**NY5**

**Mk.1 Pool: ICHE. Dep: SA Livery: Painted to livery specified by hirer**

| Veh No: | Built: | Des Code: |
|---|---|---|
| 99601 | BR Wolverton. | NY5.03 |
| 99620 | BR Wolverton. | NY5.03 |
| 99621 | BR Wolverton. | NY5.03 |
| 99622 | BR Wolverton. | NY5.03 |
| 99623 | BR Wolverton. | NY5.03 |
| 99625 | BR Wolverton. | NY5.03 |
| 99630 | BR Wolverton. | NY5.04 |
| 99631 | BR Wolverton. | NY5.17 |
| 99632 | Birmingham RC&W. | NY5.22 |
| 99633 | BR Ashford/Eastleigh. | NY5.22 |
| 99634 | BR Wolverton. | NY5.20 |
| 99635 | BR Wolverton. | NY5.20 |
| 99636 | BR Wolverton. | NY5.26 |
| 99637 | Metro-Cammell. | NY5.21 |
| 99641 | BR Wolverton. | NY5.17 |
| 99642 | BR Wolverton. | NY5.17 |
| 99645 | Pressed Steel | NY5.23 |
| 99647 | Gloucester RC&W | NY5.04 |
| 99648 | Pressed Steel | NY5.25 |
| 99650 | Cravens | NY5.24 |
| 99657 | BR York | NY5.22 |
| 99659 | BR York | NY5.22 |
| 99661 | BR Derby | NY5.24 |

## PRESERVED PRIVATE OWNER OPERATING STOCK

**Only vehicles authorised to form trains for public conveyance on chartered services are listed here. Coaches with the sole use of 'Support Vehicles' for conveying staff during movement of preserved locomotives are not included. All vehicles form Pool ICHP.**

| Veh No: | Owner: | Des Code: | Seats 1st/Std | Dep. |
|---|---|---|---|---|
| 99052 | THR | AO1.02 | 21/- | EC |
| 99120 | PULR | AO3. | 12/18 | BN |
| 99122 | PULR | AO1.22 | 42/- | BN |
| 99123 | PULR | AO1.22 | 42/- | BN |
| 99124 | PULR | AO1.22 | 42/- | BN |
| 99129 | PULR | AO3. | 12/24 | BN |
| 99130 | PULR | AO1. | 24/- | BN |
| 99131 | PULR | AO1.33 | 12/ | BN |
| 99132 | PULR | AO2.34 | -/44 | BN |
| 99160 | TCL | AO4.23 | 28 berths | OM |
| 99161 | TCL | AO4.23 | 28 berths | OM |
| 99162 | TCL | AO4.23 | 28 berths | OM |
| 99163 | TCL | AO4.23 | 28 berths | OM |
| 99164 | TCL | AO4.23 | 28 berths | OM |
| 99165 | TCL | AO4.24 | 28 berths | OM |
| 99166 | TCL | AO4.24 | 14 berths | OM |
| 99167 | TCL | AO4.25 | 18 berths | OM |
| 99168 | TCL | AO5.09 | -/- | OM |
| 99169 | TCL | AO2.39 | -/64 | OM |
| 99170 | TCL | AO2.39 | -/64 | OM |
| 99171 | TCL | AO2.39 | -/56 | OM |
| 99335 | SLOA | AO1.21 | 30/- | BN |
| 99347 | SLOA | AO1.20 | 42/- | BN |
| 99348 | SLOA | AO1.20 | 42/- | BN |
| 99349 | SLOA | AO1.20 | 42/- | BN |
| 99350 | SLOA | AO1.20 | 42/- | BN |
| 99351 | SLOA | AO1.20 | 42/- | BN |
| 99352 | SLOA | AO1.20 | 42/- | BN |
| 99353 | SLOA | AO1.20 | 42/- | BN |
| 99354 | SLOA | AO1.30 | 24/- | BN |
| 99355 | SLOA | AO3.11 | 12/18 | BN |
| 99356 | SLOA | AO3.11 | 12/18 | BN |
| 99357 | SLOA | AO1.22 | 42/- | BN |
| 99358 | PULR | AO1.22 | 42/- | BN |
| 99370 | GRAM | AO2.41 | -/31 | IS |
| 99371 | GRAM | AO2.41 | -/42 | IS |
| 99530 | VSOE | AO4.14 | 26/- | SL |
| 99531 | VSOE | AO4.15 | 26/- | SL |
| 99532 | VSOE | AO4.14 | 26/- | SL |
| 99533 | VSOE | AO5.04 | -/- | SL |
| 99534 | VSOE | AO4.17 | 20/- | SL |
| 99535 | VSOE | AO4.18 | 26/- | SL |
| 99536 | VSOE | AO4.19 | 24/- | SL |
| 99537 | VSOE | AO4.20 | 20/- | SL |
| 99538 | VSOE | AO2.31 | -/- | SL |
| 99539 | VSOE | AO4.16 | 20/- | SL |
| 99540 | VSOE | AO1.22 | 42/- | SL |
| 99541 | VSOE | AO4.19 | 24/- | SL |
| 99542 | VSOE | AO5.08 | -/- | SL |
| 99710 | TRTS | AO2.37 | -/48 | LL |
| 99712 | TRTS | AO2.37 | -/48 | LL |
| 99713 | TRTS | AO2.37 | -/48 | LL |
| 99714 | TRTS | AO3.09 | 24/18 | LL |
| 99716 | TRTS | AO2.37 | -/48 | LL |
| 99717 | TRTS | AO2.37 | -/48 | LL |
| 99718 | TRTS | AO2.37 | -/48 | LL |
| 99719 | TRTS | AO3.09 | 24/18 | LL |
| 99720 | TRTS | AO2.37 | -/24 | LL |
| 99818 | SCR | AO4.22 | -/23 | PH |
| 99819 | SCR | AO2.39 | -/64 | PH |

| | | | | |
|---|---|---|---|---|
| 99820 | SCR | AO2.39 | -/64 | PH |
| 99821 | SCR | AO2.40 | -/39 | PH |
| 99880 | THR | AO1.31 | 12/- | EC |
| 99881 | THR | AO1.32 | 19/- | EC |
| 99882 | THR | AO1.29 | 8/- | EC |
| 99883 | THR | AO1.30 | 10/- | EC |
| 99884 | THR | AO1.29 | 6/- | EC |
| 99885 | THR | AO1.30 | 8/- | EC |
| 99886 | THR | AO5.07 | -/- | EC |
| 99887 | THR | AO1.23 | 11/- | EC |

| **Operators:** | | **Liv:** |
|---|---|---|
| GRAM: | Grampian Railtours, Aberdeen. | Im |
| PULR: | Pullman Rail. | Ib |
| SCR: | Scottish Railway Preservation Society. | |
| SLOA: | Steam Locomotive Operators Association (by PULR) | Im |
| TCL: | Travelling College Ltd. | Choc. & cream |
| THR: | Thomas Hill Rotherham (by GSWR). | |
| TRTS: | Train Tours. | Green with red band |
| VSOE: | Sea Containers Ltd (Venice-Simplon Orient Express). | Ib |

## INTERCITY 125 TRAILER CAR FORMATIONS.

## EAST COAST & MIDLAND MAIN LINES

| Set no. | Sector | Depot | Booked formation | | | | | | | |
|---|---|---|---|---|---|---|---|---|---|---|
| 01 | IEC | BN | 41057 | 41058 | 40708 | 42335 | 42111 | 42112 | 42113 | 44041 |
| 02 | IEC | BN | 41059 | 41060 | 40733 | 42336 | 42115 | 42116 | 42117 | 44042 |
| 03 | IEC | BN | 41061 | 41062 | 40729 | 42337 | 42119 | 42120 | 42121 | 44043 |
| 04 | IEC | BN | 41063 | 41064 | 40754 | 42328 | 42123 | 42124 | 42125 | 44044 |
| 05 | IEC | BN | 41171 | 41173 | 40734 | 42338 | 42178 | 42127 | 42128 | 44021+ |
| 06 | IEC | NL | 41067 | 41068 | 40730 | 42331 | 42131 | 42132 | 42133 | 44046 |
| 07 | IEC | NL | 41069 | 41070 | 40751 | 42339 | 42135 | 42136 | 42137 | 44047 |
| 08 | IEC | NL | 41071 | 41072 | 40728 | 42329 | 42139 | 42140 | 42141 | 44048 |
| 10 | IEC | BN | 41075 | 41076 | 40756 | 42327 | 42147 | 42148 | 42149 | 44050 |
| 11 | IEC | NL | 41077 | 41078 | 40753 | 42324 | 42151 | 42152 | 42153 | 44051 |
| 12 | IEC | NL | 41079 | 41080 | 40700 | 42155 | 42156 | 42157 | 42100 | 44052 |
| 13 | IEC | BN | 41081 | 41082 | 40701 | 42159 | 42160 | 42161 | 42101 | 44053 |
| 14 | IEC | BN | 41083 | 41084 | 40702 | 42163 | 42164 | 42165 | 42102 | 44054 |
| 15 | IEC | BN | 41085 | 41086 | 40703 | 42169 | 42168 | 42167 | 42103 | 44055 |
| 16 | IEC | BN | 41087 | 41088 | 40706 | 42104 | 42171 | 42172 | 42173 | 44056+ |
| 17 | IEC | BN | 41089 | 41090 | 40705 | 42175 | 42176 | 42177 | 42105 | 44057 |
| 18 | IEC | BN | 41091 | 41092 | 40704 | 42179 | 42180 | 42181 | 42106 | 44058+ |
| 19 | IEC | BN | 41093 | 41094 | 40707 | 42183 | 42184 | 42185 | 42107 | 44059+ |
| 20 | IEC | BN | 41095 | 41096 | 40736 | 42326 | 42187 | 42188 | 42189 | 44060 |
| 21 | IML | NL | 41097 | 41098 | 40750 | 42158 | 42191 | 42192 | 42193 | 44061 |
| 22 | IML | NL | 41099 | 41100 | 40711 | 42235 | 42240 | 42198 | 42199 | 44063 |
| 23 | IML | NL | 41101 | 41102 | 40712 | 42201 | 42202 | 42203 | 42204 | 44064 |
| 24 | IEC | NL | 41103 | 41104 | 40713 | 42206 | 42207 | 42208 | 42209 | 44066 |
| 25 | IEC | NL | 41105 | 41106 | 40714 | 42211 | 42212 | 42213 | 42214 | 44067 |
| 26 | IEC | BN | 41113 | 41108 | 41107 | 40715 | 42217 | 42218 | 42219 | 44097+ |
| 27 | IEC | BN | 41109 | 41110 | 40716 | 42334 | 42222 | 42223 | 42224 | 44101+ |
| 28 | IML | NL | 41112 | 41111 | 40749 | 42194 | 42229 | 42227 | 42228 | 44073 |
| 29 | IEC | BN | 41120 | 41114 | 40718 | 42231 | 42232 | 42233 | 42234 | 44074 |
| 30 | IEC | BN | 41115 | 41116 | 40710 | 42330 | 42237 | 42238 | 42239 | 44075 |
| 31 | IEC | BN | 41170 | 41118 | 40720 | 42241 | 42242 | 42243 | 42244 | 44098+ |
| 32 | IEC | BN | 41119 | 41046 | 40721 | 42246 | 42247 | 42248 | 42249 | 44078+ |
| 33 | IEC | BN | 41149 | 41150 | 40739 | 42162 | 42166 | 42170 | 42174 | 44079 |
| 34 | IEC | BN | 41151 | 41152 | 40740 | 42226 | 42182 | 42186 | 42190 | 44080 |
| 35 | IEC | HT | 41153 | 41066 | 40511 | 41154 | 40741 | 42205 | 42210 | 44083 |
| 36 | IML | NL | 41155 | 41156 | 40748 | 42215 | 42220 | 42225 | 42230 | 44085 |
| 37 | IEC | NL | 41157 | 41041 | 40501 | 41158 | 40743 | 42245 | 42250 | 44086+ |
| 38 | IML | NL | 41055 | 41056 | 40709 | 42081 | 42082 | 42083 | 42126 | 44027 |
| 39 | IML | NL | 41045 | 41065 | 40738 | 42062 | 42066 | 42067 | 42068 | 44022 |
| 44 | IEC | BN | 41174 | 41172 | 40742 | 42130 | 42134 | 42138 | 42122 | 44093 |
| 45 | IML | NL | 41117 | 41176 | 41175 | 40619 | 42146 | 42150 | 42154 | 44094 |
| 46 | IML | NL | 41039 | 41040 | 40735 | 42323 | 42057 | 42058 | 42059 | 44019 |
| 47 | IML | NL | 41043 | 41044 | 40737 | 42340 | 42063 | 42064 | 42065 | 44045+ |

Spare coaches:
40505 40513 40717 40745 40746 42129 42195 42200 42341 44070 44071
44077 44100

+ Buffer fitted TGS.

## GREAT WESTERN MAINLINE and CROSS COUNTRY

| | | | | | | | | | | |
|---|---|---|---|---|---|---|---|---|---|---|
| 04 | IWR | PM | 41009 | 41010 | 40204 | 42012 | 42004 | 42013 | 42014 | 44004 |
| 05 | IWR | PM | 41011 | 41012 | 40205 | 42015 | 42005 | 42016 | 42017 | 44005 |
| 06 | IWR | PM | 41013 | 41014 | 40206 | 42018 | 42006 | 42019 | 42020 | 44006 |
| 07 | IWR | PM | 41015 | 41016 | 40207 | 42021 | 42007 | 42022 | 42023 | 44007 |
| 08 | IWR | PM | 41017 | 41018 | 40208 | 42024 | 42008 | 42025 | 42026 | 44008 |
| 09 | IWR | PM | 41019 | 41020 | 40211 | 42027 | 42009 | 42028 | 42029 | 44009 |
| 10 | IWR | PM | 41021 | 41022 | 40210 | 42030 | 42010 | 42031 | 42032 | 44010 |
| 11 | IWR | LA | 41023 | 41024 | 40755 | 42096 | 42033 | 42034 | 42035 | 44011 |
| 12 | IWR | LA | 41025 | 41026 | 40723 | 42097 | 42036 | 42037 | 42038 | 44012 |
| 13 | IWR | LA | 41027 | 41028 | 40725 | 42098 | 42039 | 42040 | 42041 | 44013 |
| 14 | IWR | LA | 41029 | 41030 | 40726 | 42099 | 42042 | 42043 | 42044 | 44014 |
| 15 | IWR | LA | 41031 | 41032 | 40727 | 42216 | 42045 | 42046 | 42047 | 44015 |
| 16 | IWR | LA | 41033 | 41034 | 40731 | 42221 | 42048 | 42049 | 42050 | 44016 |
| 17 | IWR | LA | 41035 | 41036 | 40732 | 42051 | 42342 | 42052 | 42053 | 44017 |
| 18 | IWR | LA | 41037 | 41038 | 40757 | 42054 | 42343 | 42055 | 42056 | 44018 |
| 19 | IWR | PM | 41003 | 41004 | 40752 | 42333 | 42143 | 42144 | 42145 | 44049 |
| 20 | IWR | LA | 41127 | 41128 | 40233 | 42196 | 42197 | 42060 | 42061 | 44020 |
| 23 | IWR | PM | 41005 | 41006 | 40744 | 42069 | 42070 | 42071 | 42118 | 44023 |
| 24 | IWR | PM | 41049 | 41050 | 40232 | 42325 | 42072 | 42073 | 42074 | 44024 |
| 25 | IWR | LA | 41051 | 41052 | 40231 | 42075 | 42076 | 42077 | 42078 | 44025 |
| 26 | IWR | PM | 41007 | 41008 | 40747 | 42332 | 42236 | 42079 | 42080 | 44026 |
| 28 | IWR | LA | 41121 | 41122 | 40722 | 42345 | 42251 | 42252 | 42253 | 44028 |
| 29 | IWR | PM | 41123 | 41124 | 40209 | 42255 | 42263 | 42256 | 42257 | 44029 |
| 30 | IWR | LA | 41126 | 41125 | 40724 | 42344 | 42259 | 42260 | 42261 | 44030 |
| 32 | IWR | LA | 41129 | 41130 | 40212 | 42267 | 42346 | 42268 | 42269 | 44032 |
| 33 | IWR | PM | 41131 | 41132 | 40213 | 42271 | 42347 | 42272 | 42273 | 44033 |
| 34 | IWR | LA | 41133 | 41134 | 40221 | 42275 | 42264 | 42276 | 42277 | 44034 |
| 35 | IWR | LA | 41135 | 41136 | 40422† | 42279 | 42265 | 42280 | 42281 | 44035 |
| 36 | IWR | LA | 41137 | 41138 | 40228 | 42283 | 42003 | 42284 | 42285 | 44036 |
| 37 | IWR | LA | 41139 | 41140 | 40416 | 42287 | 42348 | 42288 | 42289 | 44037 |
| 38 | IWR | LA | 41141 | 41142 | 40732 | 42291 | 42349 | 42292 | 42293 | 44038 |
| 39 | IWR | LA | 41143 | 41144 | 40418 | 42295 | 42350 | 42296 | 42297 | 44039 |
| 40 | IWR | PM | 41145 | 41146 | 40419 | 42299 | 42351 | 42300 | 42301 | 44040 |
| 41 | ICC | PM | | 41147 | 40401 | 42254 | 42258 | 42262 | 42266 | 44000 |
| 42 | ICC | PM | | 41148 | 40402 | 42270 | 42274 | 42278 | 42282 | 44062 |
| 43 | ICC | PM | | 41159 | 40403 | 42286 | 42290 | 42294 | 42298 | 44065 |
| 44 | ICC | PM | | 41160 | 40425 | 42302 | 42303 | 42304 | 42305 | 44068 |
| 45 | ICC | PM | | 41161 | 40420 | 42084 | 42085 | 42086 | 42087 | 44069 |
| 46 | ICC | LA | | 41162 | 40414 | 42088 | 42089 | 42090 | 42091 | 44072 |
| 47 | ICC | LA | | 41163 | 40415 | 42092 | 42093 | 42094 | 42095 | 44076 |
| 51 | ICC | LA | | 41165 | 40430 | 42108 | 42109 | 42110 | 42322 | 44087 |
| 52 | ICC | LA | | 41166 | 40424 | 42306 | 42307 | 42308 | 42309 | 44088 |
| 53 | ICC | LA | | 41167 | 40429 | 42310 | 42311 | 42312 | 42313 | 44089 |
| 54 | ICC | LA | | 41168 | 40426 | 42314 | 42315 | 42316 | 42317 | 44090 |
| 55 | ICC | LA | | 41169 | 40434† | 42318 | 42319 | 42320 | 42321 | 44091 |

spare coaches :
40423† 40427 40435 40436 40437 41164 42011 44081 44084

† September 1990: 40234 to LA35, 40423 to LA55, 40422 to spare.

Not accounted for:
41042 44001 44002 44003 44031 44099

Note: Spare TGS vehicles will be used for commencement of modifications to DGS for InterCity Cross-Country services.

Above: Class 431 in original 4-car (4-REP) formation passes Clapham with a Waterloo –Bournemouth semi-fast service with two Class 438 4-TC units trailing. As this book closed for press the unit was about to be reformed to form a 6-car (6-REP) unit and it will not be able to haul the non-powered TC sets. See reformation page for latest details.

Below: Renumbered during 1989 from 47665 Class 47/4 No 47820 stands at King's Cross carrying one of the many minor variations of the old standard rail blue livery. Under present policy this locomotive will be repainted to INTERCITY swallow livery at next overhaul.

# RENUMBERED AND REFORMED STOCK 1989/90.

**Renumbered Locomotives:**

| Current No: | Former No: | | | | |
|---|---|---|---|---|---|
| 08600 | 97800 | | | | |
| 20901-05 | 20041 | 20060 | 20083 | 20101 | 20219 |
| 20906 | 20225 | | | | |
| 315xx | 314xx (same last two digits) | | | | |
| 31970 | 97204 | | | | |
| 37008 | 37352 | | | | |
| 37026 | 37320 | | | | |
| 37032 | 37353 | | | | |
| 37037 | 37321 | | | | |
| 37045 | 37355 | | | | |
| 37079 | 37357 | | | | |
| 37088 | 37323 | | | | |
| 37099 | 37324 | | | | |
| 37108 | 37325 | | | | |
| 37111 | 37326 | | | | |
| 37137 | 37312 | | | | |
| 37145 | 37313 | | | | |
| 37152 | 37310 | | | | |
| 37156 | 37311 | | | | |
| 37271 | 37303 | | | | |
| 37272 | 37304 | | | | |
| 37273 | 37306 | | | | |
| 37274 | 37308 | | | | |
| 37351 | 37002 | | | | |
| 43201-29 | tba | | | | |
| 47801-04 | 47551 | 47552 | 47553 | 47591 | |
| 47805-20 | 47650-65 resp. | | | | |
| 47821-25 | 47607 | 47571 | 47620 | 47602 | 47590 |
| 47826-30 | 47637 | 47589 | 47629 | 47619 | 47649 |
| 47831-35 | 47563 | 47560 | 47608 | 47609 | 47620 |
| 47836-40 | 47618 | 47611 | 47612 | 47621 | 47613 |
| 47841-45 | 47642 | 47606 | 47623 | 47556 | 47638 |
| 47846-50 | 47647 | 47577 | 47632 | 47570 | 47648 |
| 47851-53 | 47639 | 47646 | 47614 | | |
| 47971-73 | 97480 | 97545 | 97561 | | |
| 50049 | 50149 | | | | |
| 85101-05 | 85006 | 85009 | 85010 | 85012 | 85016 |
| 85106-10 | 85021 | 85024 | 85032 | 85035 | 85036 |
| 85111/12 | 85004 | 85007 | | | |
| 86205 | 86503 | | | | |
| 86217 | 86504 | | | | |
| 86222 | 86502 | | | | |
| 86233 | 86506 | | | | |
| 86239 | 86507 | | | | |
| 86241 | 86508 | | | | |
| 86246 | 86505 | | | | |
| 86258 | 86501 | | | | |
| 866xx | 864xx (same last two digits). | | | | |

**Renumbered Diesel Multiple Units:**

| | |
|---|---|
| 141104 | 141003 |
| 141108 | 141007 |
| 141112 | 141011 |
| 141114 | 141013 |
| 141118 | 141017 |
| 1425xx | 1420xx |
| 143601-19 | 143001-19 |
| 143320-25 | 143020-25 |

**Renumbered DMU Vehicles:**

| Current No: | Former No: |
|---|---|
| 55928/29 | 53018 53015 |
| 54903/04 | 54009 54015 |
| 59110/11 | 59101/05 |
| 60154/55 | 60100 60101 (units 205001/02) |

**Reformed Diesel Electric Multiple Units:**

| | | | |
|---|---|---|---|
| 205023 | 60122 | 60669 | 60823 |
| 205024 | 60123 | 60668 | 60822 |

**Renumbered Electric Multiple Units (not reformed):**

| **Current No:** | **Former No:** | | | |
|---|---|---|---|---|
| 310107 | 310062 | | | |
| 310108 | 310048 | | | |
| 310109 | 310053 | | | |
| 310110 | 310054 | | | |
| 310111 | 310063 | | | |
| 1301-16 | 1824-251252 | 1244 | 1264 | 1241 |

**Revised EMU Formations:**

| Unit No: | Current official formation: | | | | |
|---|---|---|---|---|---|
| 302262 | 75310 | 61121 | 70130 | 75235 | |
| 302272 | 75359 | 61131 | 70111 | 75245 | |
| 302274 | 75324 | 61190 | 70221 | 75247 | |
| 302283 | 75331 | 61199 | 70131 | 75256 | |
| 302285 | 75298 | 61201 | 70190 | 75259 | |
| 302990 | 68100 | 68020 | 68207 | | |
| | (75084) | (61090) | (75082) | | |
| 302991 | 68101 | 68021 | 68208 | | |
| | (75221) | (61067) | (75217) | | |
| 302992 | 68102 | 68022 | 68209 | | |
| | (75218) | (61227) | (........) | | |
| 303048 | 75752 | 61824 | 75808 | | |
| 305414 | 75289 | 61477 | 75562 | | |
| 308144 | ..... | 61894 | 70622 | 75931 | |
| 313034 | 62562 | ..... | 62626 | | |
| 1203 | 76753 | 62391 | 71071 | 76804 | |
| 1216 | 76766 | 62404 | 71084 | 76837 | |
| 1500 | 61389 | ..... | 70302 | 61388 | |
| 1547 | 61329 | 70345 | 70272 | 61328 | |
| 1714 | 76077 | 62018 | 70696 | 76023 | |
| 1715 | 76082 | 62023 | 70701 | 76028 | |
| 2303 | 61954 | 70656 | 69347 | 61955 | |
| 2307 | 61802 | 70606 | 69343 | 61803 | |
| 2403 | 77384 | 71820 | 62941 | 71844 | 77408 |
| 2404 | 77385 | 71821 | 62939 | 71845 | 77409 |
| 2405 | 77386 | 71822 | 62944 | 71846 | 77410 |
| 2406 | 77389 | 71823 | 62942 | 71847 | 77411 |
| 2408 | 77387 | 71825 | 62945 | 71849 | 77413 |
| 2409 | 77390 | 71826 | 62946 | 71850 | 77414 |
| 2410 | 77391 | 71827 | 62948 | 71851 | 77415 |
| 2411 | 77392 | 71828 | 62940 | 71858 | 77422 |
| 2412 | 77393 | 71829 | 62947 | 71853 | 77417 |
| 2417 | 77398 | 71834 | 62953 | 71852 | 77416 |
| 3019 | 76267 | 62139 | 70799 | 76266 | |
| 3425 | 76338 | 62192 | 70874 | 76358 | |
| 5728 | 77689 | 62810 | 71527 | 77782 | |
| 5856 | 77781 | 62764 | 71692 | 77690 | |
| 6322 | 14488 | 16119 | | | |
| Spare: | 62268 | 62317 | 62319 | 62342 | 62479 |
| | 69309 | 70822 | 70837 | 70842 | 70900 |
| | 71733 | 72601 | 72700 | 76327 | 76824 |

Unit Nos

| New | Old | Current official formation: | | | |
|---|---|---|---|---|---|
| 1751 | 2101 | 76063 | 62054 | 71044 | 76059 |
| 1752 | 2102 | 76129 | 62064 | 71046 | 76069 |
| 1753 | 2103 | 76124 | 62065 | 71052 | 76070 |
| 1754 | 2104 | 76117 | 62058 | 71050 | 76051 |
| 1755 | 2105 | 76121 | 62062 | 71058 | 76067 |
| 1756 | 2106 | 76118 | 62059 | 71065 | 76064 |
| 1757 | 2107 | 76122 | 62063 | 71047 | 76068 |
| 1758 | 2108 | 76127 | 62068 | 71064 | 76073 |
| 1759 | 2109 | 76123 | 62070 | 71066 | 76075 |
| 1760 | 2110 | 76115 | 62056 | 71067 | 76061 |
| 1761 | 2111 | 76112 | 62053 | 71068 | 76058 |
| 1762 | 2112 | 76116 | 62067 | 71097 | 76072 |

| | | | | | | | |
|---|---|---|---|---|---|---|---|
| 1901 | | | | | | | |
| 1902 | Various | 62153 | 70824 | 70859 | | | |
| 1903 | Various | 62145 | 70834 | 70866 | 70853 | 70827 | 76324 |
| 1904 | Various | 62154 | 70838 | 70870 | 70845 | 70839 | 76323 |
| 1905 | | | | | | | |
| 1906 | Various | 62142 | 70830 | 71163 | 70849 | 70817 | 76322 |

| | | | | | |
|---|---|---|---|---|---|
| 2251 | 1276 | 76726 | 62364 | 69302 | 76797 |
| 2252 | 1278 | 76728 | 62366 | 69312 | 76799 |
| 2253 | 1284 | 76734 | 62372 | 69313 | 76805 |
| 2254 | 1282 | 76732 | 62370 | 69306 | 76803 |
| 2255 | 1290 | 76740 | 62378 | 69310 | 76811 |
| 2256 | 1297 | 76747 | 62385 | 69307 | 76818 |
| 2257 | 1279 | 76729 | 62367 | 69311 | 76800 |
| 2258 | 1296 | 76746 | 62384 | 69316 | 76817 |
| 2259 | 1298 | 76748 | 62386 | 69318 | 76819 |
| 2260 | 1299 | 76749 | 62387 | 69304 | 76820 |
| 2261 | 1300 | 76750 | 62388 | 69301 | 76821 |
| 2262 | 1802 | 76779 | 62417 | 69333 | 76850 |
| 3404 | 3441 | 76378 | 62261 | 70894 | 76236 |
| 3405 | 3005 | 76239 | 62271 | 70785 | 76238 |
| 3460 | 3105 | 76540 | 62211 | 70956 | 76539 |
| 3472 | 3085 | 76500 | 62244 | 70936 | 76499 |
| 3473 | 3086 | 76502 | 62245 | 70937 | 76501 |
| 3474 | 3087 | 76504 | 62246 | 70938 | 76503 |
| 3475 | 3111 | 76552 | 62270 | 70962 | 76551 |
| 3476 | 3109 | 76548 | 62247 | 70960 | 76547 |
| 3477 | 3110 | 76550 | 62248 | 70961 | 76549 |
| 3478 | 3122 | 76653 | 62125 | 71003 | 76654 |
| 3479 | 3123 | 76655 | 62272 | 71004 | 76656 |
| 3480 | 3072 | 76474 | 62323 | 70923 | 76473 |
| 3481 | 3119 | 76648 | 62324 | 70900 | 76647 |
| 3482 | 3124 | 76657 | 62320 | 71005 | 76658 |
| 3483 | 3126 | 76661 | 62233 | 71007 | 76662 |
| 3484 | 3073 | 76476 | 62325 | 70924 | 76475 |
| 3485 | 3089 | 76508 | 62327 | 70940 | 76507 |
| 3486 | 3074 | 76478 | 62234 | 70925 | 76477 |
| 3487 | 3090 | 76510 | 62250 | 70941 | 76509 |
| 3488 | 3127 | 76663 | 62235 | 71008 | 76664 |
| 3489 | 3128 | 76665 | 62251 | 71009 | 76666 |
| 3490 | 3143 | 76695 | 62328 | 71024 | 76696 |
| 3491 | 3076 | 76482 | 62329 | 70927 | 76481 |
| 3492 | 3129 | 76667 | 62344 | 71010 | 76668 |
| 3493 | 3130 | 76669 | 62237 | 71011 | 76670 |
| 3494 | 3133 | 76675 | 62330 | 71014 | 76676 |
| 3495 | 3145 | 76699 | 62331 | 71026 | 76700 |
| 3496 | 3132 | 76673 | 62334 | 71013 | 76674 |
| 3497 | 3131 | 76671 | 62346 | 71012 | 76672 |
| 3498 | 3146 | 76701 | 62333 | 71027 | 76702 |
| 3499 | 3174 | 76901 | 62347 | 71135 | 76902 |
| 3500 | 3070 | 76470 | 62455 | 70921 | 76469 |
| 3501 | 3091 | 76512 | 62332 | 70942 | 76511 |
| 3502 | 3150 | 76709 | 62252 | 71031 | 76710 |
| 3503 | 3136 | 76681 | 62251 | 71017 | 76682 |
| 3504 | 3151 | 76711 | 62351 | 71032 | 76712 |
| 3505 | 3071 | 76472 | 62352 | 70922 | 76471 |
| 3506 | 3112 | 76554 | 62337 | 70963 | 76553 |
| 3507 | 3114 | 76556 | 62232 | 70965 | 76555 |
| 3508 | 3117 | 76643 | 62273 | 70998 | 76644 |
| 3509 | 3115 | 76560 | 62275 | 70966 | 76559 |
| 3510 | 3116 | 76641 | 62318 | 70997 | 76642 |
| 3511 | 3118 | 76645 | 62276 | 70999 | 76646 |
| 3512 | 3107 | 76544 | ..... | 70958 | 76543 |
| 3513 | 3141 | 76691 | ..... | 71022 | 76692 |
| 3514 | | | | | |
| 3515 | | | | | |
| 3516 | | | | | |
| 3517 | | | | | |
| 3518 | | | | | |
| 3519 | | | | | |
| 3520 | | | | | |
| 3521 | | | | | |
| 3522 | | | | | |
| 3523 | | | | | |
| 3524 | | | | | |
| 3525 | | | | | |
| 3526 | | | | | |
| 3527 | | | | | |
| 3528 | | | | | |
| 3529 | | | | | |
| 3530 | | | | | |
| 3531 | | | | | |
| 3532 | | | | | |
| 3533 | | | | | |
| 316999 | 7001 | 67300 | 67401 | 71246 | 67301 |

**FORMATIONS OF NEW STOCK DELIVERED or ON ORDER:**

| Unit Nos: | Formations: (in sequences shown): | | | |
|---|---|---|---|---|
| 165001 to<br>165022 | 58801<br>58822 | | 58834<br>58855 | |
| 165023 to<br>165033 | 58823<br>58833 | 55404<br>55414 | 58856<br>58866 | |
| 165034 to<br>165039 | 58867<br>58872 | | 58873<br>58878 | |
| 165101 to<br>165117 | 58916<br>58932 | 55415<br>55431 | 58953<br>58969 | |
| 165118 to<br>165137 | 58933<br>58952 | | 58879<br>58898 | |
| 319161 to<br>319180 | 77458(evens)<br>77496 | 63043<br>63062 | 71929<br>71948 | 77459(odds)<br>77497 |
| 319181 to<br>319186 | 77974(evens)<br>77984 | 63093<br>63098 | 71979<br>71984 | 77973(odds)<br>77983 |
| 320301 to<br>320322 | 77899<br>77920 | 63021<br>63042 | 77921<br>77942 | |

| | | | | |
|---|---|---|---|---|
| 321347 to<br>321366 | 78131<br>78150 | 63105<br>63124 | 71991<br>72010 | 78280<br>78299 |
| 321401 to<br>321430 | 77943<br>77972 | 63063<br>63092 | 71949<br>71978 | 78095<br>78124 |
| 321431 to<br>321442 | 78300<br>78311 | 63125<br>63136 | 72011<br>72022 | 78151<br>78162 |
| 321443 to<br>321448 | 78274<br>78279 | 63099<br>63104 | 71985<br>71990 | 78125<br>78180 |
| 322481 to<br>322485 | 77985<br>77989 | 63137<br>63141 | 72023<br>72027 | 78163<br>78167 |
| (46)5001 to<br>(46)5050 | 64759(odds)<br>64857 | 72029(odds)<br>72127 | 72028(evens)<br>72126 | 64760(evens)<br>64858 |
| (46)5201 to<br>(46)5250 | 65462(evens)<br>65560 | 72719(odds)<br>72817 | 78720(evens)<br>72818 | 65463(odds)<br>65561 |
| (45)6001 to<br>(45)6024 | 64735<br>64758 | 78250<br>78273 | | |
| (483)001 to<br>(483)008 | 121<br>128 | 221<br>228 | | |

## Hauled Coaching Stock Renumbered:

| Current: | Former: | | | | | | | | | |
|---|---|---|---|---|---|---|---|---|---|---|
| 3403 | 6450 | | | | | | | | | |
| 6200-09 | 3198 | 3210 | 3191 | 3180 | 3216 | 3193 | 3183 | 3204 | 3205 | 3177 |
| 6210-19 | 3196 | 3215 | 3176 | 3208 | 3211 | 3170 | 3179 | 3184 | 3209 | 3213 |
| 6220-29 | 3175 | 3173 | 3171 | 3194 | 3195 | 3200 | 3203 | 3197 | 3201 | 3212 |
| 6230-35 | 3185 | 3189 | 3199 | 3206 | 3207 | 3190 | | | | |
| 6310 | ADB975325 | | | | | | | | | |
| 6320 | TDM395707 | | | | | | | | | |
| 6330 | ADB975629 | | | | | | | | | |
| 6332-36 | ADB975651 | | ADB975652 | | 92128 | | ADB975655 | | ADB975658 | |
| 6337-41 | ADB975660 | | 92180 | | ADB975666 | | ADB975678 | | ADB975980 | |
| 6342-44 | ADB975981 | | ADB975999 | | 92080 | | | | | |
| 6350-59 | 3088 | 3050 | 19465 | 19478 | | | | | | |
| 6800-09 | 6435 | 6442 | 6439 | 6443 | 6449 | 6436 | 6440 | 6452 | 6454 | 6455 |
| 6810-19 | 6437 | 6451 | 6448 | 6463 | 6465 | 6420 | 6461 | 6431 | 6427 | 6446 |
| 6820-29 | 6434 | 6424 | 6464 | 6428 | 6447 | 6429 | 6424 | 6425 | 6460 | 6423 |
| 11005-07 | 11905 | 11906 | 11907 | | | | | | | |
| 12169-72 | 11908 | 11909 | 11910 | 11922 | | | | | | |
| 40221 | 40421 | | | | | | | | | |
| 40228 | 40428 | | | | | | | | | |
| 40233 | 40433 | | | | | | | | | |
| 40722-27 | 40322-27 | | | | | | | | | |
| 40731 | 40331 | | | | | | | | | |
| 40755 | 40355 | | | | | | | | | |
| 44201-24 | tba | | | | | | | | | |
| 95303 | 95313 | | | | | | | | | |
| 96162-69 | 93047 | 93646 | 93880 | 93784 | 93834 | 93756 | 93978 | 93977 | | |
| 96177-82 | 93980 | 93782 | 93910 | 93843 | 93875 | 93944 | | | | |
| PULR99132 | 1861 | | | | | | | | | |
| TCL99160-69 | 18856 | 18871 | 18795 | 19194 | 18853 | 5034 | 18776 | 21238 | 18778 | 4941 |
| TCL99170/71 | 4957 | 4921 | | | | | | | | |
| SCR99819-21 | 4844 | 4871 | 9227 | | | | | | | |
| GRAM99370/71 | 9400 | 3600 | | | | | | | | |

Above: The first Railfreight Steel liveried (Fm) Class 60 locomotive, No 60008 *Moel Fammau* seen by the lifting jacks at Thornaby TMD (TE) on 7 February. Technical teething problems have delayed the class' delivery and introduction to revenue earning service but their introduction to Coal, Construction, Petroleum and Steel heavy freight duties will cause the demise of over 200 'life expired' locomotives.

Below: Portsmouth 'Greyhound' Class 421/5 4-CIG No 1825 (since renumbered 1312) awaits departure from Waterloo. These 16 units can be quickly identified by the black 'crescent' across the top of the cab front.

## NAMED ROLLING STOCK

**The following list covers named stock at the time of publication, including unofficial names carried where respectably applied. A few shunting locomotives carry pre-TOPS numbers in addition to their 'official' identity. Regrettably BR has chosen to remove many names at the time of overhaul and although InterCity were expected to apply replacement new style plates to Class 43s this has not generally been effected. Italicised names have not yet been applied.**

**Locomotives:**

| | |
|---|---|
| 08164# | Prudence |
| 08168# | D3236 |
| 08308 | Langwith |
| 08331# | Terence |
| 08434 | Midland |
| 08436 | Beighton |
| 08480 | Old Oak Common 1882–1982 |
| 08492 | Barnsley |
| 08495 | Bury |
| 08500 | Thomas |
| 08509 | Wath ETD 41F |
| 08543 | Rotherwood |
| 08562 | The Doncaster Postman |
| 08594 | Ely |
| 08600 | Ivor |
| 08602# | Clarence |
| 08629 | Wolverton |
| 08638 | Cambridge |
| 08641 | Dartmoor |
| 08642 | D3809 |
| 08645 | Friary |
| 08647# | Crimpsall |
| 08673 | Piccadilly |
| 08680 | Northern Lights |
| 08691 | Escafeld |
| 08721 | Starlet |
| 08749 | Great Central |
| 08764# | Florence |
| 08772 | Camulodunum |
| 08817 | Thornaby |
| 08833 | Liverpool Street Pilot |
| 08855 | Hatton Castle |
| 08857 | Darnall |
| 08867 | Ralph Easby |
| 08869 | The Canary |
| 08870 | Millhouses 41C |
| 08878 | Grimesthorpe 41B |
| 08879 | Earles |
| 08880 | Mexborough 41F |
| 08882 | Benachie |
| 08892 | D4122 |
| 08919 | Cadeby 41A |
| 08953 | Plymouth |
| 08954 | Penwithers |
| 08993 | Ashburnham |
| 08994 | Gwendraeth |
| 08995 | Kidwelly |
| | |
| 09008 | Aldwark |
| 09013 | Dick Hardy |
| 09014 | Shepcote |
| 09015 | City of Hereford |
| 09025 | Victory |
| 09026 | William Pearson |
| | |
| 20028 | Bedale |
| 20118 | Saltburn by the Sea |
| 20122 | Cleveland Potash |
| 20137 | Murray B. Hofmeyr |
| 20156 | HMS Endeavour |
| 20165 | Henry Pease |
| 20172 | Redmire |
| 20173 | Wensleydale |
| 20901# | Nancy |
| 20902# | Lorna |
| 20903# | Alison |
| 20904# | Janis |
| 20905# | Iona |
| 20906# | Georgina |

| | |
|---|---|
| 31102 | Cricklewood |
| 31160 | Phoenix |
| 31201 | Fina Energy |
| 31233 | Phillips-Imperial |
| 31276 | Calder Hall Power Station |
| 31413 | Severn Valley Railway |
| 31423 | Jerome K Jerome |
| 31428 | North Yorkshire Moors Railway |
| 31530 | Sister Dora |
| 31544 | Keighley & Worth Valley Railway |
| 31568 | The Enginmen's Fund |
| | |
| 33008 | Eastleigh |
| 33025 | Sultan |
| 33050 | Isle of Grain |
| 33051 | Shakespeare Cliff |
| 33052 | Ashford |
| 33056 | The Burma Star |
| 33207 | Earl Mountbatten of Burma |
| | |
| 37004 | Tiger Moth |
| 37009 | Typhoon |
| 37012 | Derwent |
| 37013 | Vampire |
| 37026 | Shap Fell |
| 37035 | Gartcosh |
| 37049 | Imperial |
| 37057 | Viking |
| 37059 | Port of Tilbury |
| 37068 | Grainflow |
| 37069 | Thornaby TMD |
| 37072 | Venum |
| 37073 | Tornado |
| 37077 | Hurricane |
| 37087 | Vulcan |
| 37088 | Clydesdale |
| 37099 | Clydebridge |
| 37108 | Lanarkshire Steel |
| 37111 | Glengarnock |
| 37113 | Radio Highland |
| 37114 | Dunrobin Castle |
| 37137 | Clyde Iron |
| 37152 | British Steel Ravenscraig |
| 37156 | British Steel Hunterston |
| 37178 | Meteor |
| 37184 | Buccanneer |
| 37188 | Jimmy Shand |
| 37190 | Dalzell |
| 37209 | Phantom |
| 37235 | Coal Merchants' Association of Scotland |
| 37240 | Golden Heart |
| 37251 | Gladiator |
| 37261 | Caithness |
| 37262 | Dounreay |
| 37275 | Stainless Pioneer |
| 37298 | Victor |
| 37358 | P & O Containers |
| 37401 | Mary Queen of Scots |
| 37402 | Oor Wullie |
| 37403 | Glendarroch |
| 37404 | Ben Cruachan |
| 37405 | Strathclyde Region |
| 37406 | The Saltire Society |
| 37407 | Loch Long |
| 37408 | Loch Rannoch |
| 37409 | Loch Awe |
| 37410 | Aluminium 100 |

| | |
|---|---|
| 37411 | Institution of Railway Signal Engineers |
| 37412 | Loch Lomond |
| 37413 | Loch Eil Outward Bound |
| 37417 | Highland Region |
| 37418 | An Comunn Gaidhealach |
| 37420 | The Scottish Hosteller |
| 37423 | Sir Murray Morrison 1874–1948 |
| 37425 | Sir Robert MacAlpine. Concrete Bob |
| 37426 | Y Lein Fach. Vale of Rheidol |
| 37427 | Bont Y Bermo |
| 37428 | David Lloyd George |
| 37429 | Eisteddfod Genedlaethol |
| 37430 | Cwmbrân |
| 37431 | County of Powys. Sir Powys |
| 37501 | Teesside Steelmaster |
| 37502 | British Steel Teesside |
| 37503 | British Steel Shelton |
| 37504 | British Steel Corby |
| 37505 | British Steel Workington |
| 37506 | British Steel Skinningrove |
| 37507 | BSC Hartlepool Pipe Mill |
| 37511 | Stockton Haulage |
| 37512 | Thornaby Demon |
| 37667 | Wensleydale |
| 37668 | Leyburn |
| 37671 | Tre Pol and Pen |
| 37672 | Freight Transport Association |
| 37675 | William Cookworthy |
| 37688 | Great Rocks |
| 37689 | Coedbach |
| 37693 | Sir William Arrol |
| 37702 | Taff Merthyr |
| 37711 | Tremorfa Steel Works |
| 37712 | Cardiff Rod Mill |
| 37799 | Sir Dyfed-County of Dyfed |
| 37800 | Glo Cymru |
| 37801 | Aberddawan. Aberthaw |
| 37888 | Petrolea |
| 37892 | Ripple Lane |
| 37901 | Mirrlees Pioneer |
| 37905 | Vulcan Enterprise |
| | |
| 43023 | County of Cornwall |
| 43026 | City of Westminster |
| 43027 | Westminster Abbey |
| 43032 | The Royal Regiment of Wales |
| 43045 | The Grammer School, Doncaster AD1350 |
| 43049 | Neville Hill |
| 43052 | City of Peterborough |
| 43053 | County of Humberside |
| 43056 | University of Bradford |
| 43060 | County of Leicestershire |
| 43061 | City of Lincoln |
| 43078 | Shildon, County Durham |
| 43084 | County of Derbyshire |
| 43093 | York Festival '88 |
| 43095 | Heaton |
| 43097 | The Light Infantry |
| 43103 | John Wesley |
| 43106 | Songs of Praise |
| 43109 | Yorkshire Evening Press |
| 43114 | The National Garden Festival, Gateshead 1990 |
| 43115 | Yorkshire Academy of Cricket |
| 43118 | Charles Wesley |
| 43131 | Worshipful Company of Carmen |

| | |
|---|---|
| 43149 | BBC Wales Today |
| 43150 | Bristol Evening Post |
| 43155 | BBC Look North |
| 43157 | Yorkshire Evening Post |
| 43169 | The National Trust |
| 43186 | Sir Francis Drake |
| 43193 | Yorkshire Post |
| 43 | *City of Culture* |
| 43 | *City of Discovery* |
| 43 | *Granite City* |
| | |
| 47002 | Sea Eagle |
| 47003 | Wild Swan |
| 47005 | Harrier |
| 47007 | Stratford |
| 47009 | Guillemot |
| 47016 | The Toleman Group |
| 47051 | Great Snipe |
| 47060 | Halewood Silver Jubilee 1988 |
| 47085 | Conidae |
| 47096 | Rook |
| 47098 | Oriole |
| 47100 | Merlin |
| 47102 | Buzzard |
| 47119 | Arcidae |
| 47120 | Osprey |
| 47121 | Potchard |
| 47123 | Jay |
| 47125 | Tonnidae |
| 47142 | The Sapper |
| 47145 | Jostinot |
| 47146 | Paridae |
| 47186 | Tinsley TMD Silver Jubilee, 41A, 1966-1990 |
| 47190 | Pectinidae |
| 47193 | Lucinidae |
| 47194 | Bullidae |
| 47195 | Muricidae |
| 47196 | Haliotidae |
| 47200 | Jackdaw |
| 47207 | Bulmers of Hereford |
| 47209 | Bittern |
| 47210 | Blue Circle Cement |
| 47217 | Kingfisher |
| 47218 | Firecrest |
| 47219 | Sandpiper |
| 47222 | Appleby Frodingham |
| 47226 | Seagull |
| 47231 | The Silcock Express |
| 47233 | Strombidae |
| 47238 | Bescot Yard |
| 47245 | Lynett |
| 47278 | Vasidae |
| 47280 | Pedigree |
| 47281 | Merddin Emrys |
| 47283 | Johnnie Walker |
| 47284 | Storm Cock/Mistlethrush |
| 47291 | The Port of Felixstowe |
| 47298 | Kestrel |
| 47307 | Bunting |
| 47310 | Raven |
| 47311 | Warrington Yard |
| 47313 | Curlew |
| 47314 | Blackcap |
| 47316 | Wren |
| 47317 | Willesden Yard |
| 47319 | Norsk Hydro |
| 47324 | Glossidae |
| 47333 | Civil Link |
| 47337 | Herbert Austin |
| 47338 | Cormoront |
| 47348 | St. Christopher's Railway Home |
| 47350 | British Petroleum |
| 47360 | Fulmar |
| 47361 | Wilton Endeavour |
| 47363 | Billingham Enterprise |
| 47365 | Diamond Jubilee |
| 47366 | The Institution of Civil Engineers |
| 47368 | Neritidae |
| 47375 | Tinsley Traction Depot. Quality Assured |
| 47376 | Skylark |
| 47379 | Total Energy |
| 47380 | Immingham |
| | |
| 47424 | The Brtöntes of Haworth |
| 47425 | Holbeck |
| 47444 | University of Nottingham |
| 47457 | Ben Line |
| 47461 | Charles Rennie Mackintosh |
| 47470 | University of Edinburgh |
| 47471 | Norman Tunna G.C. |
| 47474 | Sir Rowland Hill |
| 47484 | Isambard Kingdom Brunel |
| 47488 | Rail Riders |
| 47489 | *Crewe DMD* |
| 47490 | Bristol Bath Road |
| 47491 | Horwich Enterprise |
| 47492 | The Enterprising Scot |
| 47500 | Great Western |
| 47501 | Craftsman |
| 47503 | The Geordie |
| 47508 | S.S. Great Britain |
| 47509 | Albion |
| 47513 | Severn |
| 47515 | Night Mail |
| 47517 | Andrew Carnegie |
| 47522 | Doncaster Enterprise |
| 47526 | Northumbria |
| 47527 | Kettering |
| 47535 | University of Leicester |
| 47537 | Sir Gwynedd. County of Gwynedd |
| 47539 | Rochdale Pioneers |
| 47541 | The Queen Mother |
| 47546 | Aviemore Centre |
| 47549 | Royal Mail |
| 47550 | University of Dundee |
| 47555 | The Commonwealth Spirit |
| 47558 | Mayflower |
| 47559 | Sir Joshua Reynolds |
| 47562 | Sir William Burrell |
| 47564 | Colossus |
| 47567 | Red Star |
| 47568 | Royal Engineers Postal & Courier Services |
| 47572 | Ely Cathedral |
| 47573 | The London Standard |
| 47574 | Benjamin Gimbert G.C |
| 47575 | City of Hereford |
| 47576 | Kings Lynn |
| 47578 | Royal Society of Edinburgh |
| 47579 | James Nightall G.C |
| 47580 | County of Essex |
| 47581 | Great Eastern |
| 47582 | County of Norfolk |
| 47583 | County of Hertfordshire |
| 47584 | County of Suffolk |
| 47585 | County of Cambridgeshire |
| 47586 | Northamptonshire |
| 47588 | Carlisle Currock |
| 47592 | County of Avon |
| 47593 | Galloway Princess |
| 47595 | Confederation of British Industry |
| 47596 | Aldeburgh Festival |
| 47600 | Dewi Sant. Saint David |
| 47602 | Glorious Devon |
| 47603 | County of Somerset |
| 47604 | Women's Royal Voluntary Service |
| 47615 | Castell Caerffili. Caerphilly Castle |
| 47616 | Y Ddraig Goch. The Red Dragon |
| 47617 | University of Stirling |
| 47624 | Cyclops |
| 47626 | Atlas |
| 47627 | City of Oxford |
| 47634 | Henry Ford |
| 47635 | Jimmy Milne |
| 47636 | Sir John de Graeme |
| 47640 | University of Strathclyde |
| 47641 | Fife Region |
| 47642 | Strathisla |
| 47644 | The Permanent Way Institution |
| 47 | *Quadrant* |
| 47 | *Post Haste* |
| 47 | *Robert F.Fairlie* |
| | |
| 47701 | Saint Andrew |
| 47702 | Saint Cuthbert |
| 47703 | Saint Mungo |
| 47704 | Dunedin |
| 47705 | *University of Oxford* |
| 47706 | |
| 47707 | Holyrood |
| 47708 | Waverley |
| 47709 | The Lord Provost |
| 47710 | Sir Walter Scott |
| 47711 | Greyfriars Bobby |
| 47712 | Lady Diana Spencer |
| 47714 | *Ruskin College* |
| 47715 | Haymarket |
| 47716 | The Duke of Edinburgh's Award |
| 47717 | Tayside Region |
| | |
| 47803 | Womens' Guild |
| 47809 | Finsbury Park |
| 47821 | Royal Worcester |
| 47825 | Thomas Telford |
| 47831 | Bolton Wanderer |
| 47832 | Tamar |
| 47834 | Fire Fly |
| 47835 | Windsor Castle |
| 47836 | Fair Rosamund |
| 47841 | The Institution of Mechanical Engineers |
| 47845 | County of Kent |
| 47846 | Thor |
| | |
| 47971 | Robin Hood |
| 47973 | Midland Counties 150, 1839–1989 |
| | |
| 50001 | Dreadnought |
| 50002 | Superb |
| 50003 | Temeraire |
| 50004 | St.Vincent |
| 50005 | Collingwood |
| 50007 | Sir Edward Elgar |
| 50008 | Thunderer |
| 50009 | Conqueror |
| 50014 | Warspite |
| 50015 | Valiant |
| 50016 | Barham |
| 50017 | Royal Oak |
| 50018 | Resolution |
| 50019 | Ramillies |
| 50020 | Revenge |
| 50023 | Howe |
| 50024 | Vanguard |
| 50026 | Indomitable |
| 50027 | Lion |

50028 Tiger
50029 Renown
50030 Repulse
50031 Hood
50032 Courageous
50033 Glorious
50034 Furious
50035 Ark Royal
50036 Victorious
50037 Illustrious
50042 Triumph
50043 Eagle
50044 Exeter
50045 Achilles
50046 Ajax
50048 Dauntless
50049 Defiance
50050 Fearless

56001 Whatley
56028 West Burton Power Station
56029 Eggborough Power Station
56031 Merehead
56032 Sir de Morgannwg. County of South Glamorgan
56034 Castell Ogwr. Ogmore Castle
56037 Richard Trevithick
56038 Western Mail
56040 Oystermouth
56053 Sir Morgannwg Ganol. County of Mid Glamorgan
56062 Mountsorrel
56063 Bardon Hill
56074 Kellingley Colliery
56075 West Yorkshire Enterprise
56080 Selby Coalfield
56091 Castle Donington Power Station
56095 Harworth Colliery
56099 Fiddlers Ferry Power Station
56101 *Mutual Imperial*
56102 Scunthorpe Steel Centenary
56122 Wilton Coal Power
56123 Drax Power Station
56131 Ellington Colliery
56133 Crewe Locomotive Works
56134 Blyth Power
56135 Port of Tyne Authority

58002 Daw Mill Colliery
58003 Markham Colliery
58014 Didcot Power Station
58018 High Marnham Power Station
58019 Shirebrook Colliery
58020 Doncaster Works
58034 Bassetlaw
58039 Rugeley Power Station
58040 Cottam Power Station
58041 Ratcliffe Power Station
58042 Ironbridge Power Station
58049 Littleton Colliery
58050 Toton Traction Depot

59001 Yeoman Endeavour
59002 Yeoman Enterprise
59003 Yeoman Highlander
59004 Yeoman Challenger
59005 Kenneth J.Painter

60001 Steadfast
60002 Capability Brown
60003 Christopher Wren
60004 Lochnager
60005 Skiddaw
60006 Great Gable
60007 Robert Adam
60008 Moel Fammau
60009 Carnedd Dafydd
60010 Plynlimon
60011 Cader Idris
60012 Glyder Fawr
60013 Robert Boyle
60014 Alexander Fleming
60015 Bow Fell
60016 Langdale Pikes
60017 Arenig Fawr
60018 Moel Siabod
60019 Wild Boar Fell
60020 Great Whernside
60021 Pen-y-Ghent
60022 Ingleborough
60023 The Cheviot
60024 Charles Babbage
60025 Joseph Lister
60026 William Caxton
60027 Joseph Banks
60028 John Flamsteed
60029 Ben Nevis
60030 Cir Mhor
60031 Ben Lui
60032 William Bramwell Booth

*Other planned names:*
*Construction sub-Sector:*
Axe Edge
Black Tor
Bleklow Head
Bow Fell
Brecon Mountains
Dovestone Tor
Dunkery Beacon
Elidr Fawr
Glastonbury Tor
Hay Tor
High Willhays
Kinder Scout
Mam Tor
Shining Tor

*Steel sub-Sector*
Ben Macdui
Bidean Nam Bian
Blencathra
Carnedd Llewelyn
Crib Goch
Cross Fell
Goat Fell
Helvellyn
Pen-y-Fan
Scafell
Sgurr na Ciche
Snowdon
Tremadog
Tryfan

*Coal sub-Sector*
An Teallach
Arcuil
Ben More Assynt
Boar of Baddenoch
Braeriach
Buyachaille Etive Mor
Cairn Gorm
Cairn Toul
Canisp
Foinaven
Liathach
Quinag
Schiehallion
Slioch
Stac Pollaidh
Suilven
John Logie Baird
Thomas Barnardo
Alexander Graham Bell
William Beveridge
Jospehine Butler
Charles Darwin
Humphrey Davy
Dorothy Garrod
John Howard
James Clerk-Maxwell
John Louden McAdam
Robert Owen
Samuel Plimsoll
Adam Smith
James Watt
William Wilberforce

*Petroleum sub-Sector*
Anthony Ashley Cooper
Elizabeth Fry
Samuel Johnson
James Murray
Florence Nightingale
John Reith
Mary Somerville

73004 The Bluebell Railway
73005 Mid Hants. Watercress Line
73101 Brighton Evening Argus
73112 University of Kent at Canterbury
73117 University of Surrey
73118 The Romney Hythe and Dymchurch Railway
73119 Kentish Mercury
73129 City of Winchester
73130 City of Portsmouth
73131 County of Surrey
73134 Woking Homes 1885–1985
73138 Post Haste
73201 Broadlands
73202 Royal Observer Corps
73204 Stewarts Lane 1860–1985
73205 London Chamber of Commerce
73206 Gatwick Express
73207 County of East Sussex
73208 Croydon 1883–1983
73210 Selhurst
73211 County of West Sussex
73212 Airtour Suisse
732 *Battle of Britain*

86101 Sir William A Stanier FRS
86102 Robert A Riddles
86103 André Chapelon
86204 City of Carlisle
86205 City of Lancaster
86206 City of Stoke on Trent
86207 City of Lichfield
86208 City of Chester
86209 City of Coventry
86210 City of Edinburgh
86212 Preston Guild
86213 Lancashire Witch
86214 Sans Pareil
86215 Joseph Chamberlain
86216 Meteor
86217 Halley's Comet
86218 Planet
86219 Phoenix
86220 The Round Tabler
86221 BBC Look East
86222 Lloyd's List
86223 Norwich Union

| | |
|---|---|
| 86224 | Caledonian |
| 86225 | Hardwicke |
| 86226 | Royal Mail Midlands |
| 86227 | Sir Henry Johnson |
| 86228 | Vulcan Heritage |
| 86229 | Sir John Betjeman |
| 86230 | The Duke of Wellington |
| 86231 | Starlight Express |
| 86232 | Harold Macmillan |
| 86233 | Laurence Olivier |
| 86234 | J B Priestley O.M |
| 86235 | Novelty |
| 86236 | Josiah Wedgwood. Master Potter 1730–1795 |
| 86237 | Sir Charles Hallé |
| 86238 | European Community |
| 86239 | L.S.Lowry |
| 86240 | Bishop Eric Treacy |
| 86241 | Glenfiddich |
| 86242 | James Kennedy G.C |
| 86243 | The Boys' Brigade |
| 86244 | The Royal British Legion |
| 86245 | Dudley Castle |
| 86246 | Royal Anglian Regiment |
| 86247 | Abraham Darby |
| 86248 | Sir Clwyd – County of Clwyd |
| 86249 | County of Merseyside |
| 86250 | The Glasgow Herald |
| 86251 | The Birmingham Post |
| 86252 | The Liverpool Daily Post |
| 86253 | The Manchester Guardian |
| 86254 | William Webb Ellis |
| 86255 | Penrith Beacon |
| 86256 | Pebble Mill |
| 86257 | Snowdon |
| 86258 | Talyllyn |
| 86259 | Peter Pan |
| 86260 | Driver Wallace Oakes G.C |
| 86261 | Driver John Axon G.C |
| 86401 | Northampton Town |
| 86411 | Airey Neave |
| 86412 | Elizabeth Garrett Anderson |
| 86414 | Frank Hornby |
| 86415 | Rotary International |
| 86416 | Wigan Pier |
| 86417 | The Kingsman |
| 86428 | Aldaniti |
| 86430 | Scottish National Orchestra |
| 86434 | University of London |
| | |
| 86607 | The Institution of Electrical Engineers |
| 86608 | St. John Ambulance |
| 86613 | County of Lancashire |
| 86621 | London School of Economics |
| 86627 | The Industrial Society |
| 86632 | Brookside |
| 86633 | Wulfruna |
| | |
| 87001 | Royal Scot |
| 87002 | Royal Sovereign |
| 87003 | Patriot |
| 87004 | Britannia |
| 87005 | City of London |
| 87006 | City of Glasgow |
| 87007 | City of Manchester |
| 87008 | City of Liverpool |
| 87009 | City of Birmingham |
| 87010 | King Arthur |
| 87011 | The Black Prince |
| 87012 | The Royal Bank of Scotland |
| 87013 | John o'Gaunt |
| 87014 | Knight of the Thistle |
| 87015 | Howard of Effingham |
| 87016 | |
| 87017 | Iron Duke |
| 87018 | Lord Nelson |
| 87019 | Sir Winston Churchill |
| 87020 | North Briton |
| 87021 | Robert the Bruce |
| 87022 | Cock o' the North |
| 87023 | Velocity |
| 87024 | Lord of the Isles |
| 87025 | County of Cheshire |
| 87026 | Sir Richard Arkwright |
| 87027 | Wolf of Badenoch |
| 87028 | Lord President |
| 87029 | Earl Marischal |
| 87030 | Black Douglas |
| 87031 | Hal o' the Wynd |
| 87032 | Kenilworth |
| 87033 | Thane of Fife |
| 87034 | William Shakespeare |
| 87035 | Robert Burns |
| | |
| 87101 | Stephenson |
| | |
| 89001 | Avocet |
| | |
| 90001 | BBC Midlands Today |
| 90002 | |
| 90003 | |
| 90004 | |
| 90005 | Financial Times |
| 90006 | |
| 90007 | |
| 90008 | |
| 90009 | Royal Show |
| 90010 | 275 Railway Squadron (Volunteers) |
| 90011 | Chartered Institute of Transport |
| 90012 | |
| 90013 | |
| 90014 | The Liverpool Phil. |
| 90015 | BBC North West |
| 90019 | Penny Black |
| 900 | |
| 900 | |
| 900 | |
| 900 | |
| | |
| 91001 | Swallow |
| 91002 | |
| 91003 | |
| 91004 | The Red Arrows |
| 91005 | |
| 91006 | |
| 91007 | |
| 91008 | |
| 91009 | |
| 91010 | |
| 91011 | Terence Cuneo |
| 91012 | |
| 91013 | |
| 91014 | |
| 91015 | |
| 91016 | |
| 91017 | |
| 91018 | |
| 91019 | |
| 91020 | |
| | |
| 97403 | Ixion |
| | |
| ADB968027 | Tamworth Castle, *D7672* |

**Multiple Units:**

| | |
|---|---|
| 51899 | Aylesbury College |
| 143005 | River Tees |
| 143006 | River Wear |
| 203001 | St. Leonards (60152) |
| 319005 | Partnership for Progress (62895) |
| 321312 | Southend-on-Sea. (71891) |
| 2401 | Beaulieu. (62937) |
| 2402 | County of Hampshire. (62938) |
| 2419 | BBC South Today. (62955) |
| 24 | *Thomas Hardy* (629..) |

**Hauled Coaching Stock**

| | |
|---|---|
| 504 | Ullswater |
| 506 | Windermere |
| 546 | Coniston Water |
| 548 | Grassmere |
| 549 | Bassenthwaite Lake |
| 550 | Rydal Water |
| 551 | Buttermere |
| 552 | Emmerdale Water |
| 553 | Crummock Water |
| 586 | Derwent Water |
| 5154 | Clan Fraser |
| 5166 | Clan Mackenzie |
| 5191 | Clan Donald |
| 5212 | Capercailzie |
| 5230 | Corrikemoillie |
| 6300 | Hebridean |
| 9388 | Bailechaul |
| 9414 | Braham Seer |
| 11073 | William Ewart Gladstone |
| 11074 | Thomas Brassey |
| 11076 | John Lennon |
| 11077 | Sir Richard Arkwright |
| 11078 | John Owens |
| 11079 | Francis Eggerton |
| 11081 | Elizabeth Gaskell |
| 11083 | Kitty Wilkinson |
| 11084 | William Roscoe |
| 11086 | Henry Doulton |
| 11088 | Sir John Brunner |
| 11089 | George Stubbs |
| 11091 | Sir Stanley Matthews |
| 11092 | Ernest Rutherford |
| 11093 | L.S.Lowry |
| 11094 | Arnold Bennett |
| 99122 | Helen |
| 99123 | Grace |
| 99124 | Frances |
| 99354 | Hadrian Bar |
| 99530 | Perseus |
| 99531 | Phoenix |
| 99532 | Cygnus |
| 99534 | Ibis |
| 99535 | Minerva |
| 99536 | Zena |
| 99537 | Audrey |
| 99539 | Ione |
| 99541 | Lucille |

# Private owner locomotives. (BR TOPS number not carried on Class 08).

# STOP PRESS

As a follower of the British Rail rolling stock scene you will doubtless appreciate that changes effecting some aspects of the fleet are a daily occurrence. In recent years BR has advanced from the quill pen to a less than accurate computer system and centralised its reporting of stock alterations to singe official source. Luckily for staff and enthusiasts a large number of additional sources are able to supplement this service. In the preceding pages every effort has been made to provide the most accurate information relating to the fleet from 14 May, although compiled in advance of that date.
The following changes have been advised in the few days since production commenced. To keep this listing as short as possible only changed information is shown, with all stock *transferred in* to each depot shown, firstly where there is no change to the operating sub-Sector, thence where the sub-Sector is also changed. This is followed by a summary of changes where the *Sector and sub-Sector only* are altered.

LOCOMOTIVES:
Withdrawn: 08796
Renumbered: 31444/53/56/58 now 31544/53/56/58 (delete 314xx entries and † by 315xx entries).
Reallocated:
BS DCMC: 31105. DCMN: 31248. DCMW: 31171, 31272/90.
CD DCQA: 47531. PCDB: 31406. RXLC: 47479
CL 97251
ED DCHA: 26008, 37088, 37152. FDSE: 20118/19/22/24/37/38/56/65. FDTE: 37407. FDUE: 37113/14/28/54, 37261/62. PEDA: 47717.
EH FSAE: 09004.
IS PISA: 47518.
NL IMLP: 43074/75.
OC NWRA: 47702. RXLD: 47526/59/67.
SU DCSB: 09023.
TE FCTY: 37415/17/20, 47359. FMTY: 20046/61/93/98, 20107/12.

DCEA: 37025.
DCSA: 33208.
DMSA: 73106/07/36.
DCWA: 33109/11.
DMEA: 31405/09/20/34/35.
FEGN: 20197.
FDPC: 90021–43.
FDYX: 81010, 85107.
IEDA: 47550.
IMLP: 43108/09/54/55.
PCDA: 47512.
PCDB: 31400/04/12/14/16/26.
RXLC: 47459/62, 47503.

HAULED COACHING STOCK:
Reallocated:
BN: 3178/87, 10331, 11258/59, 12229, 12328, 12481/82/83, 82212. IEC: 13562/67/77, 13603, 17151/64.
CL: ICHH: 21269.
DY: 1954, 13568/69/78/81/96/98. ICC: 5689, 17143. IML: 9506, 13571/82.
EC: 5709, 10665/73/80/92. IXXH: 10668, 10701. PEC: 5259/86, 5368, 5459/77, 5582. RPXZ: 92028/29/31.
EN: 5913/15/24/76/83, 6011/22/29, 6105/45, 9500.
HT: PHT: 5273/82, 5325/53, 9412/23.
HQ: IXXZ: 1946/47.
IS: PIS: 5187, 5281, 5371/82, 5417, 5505/09/48/54/57/60/61/86, 6508/09/14/16/20/23/24, 17119/23/25/36.
LA: 13488/93, 13517, 17058/62. IWR: 10568/73. NSS: 5275/93. RPXW: 92088.
LL: 4845/55/57/61/86, 4909/18/22/24/25/28/33/34/37/44/47/48/52/54/56/58/62/64/65/74/76/78/82/83/86/88, 17052/54/66/75/98. 17100/03/13. ICC: 1845. ICHC: 17037/43/47. ICHD: 4915/27/39/46/49/59/61/63/66/77/79/91/93/96/98/99, 5001/02/08/29/30/33/41/44, 17042/93, 17102/17/22/29/31.
MA: 1880, 1971, 3277, 3331/44/50/51, 5522/24/30/39/66/69/90, 5605, 5914/19/35/49/77/88/96, 6006/15/18/46/47/49, 6134/38/63/65/79/80/81/83, 10207/13/22/23/24/26/27/47/54/56/59, 11060/64/65/66/69/70/73/76/79/91/93/94/96, 11100, 12029/34/36/56/60/62, 12105/07-10/20/28/39/46/50/54/57/59/60/67, 17173/74/75, 17160. ICC: 6665. ICHM: 1832/57. IWC: 3284. IXXH: 5422.
NC: IAN: 3229/35/39/41. IAND: 5369, 6506. IANR: 5929/59/64/68, 6139/60/67, 9704/07.
OM: 5436/57/64. IXXH: 17137.
OY: 3314/36. ICHD: 4930.
WB: 1805/76, 3318, 5916/30, 6008/16/25, 6153, 10234/51, 10512/27/29/79, 10665/73/80. IWC: 5287, 5346, 5467, 12010/43/55/69, IWCD: 10534/70.

IANR: 1647/71/83/86/89/91/92/96/97/99, 9702/03/14.
ICC: 5663, 6601/04/05/07/14/19.
ICCR: 1653, 1959/73/81.
ICH: 3223/26/27, 13584/86/88/89/94/95.
ICHC: 17101.
ICHM: 3228/31, 17124/26/30/34/38.
ICHS: 1853.
IML: 13565.
IWCD: 10552.
IWCR: 6060.
IXXH: 1816/42/50/65/67/69/70/71/82, 5304/14/61/64/67/70/72/95, 5403/15/30/38/59/66/86/87/96, 5522/32/36/81/89/97, 9421/27/38/41/47/54/56/57/59/64/65/69/72, 10501/38/40/60/66/73/78/89/97, 10604/06/12/79/82/84/85/86/91/93/99, 10704/07, 13230/36/37, 13341, 13564/72/74/76/79/80/90/91/92/97/99, 13602/08/10, 17051, 35469.
IXXZ: 1833/48/75/79, 4634, 9007, 13605, 25008, 26125.
RPIC: 92094/96/97/98, 92102/08/15/25/48/51/65/75/88/90/95/96/97.
RPIP: 92000/01/06/08/11/12/23/25-29/31-40/46/48/50/55/57/61/63/65/77/86/88/91, 92100/11/13/14/16/26/36/38/46/47/55/59/67/72/74/83/86/93/94, 92203.
RPIT: 92002-05/16.
RPXT: 80304/07/11.

LIVERIES:
I: 3248, 6613, 9704/07, 40747/52.

Front cover: New Class 91 No 91011 seen at King's Cross on 6 March when it was named *Terence Cuneo.* InterCity style nameplate *Terence Cuneo* on locomotive No 91011.
Back cover: York Wagon Works diesel shunter No 08500 *Thomas 1* specially painted red by works' staff.
Class 322 unit No 322481 for Stansted Express services receives the approval of NSE's director Chris Green, at BREL's York Work's.